A Guide Book of Modern United States Dollar Coins

A Complete History and Price Guide

Q. David Bowers

Foreword by
Edmund C. Moy
38th Director, United States Mint (2006–2011)

Whitman Publishing, LLC
PUBLISHING SINCE 1934
Whitman.com

A Guide Book of Modern United States Dollar Coins

© 2016 Whitman Publishing, LLC
3101 Clairmont Road, Suite G, Atlanta, GA 30329

THE OFFICIAL RED BOOK is a trademark of Whitman Publishing, LLC.

Correspondence concerning this book may be directed to
Whitman Publishing, Attn: Modern U.S. Dollar Coins, at the address above.

ISBN: 0794843980
Printed in China

Other books in the Bowers Series include: *A Guide Book of Morgan Silver Dollars; A Guide Book of Double Eagle Gold Coins; A Guide Book of United States Type Coins; A Guide Book of Modern United States Proof Coin Sets; A Guide Book of Shield and Liberty Head Nickels; A Guide Book of Flying Eagle and Indian Head Cents; A Guide Book of Washington and State Quarters; A Guide Book of Buffalo and Jefferson Nickels; A Guide Book of Lincoln Cents; A Guide Book of United States Commemorative Coins; A Guide Book of United States Tokens and Medals; A Guide Book of Gold Dollars; A Guide Book of Peace Dollars; A Guide Book of the Official Red Book of United States Coins; A Guide Book of Franklin and Kennedy Half Dollars; A Guide Book of Civil War Tokens; A Guide Book of Hard Times Tokens; A Guide Book of Mercury Dimes, Standing Liberty Quarters, and Liberty Walking Half Dollars; A Guide Book of Half Cents and Large Cents; A Guide Book of Barber Silver Coins;* and *A Guide Book of Liberty Seated Silver Coins.*

If you enjoy modern U.S. dollar coins, join the American Numismatic Association. Visit www.Whitman.com/ANA for membership information.

CONTENTS

FOREWORD

The Presidential $1 Coin Program was the first new coin program I was responsible for as director of the United States Mint. Within months of being sworn in as the 38th person to serve in that capacity, I debuted their designs to the American public, initiated their production at the Mint, and put them into circulation through the Federal Reserve System.

The program was launched little more than a year after the legislation was signed into law by President George W. Bush on December 22, 2005. A year is barely enough time to launch a single new coin, let alone a new coin series with several rotating designs each year, and one that required developing a mass-production manufacturing process for the legally required edge lettering. My head hurts just thinking about all the work that was done to get the coin into circulation on time. It was quite the challenge and I am proud of the men and women of the United States Mint who rose to the task.

Reading Dave Bowers's *Guide Book of Modern United States Dollar Coins* also brings back good memories about my experiences with dollar coins. I have fond recollections of President George Washington and me charming New Yorkers in Grand Central Station with a demonstration of how the coins worked in subway fare machines. I had the opportunity to meet several of John Adams's descendants and even tour his home (how did they sleep in those short beds?).

I remember when National Museum of the American Indian director Kevin Gover and I poured newly minted 2009 Native American dollar coins out of an authentic handmade Native American basket in the NMAI's Potomac Atrium.

I get a big smile on my face whenever I remember the great feeling I had when I got my first Eisenhower dollar coin in change. It was weighty, substantial, and large in my small hand. For a young boy, I felt that I was the richest kid on the block.

But my fondest dollar coin memory was at a members-only congressional reception for golf great Arnold Palmer when the legislation passed awarding him the Congressional Gold Medal, the highest award Congress can give. Congress commissioned the United States Mint to make the medal and I was there with my artists to start the design process. Arnie and I were chatting and I offered him a newly minted Presidential dollar coin to use as a ball marker. Laughing, he waived me off and said that he loved dollar coins and frequently gave them away as gifts. Then he pulled out a handful from his pocket and gave me one. "I bet you give away lots of coins, but how often does someone give the Mint director a coin?" Not many, and none of them were Arnold Palmer. That dollar coin is one of my favorite mementos from my time as director.

At my last congressional oversight hearing, before the House of Representatives Committee on Financial Services Subcommittee on Domestic Monetary Policy and Technology, I was questioned on why modern dollar coins have not had sustained success in the United States. Part of my answer was that, unlike most countries that successfully use a higher-denomination coin, the United States did not also eliminate the $1 bill. Most advanced economies have undergone some currency reform: eliminate the lowest-denomination coin, create a high-denomination coin, and eliminate the lowest-denomination bill.

All this is to say that collectors should take another look at these underappreciated coins. Of all the modern U.S. coins, none have undergone so many versions in such a short period of time. They come in multiple sizes, have various metal content, and are still relatively accessible. Given the growth of electronic and digital transactions, and Americans being creatures of habit used to their $1 bills, it is unlikely that a new dollar coin is in the cards when the Presidential dollar series ends.

As you can see, there are many highways and byways to explore in the world of modern U.S. dollar coins. This book is the essential guide to the subject. It is comprehensive, written for the new and seasoned collector alike, and authoritative, as one would expect from numismatic legend Q. David Bowers.

Edmund C. Moy
38th Director of the United
States Mint (2006–2011)

Edmund C. Moy is a 1979 graduate of the University of Wisconsin with majors in economics, international relations, and political science. He was a sales and marketing executive for Blue Cross Blue Shield United of Wisconsin from 1979 to 1989. Moy served in the administration of George H.W. Bush, within the Department of Health and Human Services, then worked eight years in the private sector with venture-capital firms, entrepreneurs, and corporate and nonprofit boards. In the Bush White House he was special assistant to the president for presidential personnel. In this capacity he recommended candidates to President Bush for the most senior political appointments for 11 Cabinet departments and Cabinet-rank agencies, 32 independent federal agencies, and 14 part-time presidential boards and commissions. It was during a dramatic period in American history—from September 2006 to January 2011—that Ed Moy served as 38th Director of the U.S. Mint. This put him in charge of the largest coinage factory and bullion "company" in the world, with responsibility over the main Philadelphia Mint and branch mints in Denver, San Francisco, and West Point, as well as the gold depository of Fort Knox. During Moy's directorship, the Sacagawea dollars were continued and the Presidential and Native American dollars were introduced. Today Ed Moy is an executive, strategist, and advisor in economic policy and finance/investment, and a frequent speaker and commentator on these topics. He lives in Arlington with his wife, Karen, and their daughters.

The author (left) and Mint Director Edmund C. Moy at the
American Numismatic Association convention, August 6, 2009.

PREFACE

Modern U.S. dollar coins—those dating from the 1970s to today—are popular with collectors, even though they don't share the sepia-toned romance of older silver dollars. They're not worn from being slid down countless bars in Wild West saloons; we don't imagine them being paid out of Las Vegas slot machines in streams of clinking silver. None of them have attained the legendary status of the 1804 dollar, or entered the popular imagination like the coin supposedly thrown across the Potomac River by a young George Washington. (Never mind that the first U.S. silver dollars were minted when Washington was in his 60s.) Even so, coin collectors love modern dollars. Nearly every American has seen them, even the older Eisenhower types, at one point or another; specialists study their varieties; and the U.S. Mint continues to produce them by the millions, in innovative formats and with fascinating new themes and designs.

By 2016 Whitman Publishing's Bowers Series had covered the most popularly collected earlier dollar types (in the eponymous *Guide Book of Peace Dollars*, the *Guide Book of Morgan Silver Dollars*, and the *Guide Book of Liberty Seated Silver Coins*). But there was no single book-length history and coin-by-coin study of Eisenhower, Anthony, Sacagawea, Native American, and Presidential dollars. The *Guide Book of Modern United States Dollar Coins*, volume no. 22 in the Bowers Series, remedies that situation. This new volume is a natural addition to the lineup. Every day at Whitman we're taking the pulse of the hobby community. From conversations with coin collectors, dealers, Mint officials, and others, and from our sales of folders, albums, and related products, we know that interest in modern dollar coins is strong. Eisenhower dollars have a numismatic society, the Ike Group, devoted to them. Collectors (some with profit in mind) carefully select the highest-graded coins in the series, take the time to build well-matched and visually appealing sets, compete in registries, research the history of the coins, and study interesting die varieties. Susan B. Anthony dollars make up a shorter series but they have their enthusiasts as well. And the golden dollars of 2000 to date traverse a rich landscape of Native American and presidential themes, giving collectors much to think and talk about.

The Bowers Series is named for Whitman Publishing's numismatic director, Q. David Bowers, a legend in the hobby. Not every volume in the collection is written by Dave Bowers himself (Roger W. Burdette created the work on Peace dollars, for example), but he was a natural choice for this particular subject. The author of several best-selling books on silver dollars, as well as numerous books and countless articles and columns on other coin series, Dave stays up to date on all modern coinage, including dollars. His contacts within the hobby community give him access to market insight and analysis from specialists. Over the past several years Dave and I have visited each of the U.S. Mint's currently operating facilities (Philadelphia, Denver, San Francisco, and West Point, as well as headquarters in Washington, D.C.). We have interviewed Mint officers, technicians, engineers, assayers, coin designers, manufacturing specialists, and others who work with our nation's coinage on a daily basis. By observing firsthand every aspect of production, and taking copious notes, Dave has gathered unique knowledge of the dollar coins being made today. This information is priceless not only for active coin collectors, but also for the sake of American history in general. Dave Bowers tells the story of the coins of the United States, and the coins tell the story of the nation.

To this cutting-edge modern-day research, which is ongoing as you read these words, Dave adds his photographic memory of 60-plus years as a coin dealer, collector, and researcher. He was famous as a numismatist well before the first modern U.S. dollars were minted in 1971, and he has personally known most of the designers, engravers, Mint directors, and others involved in the creation, production, and distribution of these coins.

I have written elsewhere on the subject of how Q. David Bowers manages to be so prolific as an author, in breadth and depth, across so many numismatic subjects. In the preface to the *Guide Book of Hard Times Tokens* I mentioned a few factors: his disciplined approach to writing, his insatiable curiosity, his ability to make creative mental connections, his deep network of colleagues, and his years of active experience. All of these factors were in play as Dave created the *Guide Book of Modern United States Dollar Coins.* The result is a valuable reference guide that will benefit every coin collector.

Dennis Tucker
Publisher, Whitman Publishing
Atlanta, Georgia

Author Q. David Bowers signing the guest book
during a research visit to the San Francisco Mint, 2015.

INTRODUCTION

I like Ike! I like Sacagawea too. I of course like presidents Washington and Lincoln, but I also like Buchanan and Harding even if historians don't. As to Susan B. Anthony, I have come to find her attractive, although at one time I preferred Miss Liberty. All these figures from the past are on coins, of course.

Welcome to my study of modern dollars from 1971 to date. For the coins in this book I was present at their creation, so to speak. By 1971 I had studied minting history for many years—since the early 1950s, in fact—and had visited the three mints then in operation. I also knew the key Mint officials and was a fine personal friend of Chief Engraver Frank Gasparro. After his retirement on January 6, 1981, I became a friend of his successor, Chief Engraver Elizabeth Jones. During and after that time, until the present, I have known most of the engravers on the Mint staff, sculptor-engravers and medallic sculptors, as they are designated now. I've even met some of the talented outsiders in the Mint's Artistic Infusion Program, who have designed certain of the "golden dollars" of the present century.

I have worked with Mint directors as well, including Mary Brooks, Donna Pope, Philip Diehl, Jay Johnson, Henrietta H. Fore, Edmund C. Moy, and Acting Director Richard Peterson. In 2015 I met incoming principal deputy director Rhett Jeppson and spent some time with him. I attended various events relating to dollar coins from the Eisenhower series forward. Tom Jurkowsky, director of corporate communications, who is important in Mint public relations and outreach, has been of immeasurable help, a helper par excellence. Michael J. White sent me a *box* of Mint document copies, news releases, and more—a treasure trove that resulted in my finding information that contributed to a lot of facts in this book that have never appeared in a single volume before.

Several modern authors and researchers who have studied these coins in detail have helped in many ways, including by providing quotable narrative. Charles Morgan, James Sego, Rob Ezerman, Herbert Hicks, James Wiles, and others have provided information that I would not have otherwise acquired. See the Acknowledgements on page 340 for an expanded list. I am grateful to all.

I also followed the distribution of the new dollars—the high hopes of the Treasury Department that the 1971 Eisenhower dollars would become popular, which never came to pass, but I did see them on gaming tables in Las Vegas in 1972 and 1973. Although Chief Engraver Frank Gasparro hoped that his Liberty Cap design would be used on the new mini-dollar of 1979, as did the Treasury Department, Congress had the last word, as it always does, and suffragette Susan B. Anthony was portrayed. I was in Frank's office when he had many images of her arranged around the wall and was doing his best, and with enthusiasm, to create a coin that everyone would like. This did happen, but only with collectors. The public gave a collective yawn. Try as it might the Treasury could not persuade citizens to prefer coins to dollar bills. Then there was the mystery, still unsolved, of what happened to hundreds of thousands of 1981–D and S dollars. Neither I nor the Treasury Department could find out where they went—this despite my spending hours on the telephone with Federal Reserve staff. In 1999 there was a surprise when more "Susies" were struck, even though tens of millions of 1979 and 1980 coins were still in storage. The conventional-wisdom explanation was one thing and reality was another, as I learned from a highly placed Mint official while doing research in 2015.

As some readers may remember, in 1993 my two-volume set, *Silver Dollars and Trade Dollars of the United States: A Complete Encyclopedia*, was published and soon became the standard reference on the title subjects. The Ike and Susie dollars (except for the 1999 coins) were covered in detail.

Fast-forward to 2000, when Sacagawea dollars were issued. I had never written about them in depth, but I was on the scene when they were created and first offered for sale. These were pet coins of Mint Director Jay Johnson, and he told me many stories about his trying to promote them, even through Kermit the Mint Spokesfrog (who was mainly busy croaking about State quarters).

There were no contemporary images of Sacagawea, the lady who acted as a guide for the Corps of Discovery in the Northwest, best known as the Lewis and Clark Expedition. Artist-sculptor Glenna Goodacre of Santa Fe, New Mexico, submitted a design that was chosen. For a model she chose a local university student of Blackfoot parentage, Randy'L He-dow Teton. I had several pictures taken of her and Randy'L. Later, when I ran across her again, she said that had since learned that charging for photographs had been worthwhile. If baseball players do that, why not coin models?

More than any other coins among modern dollars—although 1971 and 1972 Ikes give a good run for the money—the 2000-dated Sacagawea dollars have a complicated and somewhat complex history—involving rarities hidden in boxes of Cheerios cereal, gold strikings that circulated the Earth in orbit with astronauts, and trouble when coins of the new manganese-brass cladding turned purple and other colors! Read all about it—as they say—in the pages to follow.

In 2008 the Sacagawea dollars with Thomas D. Rogers's beautiful soaring eagle on the reverse were minted for the last time. Sacagawea endured as the obverse of the new Native American dollars introduced in 2009 and continued since that time. There is a lot to like about the "golden dollars" of the present century, but it was a mistake in my opinion to place the date and mintmark of later coin on the *edge* Displayed in an album a set of 2009-P, D, and S coins all look the same!

The Presidential dollars from 2007 to date are a separate series, actually initiating the curious edge placement of key details essential for numismatists. The Statue of Liberty reverse by talented Mint sculptor-engraver Don Everhart is nice enough, but the obverses are not as interesting as they could have been. It was proposed that each obverse depict a president in a different pose or in different surroundings, and that the reverse show a scene from his life. In 2009 the reverses of Lincoln cents showed events from the life of that president and were exceptionally interesting. Some years ago I wrote a book on American presidents for Whitman—not for numismatic readers, but for the general public. I delved into the lives of the various men, as have many historians before me. Some of this information in abbreviated form is given under each of the Presidential dollar listings. There you will find Peggy Eaton, whose flirtations caused the rearrangement of a president's Cabinet. You will also encounter a twentieth-century president who was an extreme racist, who praised the Ku Klux Klan, and denounced women who sought to vote.

The modern dollars from 1971 to date now include nearly 200 different regular dates and mints, making them a nice specialty. Although some are scarcer than others, especially among Eisenhower dollars in higher grades, all are readily available and affordable in Mint State. Writing this book and contacting a new generation of collectors and dealers who have studied them has been a very rewarding experience, as has been a close interface with the U.S. Mint staff over a long period of years, as noted.

Inspired by what I have learned about "golden dollars" from 2000 to date, and already liking Ikes and Susies, I set about forming a collection of them. Surprisingly, a set of basic dates and mintmarks, in Mint State and Proof, costs far less than a thousand dollars. Then there were two special coins. One, a 2000-P dollar presented to Glenna Goodacre, was gifted to me years ago by Jeff Garrett. I took it out of hiding, thus saving a lot of money as I built my collection. Then there was another variety of 2000-P connected with the earlier-mentioned General Mills cereal. I wrote out a strong four-figure check for it. Gulp! If there is any consolation, even though it is one of the prime rarities of our era, it cost only a fraction of what I paid for my 1787 Columbia and Washington medal. (Am I piquing your interest? I love writing, and some years ago the Columbia and Washington medal was showcased in a book I wrote with Katherine Jaeger, *100 Greatest American Medals and Tokens,* one of my favorites.)

I hope you enjoy the chapters to follow and learn a lot you did not know about, perhaps including a 1971 Eisenhower dollar that has a "friendly eagle" on the reverse—just like I did when I was doing research for this book.

The standard-issue 2000-P Sacagawea dollar (top) has two low-mintage variants
available to collectors. Presentation copies (middle), given to designer Glenna
Goodacre and subsequently released into the marketplace, have a distinguishing finish,
while versions distributed in Cheerios boxes (bottom) show distinctly bold tail feathers.

SILVER DOLLARS, 1794–1935

Although the United States did not coin silver dollars until 1794, by that time the dollar had been a familiar monetary unit for many years. Dollar-sized coins, also called crowns, talers, and related names, had been made for centuries in Europe and its colonies. In widest use in America was the Spanish milled dollar or 8 reales, made not only in Spain but also in Mexico and the Spanish-American colonies of Central and South America. The *real* (pronounced "ray-AHL") coin, worth 12-1/2 cents, was known as a bit. A 2-reales coin, two bits or a quarter of a dollar, was worth 25 cents, and a 4-reales coin was worth a half dollar.

These coins were legal tender in the United States until the Act of February 21, 1857, repealed their status, effective two years later but subsequently extended for six months. From 1794 through the late 1850s, 8-reales were plentiful in commerce while federal dollars were seldom seen as they were mainly used in the export trade.

Various silver and gold coins of other countries were legal tender as well, including many issues of Great Britain and France. Coins of the same denomination and from the same country could vary in silver content depending on when they were made. As the silver content and denominations of these foreign coins changed from time to time, metropolitan and financial papers carried columns headed "Prices Current," giving exchange values.

Many merchants, towns, and other entities continued reckoning in Spanish dollars or British pounds, shillings, and pence into the early 1800s.

When the United Colonies began issuing their own paper money in 1775 it was denominated in Spanish milled dollars. Such notes were produced through 1778 and in denominations up to $80.

A Spanish-American silver 8 reales or dollar, 1759, of King Ferdinand VI, struck at the Mexico Mint with an M̥ mintmark. The obverse depicts the Pillars of Hercules, the mythical posts at each side of the entrance to the Mediterranean Sea from the Atlantic Ocean. (shown at 125%)

Later bills were imprinted with "United States of America." As the fledgling American government had few silver or gold coins to back the notes, they depreciated to the point at which it took $40 or more in Continental Currency to exchange for one Spanish silver dollar. As citizens were uncertain of the financial strength of the Treasury, no more federal notes were issued in quantity until 1861.

In the same era certain of the colonies, later becoming states, issued their own paper. Beginning in 1782 state-chartered banks issued paper currency. By the time the federal government issued Demand Notes in 1861 to help finance the Civil War, about 3,000 state-chartered banks had distributed countless millions of notes. Popular denominations included $1, $2, $3, $5, $10, and $20. Bills of $50 and $100 were not often seen, and those with values of $500 and $1000 were mainly used in bank-to-bank transactions.

Continental Currency $8 note issued by the United Colonies, February 17, 1776, payable in Spanish milled dollars. The congress that would form the United States of America actually had virtually no coin reserves to redeem such bills at face value.

$1 note of the Wolfborough [sic] Bank of Wolfeboro, New Hampshire, 1838. Daniel Pickering, the bank's president, was a leading entrepreneur in the town and in 1850 built the Pavilion, a grand hotel on the shore of Lake Winnipesaukee.

The First Bank of the United States, a private entity in which the government was a stockholder, was chartered in 1791 and did business for 20 years until its charter expired. The Second Bank of the United States was chartered in 1816 and also operated for 20 years. The various branches of these banks issued many notes, including of the $1 denomination. Only a few genuine bills survive to the present day, although counterfeits are seen with frequency.

The Philadelphia Mint

The Mint Act of April 2, 1792, authorized the coinage of copper half cents and cents, silver half dimes, dimes, quarters, half dollars, and dollars, and gold $2.50, $5, and $10 coins. The production of precious-metal coins could not take place until a surety bond of $10,000 was posted by chief coiner Henry Voigt and assayer Albion Cox. These sums could not be met at the time. Accordingly, the coinage for 1793, the first year the Mint was in full operation, consisted only of copper coins. The first produced were cents, struck in February, delivered by the coiner on March 1, and released into circulation March 15.

As no engraver had been appointed yet, it fell to the chief coiner, Henry Voigt, to engrave the dies.[1] These were produced in quantity through the spring and summer. In late June or early July Joseph Wright was appointed to the post of engraver. Wright, a highly trained artist in the private sector, may have created the high-relief version of Miss Liberty in combination with a wreath reverse and is definitely credited with the Liberty Cap design. Unfortunately, he contracted yellow fever and passed away in September 1793. Otherwise later designs of United States coins might well be different from what we know today. Wright's legacy of Miss Liberty with a cap and pole, inspired by the famous Libertas Americana medal of 1782, lived on and was used

The Philadelphia Mint in the 1790s. The front building, actually two older buildings connected, served as the offices. Coining was done in the large building behind it, the foundation of which was first laid on July 31, 1792. At the back of the property was a horse-powered rolling mill to convert ingots into strips of metal. (George L. Osborn sketch, 1974)

in copper issues for the next several years. Half cents of the Liberty Cap design were issued in July. Two centuries later, in 1979, Chief Engraver Frank Gasparro proposed reviving the Liberty Cap motif for use on the forthcoming "mini dollar," but Congress mandated that the portrait of suffragette Susan B. Anthony be used.

Robert Scot (often misspelled *Scott* in contemporary directories), who was born in Scotland and trained as a watchmaker, came to Philadelphia in the early 1780s. He was hired as the Mint engraver on November 23, 1793. By this time he had produced many line engravings, including maps and portraits, for clients. Scot would continue in the post for many years, until his death in November 1823. On the following December 31 his estate was paid $100 for one month's salary to close out his account. While holding the engravership he also did extensive outside work, including for Thomas Dobson's edition of *Rees' Encyclopedia*, published in Philadelphia from 1794 to 1803. John Reich, who had done contract work for the Mint since 1800, was signed as assistant engraver in 1807 and produced most of the new federal coin designs after that time, but none relating to silver dollars.

The first cents issued in March 1793 depicted Miss Liberty on the obverse and a chain of 15 links on the reverse. (shown at 150%)

1793 Sheldon-9, the second major design of the cent. The obverse and reverse are in high relief from masterfully engraved dies. These are known as Wreath cents today and exist in several varieties. (shown at 150%)

The Liberty Cap design by Joseph Wright, a highly accomplished artist in the private sector who joined the Mint in the summer of 1793, is the rarest of the three major types of the year. (shown at 150%)

The First Silver Dollars

A congressional act of March 3, 1794, had reduced the surety-bond requirements to $5,000 for chief coiner Voigt and just $1,000 for assayer Cox. Mint Director David Rittenhouse, a man of means, guaranteed the bond for Voigt, while Charles Gilchrist stood as guarantor for Cox. All was set to produce silver coins. While the coinage of half cents and cents was done for the Mint's own account and a profit was registered on the difference between face value and the cost of copper, silver and gold coins were minted only at the specific request of depositors. In the early 1790s the Mint had no bullion account of its own. A depositor of silver or gold had to call at the Mint at a later time to receive coins of the asked-for denominations.

In November 1794 about 2,000 silver dollars were made, the first coinage of the denomination, but only 1,758 were found to be suitable for circulation. The others were rejected and held back. The obverse featured what numismatists call the Flowing Hair design, with Miss Liberty facing right and tresses of hair streaming to the left. A few of the new dollars were carried north to Portsmouth in the Granite State, where the *New Hampshire Gazette* reported the following on December 2:

> Some of the dollars now coining at the Mint of the United States have found their way to this town. A correspondent put one into the editor's hands yesterday. Its weight is equal to that of a Spanish dollar, encircled by *Fifteen Stars*, and has the word "LIBERTY" at the top, and the date, 1794, at the bottom. On the reverse, is the *Bald Eagle*, enclosed in an *Olive Branch*, round which are the words "One Dollar, or Unit, Hundred Cents." The *tout ensemble* has a pleasing effect to a connoisseur; but the touches of the graver are too delicate, and there is a want of that boldness of execution which is necessary to durability and currency.

The 1794 dollars passed into the channels of commerce where in time most became very worn. When numismatics became a widely popular hobby in the United States beginning in the 1850s, bankers and exchange houses picked these dollars out of deposits, as they were worth a premium. Today somewhere between 135 and 150 are estimated to exist.

All 1794 and 1795 half dollars and dollars have eight stars arranged to the left on the obverse and seven to the right. Later star counts and arrangements varied. The reverse depicts an eagle perched on a small cloud enclosed within an open wreath. Half dime dies were also prepared in 1794, but they were not used until 1795. Numismatists view the Flowing Hair coins to be of special desirability, the first entries in a type set of American silver issues.

This 1794 dollar was obtained in the year of issue or in early 1795 by William Strickland, a visitor from England who collected coins and other objects. It later passed to the Roland Winn family and was in the Lord St. Oswald Collection auctioned by Christie's in London in 1964. Later, it was acquired by D. Brent Pogue. It crossed the auction block in September 2015. (shown at 125%)

Draped Bust Coinages

For most of 1795 the Flowing Hair design was used, creating well over two dozen varieties and die combinations. In the autumn it was replaced by the Draped Bust motif, said by some to have been based on a Gilbert Stuart sketch of a Philadelphia society lady. In catalogs of years ago it was popular to call the obverse design the Fillet Head or Fillet Bust, *fillet* meaning ribbon and pertaining to the band tying Miss Liberty's hair at the back of her head. The perched eagle on the reverse was modified slightly from the earlier Flowing Hair version. Coins of this design were minted through early 1798.

In 1798 the reverse of the dollar was changed to the Heraldic Eagle or Large Eagle type based on the Great Seal of the United States. This motif had been introduced in 1796 on the quarter eagle, or gold $2.50 coin.[2] From 1798 through 1803, extending into 1804, coinage of silver dollars was very heavy. In early 1804, 19,570 coins were made from earlier-dated dies, presumably of 1803.

The availability of dollars in quantity had an unintended side effect. It had been normal practice for importers of foreign goods to send Spanish-American dollars in exchange, but the availability of the United States' version made it easier to use the domestic product. Many of the U.S. dollars were then sent to the East Indies to pay for spices and to the treaty port of Canton in China to pay for Eastern luxury goods.

**In autumn 1795 the Draped Bust obverse was
introduced, perhaps based on a sketch by Gilbert Stuart.
The reverse was modified slightly. (shown at 125%)**

**In 1798 the reverse was changed to the Heraldic Eagle or
Large Eagle design. This motif was continued through 1804, in
which year coinage of silver dollars was suspended. (shown at 125%)**

Many other dollars went to the West Indies. These dollars rarely returned and were thus lost to the nation as coins, unable to serve in domestic commerce.

As noted, in the early years the Mint struck silver and gold coins to the order of depositors of those metals. While the recipients of such pieces could do what they wished with them, it was the Treasury Department's hope and intention that the Mint would produce enough coins so that U.S. denominations would take the place of the overwhelming quantities of Spanish-American gold and silver coins in domestic circulation. The one-way shipments of silver dollars and $10 gold eagles—the largest and easiest to handle denominations—to foreign lands did no good for everyday business in the United States. By executive order made at the request of the Bank of the United States the mintage of $1 and $10 coins was stopped partway through 1804. Dollars would not be coined again for circulation until 1836, and it was not until 1838 that $10 pieces reappeared.

After 1804 the silver half dollar and gold $5 half eagle were the largest precious-metal coins of the realm being currently minted. Most half dollars remained stateside, but the vast majority of half eagles were exported, including nearly all struck from 1821 through early 1834, a time when no gold coins were seen in domestic commerce.

The 1804 Silver Dollar

Although there are silver dollars dated 1804, such pieces bearing this date were not minted for the first time until 1834. In that year it was desired to create some special diplomatic gifts to present on behalf of the president of the United States to foreign dignitaries on the far side of the world. These included maps, glassware, fine clothing, ornate swords, and other items. It was thought that for each recipient a fine set of American coinage mounted in an appropriate case would be truly representative of the United States. Two sets—one displayed in a red leather case and the other in a case of yellow leather—are known to have been presented: one to the sultan of Muscat and the other to the king of Siam.

Chief coiner Adam Eckfeldt worked with others to assemble one each of the current coins, each in mirror Proof finish. These comprised the half cent, cent, half dime, dime, quarter dollar, half dollar, gold $2.50, and gold $5. The Coinage Act of April 2, 1792, had provided for these and two other denominations, the silver dollar and the gold eagle or $10 coin. By 1834 the dollar and eagle were history, as none had been struck since three decades earlier in 1804.

What to do?

**A Proof 1804-dated silver dollar that was part of a set
presented to the sultan of Muscat in 1835. (shown at 125%)**

Seeking to reflect the history of American coinage correctly, Eckfeldt proposed including a dollar and an eagle of 1804, but none were on hand. Checking the *Annual Report of the Director of the Mint*, 1804, he learned that 19,570 silver dollars and 3,757 gold eagles had been struck in that year. New dies for each were made in 1834 with a mirror finish, and examples of the coins were struck. The 1804 eagle dies were left-over dies from 1804/1805—the obverse dated 180 with the plain 4 added from the 1834 half dollar punch set. The reverse was a *half dollar* reverse of 1805! The silver dollar has evenly beaded dentils and a rim. The eagle has the old style with no rim and irregular dentils. What Eckfeldt did not know, as there were no numismatic or other relevant guides in print, was that the dollars made in 1804 were from earlier-dated dies. Thus, there was no such coin as an 1804-dated dollar until 1834. However, there had been a mintage of 1804-dated eagles in that calendar year.

Early in 1835 two more Proof sets were ordered, intended for presentation in Cochin-China (today's Vietnam) and Japan. These were ready just before the USS *Peacock* was set to unfurl its sails to carry Edmund Roberts and his contingent on special assignment from the Andrew Jackson administration to visit dignitaries on the far side of the world. Thusly four sets were made. The last two sets were never presented, and what happened to them is not known today.

The existence of an 1804-dated dollar was not known to numismatists until 1842, when one was illustrated in the book by Jacob R. Eckfeldt and William E. DuBois published that year, *A Manual of Gold and Silver Coins of All Nations, Struck Within the Past Century*. This piqued the interest of Matthew A. Stickney, a Massachusetts numismatist who collected coins by date but did not have an 1804 dollar. He contacted the Mint, and in 1843 paid a visit and swapped some other coins for a specimen.

Today eight 1804-dated dollars are known from the dies made in 1834. At a later time, into the 1870s, restrikes were made with the same obverse die and another reverse die. Six of these are known today. As a class the 1804 dollar, nicknamed "The King of American Coins," has gained a fame all its own.

Gobrecht and Liberty Seated Silver Dollars

In 1835 the Treasury Department explored the idea of issuing more silver dollars for general circulation. It had been many years since the Flowing Hair and Draped Bust coins of the late 1700s and early 1800s centuries were coined, and few of those remained in circulation. The needs of commerce had been satisfied by Spanish-American 8-reales "dollars" and their fractional parts. To a lesser extent other dollar-sized coins that were legal tender played a part. By 1835 William Kneass was the engraver at the Mint and had been since his appointment in 1824 to succeed the late Robert Scot. In 1834 he had redesigned the quarter eagle and half eagle—the only gold denominations then being made—with the Classic Head motif, actually an adaptation of the portrait created years earlier by assistant engraver John Reich for use on the 1808 copper cent and later used on half cents as well.

In May 1835 Mint Director Samuel Moore, who had held the post since July 1824, resigned his position and on the 26th of that month his brother-in-law Dr. Robert Maskell Patterson was appointed. For the next month or so an easy transition was made. It was anticipated that activities would be busier than ever, as Congress had provided for the establishment of three branch mints, in New Orleans, Louisiana;

Charlotte, North Carolina; and Dahlonega, Georgia. Each would need a supply of dies and related equipment. Engraver Kneass was getting along in years. On June 16, Moore, still concerned with Mint matters, wrote to Secretary of the Treasury Levi Woodbury seeking permission to hire Christian Gobrecht as a member of the Mint staff. Gobrecht had been an engraver of bank-note plates and medal dies for many years, and his art was considered to be of a high order of excellence. Moore's recommendation was followed, and Gobrecht joined as "second" engraver (preferring that designation over "assistant") in September. Kneass had a debilitating stroke soon afterward and was unable to do much work.

Moore and Patterson both desired to begin work on a new dollar, one with Miss Liberty in a seated position on the obverse and a rendition on the reverse of the traditional eagle. Thomas Sully, a Philadelphia artist of renown, was enlisted to draw the obverse design, and Titian Peale, another local artist of talent, was assigned the reverse. In time, accepted sketches and models of both sides were created. The obverse design became known as Liberty Seated and the reverse, with the national bird in flight, the Flying Eagle.

Dies were prepared and in late 1836 the first coinage was accomplished—1,000 coins with mirror Proof fields and plain edges, unusual for coins intended for circulation. Most were deposited in a local bank and later paid out at face value. In early 1836, 600 more were struck from 1836-dated dies oriented in a different alignment. At least some of these 600 coins had reeded edges, an answer to the criticism that the plain-edge coins were "too medallic." When coin collecting became a popular hobby in the 1850s many bullion brokers and others retrieved Gobrecht dollars for the slight premium value they had at the time.

In 1839 it is thought that 300 more Gobrecht dollars were made for circulation. These had stars on the obverse, an eagle in a plain field on the reverse, and reeded edges. As with the two circulation issues of Gobrecht dollars and various associated patterns, combined with large numbers of restrikes made beginning in 1859, the order of striking and die alignments created puzzles that numismatists have been sorting out in recent times.

In 1836 the Gobrecht silver dollar with starless obverse and Flying Eagle reverse was made. In that year 1,000 were struck, most of which were put into circulation. (shown at 125%)

In 1840 the first large mintage of new dollars was made for circulation. The obverse depicted a modified Liberty Seated design with drapery at her elbow, and the reverse showed a perched eagle similar to that used on quarter dollars and half dollars in 1838 and 1839. The mintage for that year was 61,005. All went into circulation, there being no numismatic interest in such pieces as the time. Interested collectors opted for Proofs, of which a small number were made.

Contemporary accounts reveal that many of these coins were used as bullion pieces in the export trade. It seems that from the outset banks and exchange brokers charged several cents premium for such pieces. For quantity coins in everyday circulation, half dollars were the usually-seen highest denomination.

The discovery of gold at Sutter's Mill on the American River on January 24, 1848, ignited the California Gold Rush. In the next year thousands of "Forty Niners" arrived by land and sea to seek their fortunes. Large quantities of bullion reached the East, then went to Europe, causing gold to become more "common" in its ratio to silver, the standard being that 1 ounce of gold was equal in value to 15-1/2 ounces in silver. The price of silver rose on international markets to the point at which it cost more than face value to mint silver coins—the denominations in use at the time being the half dime, dime, quarter dollar, half dollar, and silver dollar. Hoarders and speculators retrieved what they could from circulation, to derive a few cents of profit on every

1839 Gobrecht dollar. (shown at 125%)

Gobrecht silver dollars with the Liberty Seated obverse and a reverse depicting a perched eagle were first made in 1840. This type, without motto on the reverse, was used through 1865. (shown at 125%)

dollar of face value. In 1851 the silver three-cent piece or trime was introduced. Containing just 75% silver instead of the standard 90% in other coins, they were not attractive to hoarders and were able to circulate freely.

The Coinage Act of February 21, 1853, reduced the silver content of the coins from the half dime to the half dollar, but not the dollar. After that point these silver coins became a familiar sight in circulation once again. Liberty Seated silver dollars still cost more than face value to produce and were made only to the order of bullion depositors who valued them for their silver content; their face value was irrelevant. The vast majority was shipped to Europe and to China and melted. None circulated domestically. Today, all Liberty Seated silver dollars after 1849 are scarce, and many are rare, despite generous mintages.

In 1866 the motto IN GOD WE TRUST was added to the reverse of all silver coins from the quarter to the dollar and all gold coins from the half eagle to the double eagle. That notation had first appeared on circulating coins in 1864 on the new bronze two-cent piece.

The Coinage Act of February 12, 1873, eliminated the standard or Liberty Seated silver dollar. A new denomination was introduced—the trade dollar specifically made for export to China. On these, Liberty was seated on bales on the obverse, and on the reverse a new-style eagle was shown. These were made in quantity through early 1878. After that time Proofs were made for collectors until 1883, plus a secret mintage of 1884 and 1885 coins for a dealer with close ties to the Mint.

**In 1866 the motto IN GOD WE TRUST was
added to the reverse of the dollar. (shown at 125%)**

**Trade dollars weighing 420 grains were minted for the
export trade to China from 1873 to 1878. (shown at 125%)**

Morgan and Peace Silver Dollars

Beginning in 1870 there were major disruptions in the silver market. In Europe several countries including the newly formed German Empire discontinued making coins that were nearly of full silver content, freeing large amounts of bullion. Prices on the international market dropped. In the same era, production of silver in the American West increased with the output of existing mines plus many new ore discoveries. The atmosphere of silver prosperity of the 1860s changed to gloom in some areas in the 1870s. The situation was unfortunate and perplexing to those in the mining and refining industries.

Silver-mining interests in the West felt that if Uncle Sam would purchase an unlimited amount of silver as it became available and convert it to coins, the problem would be solved. However, the Treasury Department had no need for more silver coins. Millions of them had been hoarded by the public since 1862, when the outcome of the Civil War was uncertain. In 1876 these hoarded coins were dumped back into circulation. There was a glut.

Not to worry. Politics reared its head, and on February 28, 1878, the Bland-Allison Act was passed, mandating that the Treasury Department buy two to four million ounces of silver bullion at the market price each month and convert it into dollars. The trade dollar was discontinued.

A design created in 1877 by U.S. Mint assistant engraver George T. Morgan for a pattern half dollar was adapted for use on the dollar. Coinage in quantity began in March 1878. As there was no need for millions of silver dollars in circulation, they were piled up in 1,000-coin bags in Mint and Treasury vaults. At one time many were even stored in the Philadelphia Post Office!

Finally, in 1904 the supply of silver bullion under the 1878 and later acts ran out, and mintage of dollars ceased. By that time hundreds of millions of Morgan-design dollars were in storage. There was no accounting of what dates, mintmarks, or varieties were involved. The next chapter in the silver-dollar chronicle involved the Pittman Act of April 23, 1918. This was legislation "to conserve the gold supply of the United States; to permit the settlement in silver of trade balances adverse to the United States; to provide silver for subsidiary coinage and for commercial use; to assist foreign governments at war with the enemies of the United States; and for the above purposes to stabilize the price and encourage the production of silver."

Great Britain, a friend of the United States and at the time at war with Germany, claimed to be in urgent need of silver for use in

Too much silver: the Boston & Colorado Gold and Silver Smelting Company, Black Hawk, Colorado, with a pile of 30 silver ingots weighing 2,200 pounds.

colonial India. The only possible source of sufficient metal to meet the war emergency, it was said, was the United States Treasury stock of silver dollars. Congress therefore passed the act of April 23, 1918, which authorized the melting or breaking up and sale as bullion of a quantity not to exceed 350,000,000 silver dollars from those in storage. In addition to the 259,121,554 silver dollars eventually melted to create bullion sold to Great Britain, 11,111,168 silver dollars were melted and assigned for subsidiary silver coinage—current dimes, quarters, and half dollars.

Certain of the melted silver dollars came from these sources, these being the *bullion* values of the coins:

Mint stock from the Philadelphia Mint: $58,534,554.

Mint stock from the San Francisco Mint: $39,001,000.

Transferred from the Treasury at Washington to the Philadelphia Mint: $87,686,000.

Transferred from the Treasury at Washington to the San Francisco Mint: $25,000,000.

Transferred from Sub-Treasury at New York to the New York Assay Office: $26,500,000.

Transferred from the New Orleans Mint to the Philadelphia Mint: $12,400,000.

Transferred from the New Orleans Mint to the San Francisco Mint: $10,000,000.

By that time the Treasury in Washington had in storage vast quantities of undistributed Carson City coins as well as coins from other mints, with no inventory or accounting. What the Sub-Treasury had is not known, but many may have been coins that had once been in circulation. The face value of many coins from the several sources:

Face value of dollars melted for sale as bullion from the Philadelphia Mint: $158,620,554.

Face value of dollars melted for sale as bullion from the San Francisco Mint: $74,001,000.

Face value of dollars melted for sale as bullion from the New York Assay Office: $26,500,000.

Silver dollars of the George T. Morgan design were minted continuously from 1878 to 1904 and again in 1921. (shown at 125%)

In addition to the above there were other transactions. In total, 270,232,722 silver dollars of earlier dates were melted.

Not long afterward, Congress passed an act to purchase domestically produced silver bullion to replace the silver dollars melted for sale to Great Britain (but not those melted for domestic coinage), part of the logic being that they were needed as backing for Silver Certificates. At the time there were still large quantities of earlier dollars in storage that had escaped the Pittman Act. From later government records:

> The quantity of silver required for recoining 259,121,554 silver dollars of exact legal silver content, disregarding the question of operative losses, was 200,414,327.07 fine ounces. Monthly receipts of purchased silver by the mint service institutions during the three-year period from May 1920 to June 1923, averaged approximately 5,000,000 ounces, the purchases absorbing practically the entire silver production of the United States for this period. These purchases were made at the fixed price of $1 per fine ounce, *while the market rate during this time was usually below 70 cents.*[3]

In 1921 a hurry-up call was made to strike more silver dollars as quickly as possible. It was thought that the master hubs and dies for the Morgan dollar had been destroyed earlier, as with so many coins in storage there was no conceivable reason that any others would ever be made.[4] Accordingly, in 1921 new hubs and masters were made slightly different in detail from the earlier ones. The Philadelphia, Denver, and San Francisco mints each turned out millions of coins.

In the meantime, there had been a movement within the American Numismatic Association and elsewhere to create a new silver dollar design commemorating the end of the World War with the 1919 Treaty of Versailles. Several "peace" designs were proposed. One by Anthony de Francisci, a sculptor in the private sector, was adopted, and coinage commenced in December 1921, after which the Morgan design was retired, presumably for all time.

The original 1921 Peace dollar design had high-relief features on the obverse in particular, with the result that the details at the center did not strike up properly. In 1922 the Mint lowered the relief. Coinage of Peace dollars continued intermittently through 1935.

Peace silver dollars were minted from 1921 to 1928 and again in 1934 and 1935. (shown at 125%)

Coins in Commerce

From the late 1800s through the early 1960s silver dollars were a standard part of numismatics. For the Morgan and Peace coins, banks typically had from a few thousand coins to many 1,000-coin bags of dollars in their vaults—often with unsorted miscellaneous dates and mintmarks. For collectors who visited banks to look through what was on hand, most dates and mintmarks could be found for face value, although Carson City varieties in particular were scarce. Grades ranged from well-worn to Mint State.

In the meantime, silver dollars of these two types were rarely seen in general commerce in most regions of the country, certain Rocky Mountain states being exceptions. As a resident of the East I don't recall ever receiving a silver dollar in change. In Nevada silver dollars were in wide use on gaming tables, adding to the romance of playing roulette or poker. By the 1940s, Nevada casinos were the main users of such coins. Silver dollars saw limited circulation in Montana, Idaho, and certain nearby areas. In the meantime, many collectors endeavored to build collections of Morgan and Peace dollars by date and mintmark. The *Guide Book of United States Coins*, the first edition of which was released in 1946, became the standard source for market values.

In November 1962 a long-sealed (since 1929) vault at the Philadelphia Mint was opened in order to tap reserves of silver dollars, popular for banks to pay out during the holiday season. The coins had been put there from a shipment from a vault in the inactive (since 1909) New Orleans Mint. A few hundred 1,000-coin bags of sparkling new 1903-O Morgan dollars were casually given out. At the time this date/mintmark was the rarest and most famous of all coins in the series—so rare that it was estimated that no more than a dozen or two dozen Mint State coins existed! The 1903-O listed for $1,500 in the *Guide Book*, the top price level for any Morgan dollar.

This was like finding money in the streets, a nationwide silver rush occurred, and several hundred million silver dollars of various dates and mintmarks were paid out from Treasury and bank vaults.

The End of Silver Dollars

In step with the foregoing, by 1964 there was widespread recognition that the price of silver on international markets was going to rise above the $1.2727 melt-down worth of silver currently in 90% silver coins. This sharply accelerated the rush to buy silver dollars from banks and from the Treasury Department. There was nothing for an individual buyer to lose: a silver dollar would still be worth a dollar and could potentially be worth more in silver value.

On Wednesday, March 24, 1964, Secretary of the Treasury Douglas Dillon declared that, effective immediately, Silver Certificates could not be redeemed for silver dollars, and no more dollar coins would be paid out. The great silver dollar rush had ended. The Treasury took stock of its remaining pieces and found about 3,000,000 Carson City dollars on hand—Mint State, low-mintage issues that the Department later auctioned over a period of time.

This dollar bonanza encouraged tens of thousands of people to discover numismatics and become serious collectors, while hundreds of thousands more developed a casual interest—perhaps setting aside a few dozen or even a bag or two of dollars.

Meanwhile in 1964, other silver coins continued to be made, including the new Kennedy half dollar. By year's end the Philadelphia Mint had struck 273,304,004 of the new half dollars for circulation, and the Denver Mint made an additional

156,205,446. All or nearly all disappeared into the hands of the public and speculators, and it was widely reported that no one had received even a single coin in pocket change. In the autumn Secretary Dillon stated that the Treasury was investigating alternative metals for striking coins from dimes to half dollars.

In the spring and early summer of 1964 there was a strong call for more silver dollars by the public and also by Nevada casinos. None of the coins had been minted for circulation since 1935. Legislation passed on August 4, 1964, provided for the coinage of 45 million silver dollars. At the Philadelphia Mint hubs and dies were made for a new silver dollar issue of 1964. Examples of 1964-dated Morgan dollars and Peace dollars were made as trials. At the Denver Mint 316,076 Peace-design coins were struck with D mintmarks. None were officially released, although some accounts stated that Mint employees were allowed to buy them. No example has ever been publicized.

New silver dollars were not to be, at least for the time being.

Thus was set the scenario for modern metallic dollars commencing with the Dwight D. Eisenhower coins in 1971.

Galvano for a Morgan dollar
dated 1964, when possibilities
for a new dollar included revival
of the 1878–1921 design.

Die for the 1964 Peace silver dollar.

COLLECTING MODERN U.S. DOLLAR COINS

The field or panorama of dollars from the first 1971 Eisenhower issues up to the latest Sacagawea, Native American, and Presidential coins comprises nearly 200 dates and mintmarks—or more than all of the 1836 to 1935 Liberty Seated, Morgan, and Peace dollar varieties listed in the *Guide Book* combined! Whereas a set of these early dollars in MS–63 to 65 and PF-65 grades would cost at least several million dollars, with one (the 1870-S) unknown at this level, a full set of *Guide Book*–listed Eisenhower, Susan B. Anthony, Sacagawea, Native American, and Presidential dollars costs less than $1,000!

The field is large, interesting, and, as you will learn in the following chapters, filled with some surprises.

Eisenhower Dollars

(shown at 125%)

First minted in 1971, Eisenhower dollars were hailed on several fronts. Nevada casinos, which had been using metal tokens and composition chips since 1965, could at last return to having dollar coins on their tables. Unexpectedly to observers the use of Ike dollars, as they were nicknamed, lasted for a relatively short time, after which casinos went back to using colorful chips with their name imprinted on each.

Another aspect of the early Eisenhower coin excitement, especially in Treasury Department circles, was that metal dollars, which could last close to 20 years or even more in circulation, would replace paper dollar bills that had a life of only about 18 months. This change did not happen, as the longtime position of the Crane Paper Co. as a supplier to the Bureau of Engraving and Printing had deep and seemingly sacred political connections. In time, Canada, Great Britain, and other countries replaced their lowest-denomination paper currency with coins, but despite many attempts (as related in the following chapters), paper dollars are still here, whereas metal dollars are hardly ever seen in commerce. Further casting a shadow on the use of metal dollars in American commerce anytime soon is new paper of improved strength and endurance.

Another factor at the launch of the Eisenhower dollar was numismatic interest. Although the design was not a favorite of everyone, there was a strong collector demand for the varieties issued from the Philadelphia, Denver, and San Francisco mints. This was particularly true in the first several years. During the over-promoted 1776–1976 Bicentennial and afterward, interest slumped and new collectors were fewer. All along the way the discoveries of interesting die varieties, some differing only minutely, was continually covered by *Coin World* and *Numismatic News*, the two weekly publications, plus other media. In time, several reference books on Eisenhower dollars were published (see the bibliography), the Internet added information, and the Ike Group Web site was formed by Rob Ezerman as a forum for specialists who enjoy coins with minor variations.

Today, Eisenhower dollars are very widely and enthusiastically collected. With a few exceptions, the major varieties can be collected in gem (MS-65) or finer grade and Proof-65 or finer, for relatively little expense. Certain variations in the dies, especially for 1971 and 1972, including the charmingly named 1971-D Friendly Eagle, can be added to a basic collection for reasonable cost. For me the stories that go with each issue and the American scene at the time add a lot of interest to a set of these coins.

If your interest is piqued, a local coin show or coin shop is a good place to get started. Most have a nice variety of coins and albums. There are also many offerings on eBay and in other Internet auctions.

Susan B. Anthony Dollars

(shown at 125%)

Forming a collection of Susan B. Anthony dollars, of 1979 to 1981 and then with a jump to 1999, can be done as quickly as a wink. There is but one scarce (sort of) variety, the 1979, Wide Rim, issue. The story is that the border on early strikes, called the Narrow Rim issue, was thin, with a large gap between it and the date. It was widened on later coins, making the date appear nearer. Because of this visual cue, these are also sometimes referred to as Near Date and Far Date, although the date did not change location.

The 1999 coins came as a surprise to numismatists, especially as tens of millions or even more Anthony dollars were still languishing in Treasury vaults. However, demand for dollars was increasing rapidly through use in buses and vending machines—so the official story went. But, the official story was a disguise for something else, as I learned in 2015 and as is related in chapter 5.

I don't think anyone can make a deep specialty in this brief series, but a few die varieties lend interest.

When asked by a *New York Times* reporter in 1923, "Why did you want to climb Mount Everest," George Mallory retorted, "Because it's there." Similarly, perhaps the reason to collect "Susie" dollars, as we call them, is because they are there. A collection of modern dollars would not be complete without them.

Sacagawea Dollars

(shown at 125%)

The Susan B. Anthony mini-dollar, as it was often called, never became popular in commerce and never replaced the paper dollar. However, lessons had been learned, and an essentially new group of legislators—different from those who conceived the SBA dollars years earlier—jumped on the idea that a small-diameter dollar, if configured differently, would replace the paper dollar bill. This time around it would not be likely to be confused with the quarter as it was a new coin format with a golden-color surface and a plain edge.

Sacagawea, the Native American interpreter who traveled as an interpreter (not a *guide*, as per popular wisdom) with the Lewis and Clark Expedition in the upper reaches of the Missouri River and Northwest, was the hands-on favorite for the obverse motif, and an American eagle in flight served well on the other side.

The story of the first year of the Sacagawea dollar would make a good *book* by itself! Well, almost. In 2000 enough coins were made to furnish three for every man, woman, and child in America. The expectation was that soon purses and pockets would be jingling and jangling with them. The ideal "golden" surface proved to be less than that, and problems developed. Then there are the stories of coins struck in real gold and flown on a space mission, the unintended special coins made for obverse designer Glenna Goodacre, the puzzle of coins turning to different colors, and more—not to overlook how much citizens of *Ecuador* liked them. Oops! I forgot to mention the special Cheerios cereal coins—see chapter 6!

The Sacagawea dollar was a win-win product for the U.S. Mint and the financial statements of the Treasury Department as each one yielded a large profit over the cost of metal and striking. The only problem from a logical viewpoint was that merchants and others did not use them in commerce. Countless millions piled up in Treasury vaults. A stop was put to this in 2002. Later varieties were limited to numismatic strikes sold at a premium. By 2008, when the last pieces left the coining presses, a nice series had been created—one that was and still is dear to collectors. Today a basic run of Sacagawea dollar dates and mintmarks from 2000 to 2008 in gem Mint State and Proof preservation costs less than $200. There is room for such a display in every collection.

Native American Dollars

(shown at 125%)

Launched in 2009 the Native American dollars continued the popular Sacagawea obverse motif. In a decision that certainly was not run by or approved by numismatists, Congress mandated that the Mint place the date and mintmark on the edge—where it cannot be seen in an album or in most holders.[1] The idea was that it would be cheaper not to make dated and mintmarked dies each year. The same had been done in 2008 with the Presidential dollars (see next listing). This move was a major deterrent to collectors enjoying such coins and being able to identify them at a glance.

The reverse each year is different—portraying an aspect of the life, activities, or experience of various Native American tribes and individuals. The result has been a series that is interesting and attractive to contemplate on both sides. As you read these words the series continues. The Mint created a rarity, relatively speaking, when in 2015 it issued a 2015-W coin, the first ever "golden dollar" struck at the West Point Mint and intended for sale. Only 90,000 were minted, making it about *30 times rarer* than earlier coins with mintages of 3 million so. The unique aspect of the W mintmark was featured quietly with the result that most collectors did not learn about these coins until after they were sold out. Although this is the key to the series, and so by far, it still is very affordable.

A full set of standard dates and mintmarks from 2009 to date, graded MS–63 to 65 or so, costs little more than $100, to which can be added the 2015-W for modest additional cost. Again, there is room for a set of Native American dollars in every collection. As of press time this is the only series of regular dollar coins that is scheduled to continue after 2016. There is a lot to like with these coins, a continuation in a way of the Sacagawea dollar series.

Presidential Dollars

(shown at 125%)

The Presidential dollars series began in 2007 with the George Washington coin, followed in the same year by those with portraits of John Adams, Thomas Jefferson, and James Madison. At the rate of four coins per year the series ran into 2016. The requirement was that to be honored a president had to have been dead for two years. That left three candidates for the last year—Richard M. Nixon, Gerald Ford, and Ronald Reagan. Not eligible were the living past presidents Jimmy Carter, George H.W. Bush, George W. Bush, and Bill Clinton, or current president Barack Obama.

Each Presidential dollar has a standard reverse—a view of the Statue of Liberty, by Don Everhart—nice enough if it had been used once instead of continuously. As was remarked by others at the time, it would have been desirable to have each coin depict a scene from the honored president's administration. Had the numismatic community—people constituting by far the greatest demand for such coins—been considered, the situation might have been different.

The obverse features a portrait of each president— adaptations of the images used on various presidential medals issued by the Mint in past years. The dates and mintmarks are on the edges, making quick identification a challenge, a slip-up in logic, it would seem.

A complete set of Mint State and Proof coins is inexpensive, if you ignore a few special strikings made in 2015 and 2016, but even those are quite affordable to most buyers.

The edge lettering from a 2007 Proof Presidential dollar.

Toning on Coins

There is a strong market for silver-clad and silver coins with attractive toning. This is true not only for Eisenhower dollars, but also for Peace, Morgan, and earlier dollar designs. Be careful when paying a sharp premium for toned coins, as the toning might be artificially applied rather than a result of natural circumstances. A bright Morgan, Peace, or Eisenhower dollar can be do-it-yourself toned by placing it on a piece of freshly sawn oak and putting it in a small sealed container. Rainbow toning can be deliberately added by a combination of low heat and time to "age."

Certified Coins

In recent times some collectors of modern dollars and other coins have felt that unless a coin is certified it is not worth owning. Advertisements have fostered this feeling. To old-timers this attitude seems strange and takes away from the basic enjoyment of building sets.

The fact is that all standard dates and mintmarks of dollars from the 1971 Eisenhower coins to the latest issues are *very common* in Mint State. At the MS-65 level a couple of Eisenhower dollars are slightly scarce. "This is a coin that was not typically born nice," commented numismatist Charles Morgan, who has devoted years of study to this series and is a major contributor to the Eisenhower dollar information present text.[2] As such, coins offered as MS-65 or finer can vary widely in eye appeal. I have seen many instances in which coins certified as MS-63 have nicer strike and eye appeal than do those labeled MS-65. Cherrypicking for quality is highly recommended! The secret is that most buyers consider only the label, and really choice coins are apt to cost no more, except in the effort of hunting them down.

Proof Eisenhowers are on the long side of Proof-65 unless they have been cleaned, and those of the Susan B. Anthony and later are easy to find in high Proof grades. Certain holders have been marketed with promotional comments such as "First Strike," "Early Strike," and the like, which generally add little or nothing to their resale value. "These labels are more a benefit to marketing companies than to collectors and a quick look at the population reports will show that the majority of modern coins submitted for certification wind up in 'First Strike' holders," Charles Morgan observed, echoing the comments of several other contributors to this study.[3]

As for the traditional definition of the term, the U.S. Mint has stated on a number of occasions that it keeps no track of which coins were struck first or earliest in the shipments it makes.

I hereby state, and clearly, that I am a great fan of certified coins for early issues such as Liberty Seated, Morgan, and Peace dollars, as for many coins the difference in values can be very great between two adjacent grades. For example, a recent edition of *A Guide Book of United States Coins* lists the values of a 1928-S Peace silver dollar as MS-63 $525, MS-64 $1,200, and MS-65 $22,000. As grading is largely a matter of opinion, and as opinions can differ even when the same coin is resubmitted to the same grading service, in this instance I would opt for a hand-picked 63 or 64 and instead of buying a 65 would use the money to start on another series of coins.[4]

With dollars from Eisenhower to date I suggest that you proceed with caution when it comes to certified coins. While there are, on many occasions, beautiful coins in high-grade holders, there are so many risks involved with paying today's going rates for conditionally rare modern coins.

Unless you are concentrating on building a registry set with PCGS or NGC, where *numbers* and not *eye appeal* count, a better option is to form beautiful sets in a group of albums with pages, store and carry them easily, and more easily enjoy them. My personal collection is in album pages except for a handful of special modern Enhanced Uncirculated and Reverse Proof coins that were made without much advance publicity by the Mint, with the result that albums do not include spaces for them.

It is annoying that when I look at, for example, my 2013 Native American dollars in an album, I can't tell the difference between the P and the D issue as the mintmarks are invisible unless I make an effort to take the coins out, and the S coin is identifiable as only Proofs were made in San Francisco. It would be nice if the sole remaining active series—the Native American dollars—would be revised to have the dates and mintmarks easily available. But it would be equally, if not more, annoying to me to have to pull out dozens of boxes of certified coin holders in order to look at my collection. Again I give a nod to those building registry sets, as holders come with that territory.

Another thing that certified-coin collectors need to keep in mind is that to date so few coins of each issue have been submitted to certification that published data—or census—for each coin is woefully incomplete. To provide an illustration, let's take a look at the PCGS figures for the 1973-D Eisenhower dollar, which are current as of October 2015: MS-60 (none); MS-61 (1); MS-62 (11); MS-63 (147); MS-64 (980); MS-65 (1,362); MS-66 (296); and MS-67 (11).

Charles Morgan shares this analysis:

> If someone were to look at these numbers and come to the conclusion that most 1973-D Eisenhower dollars would grade MS-65, they would be incorrect. If they looked at the numbers and surmised that Eisenhower dollars 1973-D were scarce because only a 2,800 have been certified (compared to almost 5,750 1893-S Morgan dollars, for instance), they'd be quite wrong as well!
>
> The reason why the certified population for modern coins resemble this "bell curve" pattern is because the quality of coins that are submitted for certification

naturally fall within the parameters of *what would be profitable for the submitter*. At present, MS-64 coins are a "break even" point for high-volume submitters, MS-65 coins are marginally profitable, MS-66 coins are very profitable, and MS-67 coins are extremely profitable—but as you can see based on the numbers, getting an MS-67 coin back from PCGS up to this point has been a very unlikely outcome.

Of course that fact could change at any time. PCGS could loosen their standards for what constitutes coins in these higher grades—a phenomena known as grade-flation—or large amounts of hitherto unsubmitted high-grade coins could turn up in the marketplace (the total number of coins certified is but a fraction of a percent of the issue's 2,000,000-coin mintage).

Those willing to participate in the high-grade modern-coin certified market need to understand this fact as well: In order for the top-population coins to maintain their value, buyers have to exist to accommodate each coin that gets made. If the number of high-grade coins being certified outnumber the number of willing buyers, then the prices will decline. This is simple supply-and-demand economics.

With so few dealers supporting the back end of the modern-coin market, it is collectors that carry all of the risks associated with buying and holding these high-priced modern condition rarities.[5]

The preceding explanation has few parallels in any modern rare-coin text I have ever seen. Population reports are difficult for most hobby newcomers to understand. By way of analogy: among Barber quarters minted from 1892 to 1916, by far the rarest issue is the 1901-S. However, population reports show that more well-worn 1901-S quarters have been certified than for any other in the Barber series! The explanation is that a 1901-S in Very Good condition is a very valuable coin, which makes the expense of certification worthwhile, whereas a Very Good common-date 1901 Philadelphia Mint quarter is valued at very little, so it's not profitable to pay for certification.

Certified Proofs furnish another example. As of October 2015 PCGS had certified the following quantities of Deep Cameo Proof 2012-S Chester A. Arthur Presidential dollars: Below PF-68 (none); PF-68 (18); PF-69 (1,958); and PF-70 (368).

This mainly tells us that most certified coins of this variety are superb gems, and there are enough PF-69 coins to go around to satisfy the demand for them. Plus, as 1,438,710 Proofs were coined, fewer than 1% have been certified by PCGS. What does this say about the quantities of others that might be certified someday?

More from Charles Morgan:

Collectors of certified modern coins need to be aware of a few things. The first thing is that high-value modern coins are targets for bulk submitters to the third-party grading services. If you can make $10,000 with a high-grade coin that costs you a few dollars to buy "in the raw," why wouldn't you submit that coin over and over again? The services are notoriously imprecise with their grading judgments. Today's MS-65 could be tomorrow's MS-66 or MS-67. Believe me, it happens, and it happens in part because of the way the services are set up. The modern grading line is usually staffed by different graders than the traditional line. Many submitters I know use bulk grading to set a baseline on grades for modern coins and then submit the same coins again through the regular modern grading line or at coin shows (paying upwards of $100 per coin) to upgrade the coin. Of course, this only pays when the resulting grade is profitable.

We (my co-researcher Hubert Walker and I) coined the term *terminal point* to describe the lowest grade where a coin is still profitable for grade submission. You will notice pretty quickly what this point is for most modern issues as the density of coins submitted usually bottoms out near that point. Anything graded below it is either an esoteric mint error or an error in judgment on the part of the submitter. This is why there are so few Ike dollars certified in low Mint State grades.[6]

Leaving the Morgan commentary, I continue: Realize that a coin that is common and cheap in MS-65 can cost $1,000 or more in today's market if only a few have been certified at the 68 or higher level. Also be aware that most dealers will not buy these ultra-high-grade coins at strong prices for their inventories, but only if they have customers for them. The aftermarket is very thin.

The more *aware* you can be, the more wisely you will spend your money. This will engender a deep sense of satisfaction and comfort as you go onward in numismatics.

3

3 3 3 3 3 3 3 3 3 3

THE AMERICAN SCENE, 1971 TO DATE

The Year 1971

CURRENT EVENTS. President Richard M. Nixon (inaugurated in 1969) occupied the White House, war was raging in Vietnam, and inflation was rampant in the United States. In particular many Americans, especially men of draft age, often protested about the war, which seemed to have no plan. A group of 700 Vietnam War veterans gathered at the Capitol Building in Washington, D.C. and threw their battle medals at the building to show their growing disgust with the war. Many wondered why we were involved at all in a conflict on the far side of the world that did not involve many American interests but took tens of thousands of American casualties.

In an attempt to stop inflation, President Nixon imposed a 90-day freeze on wages and prices on August 15, 1971. As an indication of national priorities, a study found that through taxes the average American taxpayer gave the U.S. government $7 for medical research (part of $315 for health-related activities), $30 for space exploration, and $30 for highway construction, but $400 for defense and $125 for the Vietnam War. During the year the price of gold bullion dropped 32%.

American research was halted on the supersonic transport plane (SST), leaving the field open to Russia with its TU-104 and to Britain and France with their Concorde. As it turned out, only the Concorde ever saw commercial use. On September 26, Japanese emperor Hirohito met President Nixon in Anchorage, Alaska. This was the first time a Japanese monarch and a U.S. president ever exchanged greetings in person.

The United States ceased giving licenses for commercial whale hunting on March 1, 1971. The Apollo 14 space mission was launched on January 31 and landed on the Moon on February 5, returning to earth on February 9 and landing in the South Pacific. The Mariner 9

The launch of the Apollo 14 space mission.

space probe was launched from Cape Kennedy, Florida, on May 30 toward Mars and sent back many images during its journey. Space exploration had been made a national priority by former President John F. Kennedy earlier in the previous decade when it was realized that America was severely behind Russia in this technology. By 1971 the contest had somewhat evened out.

Popular books of the year included *The Exorcist, Eleanor and Franklin, Bury My Heart at Wounded Knee, Honor Thy Father, The Winds of War*, and *Rabbit Redux*. Beginning on June 13, 1971, excerpts from *The Pentagon Papers* were printed in *The New York Times*, revealing an inside view of U.S. defense activities. Films included *A Clockwork Orange*, Woody Allen's *Bananas, Carnal Knowledge, The French Connection, Fiddler on the Roof*, and *The Last Picture Show*.

Mainland China joined the United Nations at the expense of Taiwan, which was forced out of the U.N. as a result of mainland China's admittance; the state of Bangladesh was carved out of Pakistan; and the dictator Idi Amin seized power of Uganda through a military coup.

THE NUMISMATIC SCENE. Citizens still could not legally own gold bullion—the result of regulations imposed by the government in 1933 and 1934. As domestic inflation and the war seemed to have no end, many citizens bought gold in the form of double eagles and other coins. This helped revive the numismatic market, which had been in a slump since 1965.

In Colorado Springs the American Numismatic Association's (ANA) journal, *The Numismatist*, included Ed Rochette as editor, Colonel Adna G. Wilde as executive director, and Herbert M. Bergen as president. In Bergen's January message he called for governor nominees "who are qualified by sufficient years of membership and experience in the operation of ANA to insure their capability to properly and adequately serve as governors of such a large organization." In the biannual election John Jay Pittman became the new president and took office in August. The third annual ANA Summer Seminar had a record attendance of 47 students. The ANA had a balanced budget and for the most recent fiscal year showed a surplus of $2,232.63. The annual convention was held in Washington, D.C., and attracted 10,570 visitors.[1] Eva Adams, a former Mint director, was elected to the ANA Board, stirring controversy.[2]

In Iola, Wisconsin, Chet Krause and Cliff Mishler, the two leading figures at *Numismatic News*, had a close connection with the Treasury Department and the Mint, and did many positive things to

On its Silver Anniversary, Red Book salutes the panel!

The 1972 Silver Anniversary Edition of the Guide Book of United States Coins is now available. Like those preceding it, the 25th edition derives a large measure of its authority from Whitman's Panel of numismatic experts. This Panel represents some of the most respected names in coins, and their familiarity with the subject and the market make them supremely qualified. The gentlemen on this page have all served as panelists for twenty years or more. Our congratulations and thanks. They have aided immeasurably in making the Red Book what it is—the one indispensable volume to the coin hobbyist.—R. S. Yeoman, Editor.

See your dealer today. 256 pp. $2.50

WESTERN PUBLISHING COMPANY, INC. Racine, Wisconsin 53404

In July 1971, as Whitman Publishing was celebrating the 25th anniversary of the hobby's popular *Guide Book of United States Coins* (the "Red Book"), the company honored numismatic panelists who had worked on the book for 20 or more years. These included such luminaries as R.S. Yeoman, Aubree Bebee, Arthur and Paul Kagin, Abe Kosoff, and others.

influence numismatics. Margo Russell, editor of *Coin World* in Sidney, Ohio, was a newshound *par excellence* and tracked down much information about the new Eisenhower dollars as well as other events.

The Comprehensive Catalog and Encyclopedia of Morgan and Peace Dollars, by Leroy C. Van Allen and A. George Mallis, was published and in time would create widespread interest in collecting dollars by minute die varieties. Silver bars for investment were popular. A 100-ounce bar was advertised for $230. Bags of 1,000 Morgan and Peace dollars traded frequently. The General Services Administration (GSA) announced it would sell 2.8 million long-stored silver dollars, mostly from the Carson City Mint. In time through a series of sales all were distributed. Scattered pre-1965 silver coins could be found in circulation now and again, but most were gone. Half dollars no longer circulated to any extent.

The Philadelphia Mint purchased an improved Janvier engraving machine, a precision device that made master hubs from artists' models.

The Year 1972

CURRENT EVENTS. On January 5, 1972, President Richard M. Nixon signed a $5.5 billion bill for a program to develop a reusable space shuttle. The Apollo 16 Moon mission was successful. Nixon visited China and conducted negotiations to reduce hostilities and to increase scientific and cultural relations because, since the late 1940s, U.S. relations with China had been cold and distant.

On March 22 the Equal Rights Amendment to the Constitution was passed, prohibiting discrimination on the basis of sex; however, by the end of the year only 22 of the required 38 states had ratified the amendment, and by June 30, 1982, the amendment would die. In ensuing years there were many areas in which minorities, especially African Americans, were still discriminated against. In May, President Nixon became the first U.S. chief executive to visit Moscow. He signed a number of important agreements and met with Leonid L. Brezhnev. The Vietnam War continued to rage and full-scale bombing, which had been suspended, was resumed on December 18. Matters went from bad to worse—B-52 bombing raids were increased, protests continued, casualties mounted, and the hope for peace seemed distant.

On June 17 five men were caught in a burglary attempt at the Democratic Party headquarters in the Watergate Apartments in Washington, D.C. On August 1, 1972, *Washington Post* reporters Robert

U.S. Representative Martha Griffiths proposed the legislation that led to the Equal Rights Amendment passing both houses of Congress. The amendment fell five states short of ratification, and additional states withdrew their approval when ratification failed. Shockingly, there is still no language in the Constitution guaranteeing equal rights to women.

Woodward and Carl Bernstein reported a financial connection between the Watergate break in and Nixon's Committee for the Re-Election of the President (popularly if inaccurately known as CREEP). On August 29, 1972, President Nixon announced that a White House investigation of the Watergate situation revealed that administration officials were not connected in any way with it. A White House spokesman called the *Washington Post* stories "shabby journalism," "mudslinging," and "unfounded and unsubstantiated allegations." By election time the depth of the scandal was not fully realized, and President Richard Nixon and Vice President Spiro T. Agnew were re-elected on November 7, 1972, beating Democratic candidates George S. McGovern and R. Sargent Shriver. Although Nixon proclaimed his honesty over and over again and famously stated "I am not a crook," over the next two years the majority

The "dirty tricks" of the Watergate scandal would come to light in 1972. More than 40 years later, in 2016, President Richard Nixon would be commemorated on a Presidential dollar coin.

of his top advisors would commit perjury and Nixon himself would resign rather than face investigation. Many fine accomplishments, particularly in international relations, were overshadowed by disgrace when the Nixon administration finally toppled. In the meantime, Nixon participated in various events involving Eisenhower dollars.

The compact disc (CD) was developed by RCA, which was enlightened about its future. The Philips audio cassette was all the range for recorded music, replacing the reel-to-reel tape recorder. Clumsy eight-track cartridges for use in automobiles achieved modest sales.

On November 14, 1972, the Dow-Jones Industrial Average of blue-chip stock prices closed above 1,000 for the first time in history, reaching 1,003.16.

THE NUMISMATIC SCENE. In March the ANA regretfully accepted the resignation of Executive Vice President Colonel Adna G. Wilde and named Edward Rochette as his successor, whose title was later changed to executive director. In succeeding years Rochette did much to improve and enhance many aspects of the organization. The ANA had more than 25,000 members worldwide and was growing. On June 15, the ANA began operations of the American Numismatic Association Certification Service (ANACS). Through the ANACS coins could be submitted and, for a fee, would be returned with a photographic certificate if found to be genuine. This was based in Washington, D.C., and was under the direction of Charles Hoskins.

"Whizzing," or the treatment of circulated coins with a high-speed steel brush to make them appear Uncirculated, was endemic. In his "Featuring Fakes" column Virgil Hancock mounted a campaign to stop the practice. The ANA practice of expelling some members who overgraded or caused problems was enforced erratically and inconsistently, creating complaints. In time this was largely "solved" by decreasing the number of expulsions. The ANA annual summer convention was held in New Orleans.

World-Wide Coin Investments of Atlanta, Georgia, announced the simultaneous purchase of the Hydeman specimen of the famous 1913 Liberty Head nickel and the Idler specimen of the "King of American Coins," the 1804 dollar. Both coins were purchased from professional numismatist Abe Kosoff for the then-lofty price of $180,000.

The coin market was active, and much attention was focused on gold coins. The new 1972 Doubled-Die cent created a sensation. Silver dollars were popular, as they had been for the past decade. Using television and other media, the Franklin Mint sold millions of medals to the public.

Grading was the leading topic of debate, and it seemed that just about everyone had different ideas on the subject. Dr. William H. Sheldon's 70-point grading scale, conceived in 1949 as a market-price formula for 1793–1814 large cents, was expanded, altered, and used in many different ways. Before long, such grades unknown to Sheldon, as MS-61, MS-62, etc., were in vogue, often accompanied by plus or minus signs, sometimes in multiple, as MS-61++. Coin marketing was becoming the message and traditional aspects of the hobby—such as art, history, romance, and the excitement of completing a set or series—were left behind, as just two things became important: grade and price. Some called the art and science of numismatics an *industry*. The collecting world changed, perhaps forever. In the meantime, dedicated enthusiasts who were members of specialized societies for tokens, medals, paper money, copper coins, and other issues had a good time.

The Year 1973

CURRENT EVENTS. On January 28, 1973, a cease-fire in Vietnam ended the direct involvement of U.S. ground troops in the military action there. The Watergate scandal continued. Still proclaiming his high morals, honesty, religious scruples, and other lofty attributes, Nixon sank in a quagmire of disgrace. On October 10, 1973, Vice President Spiro T. Agnew resigned under pressure and pleaded *nolo contendere* to income tax evasion. President Nixon chose Gerald R. Ford, House Republican leader, to be vice president, and Ford took office on December 3.

On March 1 the Xerox Palo Alto Research Center released the Xerox Alto. A precursor to personal computers, the Alto introduced the "mouse" and screen icons. Xerox manufactured 2,000 of these after the initial success of its 30-unit pilot run, but ultimately they did not seem to see much potential in computers for home use and abandoned the idea. In April a committee of U.S. manufacturers and grocers recommended the adoption of a Universal Product Code (UPC), which became known as the bar code. The oil crisis began in earnest, with prices rocketing sky-high and mile-long lines forming at service stations; rationing and gas purchase limits were right around the corner. Inflation continued, and the value of gold bullion rose sharply on international markets.

The Xerox Alto.

THE NUMISMATIC SCENE. In October, the Numismatic Museum at the old San Francisco Mint (operated for coining purposes 1874–1937) was dedicated.[3] President Nixon signed the Hobby Protection Act, making it the law of the land. This helped curtail counterfeits but was not strongly enforced. Very little had been done by the government to stop quantities of Chinese and other foreign-made counterfeits from entering the market. Whizzed coins continued to be a problem, and coin grading varied all over the place. Articles on coin grading were numerous. The problem was the need to develop a system that people without numismatic knowledge or experience could use on a consistent basis. This goal never came close to being achieved, but in time standards giving approximations became popular. Most coin buyers did not want to take the time to become educated.

The collecting of mint errors was a popular specialty by this time, and during the decade much was said in print about such pieces. David L. Ganz was one of America's most popular writers and was the author of more than 200 published articles in the preceding eight years. The Franklin Mint continued to sell millions of medals to the public and also made donations to numismatic groups.

ANACS expanded its service of inspecting coins and pronouncing upon their authenticity or lack thereof. The market continued its strength, and "trophy" rarities were very much in demand. Silver dollars were among the most actively sought series. Gold coins in particular were dynamic, both in the sales of legally permitted modern coins (the South African Krugerrand) and in quantities of

In the early 1970s the Philadelphia Mint issued a series of bronze and silver medals authorized by the American Revolution Bicentennial Administration.

earlier federal coins, particularly $20 double eagles. For investors—now back in the marketplace in force—Uncirculated and Proof coins were popular once again.

Arthur M. Fitts III, a graduate of Phillips Exeter Academy and Harvard who distinguished himself in many numismatic endeavors, moved to Colorado Springs to be the assistant to Executive Director Ed Rochette. N. Neil Harris became editor of *The Numismatist*.

The Young Numismatists program of the ANA, catering to ages 11 to 20, was very popular. The annual ANA convention was held in Boston where a reported 13,926 people attended the show. In the election race for ANA president Virginia Culver with 6,677 votes bested Grover Criswell with 5,922. Other governors elected to serve on the Board, and the number of votes they received, included: Miss Eva B. Adams, 9,609; John J. Pittman, 9,433; Maurice M. Gould, 8,213; Glenn B. Smedley, 7,578; Kenneth L. Hallenbeck Jr., 6,784; Adna G. Wilde Jr., 6,101; and Eldridge G. Jones, 5,726. More than 14,000 votes were cast. Culver's two-year administration proved to be one of the most effective and enlightened in association history. ANA membership stood at 26,462.

The Year 1974

CURRENT EVENTS. The early part of 1974 was dominated by the growing Watergate scandal. One by one, Nixon staffers were implicated in massive lies and cover-ups, and the president's credibility was undermined. Nixon, standing above it all, did little to help those who had tried to help him, and finally resigned the presidency on August 9. Gerald R. Ford, who had been named by Nixon to the office of vice president and who had served since December 1973, took office as the 38th president of the United

States. Ford became the first person ever to achieve that position without being elected either to the vice presidency or the presidency. Ford's tenure would be short-lived, and in 1976 he would be narrowly beaten in his bid for election by Democratic contender Jimmy Carter. President Ford pardoned Nixon on September 8, 1974, for any crimes he may have committed while in office—an action widely condemned by American citizens who realized that no ordinary law-abiding person would ever receive the same treatment. Public faith in the executive office hit an all-time low.

In California Patty Hearst, an heiress to the William Randolph Hearst fortune, was kidnapped by members of the Symbionese Liberation Army (SLA), a radical political splinter group. Meanwhile, in the sports world, the irrepressible Muhammad Ali won the World Heavyweight boxing title for the second time.

Patty Hearst was brainwashed by her captors into joining their organization and participating in a heist.

A 10.3% inflation rate contributed to a 20% slump in automobile sales, while housing dropped 40% and unemployment hit 7.2% by December 1974. The threat of a depression loomed great, but it did not materialize. On October 8 President Ford announced a program called Whip Inflation Now (WIN) to help stem rising oil prices. The energy crisis gripped the country and would dominate much of America's economy and international politics over the next 15 years. On the lighter side, on April 18 Henry "Hank" Aaron of the Atlanta Braves hit his 715th career home run.

THE NUMISMATIC SCENE. Commemoratives, gold coins, silver dollars, "type" coins, and other series—especially coins in Uncirculated and Proof grades—were becoming popular once again as an investment. Increasing emphasis was being paid to coins in outstanding preservation, and early (especially pre-1860) pieces with legitimate claims to being "condition rarities" began to sell for record prices in auctions. The weekly *Coin Dealer Newsletter* was the main source for ever-changing prices, but electronic trading networks were important as well. The three most publicized features of coin collecting were investment, investment, and investment. Prices were rising, and values of five years earlier in 1969 seemed in retrospect to have been incredible bargains.

The price of copper was increasing, and from October 17, 1973, to March 29, 1974, the Philadelphia Mint struck 1,441,039 1974-dated cents in aluminum. Mint Director Mary T. Brooks gave 16 to congressmen and others. The idea was scratched, and Brooks attempted to get them back, but two could not be found.[4] Cents were becoming scarce in circulation, and Brooks announced "Penny Redemption Month," which was later extended. It was pointed out that when American's are alerted to a potential coin shortage they rush to create one! However, little public attention was paid to the program.

Neil Harris was named as editor of *The Numismatist*, replacing Ed Rochette, who was named the new director. Florence M. Schook was named administrator of the Young Numismatist Correspondence Course. Schook would direct and expand the YN group for many years afterward. Along the way many youngsters developed a great interest in numismatics. Some went on to become professionals. Much print was devoted to revisions of the ANA bylaws with the eventual result that they became more complicated than ever. Most of this was covertly directed towards preventing directors from serving for many years, as Grover Criswell and John Jay Pittman were doing.[5] Often at ANA Board meetings open to the public Margo Russell, editor of *Coin World*, would be the only person to attend. On the positive side, membership crossed the 30,000 mark—an all-time record.

Virgil Hancock via his "Featuring Fakes" column in *The Numismatist* attracted a lot of attention and did much good. Certain aspects of his research were flawed and his statements were proved to be false, taking away from his accomplishments. As an example, he lashed out at Hal Birt and Dick Wagner who had dared question him: "When in the June issue I read the 'Die Stress Detection' article by my friend Hal Birt and Dick Wagner, I thought my eyesight suddenly had gone bad, or else that authors Birt and Wagner had written a satire on counterfeit detection. So I read the thing again! Nope, they seemed serious . . . but 100% wrong!"

On December 31, 1974, American ownership of gold bullion became legal for the first time since the early 1930s, but the reaction from the numismatic community was an unexpected letdown. The prices of gold coins dropped and remained low for the next several years.[6]

Artist John Mercanti joined the engraving staff of the Philadelphia Mint in 1974. He would work there for nearly 40 years, retiring as chief engraver in 2010.

The Year 1975

CURRENT EVENTS. The oil crisis continued to be a problem. Prices were controlled by OPEC, a consortium of oil-producing nations dominated by Saudi Arabia. Inflation remained out of control at 9.2% for the year. Unemployment was at 8.5%. Average income for an American was $14,100 per year, and the average cost of a new home was $39,300. A Ford Mustang II was listed at $4,105.

The Vietnam War ended when Communist forces captured Saigon and South Vietnam surrendered unconditionally. Construction began on the Trans-Alaska pipeline. Computer geniuses Bill Gates and Paul Allen registered the Microsoft trademark. The digital camera was invented at Eastman Kodak, but the firm believed that regular film would always be more important. The first laser printer was made.

Popular movies included *Jaws, The Towering Inferno, The Godfather Part II*, and *One Flew over the Cuckoo's Nest. Saturday Night Live* made its debut on NBC with George Carlin as host. Popular musicians and groups included Aerosmith, Bob Dylan, The Eagles, Jefferson Starship, Elton John, Led Zeppelin, John Lennon, Pink Floyd, Paul Simon, Bruce Springsteen, and The Who.

THE NUMISMATIC SCENE. The Franklin Mint was riding higher than ever and as such sponsored events and made donations to the ANA. At one minute after midnight on December 31, 1974, a minute into 1975, the Franklin Mint struck the first gold coin in America since 1933—a 100 balboa for the Republic of Panama. Beginning on January 6, the U.S. Treasury sold large quantities of gold at auction. 753,000 ounces of gold were sold for an average price of $165.65, and proceeds from the sale brought a total of $124.8 million. The government had hoped to sell two million ounces and, as such, all bids of $153 or higher were accepted. The West Point Bullion Depository began the minting of one-cent pieces. These lacked mintmarks and had the same appearance as Philadelphia cents.

The ANA dedicated its new museum on January 18. The next day the first Numismatic Round Table was held. Chaired by ANA president Culver, it was titled "Problems-Projects-Priorities." In addition to all members of the ANA Board and five staff officers, those who took part in the exploratory discussion included U.S. Mint Director Mary Brooks and her assistant, Roy Cahoon, Q. David Bowers of Bowers and Ruddy Galleries, Kenneth Bressett of Whitman Publishing, Dennis Forgue of RARCOA, Arnold Jeffcoat of *Numismatic News Weekly*, William Krieg of the Franklin Mint, William Louth of Medallic Art Co., Ray Merena of Paramount International Coin Corp., James Miller of *COINage* magazine, Margo Russell of *Coin World*, coin dealer J. Paul Scheetz, and John Smies representing the Professional Numismatists Guild. Most had attended the museum opening the day before.

Topics of discussion at the round table included legislation passed by states and the federal government that was unfavorable to numismatics, potential taxes on silver and gold bullion, coin grading, and the future of the hobby.

At a board meeting held in March the ANA budget for fiscal year 1974–1975 was adopted, with a deficit of more than $17,000. A grading committee was formed. In *The Numismatist* Virgil Hancock's "Featuring Fakes" often contained false information due to his publishing first without research. He was often subjected to the embarrassment of readers pointing out his mistakes.

The second Numismatic Round Table was held in Chicago on May 14 and was a great success. Topics included proposing a Bicentennial gold coin, setting up an ANA information bureau to provide information to media, the ANA Grading Board, holding regional seminars, and the method of allocating bourse tables at conventions. At the summer convention it was announced that Virgil Hancock had been elected president. In his first message he proposed radical changes in the ANA election procedures. In the ensuing two years he often clashed sharply with the board and anyone who suggested that his ideas were not feasible. On the plus side he asked veteran dealer Abe Kosoff, founder of the Professional Numismatists Guild, to survey dealers, collectors, and others in an effort to create a grading system that would be endorsed by the ANA.

It was reported that the association now had 30,585 members. The annual convention was held at the Los Angeles Marriott Hotel not far from the airport.

The Year 1976

CURRENT EVENTS. President Gerald Ford created a board on February 17 to oversee foreign and U.S. intelligence operations overseas. The next day he placed limits on surveillance of U.S. citizens by government agencies. (Little did he anticipate that secret surveillance of just about everything in America would be pervasive in the 21st century.) His administration accomplished many good things, but being Republican it suffered from the backlash of Watergate, and in the election in November Ford and his running mate, Senator Robert J. Dole, were narrowly defeated by Jimmy Carter and Walter F. Mondale.

The economy was worrisome, inflation was rampant, and unemployment seemed to be getting worse. In Carter, people saw an attractive alternative. Conrail, set up by the government, took over the operation of six railroads in the Northeast. In time the

Amtrak passenger rail system was put into place. The Concorde SST started supersonic service between the United States and Europe on May 24. Barbara Walters signed a five-year contract for $5 million with NBC on April 22, becoming the first anchor woman on a major network news program. In 1976, a strong anti-war, anti-Vietnam sentiment persisted, causing emotional problems for many returning veterans who faced an unappreciative welcome and even contempt back home in America. In a historic bit of Cold-War diplomacy, American astronauts and Soviet cosmonauts docked their space-ships, exchanged information and observa-

Barbara Walters, the first female anchor on a major network news program, along with her co-anchors.

tions, and actually lived with the "enemy" for a few days. In the world of sports, Muhammad Ali was still the heavyweight champ of the boxing world.

Sylvester Stallone's low-budget movie *Rocky* was released, and quickly became one of the most popular films in history. Alex Haley's novel *Roots* was published as non-fiction, and was subsequently moved to the fiction category in the *New York Times* best-seller list when it was revealed that certain details were contrived. Later, a dramatization of *Roots* broke television viewership records.

The 1976 Bicentennial of American independence was duly commemorated on coinage but was largely overlooked on the national scene. Local July 4 bicentennial celebrations were staged around the country, and in New York harbor more than a dozen tall ships and many military vessels were on display. A grand exposition had been suggested for Philadelphia, but before serious planning could get underway critics maintained that the money could better be used to fight poverty and for welfare. Thus, the city that had hosted the 1876 Centennial Exhibition had no 1976 counterpart.

THE NUMISMATIC SCENE. The coin market was alive and well with emphasis mainly on the investment angle. Many dealers who had entered the field in the 1970s were telemarketers and promoters with little traditional interest in numismatics. The Treasury Department revived the discontinued $2 bill with a new issue featuring the signing of the Declaration of Independence as the back design.

President Virgil Hancock continued to argue with those who opposed many of his ideas, including a majority of the Board of Governors. Board meetings were often punctuated by violent confrontations. There had never been an administration like this in the entire history of the ANA dating back to 1891. The accomplishments of board members, of Ed Rochette who managed Headquarters,and others, were seldom mentioned as Hancock wanted all of the limelight for himself.

Abe Kosoff sent out many inquiries in his effort to develop a grading system. Once this was done Hancock planned to set up a grading board. Kosoff suggested that the Sheldon 1 to 70 formula be used and that sharpness of strike and quality of the planchet be factored in. There were many differences of opinion. A draft version of the official ANA grading guide was sent to Kenneth Bressett at Whitman Publishing, and was reviewed by Q. David Bowers and Harvey G. Stack, who had followed the progress since the beginning. Much information was found to be illogical, inconsistent, and incorrect. They also learned that no ANA governors had read it![7] In a time-consuming task involving much correspondence and discussion, Bressett essentially rewrote it, Bowers did the introductory narrative, and Kosoff approved the final version. Extensively revised, the *Official American Numismatic Association Grading Standards for United States Coins* was launched two years later in November 1978 to a great reception.

ANACS moved from Washington to Colorado Springs. John Hunter was the only staff member to relocate. Ed Fleishmann was hired as chief authenticator. Florence Schook's Young Numismatist Program had more than 600 members earn course completion certificates. Separately, Kenneth Hallenbeck reported that his work on the ANA Correspondence Course was suffering from lack of participation by authors. This idea continued for years before it was finally dropped. At the end of the fiscal year the ANA had $156,108 revenue in excess of expenses and had investments totaling more than $2 million. The annual summer convention was held in the Americana Hotel at Times Square with a reported record attendance of more than 21,000. In the Imperial Ballroom 200 dealers set up. The auction was conducted by Stack's.

Amos Press released the *Coin World Almanac*, an 834-page reference with 23 chapters priced at $10. Countless facts were now at hand for easy access in an era when the Internet was in the distant future. Two monthly Amos Press publications, *World Coins* and *Numismatic Scrapbook*, were merged into the weekly *Coin World*. Numismatic literature and out-of-print books and catalogs were becoming popular. George F. Kolbe held his first auction of such items. Frank and Laurese Katen offered similar publications at fixed prices.

In addition to Bicentennial *coins*, the United States released several bronze, silver, and gold *medals* in 1976 to mark the nation's 200th year of independence. These are studied in depth in *American Gold and Silver* (Tucker). The gold medal here is pictured at half size.

In April 1976 the family of the late Louis E. Eliasberg placed his unique collection on display at the Philadelphia Mint, where it remained through June 1977.

The Year 1977

CURRENT EVENTS. As one of his first official acts after his January inauguration, President Jimmy Carter pardoned most of the draft resisters to the Vietnam War. On September 7, Carter signed two treaties transferring control of the Panama Canal to Panama, an act that caused great dissent among U.S. citizens who felt that Carter was wrong in giving away rights to the strategic area. On June 6, 1977, the *Washington Post* reported that the United States had developed a neutron bomb that would kill people with its radiation but would do minimal damage to property.

Unemployment remained high at 7%. Coffee prices rose and hit $5 per pound retail, causing an increase in tea consumption. On March 9 the Food and Drug Administration suggested that saccharin might cause cancer and proposed a ban that was postponed for 18 months pending new tests. On July 28, the 799-mile Trans-Alaska oil pipeline connected Prudhoe Bay to the port of Valdez. The stock market was in a slump, and the Dow-Jones Industrial Average declined more than 165 points during the year and closed at 831.17, which was below the closing price in 1964.

Two films were hits at the box office—the very first *Star Wars* and *Close Encounters of the Third Kind. The Thorn Birds,* a novel by Colleen McCullough, became a best seller. Former Secretary of State Henry Kissinger sold his memoirs for $2 million, matching the figure guaranteed in a contract signed on September 29, 1976, by Richard Nixon for *his* memoirs. On March 9, former president Gerald R. Ford and his wife Betty were reported to have signed contracts for their memoirs for about $1 million each. Attendance at professional sports burgeoned, with an increase of 24% in baseball attendance over the preceding year.

Rocket scientist Wernher Von Braun passed away in 1977, as did the "King of Rock 'n' Roll," Elvis Presley, who died in his palatial Graceland estate in Memphis, the victim of a drug overdose. Additionally, two of the greatest funnymen of all time passed away, Charlie Chaplin and Groucho Marx.

On January 24, 1977, Indiana became the 35th and last state to ratify the Equal Rights Amendment. The movement to amend the Constitution of the United States to guarantee the rights of women traces its origins back to 1923, but it was in the 1970s with a highly mobilized women's rights movement that the effort gained steam. The women's rights movement would go on to play a major role in the selection of the Ike dollar's replacement in 1979.

THE NUMISMATIC SCENE. On February 11, Mary Brooks resigned as director of the Mint after more than seven years in the position, during which time she had constantly interacted with the numismatic community. Frank H. MacDonald became acting director of the Mint. On October 26, President Jimmy Carter appointed Stella B. Hackel director of the Mint, and on November 12 she was sworn in by Secretary of the Treasury W. Michael Blumenthal. A lawyer by practice, she was from Rutland, Vermont. A large quantity of undistributed coins remained on hand, and many were held in storage at the West Point Bullion Depository, the San Francisco Assay Office, and at the Rocky Mountain Arsenal in Denver.

Q. David Bowers was elected as the president of the Professional Numismatists Guild for a two-year term. The coin market was hot, prices continued to rise, and anyone buying coins for investment, no matter what the price, could do no wrong—or so it seemed at the time.

The coin market emerged from a quiet period and became dynamic. Activity was intense, and prices rose across the board. Long-stored silver dollars from the estate of Nevada-eccentric Laverne Redfield, heavily concentrated on San Francisco varieties from 1878 to 1904, were marketed with great success. The Louis E. Eliasberg Collection, which had been on view at the Philadelphia Mint in 1976, continued to attract visitors in 1977, courtesy of the late collectors' sons and heirs, Louis Jr. and Richard.

The final medal (1977) issued for the U.S. Assay Commission was a pewter piece featuring Martha Washington. (shown reduced)

The *Annual Report of the Director of the Mint* stated this with regard to San Francisco coins:

> Chrome-plated dies of the reverse of 1-cent and 5-cent coins that had been used for Proof coins and retired for wear are now being used to produce circulating coins. In addition to saving the cost of producing new dies, previous testing showed the die life to be equal or superior to unplated dies. Tests during the fiscal year on 25-cent, 50-cent, and 1-dollar retired reverse Proof dies have also yielded above average die life. Testing to determine the feasibility of chrome plating all dies used for circulating coinage is in progress. Chrome plating cost will be weighed against die life.

Virgil Hancock occupied the president's chair and continued to run a one-man show with his Board of Governors in the background. The efforts of Vice President Grover C. Criswell were rarely credited, nor did other Board members receive much attention, at least not in print. Representing the "loyal opposition" to many of Hancock's new ideas was Adna G. Wilde Jr., former executive director of the ANA, a man who would be president in the future. In August at the annual convention held this year in Atlanta it was announced that Criswell would be the new ANA president, a foregone conclusion as he had been unopposed. The association now had close to 34,000 members, but dropouts reached record levels as several thousand members felt that Hancock had stirred up too much controversy and bitterness.

The Year 1978

CURRENT EVENTS. On January 6, President Jimmy Carter returned from a tour of Europe, India, and the Middle East. The troubled economy at home would plague Carter's administration from beginning to end. Inflation continued rampant, and on April 11 Carter stated that federal employees would be given pay increases no greater than 5.5%. On May 6 Carter declared that organized medicine and the American Medical Association were barriers to better healthcare. Meanwhile and continuing for years after, medical costs rose and government programs were beset with inefficiency and ballooning costs. Doctors became enmeshed in a morass of red tape, all of which cost patients more money and did nothing to advance medical progress. Welfare programs were inefficient and often cost the government $2 in expenses to administer $1 worth of aid. American taxpayers footed the bill.

President Carter is greeted by well-wishers in Germany on his goodwill tour.

New York City, facing bankruptcy, received a federal loan guarantee of $1.65 billion for its bonds. On December 15, Cleveland, Ohio, could not pay $15.5 million in short-term notes, becoming the first of several cities to default in modern times—nothing like this had happened since the 1930s. The inflation continued to increase, this year at the rate of 8%, but productivity increased only 0.4%. The annual U.S. trade deficit increased and continued to be a problem.

The value of the U.S. dollar fell on the international markets, and President Carter announced steps to counter this, including large sales of U.S. gold from federal holdings.

THE NUMISMATIC SCENE. The coin market was wild, all bets were off, and investors fell all over themselves in the scramble to buy anything that was round in shape with a brilliant surface. The greatest numismatic boom in history was in progress. Now articles on rare coins were commonplace in financial journals, and watchers of financial news on television were apt to see convincing actors, or even rare-coin dealers, pitching double eagles, silver dollars, and other sure-fire profit makers. In Texas the Hunt brothers attempted to corner the market for silver bullion. As a result, untold millions of worn 20th-century silver coins went to the melting pot as their metal value exceeded their worth to numismatists.

Ruthann Brettell, a long-time ANA employee, was named as assistant to Executive Vice President Ed Rochette and assumed responsibility for planning conventions and overseeing finances. Kenneth L. Hallenbeck was named as another assistant and became curator of the ANA Museum. William C. Henderson had been treasurer and continued in the post, earning great admiration and respect. Mary Thompson organized matters for ANACS. Geneva Karlson was librarian.

The summer ANA convention was held in Houston with about 8,000 in attendance. Membership stood at 29,369 at the end of the fiscal year, reflecting the greatest short-term slump in the association's history. Adding new members became the number one priority. Operations recorded a $20,000 surplus, despite record legal fees of more than $150,000, including for suits by dealers who had not been awarded bourse tables at last year's convention. It was announced that ANACS was creating a plan to grade coins for a fee.

In a thinly disguised move to keep certain people, namely Grover Criswell and John J. Pittman, from serving as governors for a long string of years the Board of Governors adopted by-laws saying that each board seat was to be numbered. In this way a particular candidate could be directly challenged. The unintended consequence in later years was that those who hoped to gain seats did not run against popular figures! This move and other restrictions later (some still in place today, including term limits) restricted the long-term franchise of members to elect the individuals they thought best qualified for office.

The Year 1979

CURRENT EVENTS. The energy crisis worsened due to the political situation in Iran. On July 15, President Carter announced an energy conservation program which would limit oil imports and reduce domestic use. Congress passed a bill authorizing $1.5 billion to bail out the Chrysler Corporation from its economic woes, following a presentation by its president, Lee Iacocca, who became an American folk hero as he subsequently turned the fortunes of the Chrysler Corporation around. Suggestions were made that he could run the country and should throw his hat in the ring for president.

Problems continued in the economy, with the biggest increase in the consumer price index in 33 years—13.3%—known as "double-digit inflation." The stock market remained stable with the Dow-Jones Industrial Average standing at 838.4 at the end of the year, an increase of 4.2% over the preceding 12 months, although a record 8.2 billion shares were traded.

The government continued its campaign against cigarette smoking and on January 11, Surgeon General Julius B. Richmond declared that cigarettes were "the single most important environmental factor contributing to early death." Meanwhile, the U.S. government continued paying subsidies to the tobacco industry.

On March 28, a malfunction occurred at the Three Mile Island nuclear plant at the Susquehanna River near Harrisburg, Pennsylvania, and the facility was shut down. Fears arose that a massive radiation leak might occur, but it never happened. The space probe Pioneer II, launched in 1973, traveled by Saturn and discovered two new rings and an 11th moon. In October, Pope John Paul II visited the Eastern and Midwestern United States, becoming the first pope to be greeted by a president in the White House.

In Iran Shah Mohammad Reza Pahlavi was overthrown, and Ayatollah Ruhollah Khomeini established a dictatorship. Many Iranians, especially those involved in business, fled—including to the United States. In November, revolutionaries took over the U.S. Embassy in Tehran and imprisoned more than 50 hostages. On March 26 a peace treaty was signed between Egypt and Israel, ending 30 years of war. The Soviets invaded Afghanistan in December. Although there had been unsettled conditions in the Middle East for many years, 1979 was perhaps the launching point for what developed into a seemingly endless series of conflicts, wars, and human tragedy that has lasted through the present day.

To rescue six American diplomats who evaded capture during the seizure of the United States embassy in Tehran, the CIA created a fake movie-production company in Hollywood— "Studio Six Productions"—and delivered disguises and documents that made possible the diplomats' escape from Iran in 1980 under the pretext of working on the film "Argo."

The Numismatic Scene. The rare-coin market experienced unbridled speculation and inflation, with many prices increasing to multiples of what they had been just a few years earlier. In November, the Garrett Collection of U.S. Coins, auctioned by Bowers and Ruddy Galleries on behalf of The Johns Hopkins University, saw $725,000 paid for the finest-known specimen of the 1787 Brasher doubloon—a world's record price for any coin at auction, a figure that would stand for nearly a decade.

The Mint released a customer survey that showed that a majority were aged 36 to 65, had family incomes of more than $10,000 per year, had some college education, and had been collecting for five years or more. More than 40% reported that two or more people in their household collected coins.[8]

On March 31 the mints closed down due to bad timing in federal funding. The closure was temporary. The U.S. Mint announced that the P mintmark would be placed on all coins manufactured, except cents, beginning in 1980.

In October the Federal Reserve raised the discount rate to 12% in an effort to control the money supply, causing stock and bond prices to drop. Many banks raised the prime rate to 14.5%. Fear of holding money increased, and people rushed to acquire tangible things including gold and silver, which rose to record prices. The Hunt brothers, Texas billionaires, continued to endeavor to corner the world market on silver bullion. Wild speculation in gold pushed the price of bullion up 135% during the year to more than $800 per ounce (the price crashed in 1980).

The ANA Certification Service (ANACS) expanded into the grading of coins for a fee, soon bringing unprecedented revenue into the ANA treasury. The annual convention was held in St. Louis.

The Year 1980

Current Events. The Jimmy Carter administration experienced a great deal of difficulty in 1980 despite the president's well-meaning and honest intentions. Hostages were still being held at the U.S. Embassy in Iran, casting a cloud over the international scene. Soviet occupation of Afghanistan was agonizing, and relations between the United States and the U.S.S.R. became very cold. To many observers Jimmy Carter seemed to occupy an office larger than he was capable of managing, and he seemed unable to cope with its many problems. Carter canceled a grain order to Russia in protest of the Afghanistan situation, withdrew sales of high-technology equipment, and declared that the United States would boycott the 1980 Olympic Games in Russia. On January 23, 1980, Carter stated that force would be used if necessary to keep supply routes open to the Persian Gulf. In February an FBI sting operation called ABSCAM incriminated 31 public officials, including one senator and six representatives, who were receiving bribes or undeclared special favors.

Guests of the 1980 Olympiad are greeted by the representatives of the fifteen republics of the USSR. 65 countries boycotted the games to protest the Soviet war in Afghanistan.

In a humanitarian move, Carter signed the Refugee Act of 1980 on March 17, broadening the term to include people from any part of the world, and increasing the maximum admitted annually to 320,000 from 290,000. On April 7, diplomatic relations with Iran were suspended. On April 24 a rescue mission to free the hostages failed, and eight were killed in a plane crash associated with the mission. President Carter deregulated certain trucking rates on July 1 and certain railroad rates on October 14. The Republicans nominated Ronald W. Reagan for president and George Bush for vice president, while the Democrats ran the Carter-Mondale ticket for reelection. Reagan's powerful campaign, coupled with widespread dissatisfaction with the incumbent, scored a Republican victory on November 4.

Inflation continued rampant and by the end of the year had increased to 12.4%, the second year of double-digit inflation, causing annuities and pensions to lose their value and increasing concern over the soundness of the American dollar. Unemployment reached 7.1%, automobile sales were at their lowest in 19 years, and the Ford Motor Company reported losses of $575 million, the largest ever sustained by an American corporation. The country's largest corporation, Exxon, attained $79.1 billion in sales; General Motors was the second largest.

Mt. St. Helens in Washington State erupted on May 18, flattening timber for miles around. The volcano, inactive since 1857, filled the air in the northwestern United States with clouds of microscopic dust. On November 28, Las Vegas' MGM Grand Hotel caught fire, killing 84 people. West Point, the Naval Academy, and the Air Force Academy all graduated their first women cadets. Voyager I (launched in September 1977) flew close to Saturn and found additional rings and three new moons; 15 moons were now known.

On Broadway it was the year for revivals, and *The Music Man*, *Brigadoon*, and *West Side Story* were staged. Ted Turner launched the Cable News Network (CNN), which would revolutionize non-stop news on television. The November 21 "Who Shot J.R.?" episode of *Dallas*, a popular television soap opera, drew more viewers than any other single television program in U.S. history. In theaters *Coal Miner's Daughter* was high on the popularity charts. The Supreme Court ruled that genetically-engineered organisms could be patented.

The United States withdrew from the Summer Olympics, as did some 50 other nations. However, in February at the Winter Olympics in Lake Placid, New York, the U.S. hockey team beat the Finnish and Russian hockey teams and won a gold medal. American athlete Eric Heiden won five gold medals in speed skating.

THE NUMISMATIC SCENE. Rampant speculation continued and created rise in the price of silver and gold to peaks of $50.35 and $873 per ounce respectively. In *The Coin Dealer Newsletter*, January 18, 1980, Allen Harriman remarked: "With both silver and gold bullion soaring into new uncharted ranges, trading in many areas of the coin market becomes more

Mount St. Helens erupting in 1980.

uncertain each day—if not each hour!" Prices peaked early in 1980, some say on April 18 at the Central States Numismatic Society Convention in Lincoln, Nebraska.[9] Prices began a fall which would continue for the next several years, bottoming out between 1982 and 1983.

First CoinVestors, Inc., and other firms prospered by telemarketing and mail campaigns to sell coins as investments to uneducated buyers, usually at prices above numismatic market values. Such firms multiplied, and many still exist.

In the meantime the market for collector-oriented (not investor) coins—colonials, early silver and copper issues, Liberty Seated coins, tokens, medals, and more remained strong. The Garrett Collection sold for The Johns Hopkins University by Bowers and Ruddy Galleries, Inc., continued to break price records as buyers ignored economic and numismatic conditions to bid for many gems. When the last of the four sales was held in 1981, the collection grossed $25,000,000—the largest amount ever realized for any rare coin collection at auction.

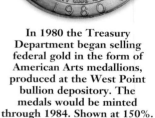

The ANA board of governors expanded the official grading standards in the Uncirculated range to include intermediate grades MS-63 and MS-67. The Numismatic Bibliomania Society, a club for devotees of numismatic literature, was formed.

In July Mint Director Stella B. Hackel revealed a new plan for mintmarks, noting that a P mintmark would appear on all coins from the cent to the dollar

In 1980 the Treasury Department began selling federal gold in the form of American Arts medallions, produced at the West Point bullion depository. The medals would be minted through 1984. Shown at 150%.

made at Philadelphia in 1980—except this: "In 1980, one-cent coins produced for circulation in Philadelphia, Denver, San Francisco, and the West Point Bullion Depository will bear no mintmarks." The last did not happen, except for West Point (later renamed West Point Mint). Years later the W mintmark was added to certain legal tender coins, but never to cents. The West Point facility began striking ounce and half-ounce American Arts gold medallions. Collectors generally ignored these as they were not coins with a face value, and the program ended in 1984. For more information on these gold medallions, see *American Gold and Silver: U.S. Mint Collector and Investor Coins and Medals, Bicentennial to Date*, by Dennis Tucker.

The Year 1981

CURRENT EVENTS. Former movie star Ronald Reagan was inaugurated as President of the United States of America on January 20. Jimmy Carter went into retirement, becoming involved in many social causes. Carter was regarded as "a good person" who was overwhelmed by national and international situations during his presidency. Also on January 20, Iran released the 52 remaining captives who had been held at the U.S. Embassy in Tehran since November 1979. The Republicans would later be accused of staging the timing to coincide with the inauguration.

In an attempt to improve economic conditions, on February 18 President Reagan recommended a cut of $41 billion to the federal budget drafted by Carter, and also proposed income tax decreases. Reagan was shot and wounded on March 30 by John Hinckley Jr. Several men accompanying the president were also wounded, most seriously was Press Secretary Jim Brady. This event eventually resulted in the Brady Law restricting the use of certain small firearms, however, the National Rifle Association (NRA) prevented Congress from passing laws that would prevent wide segments of the population from carrying concealed weapons unless their backgrounds were carefully checked. Over the next 35 years killings in city streets would sharply increase as would other senseless killings elsewhere. In the meantime, drug laws—some of them mandating incarceration for seemingly minor offences—caused America to jail a higher percentage of its citizens than any other nation in the world. Many of the incarcerated were youthful offenders who would have benefited more from counseling and rehabilitation. Auto-Immune Deficiency Syndrome (AIDS) was defined.

In April the United States agreed to sell $1 billion worth of military hardware to Saudi Arabia against strong protests from Israel. The 15-month embargo on grain shipments to the U.S.S.R. was lifted on April 24, although the Afghanistan situation was not resolved. U.S. arms sales to the People's Republic of China were permitted in an attempt to establish closer relations between the countries. On August 19 U.S. Navy planes shot down two Libyan fighters about 60 miles off the coast of Libya after the fighters, claiming sovereignty over the area, opened fire. President Reagan, who was asleep during the engagement, was briefed on the situation the next morning. Relations with Russia worsened as martial law was imposed in Poland and the Solidarity movement there was outlawed.

The economy weakened, and a world-wide recession dampened markets for collectibles, including coins and art. The real estate market fell. Car sales plummeted. National unemployment was at 7.4%. The inflation rate in 1981, however, was 14%, making double-digit increases for three years in a row. Reagan lifted price controls on oil and prices bounded upward. Airlines operated at a record loss. On August 3 13,000 air traffic controllers went on strike nationwide. President Reagan announced that unless they returned to work on August 5 they would be fired. Those who did not return to work were eventually replaced; America's labor unions had lost power and would continue to do so.

Actor Rock Hudson, a close friend of the Reagans', would die from AIDS-related complications at the beginning of Reagan's second term. Hudson's death allowed America to personalize the tragedy of the AIDS epidemic, which was disproportionately affecting the gay community.

In the White House, Nancy Reagan dazzled fashion reporters with lavish expenditures on fancy clothes. Not since the Kennedy administration had there been such an interest in this area. Maya Yang Lin, a Yale undergraduate student in architecture, won a nationwide competition to design the Vietnam War Memorial. "The Wall," as it came to be known, was subsequently built in Washington, D.C., and the names of all who died in the war or went missing in action were inscribed on its surfaces.

Cable television became increasingly popular, in time replacing TV sets that gained signals by way of antennas. MTV began business with round-the-clock music programming. Popular films included *Raiders of the Lost Ark*, *Chariots of Fire*, and *On Golden Pond*. Orlando, Florida, anchored by nearby Walt Disney World, was the world's most popular amusement location and had air service to many cities. IBM marketed its first personal computer, which used the MS-DOS (Microsoft Disc Operating System) that computer genius Bill Gates developed and offered to sell for a modest sum. IBM thought it was best to license, but Gates turned them down and went on with associates and founded the Microsoft Corporation. Years later his company would make him the world's wealthiest person.

THE NUMISMATIC SCENE. The coin market still faced a year or two of decline in series that had experienced strong run-ups in recent times, although solidly collectible issues such as colonials, half cents, large cents, Liberty Seated issues, etc., held their values fairly well, some even increased. High-grade silver dollars, gold coins, and other issues which had shared in the investment boom experienced widespread reductions. After about 1983 prices would gradually rebuild. Coin grading took many forms. The two main references in print were *Official ANA Grading Standards of United States Coins*, by Abe Kosoff and Kenneth E. Bressett, with introductory material by Q. David Bowers; and *Photograde*, by James F. Ruddy, but individual interpretations of Mint State and Proof levels varied widely. Standardization of interpretations did not tighten until 1986, when the Professional Coin Grading Service (PCGS) was founded, and many individual differences still continued beyond this point.

The director of the Mint was Stella B. Hackel Sims (usually referred to as Stella Hackel), who served from November 1977 through April 1981. From July 1981 through July 1991 the director was Donna Pope. Mrs. Pope would guide the Mint through many commemorative coin programs beginning with the 1982 commemorative half dollar observing the 250th anniversary of George Washington's birth. During the decade, Elizabeth Jones, appointed chief engraver, would be lauded for her artistic talents.

The George Washington Commemorative Coin Act was signed into law in 1981. Congress ended the nearly 30-year absence of new commemorative coins by authorizing a silver half dollar for the 250th anniversary of Washington's birth. Minting would begin in 1982. Shown at 125%.

No dollar coins were made from 1982 to 1998. Many events took place between 1981, when the last Susan B. Anthony dollars were coined in the early series, and 1999, the year of the new series. Delineating these is beyond the scope of the present text.

The Year 1999

CURRENT EVENTS. In 1999 President William Jefferson Clinton was the subject of criticism for lying under oath and having sexual encounters with an aide, among other things, and was subject to an impeachment procedure. Early in the year the Senate, largely voting along party lines, acquitted him. In April two students stormed Columbine High School in Littleton, Colorado, and killed 13 people before killing themselves. John F. Kennedy Jr., his wife, and his sister-in-law were killed when their private plane was lost at sea near Martha's Vineyard, Massachusetts.

The amateur film, *The Blair Witch Project*, cost $35,000 to make and grossed more than $125,000 at the box office. The Internet, which had become increasingly popular, had more than 150,000,000 users worldwide. Home computers were all the rage with Apple and PC systems.

Stock market investors scrambled to buy new dot.com offerings, sending the NASDAQ average to new highs. The officials of most such companies had glowing visions of profits but no realistic business plans. In Europe the Euro coin made its debut in many countries, England and Switzerland notably excepted. Henceforth the American dollar was measured against that currency. Automobiles made in Japan and Germany captured much of the market, including most luxury vehicles. The old-line American marques such as Cadillac and Lincoln had reduced appeal to younger buyers.

A tourist poses in front of the euro symbol outside the European Central Bank in Frankfurt, Germany.

THE NUMISMATIC SCENE. In one of the most dramatic programs ever instituted by the Treasury Department, largely based on congressional testimony given by Harvey Stack of Stack's, New York City, the State Quarter Program was launched. Five different states would be honored each year, in the order in which they ratified the Constitution, the first being Delaware. The program was planned to continue for ten years, until all states had been covered. The plan called for designs to be created within the individual states by artists, members of the public, and others who were to submit ideas to be reviewed and then finalized by the governors of the states. The eventual result was fifty different designs, no two alike, which delighted numismatists who gave many reviews and opinions concerning the beauty or lack thereof. Each of the quarters had a special launch ceremony covered with fanfare. Great excitement prevailed from beginning to end, and much was done for the entire numismatic hobby.

Allen Stanford, who conducted Superior Galleries in Beverly Hills, was found to have run a Ponzi scheme involving banking, sports, real estate, and other ventures in North America, including rare coins. He was subsequently convicted to serve 110 years in prison.

The Internet, in use in recent years, hit its stride in numismatics, and many different collectors, clubs, dealers, and others posted websites offering information or coins for sale. Other entities outside of numismatics, including general information, antique, and auction sites, invited numismatists to add listings. The coin market continued to be strong.

The Year 2000

CURRENT EVENTS. The presidential election was given to Republican George W. Bush whose campaign against Democrat Al Gore ended in confusion as to how votes were counted in the swing state of Florida. On December 12 the Supreme Court voted 5 to 4 in Bush's favor. The Clinton administration had been an economic success with the federal budget showing a surplus, and the unemployment rate at just 3.5%. Although the new millennium would officially begin on January 1, 2001, on January 1, 2000, it was widely celebrated. The "Y2K scare" that computers would crash worldwide and data would be lost proved to be unfounded. Ever since the Gulf War of the early 1990s, conditions in the Middle East had been more unsettled than usual, the news of which was constantly in the media.

Amateur investors were important in the stock market, parlaying savings, inheritances, and bonuses into fortunes by day trading—sometimes at desks gladly provided to them by many brokerage houses. Dot-com companies, these being existing or planned ventures with Internet businesses as their models, were the darlings. In January America Online (AOL) agreed to buy traditional media Time Warner for $165 billion to the amazement of many onlookers. The NASDAQ soared to a record 6048 on March 10. Later that month the bubble burst, and many such companies collapsed. It was not until the 2010s with a new group of investors that dot-com stocks again soared in the market (but with only a small percentage of them yielding a profit to buyers).

The economy continued to be excellent, showing admirable control of the budget and an unemployment rate of just 4%. A first-class stamp now cost 34¢.

Stephen King's latest novel, *Riding the Bullet*, was offered as an Internet download for $2.50, and more than 500,000 copies were sold. Coming years would see the Internet take the place of many traditional printed texts, especially encyclopedias and reference works. Scientists deciphered the human genome, and it was expected that this would make great advances in medicine possible.

Around the world, people put on special events and built special structures to celebrate the new millennium in the year 2000. Here is London's Millennium Dome as it appeared that year.

THE NUMISMATIC SCENE. Recovered gold coins, ingots, and other treasure from the SS *Central America*, lost at sea off the coast of North Carolina on September 12, 1857, had been recovered and were being offered to the public by Dwight N. Manley and his California Gold Marketing Group. At the ANA Convention in Philadelphia the "Ship of Gold" exhibit, with a replica of the side of the ship, was a sensation and was spread across the entrance to the bourse. A program on the *Central America* discovery was given by finder-scientist Bob Evans, with Dave Bowers assisting, and drew a record audience of 400. In *Coin World* editor Beth Deisher called it "The Story of the Year."

The coin market was strong. Coins certified by PCGS and NGC in particular were in demand, and by this time most expensive coins were bought and sold in plastic "slabs." Breaking the coins out of their holders and resubmitting them to the same services became an industry in itself, and in coming years many coins graduated a grade point or two upward.

The Year 2001

CURRENT EVENTS. In the twilight of his presidency Bill Clinton pardoned billionaire fugitive Marc Rich, a donor to certain of his projects. His administration ended with a budget surplus, and on January 20 George Bush was inaugurated.

On the morning of September 11, 19 youthful Islamic terrorists gained control of four large jetliners. Two of the planes were crashed into the twin towers of the World Trade Center complex in New York City and another crashed into the west side of the Pentagon. The last plane, Flight 93, was headed towards Washington, D.C., but passengers wrestled to take over control from the hijackers and it instead went down in a field near Shanksville, Pennsylvania. Almost 3,000 people were killed, and thus began the War on Terror. The nation would never be the same.

In 2000 the U.S. Mint issued its first—and, so far, only—bimetallic silver-and-gold commemorative coin, a $10 piece honoring the bicentennial of the Library of Congress. Shown at 150%.

The North Pool of the National September 11 Memorial & Museum commemorates those who died in the terrorist attack, while behind it stands One World Trade Center, also known as Freedom Tower, the main building of the rebuilt World Trade Center complex.

The budget surplus dwindled and was attributed to Bush administration tax cuts and a slowing economy. Wall Street was still licking its wounds from the dot-com bubble. Certain officers of Enron, a large energy firm based in Houston, were found guilty of massive fraud assisted by incorrect oversight by the local office of Arthur Andersen. In a sorry situation, the government forced all offices of the national accounting firm to close, with unfortunate consequences to many fine employees not involved in the scandal.

Global warming and climate change stirred many debates and would continue to do so into the next decades. On the literary front the *Harry Potter* novels by J.K. Rowling (first published in the United Kingdom in 1997 and in the United States in 1998) were immensely popular by this time with the younger set and parents alike.

THE NUMISMATIC SCENE. New Schuler presses made in Germany were introduced into service at the mints. These sophisticated devices mounted die pairs vertically, blank planchets dropped down a chute, were struck, fell to the bottom onto a small conveyor belt that dumped them into a bin at the end of the machine. The process was faster than the eye could follow. These presses are in service at the mints today.

State quarters continued their popularity and brought many new faces into the numismatic community. Interest in new commemorative coins sold at a premium was less than in recent years. Capitol Visitor Center commemorative coins sold just 27% of the amount authorized. The production of commemoratives that proved to be uninteresting to buyers brought complaints to the Mint, but it was Congress, not the Mint, that authorized such pieces and directed the Mint to strike them.

In March, *Coin World* reported a paid circulation of 90,767 and estimated that nearly 500,000 people were serious collectors. The American Numismatic Association had 30,167 members. The U.S. Mint had more than 1.8 million people on its mailing list, but most of those limited their purchases to Mint products. More than 1 million citizens collected or at least saved State quarters. *A Guide Book of United States Coins* continued to sell hundreds of thousands of copies each year.

The ANA experienced challenges. Membership and convention attendance were in decline and there were budget and financial difficulties. In another aspect of the hobby, very common modern coins if graded MS–68 to 70 by PCGS or NGC sometimes sold for thousands of dollars to collectors building registry sets, a relatively new aspect of the hobby that did much to prop up the market.

In September 2001 numismatist Don Bailey (right, author of the *Whitman Encyclopedia of Mexican Money*) was awarded the Mexican Order of the Aztec Eagle. Here, numismatists Clyde Hubbard (left) and Alberto Hidalgo examine the award.

The Year 2002

CURRENT EVENTS. President George W. Bush, in his first State of the Union speech, called North Korea, Iran, and Iraq "the axis of evil." President Bush signed an order to allow the National Security Agency (NSA) to spy, without a warrant, on any-one suspected of terrorist activity. Unknown to citizens, this program went far beyond its intent and spied on millions of Americans who were not under suspicion. Years later Edward Snowden exposed the system to the amazement of just about everyone (see 2013 entry). The rape and molestation of children by Catholic priests and others was the subject of many articles and much media attention, as it would continue to be for years.

The collapse of Enron due to fraud continued. The Houston office of accounting firm Arthur Andersen was implicated, and the government completely shut down the nationwide operations of the otherwise well-respected company, a move which seemed unfortunate to many observers at the time. Tyco, Qwest, Global Crossing, ImClone, and other public companies were found to have engaged in transactions ranging from questionable to fraudulent. *Spider-Man* was a box office sensation, taking in more than $406 million. AIDS, first identified in 1981, claimed many lives, spurring intense med-ical research to combat the disease.

The economy was strong, with rising prices in the housing market in particular, fueled by the easy availability of mortgages to those who had marginal credit (it was later revealed that many documents were falsified). Walmart continued to be the nation's leading retailer by far, as it had been in recent years.

Around the world humanitarian efforts by various groups continued to raise money to combat the global HIV/AIDS epidemic. Ongoing efforts to fight AIDS include research for a cure, relief for those with the disease, and educating communities on safety measures and AIDS myths to reduce the transmission of the disease.

THE NUMISMATIC SCENE. The 2002-D Tennessee quarters had the lowest mintage in the State series up to this point—"lowest" being relative, as 286,468,000 pieces is nearly one for every man, woman, and child in the United States. Unlike the Sacagawea dollars, State quarters circulated widely. Kennedy half dollars had been struck continuously since 1964, but they were rarely seen in circulation.

A survey of adjectives used in *Coin World* advertisements to sell high-grade coins included "megagem," "mind boggling," "premier plus," and even "extraterrestrial."[10] "Coin doctors," as they were tagged, made large profits by adding artificial toning, especially with "rainbow" colors, to coins. This artificial toning added to sales appeal and in many instances masked friction and other marks.

The Stack's/Sotheby's sale of a 1933 double eagle for $7.59 million shattered worldwide records. In the auction market, "ultra-grade" certified coins, especially if graded by PCGS or NGC, raised eyebrows—pieces that were common and also inexpensive in gem grades such as MS–65 and 66 sold for astronomical prices if they were close to or at MS-70, even though only a tiny fraction of the available coins had been submitted for grading.

A commemorative silver dollar in 2002 celebrated the bicentennial of the West Point military academy. Naturally they were struck at the West Point Mint.

The Year 2003

CURRENT EVENTS. The *Columbia* space shuttle, which in the summer of 1999 had carried 12 *gold* Sacagawea dollars, exploded on February 1 as it crossed the Southwest, killing the seven astronauts aboard. The federal budget had been running at a deficit, a combination of expenses attributable to security from terrorists, lower tax rates, and increased spending, and much deeper deficits were projected. By the end of the year it would reach unprecedented levels. Experienced economists worried that such programs as Social Security and Medicare would eventually run out of funding. Unemployment was at 6%. The fine print in financial instruments including tranches and derivatives was becoming so complex that in many instances bankers and investment funds could not understand them.

Based on unverified information provided by advisors, President Bush informed the public that Iraqi dictator Saddam Hussein possessed "weapons of mass destruction," and an invasion of Iraq was launched. It was thought that the Iraqis would warmly welcome this mass intervention by the United States. The war dragged into a prolonged encounter that divided America.

The Internet was now a part of the lives of most Americans. Copyrights were routinely ignored, and the music industry filed suits against some who illegally downloaded songs, including a 12-year-old girl. *The DaVinci Code*, by Dan Brown, was a best-selling novel, and *Harry Potter* books continued to fly off the shelves.

THE NUMISMATIC SCENE. Ultra-grade coins sometimes brought headline prices, such as $39,100 for a Proof-70 (PCGS) 1963 Lincoln cent. "No one can convince me that a Proof Lincoln cent from the early 1960s is worth what amounts to a whole year's salary," commented Ed Reiter, editor of *COINage* magazine. Registry-set competition created many record prices for modern coins that were very common in grades two or three points lower. On January 1, Christopher Cipoletti was named as the new executive director of the ANA. The summer convention, named the World's Fair of Money, was held in Baltimore and was the most active in recent years.

Most gold ingots and more than 5,500 Mint State 1857-S double eagles from the SS *Central America* treasure had found buyers by this time, and many had been resold at a profit.

The eBay Internet auction site founded in 1995 had become a major venue for coin sales by 2003, with countless quantities of offered items. There was no rigorous check and balance in place, and many counterfeits were offered, although these were just a small proportion of overall transactions.

The U.S. Mint issued its first-ever *series* of silver national medals in 2003—a four-medal set honoring the centennial of the National Wildlife Refuge System and President Theodore Roosevelt. (See Tucker's *American Gold and Silver* for more information.)

The Year 2004

CURRENT EVENTS. In the presidential election it was incumbent George W. Bush and Democratic challenger John Kerry. Bush won easily. The situation in Iraq went from bad to worse—the Senate Intelligence Committee reported that Iraq did not have weapons of mass destruction and, in essence, the invasion was conducted on false premises. Photographs of American soldiers, a woman in particular, abusing and sexually humiliating Iraqi prisoners brought worldwide condemnation on the United States.

Google went public in August, making the founders, Sergey Brin and Larry Page, billionaires. Google went on to do many things for the public good and for the benefit of Internet users—a model company that attracted wide admiration. They were also listed in the stock market. The Internet auction site eBay had established itself by this time as the major seller of collectibles with the unintended result that mom and pop antique shops that had dotted the landscape were mostly gone.

The exposure of the right breast of Janet Jackson during Super Bowl XLVIII caused a media sensation and was called a "wardrobe malfunction," to the amusement of all. The World Series was won by the Boston Red Sox, the first time since 1918. Google, the Internet search company, was listed in the stock market.

Google founders Sergey Brin and Larry Page developed the PageRank algorithm, which sorts Internet search results to return the most relevant pages to the querent.

THE NUMISMATIC SCENE. The American Numismatic Society moved from its two-story building at 155th and Broadway to a large office building at 140 William Street in lower Manhattan, largely the gift of numismatist-philanthropist Donald Partrick. The Mint began its Artistic Infusion Program whereby talented artists and sculptors in the private sector were invited to submit coin and medal designs to be finessed by the engraving department staff, already an incredible pool of accomplished people. Mint officials and representatives from the National Endowment for the Arts selected 18 "master designers" and six graduate art students as "associate designers" from more than 300 applicants. Later in the year a second call for artists took place. The Mint began its two-year Westward Journey Nickel Series with designs related to the Lewis and Clark Expedition of a century earlier.

The world of coin shows and auctions had been changing in recent times and continued to do so. Collectors found it more convenient to buy and bid from home than to attend distant events. Similarly, most dealers had websites and could sell coins with little effort and no travel required. Air travel with tight inspection systems and often long delays in security lines added to the problem. Mark Ferguson, the *Coin World* analyst who conducted "Coin Values," urged buyers to beware of common coins bringing high prices if in high grades. "Values listed in Coin Values, especially for MS-66 and MS-67 Washington quarters, reflect these higher values, and are to be used as a guide only."[11] Large quantities of modern forgeries made in China caused many problems, especially to buyers seeking bargains. Gold and silver bullion coins continued to be popular, as they had been since the American Eagle program began in 1986. Gold in particular attracted a lot of attention, and "gold bugs," as enthusiasts were sometimes called, were seen at many conventions. The Baltimore Coin and Currency Convention run by Gordon Berg and Ed Kuzmar drew more than 10,000 visitors in December. American Numismatic Rarities, established in 2003 with Christine Karstedt as president, conducted auctions at this and other Baltimore shows.

The Year 2005

CURRENT EVENTS. The Internet continued to draw people away from public events, and attendance at National Parks, theaters, sporting events, and even rock concerts continued a steady decline. In late August, Hurricane Katrina ravaged the Gulf Coast and inland cities, including New Orleans, causing more than 1,000 fatalities and leaving millions without homes. Municipal and federal facilities were poorly prepared to cope with the disaster.

In Iraq the death count of American soldiers crossed the 2,000 mark. The war seemed to have no plan, nor was there an end in sight. *Freakonomics* was a best seller in bookstores. Cancer replaced heart disease as the number one killer of people under 85 years of age.

Entertainment glitterati included Ben Affleck, Tom Cruise, Jennifer Aniston, Jennifer Lopez, and Brad Pitt among many others. On the Internet several Web sites catered to followers of the stars of screen and stage. Drugs, abuse of children by priests, abortion, creationism, voting registration restrictions, immigration, and other social matters made the news constantly.

Storm-tossed cars in Meraux, Louisiana, following Hurricane Katrina.

THE NUMISMATIC SCENE. The Mint continued its Westward Journey Nickel Series. An error of historical fact occurred on the 2005 nickel inscribed OCEAN IN VIEW, a description from the expedition's journal, which had it as "Ocian in view." When asked with why the journal wording was altered, a Mint spokesperson said, "Otherwise we would have been criticized for misspelling the word." Surely, this would have been the case.

The Mint announced that beginning this year the Mint sets of Uncirculated coins sold to collectors would have a "satin finish," caused by blasting the dies with a mixture of sand and glass beads. These would be struck at the rate of 300 coins per minute on presses with 300 tons of pressure, in contrast with normal circulation production at the rate of 750 per minute on 150-ton presses. Collectors discovered that the satin finish was not consistent, but high quality coins resulted. By this time the general quality of regular, commemorative, and bullion coins sold at a premium was superb, and the majority graded 67 or higher.

Some satin coins were labeled SP (Specimen) or SMS (Special Mint Set) by certain grading services. Scott Schechter of NGC commented to the effect that there were problems: "The 2005 Mint Sets that NGC has examined show a wide variety of production and handling quality," Schechter said. "Even within a single set, coins can range from heavily frosted to mostly brilliant. While some coins are obvious specimens, others closely resemble regular circulating issues. Because of the inconsistency in quality of these coins, to assure that coins submitted to NGC receive the SMS designation, they must be submitted in their original Mint packaging." Further, some coins had scratches, nicks, gouges, and abrasions.[12]

The Mint had been selling platinum bullion coins since 1997, these denominated $10, $25, $50, and $100. These had attracted relatively little numismatic interest, and in 2004 sales had dropped 27.5% from the year before, mainly because the rise in price of the metal on international markets. In 2005 there were two options: 2005 (Philadelphia Mint) Uncirculated and 2005-W (West Point) Proof. Fewer than 6,500 were sold of each. The aftermarket for earlier coins dating back to 1997 was mostly based on their melt-down value plus a nominal percentage.

The ANA World's Fair of Money was held in San Francisco and had a poor turnout, some said because other than from that city and its suburbs there were few population centers within a half-day drive. "The results are in. It was a bust," stated reader R. Mittelbach in a letter to *Coin World*.

The May 29, 2005, issue of the *Atlanta Journal-Constitution* reported on the Whitman Coin and Collectibles Atlanta Expo held at the Cobb Galleria Centre.

Not only was it lightly attended and business was slow, but sometimes 100 or more people stood in long lines to register.[13] David Harper, editor of *Numismatic News*, quoted several dealers. Andy Skrabalac said "T'was no public." Leon Hendrickson, usually busy at shows, said, "Truthfully, very slow." Harper attended a U.S. Mint program and reported that the room had five Mint officials, four numismatic editors, and just three members of the public.[14] In subsequent years the ANA would enjoy much more successful shows in Chicago and other cities.

Washington quarters from 1932 to 1998 became increasingly popular as buyers of the later State coins investigated the earlier issues. The market was strong overall, fueled by high prices for coins graded on the long side of MS-65 and PF-65. Still, many coins, commemoratives in particular, were cheaper in 2005 than they had been at the height of the "Wall Street investment market" in 1989. "Gradeflation" was endemic, with the result that countless coins graded by PCGS and NGC a few years earlier now received higher grades when "cracked out" (as the term goes) and resubmitted to the same services. Many MS-63 and MS-64 coins of yesteryear were now MS-65.

In *Penny-Wise*, journal of the Early American Coppers group, editor Dr. Harry E. Salyards wrote that collecting early coins by die varieties was becoming an increasingly popular pursuit with many opportunities to buy rare varieties that were not recognized by the seller.[15] Similarly, collecting coins described in the *Cherrypickers' Guide to Rare Die Varieties* by Bill Fivaz and J.T. Stanton attracted many enthusiasts. Whereas people buying coins as an investment tended to leave the hobby quickly, collectors of die varieties were apt to remain in numismatics for many years.

The Year 2006

CURRENT EVENTS. Space exploration achieved many triumphs during this decade and extending to the next, including photographic exploration of the planets Jupiter and Saturn, some of which were found to have volcanic activity, ice, and other unexpected characteristics. The International Space Station (ISS) was manned by astronauts from several countries, mainly the United States and Russia. Shuttle flights, which had been canceled after the *Columbia* disaster, were resumed with *Discovery*, which was a regular supplier to the ISS. Pluto lost its status as the ninth planet and was reclassified as a dwarf planet. The Patriot Act, earlier legislation initially introduced to help deter terrorism, was being used as an excuse by government agencies to close access to many facilities.

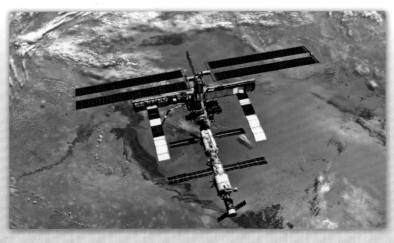

The International Space Station over the Caspian Sea.

Whether human stem cells should be used for embryonic research was a hotly debated topic. An eight-year, $415 million federal study found, to the surprise of the medical community, that a low-fat diet does not decrease the risk of heart disease, cancer, or stroke. On the financial front there was much reckless lending by banks and others, including reverse mortgages, regular mortgages with inflated appraisals, and other misdeeds, often bundling them and selling them as packages to investors. Many borrowers were not fully aware of the dangers.[16]

THE NUMISMATIC SCENE. Rising metal costs, long a problem on various occasions for the Mint, came to the fore with the value of copper and nickel increasing on the international markets. For Edmund C. Moy, who was sworn in as Mint Director on September 5, this was one of several challenges he faced. To buy one of each Mint product for sale to collectors and investors in 2006, in Uncirculated and Proof finishes, cost $14,804.[17]

New grading services sprung up like mushrooms after a rain and were often set up to gull unsuspecting buyers on the Internet, particularly on eBay. Then and now such services were unregulated.[18] Television sales shows hawked "rare" coins that were usually not rare and at prices well above what a knowledgeable collector would pay from a reputable dealer. *Inside Edition*, a syndicated television program, made sample purchases from two shopping networks and had them examined by experts, including Scott A. Travers. An "Ultimate Nickel Set" costing $69 was valued at just $2.05, and a special set of State quarters costing $99.96 was really worth $28.55.[19] Again, there was no regulation. Anyone could advertise as a professional coin dealer or grading expert.

David L. Ganz in "Coin Investment Performance," *Numismatic News*, March 7 delineated that a carefully purchased "basket" of rare coins of quality yielded an average annual increase of 13.5% over a 68-year period.

The Bureau of Engraving and Printing had been preparing special offerings to collectors for many years. These included matching low-serial-number notes from all 12 Federal Reserve Banks. A 12-note set of $50 bills was priced at $1,095 with a limit of 500 sets made. Another offering was Year of the Dog notes with 8888, considered a lucky number in Chinese culture.

In Denver, celebrating the 60th anniversary of the Red Book at the 2006 American Numismatic Association World's Fair of Money, Whitman publisher Dennis Tucker presented a .900 fine gold medal to Kenneth Bressett. A limited edition of 500 pieces struck in nickel-silver was made available to the general public. This was also the year the U.S. Mint's new 24-karat bullion-coin program, the American Gold Buffalo, started.

The ANA continued to be embroiled in internal problems; at the start of the year it was deeply involved in a lawsuit against several former employees. Other suits would emerge. Governor Walter Ostromecki was tossed off the board by the vote of other governors who would not give a reason why. *Coin World* editor Beth Deisher endeavored to get to the bottom of what developed into a great mess and, in effect, was told to mind her own business.

The Year 2007

CURRENT EVENTS. Problems arose left and right in the mortgage, banking, and other financial businesses. Old-line, long-established firms had participated in giving inflated mortgages and other questionable investments. Some tried to bail out. The worst was yet to come. The real estate market continued the rise of the previous year, fueled by over-appraisals, the granting of loans to people who could not afford properties, secret kickbacks to mortgage lenders, and more. In new developments, it was not usual for a speculator to buy multiple condos or houses and then "flip" them at a profit, even before they were ready for occupancy. Toward the end of the year many swindles were revealed.

A poll published by *The Economist* ranked the United States down at No. 97 in a list of the most peaceful countries (Norway was first). By June, candidates of the Republican and Democratic parties were campaigning heavily for the November 2008 presidential election, more than a year away. The Iraq war, still in progress, was the prime topic of discussion and debate.

Global warming was the new hot topic of the era, and whether it did or did not exist was the subject of many debates. In the meantime the ice caps of the Arctic and Antarctic were melting at alarming rates. Microsoft and their Windows operating systems, including Vista, dominated the world of personal computers, but Apple systems had also developed a strong following and their computers seemed to have fewer problems with "hacking" and unwarranted intrusions. On March 7 the Mega Millions jackpot of $370 million set a world record. Boeing launched its new 787 Dreamliner plane.

In July the Dow-Jones Industrial Average crossed 14,000 for the first time, and on October 9 it hit a new record of 14,164. This remained the high until March 2013! High interest rates and a falling real-estate market threw many properties into default on sub-prime mortgages. Some hedge funds, thought to be a particularly

Norway is the home of the Nobel Peace Prize. In 2007 the prize was awarded to former U.S. vice president Al Gore for his work combating global climate change. Gore shared the prize with the Intergovernmental Panel on Climate Change. Rajendra Pachauri accepted for the IPCC.

smart way to invest, ran into problems, such as two operated by Bear Stearns that caused the company to be sold at a fire-sale price to JPMorgan Chase.[20]

THE NUMISMATIC SCENE. The overall market weakened when the passion for "trophy coins" eased, although there were many exceptions in the auction room. With higher interest rates and slower sales, many dealers were short on funds. Interest in "collector coins," these being key issues in popular series, in grades from Good to lower Mint State, enjoyed a strong market. Outside of the higher-grade coins of the silver and gold federal series, there was great strength in tokens, medals, and paper money. Realization of the John J. Ford Jr. Collection, which consisted nearly entirely of these (and not regular coins), crossed the $50 million mark at Stack's, making it the most valuable collection ever sold. The Internet continued to be dynamic, taking market share from conventions, coin stores, and mail-order catalog listings. On a superficial level citizens still loved to collect State quarters as they were released at the rate of four a year. The U.S. Mint offered dozens of coin-purchase options and enjoyed a brisk business. Investors, a separate breed from collectors, continued to bid high prices for modern coins in ultra grades as well as double eagles and other common gold. Specialists, the old guard of the hobby, were as active as ever in areas from copper cents to colonials to paper money to tokens and medals. Whitman Publishing and Krause Publications each offered new and backlist titles covering about every aspect of numismatics from ancient to modern.

The Internet became more important than ever. Whereas in the 1990s the sign of a good auction was a filled gallery, by 2007 it was not unusual for leading firms to have just a handful of bidders in the audience and a potential audience of millions worldwide on the Internet. There were many Internet-only or virtual auctions, including on eBay, with no catalogs or printed material. In his "Coin Values" column market analyst Mark Ferguson commented:

> These days, physical attendance is not a good indication of participation; many now bid online. One dealer said he's moving away from sitting in long auction sessions, where one often is carried away in raising bids during the heat of the floor action. He said he's making more rational bids via the Internet and now enjoys dinners with his wife while the auctions take place. After years of long hours working coin shows and then auctions in the evening, more dealers have been conspicuously absent from the floor sessions as they submit their bids electronically, through a colleague or the auction companies themselves, prior to the beginning of floor bidding.[21]

Problems worsened at ANA Headquarters where deep financial losses were the rule. An article in the Colorado Springs *Gazette*, by Debbie Kelley, included this: "According to forms filed with the Internal Revenue Service, the ANA posted a loss of $1 million in the 2002 fiscal year. The deficit dropped to $975,000 in 2003 and $266,000 in 2004. Filings for 2006 have not been made, but estimates show a loss of $714,000 for 2005, nearly double the organization's projections." Executive Director Chris Cipoletti was fired, resulting in yet another lawsuit.

American Numismatic Association members who went to the 2007 World's Fair of Money banquet received a ticket good for a free copy of a special ANA Edition of the Red Book. (The show was held in Milwaukee, Wisconsin, and Whitman Publishing, which issues the Red Book, started in nearby Racine.)

THE RED BOOK COMES HOME TO WISCONSIN
ANA WORLD'S FAIR OF MONEY ★ 2007

The Year 2008

CURRENT EVENTS. President George W. Bush toured the Middle East and stopped in many countries. Pope Benedict XVI visited the United States. The SpaceX Falcon became the first private space-launch vehicle to achieve orbit around the Earth. American troops fought wars in Afghanistan and Iraq, seemingly without a firm plan.

The economy entered a recession, prices fell, unemployment rose, and the wild lending practices for mortgages, often with false documentation, contributed to many citizens owing more on their houses than they were worth. The stock market fell. The Federal Reserve cut its rediscount rate to banks to 2.25%. In December the Dow-Jones Industrial Average dropped 680 points, the fourth greatest one-day fall in its history. A bear market was raging. Lehman Brothers, an old-line investment firm was in dire straits and would soon be bankrupt. Merrill Lynch, also hard hit, was bought by Bank of America. Bernard Madoff, praised as one of America's most successful financial advisors, was charged with massive fraud extending over a period of many years. On December 31 the Dow-Jones Industrial Average closed at 8,776.38.

Bernard Madoff was charged with criminal activity after it was revealed that his investment strategy was actually a pyramid scheme.

In this election year many candidates campaigned for nominations. Joe Biden, an early favorite, dropped out in January and later was tapped by Barack Obama to be his vice presidential running mate. Hillary Clinton, who did well on her tours and won primaries, dropped out. John McCain secured the Republican nomination and picked Sarah Palin, the then-relatively unknown governor of Alaska, as his running mate. Mitt Romney, an early hopeful, exited early in the year. Obama won the election on November 4, promising change, the closing of the Guantanamo prisoner of war camp, and withdrawal from the war in the Middle East. At the time the unemployment rate was 6.1%, the inflation rate was 4.9%, and the federal budget had been running at a deficit through the entire previous administration.

THE NUMISMATIC SCENE. Gold coins were in strong demand and it was not long before the price of bullion eclipsed its $873 high of January 1980. The American Numismatic Association management was deeply embroiled in controversy. In January, President Barry Stuppler said the organization was in a "transitional phase." Further, "Finances were becoming strained due to exorbitant legal costs which exceeded budget outlays by about $500,000, overstated revenue projections and understated expenses." Lawsuits included one from former executive director Christopher Cipoletti and four from commercial grading services. Membership numbers experienced a sharp decline. On March 6 the Board announced that Larry Shepherd, a well-liked dealer with extensive business experience, had been chosen from 37 applicants as the

A suite of three different commemorative coins (a half dollar, pictured, plus a silver dollar and $5 gold piece) celebrated the American bald eagle as a national emblem in 2008.

new director. By that time the ANA had had five consecutive years of budget deficits. Stuppler said Shepherd stood out from a "well-qualified pool of applicants," and "is well respected in the numismatic community with a well-earned reputation for integrity. We look forward to his leadership at this critical time in the ANA's history."[22]

The doctoring of coins was a popular subject for debate. Countless Morgan dollars in particular now had rainbow and other colorful toning on both sides, far more than had ever been seen in the market before. "Gradeflation" was endemic, and across the board the leading certification services often bumped MS-63 to MS-64, MS-64 to MS-65, and so on. This was a win-win situation for the owners of the coins, who came to believe their coins were worth more, and for the grading services that collected more fees.

The coin market was very strong. Market analyst Mark Ferguson reported: "The American Numismatic Association's 2008 World's Fair of Money held in Baltimore during the final week of July was amazingly crowded and posted stronger sales than many expected in light of current general economic conditions. Baltimore's central location on the highly populated East Coast enabled many people to conveniently attend the convention. Baltimore is also very convenient for attendees who live in Europe. The 'buzz' that people feel when a coin show is going very well was definitely in the air. During most of the public hours the bourse was so crowded that it was difficult to get to some tables to talk to or do business with the dealers."[23]

The Year 2009

CURRENT EVENTS. The economy continued to be in recession. Many if not most financial institutions and securities businesses experienced losses, and some failed. Problems continued with mortgages, and the Federal Reserve submitted some banks to "stress tests." AIG reported nearly $62 billion in insurance losses, and the government gave it an additional $30 billion in aid beyond what it had received earlier. High interest rates on credit cards attracted federal scrutiny, but not much was done about the problem. In October the unemployment rate was 10%, the highest since 1983.

In January U.S. Airways Flight 1549 out of LaGuardia Airport in New York City lost power in both engines when it hit a flock of birds. The pilot glided the plane down to the Hudson River and all 155 passengers and crew were rescued, "the miracle on the Hudson" it was called. Circuit City, an electronics and appliance chain with 567 stores, closed its doors with the loss of 34,000 jobs.

Pilot Chesley B. "Sully" Sullenberger landed the damaged plane on the Hudson River, where nearby boats and ferries rescued all 155 souls. Here, the Army Corps of Engineers retrieves the plane.

Citizens shooting innocent people with handguns made news headlines on a regular basis this year and in the era. Serious gun controls were few and far between. Golf champion Tiger Woods was involved in a car accident near his home, an incident that led to the exposure of the affairs the married man with two children had been having with about a dozen women. Corporate sponsors dropped him. In the Middle East the United States continued the war in Afghanistan that began in 2001 and with the Iraq war started in 2003. Fewer and fewer residents in either country liked the United States.

THE NUMISMATIC SCENE. Going into the new year the Federal Reserve placed orders for just 3 billion coins for 2009, down from 10.1 billion in 2008. "The U.S. Mint isn't about to tell its workers in Philadelphia and Denver to take a six-month vacation, but it could judging from the coin demand target it is aiming for in 2009," commented David Harper, editor of *Numismatic News*.[24] The Mint established a hiring freeze, and employment during the year dropped 10%. The 110th Congress considered 129 bills relating to coins and medals and passed 17 of them. There were too many commemoratives, many collectors said. Four different reverse designs were used on Lincoln cents to observe the 200th anniversary of the president's birth. The nationwide recession prevented the Federal Reserve from releasing large quantities across the country, and for a time they were scarce in circulation.

The ANA World's Fair of Money, held in Los Angeles in August, prompted *Numismatic News* editor David Harper to comment: "Wide aisles that looked empty and lack of an audible buzz for much of the event earned the August 5–9 American Numismatic Association World's Fair of Money in Los Angeles a mediocre rating at best from dealer attendees."[25] A hot ticket at the show, however, were the new Proof MMIX $20 gold coins, which were sold in quantities, and were sometimes taken on luggage carts to NGC and PCGS who provided on-site grading. Mint Director Edmund C. Moy was on hand to meet and greet collectors. In fiscal year 2009 the Mint had 1,060,000 names on its customer list. On the plus side Executive Director Larry Shepherd proudly reported that the ANA budget did not show a deficit. Cliff Mishler, a long-time executive with Krause Publications, now retired and a popular author, was sworn in as the president of the ANA.

In the marketplace prices dropped on a number of coins that were "conditionally rare"—common enough as MS–65 or 66, but with few certified MS-68 or higher. "That market has always been very thin and artificially bolstered. Generally, the coins themselves are not really rare—just "rare" in their ultra-high slab grades. So why the surprise when prices drop due to lower demand?" wrote Alan V. Weinberg in a letter to the editor of *Coin World*.[26]

The Year 2010

CURRENT EVENTS. Military actions continued in the Middle East with no end in sight. America's military budget was multiples of that of either China or Russia, and domestically more people were in jail per capita than in any other leading Western country. Most crimes involved drugs, a modern-day reiteration of Prohibition. Gay rights, abortion, gun control, prejudice, and draconian penalties were topics of debate.

In March the Deepwater Horizon oil drilling platform exploded, killing 11 workers and spilling large quantities of oil into the Gulf of Mexico. For the next five years the owner, British Petroleum (BP), would be involved in countless lawsuits and claims for damages. WikiLeaks published without authorization more than 400,000 documents and diplomatic cables relating to government military and security affairs.

Texting on cell phones while driving had caused many accidents by this point, leading to the banning of the practice in some states. Much to the delight of the media the Supreme Court lifted restrictions on political expenditures by corporations, unions, and certain other. This ruling would reshape the political landscape in its entirety.

In 2010 world sales of gold was estimated at $150 billion. With 8,134 tons, the United States had the largest holding.[27] On May 6 the anomalous "flash crash" temporarily shaved 1,000 points off of the Dow-Jones Industrial Average. Tesla Motors, established by Elon Musk, attracted attention with news about its sophisticated all-electric car. Caffeine-laced high-energy drinks attracted unfavorable attention. Electronic cigarettes increased in popularity. The Tea

The Tesla Roadster was the first highway-capable electric vehicle in serial production in North America or Europe.

Party political movement, which gained attention during the 2009 political season, held its first convention in 2010. Per the decennial census the population of the United States was 308,745,538, up 9.7% for the decade.

Collectibles of nearly all kinds enjoyed a strong market, ranging from coins to automobiles to art. Action on eBay and other activity on the Internet were largely responsible. Citizens saddled with stock losses found comfort in owning collectibles or, for some, expensive designer watches, handbags, and automobiles.

THE NUMISMATIC SCENE. The new America the Beautiful quarters made their debut, featuring National Parks or important monuments if a state had no National Park. These were released at the rate of five per year, similar to the State quarters that started in 1999. The new program did not catch on, however, and public interest was relatively low. A parallel program of striking the new quarter designs in five-ounce, three-inch format was announced. Special Gräbener presses made in Germany were used to stamp these out one at a time as an attendant fed the planchets.

The ANA announced that its summer World's Fair of Money would be expanded to cover 10 days. The idea was tried, but was later discontinued as it was learned that most collectors stayed only two or three days. Collectors Acceptance Corporation (CAC) prospered by grading the grading services—by affixing little green stickers to PCGS and NGC certified coins that it felt were nice examples of their grades.

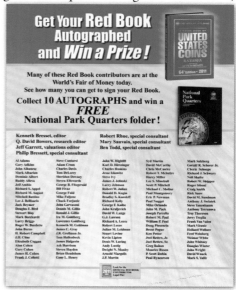

Visitors to the 2010 American Numismatic Association World's Fair of Money in Boston received a free coin folder for collecting 10 or more autographs of Red Book contributors.

Three much-discussed challenges were the graying of the hobby (youngsters were busy with computers, iPhones, and the like); the dropping of coin show attendance; and the improvement of coin designs. Fortunately, the overall market for choice and rare coins, tokens, medals, and paper money remained strong.

The Year 2011

CURRENT EVENTS. According to *The Economist*, October 22: "In America, 17.1% of citizens below 25 were out of work. Across the European Union youth employment averaged 20.9%. In Spain it is a staggering 46.2%. Only in Germany, the Netherlands, and Austria was the rate in single digits."[28] Wall Street was still suffering from the dot-com bubble and the questionable nature of many mortgage and other financial deals. Trading in derivatives, tranches, and other esoteric units prompted Warren Buffett, financial wizard at Berkshire Hathaway, to state that he could not understand some of the financial statements he reviewed. He viewed the house of Goldman Sachs to be a good investment in the current market uncertainty and in this era invested $5 billion in it.

On the 10th anniversary of the World Trade Center tragedy stringent security restrictions remained in place in many areas. Long lines at airport check-ins had become particularly annoying to many, in combination with airlines adding fees, reducing amenities, and giving less legroom unless a premium was paid. Osama bin Laden, head of the Al Qaeda terrorist organization and mastermind of the 2001 destruction of the World Trade Center was killed by an American military operation that found him hiding in Pakistan. America was spending much more on the military than the next several nations combined.

In Tucson a deranged gunman killed six people and wounded 14, including U.S. Representative Gabrielle Giffords, who in the next several years was able to partially recover. Largely uncontrolled use of handguns by citizens raised the crime rate across the country, particularly in larger cities. As part of budget constraints the government cut funding for National Public Radio (NPR). Organizations devoted to art, literature, music, education, and science suffered with reduced budgets. What might have been the Golden Age for America did not happen.

In China and Japan, modern trains routinely traveled more than 200 miles per hour. In America much infrastructure was in need of upgrading, including the Boston to Washington line used by Amtrak's Acela Express.

After two years of intense rehabilitation from a gunshot wound to the head, former U.S. representative Gabrielle Giffords speaks with President Obama and her husband, astronaut Mark Kelly, before testifying on gun violence to the Senate Judiciary Committee.

THE NUMISMATIC SCENE. In January, at the Florida United Numismatists (FUN) convention in Orlando, Florida, Scott Purvis of CoinLink (an online numismatic directory Web site founded in 1995) and David Lisot of Cointelivision announced the formation of a new online numismatic venture called CoinWeek, whose purpose was to bring together the best in feature articles, news, numismatic information, and video and publish it on a free-to-use online Web site.

In February it was reported that the ANA membership totaled 28,500, "toward the lower range of 28,000 to 32,000 that has prevailed for the past 20 years."[29] Membership in Early American Coppers, a specialty group focusing on half cents and large cents, was about 1,330 and had held steady in recent years. The price of gold hit a record high of $1,923 an ounce in early September. At a coin convention seminar the moderator asked the audience, "How many people see the price of gold at $5,000 in five years?" All hands but one were raised.

In remembrance of 9/11, the mints at Philadelphia and West Point struck silver national medals sold for the benefit of the National September 11 Memorial & Museum at the World Trade Center site (see Tucker's *American Gold and Silver*, 2016).

Under the provisions of the Coin Modernization, Oversight, and Continuity Act of 2010, Public Law 111-302, in December 2011 the Mint began striking coins from nonsense dies in various substances other than copper and nickel, which were causing losses in cent and nickel production. No specific information was given, and none of the trial strikings were released, although giving one each to the National Numismatic Collection would have been a worthwhile move.

A 2011 Proof silver national medal (congressionally authorized and struck at Philadelphia and West Point) marked the 10th anniversary of World Trade Center terrorist attacks. Sales benefited the National September 11 Memorial & Museum.

According to the *Latino Daily News* in 2014, "Approximately $167 million in $1 U.S. coins was imported by Ecuador in 2011 and will start to circulate throughout the country on May 21 [2012]."[30]

"For the first time in more than three decades the U.S. Mint has in its top career leader a person with both experience in manufacturing and executive experience in leading a large business organization. Richard 'Dick' Peterson currently is holding down the two top posts at the Mint. He is deputy Mint director—the top career position—and acting Mint director."[31] In view of the rising price of copper and silver the Mint did extensive research on using alternative metals for coinage, Peterson reported in March. "The U.S. Mint's research and development into alternative metals for the production of all six circulating coin denominations will not result in a change in diameter, weight or electronic signature."[32] A complete collection of every coin and surface finish issued in 2011 cost $23,500.

The General Accountability Office reported that 1.1 billion dollar coins were in Treasury vaults. A proposal to phase out the dollar bill and replace it with a dollar coin was potentially gaining steam as the "super committee" looked to find ways to save the government money. "Lobbying interests on both sides are ramping up their efforts in the expectation that Congress could decide the issue after more than 25 years of debate. Mining interests, vending companies, and mass transit agencies support the coin. Paper and ink producers and some small retailers oppose it."[33] Once again, nothing happened with this proposal.

In 2011 the American Numismatic Association expanded its National Money Show—an annual coin convention held in the spring—to also include a fall event, held in Pittsburgh. This experiment would continue in 2012 with a fall National Money Show held in Dallas, after which the Association returned to its old schedule of two annual conventions (the National Money Show in the spring, and the larger World's Fair of Money in the summer).

The Year 2012

CURRENT EVENTS. Advances in the retrieval oil by injecting liquid under high pressure, known as fracking, had done much to alleviate American dependence on foreign countries for fuel. Wind power had been popular in recent times and would continue to be so. Solar energy was being increasingly tapped, with government incentives helping. The robotic *Curiosity* rover, launched by NASA, landed on Mars. It carried with it a circulated 1909 V.D.B. Lincoln cent, the surface color of which was used to calibrate an optical device. NASA and SpaceX jointly launched the Dragon C2+, also known as the SpaceX COTS Demo Flight 2 (COTS 2), that made the first commercial rendezvous to the International Space Station.

E-books downloadable on the Internet became more popular than ever, but captured just a small proportion of the overall publishing market. The *Encyclopædia Britannica* stopped printing hard-copy editions. The computer system of Zappos, an online seller of shoes, was compromised. This would not, however, be the last Internet-hacking scenario. Security breaches on the Internet were common. Abuses by telemarketers made headlines as did unsolicited calls to numbers registered on the federal Do Not Call (DNC) list. Certain political campaign calls were exempt.

The *Curiosity* rover on the surface of Mars.

This photograph of a 1909 V.D.B. Lincoln cent was taken by the *Curiosity* rover on Mars.

The Scream, a painting by Edvard Munch, crossed the auction block at $120 million, setting a new record for art at auction. San Francisco set a $10 per hour minimum wage, the highest in the country, an action that precipitated a call for McDonalds (in particular) and other nationwide business to raise their levels.

Pennsylvania State University became involved in a scandal involving former coach Jerry Sandusky having been indicted on 52 counts of child molestation. He would later be convicted of 45 counts of sexual abuse. Sexual abuse by Scout leaders and Catholic priests was also in the news. State prisons in particular and hospitals run for profit were a controversial subject in this era. The desire to keep prisons filled was viewed by many as being opposed to the rights of prisoners for early release. In Florida unarmed Trayvon Martin, a 17-year-old African-American boy, was fatally shot while walking home through his neighborhood by a member of the neighborhood watch, energizing a nationwide debate on crime and the policing of black bodies. In Newtown, Connecticut, a crazed young man went into an elementary school and shot and killed 27 people, including 20 children aged 6 and 7.

Tropical storm Sandy ravaged the East Coast and caused storm surge damage that closed down parts of lower Manhattan. In retailing, leading chains were Walmart, Target, and Best Buy. Eastman Kodak filed for bankruptcy. Curiously, it had invented the electronic camera but failed to recognize its potential. By 2012 most optical equipment sold in America was made in Japan. Abusive telemarketing annoyed just about everyone with unsolicited robotic calls. One of the darlings of the market was Berkshire Hathaway, whose CEO Warren Buffett was an American financial legend and icon. On February 21 the Dow-Jones Industrial Average crossed the 13,000 mark in a climb towards the 14,000+ level it had achieved in 2007 prior to the recession. It is not a very reliable indicator long term, as its component stocks have been changed frequently.

It was an election year. President Barack Obama sought to return to the White House. Multiple Republican contenders sought recognition in primaries, including Rick Santorum, Jon Huntsman, Rick Perry, and others. The nod went to Mitt Romney, who would lose in November, some said because he wavered back and forth on some positions.

THE NUMISMATIC SCENE. Pressure to eliminate the penny continued. Both cents and nickels cost more than face value to produce, creating a loss for the Mint. Otherwise, the Mint profited handsomely from seigniorage—the profit difference between cost and face value. Such profit had brought hundreds of millions of dollars to the Mint during the period in which dollar coins were made in quantity, beginning with the Susan B. Anthony coins in 1979. Now in 2012 the gravy-train ride was over, and dollar coins were made in much lower numbers, mainly to accommodate collectors. In January two resolutions were introduced into the House of Representatives to use steel for cents and nickels. At a public forum at the ANA World's Fair of Money in August Deputy Mint Director Richard Peterson said that research into materials to be used for coinage had come down to aluminum, iron, and steel, and that non-metallic compositions were not being considered. In 2012 President Obama nominated Bibiana Boerio, formerly an executive with Ford Motor

U.S. infantry soldiers were honored by a 2012 commemorative silver dollar.

Co., to be director of the Mint. Nothing happened, and Peterson continued as Deputy Director of the Mint, filling the position admirably.

The price of gold closed at $1,647.70 on January, a drop of about 15% from the previous year's high. Sales of American Eagle gold coins remained strong. Political unrest in foreign countries and the continuing wars in the Middle East fueled public uncertainty and the desire to hold "hard" assets.

Beth Deisher retired as *Coin World* editor in April, having been on the staff for 27 years and editor since 1985, succeeding Margo Russell. Steve Roach was the next editor, until 2015 when he moved to be editor-at-large, and Bill Gibbs, a long-time staff member, took his place. On May 25 the ANA Board of Governors named Jeff Shevlin as the latest executive director of the 120-plus–year-old association. "Shevlin will oversee 34 employees, a nearly $6 million budget, and major projects that include installing a Kids Zone at the Edward C. Rochette Money Museum and relaunching a new Internet site in the next year."[34]

The Year 2013

CURRENT EVENTS. President Barack Obama was inaugurated in January to his second term in office and later in the year launched the Affordable Care Act, dubbed *Obamacare*. The roll-out was wrought with technological kinks, however, due to the sheer number of people trying to sign up on its Web site, HealthCare.gov.

Two Chechen brothers living in Massachusetts exploded two bombs made with pressure cookers to kill 3 and wound 264 innocent people. The elder brother was soon killed in an accident, and the younger was sentenced to death in a 2015 trial. An eight-story factory in Bangladesh collapsed, killing 1,129 and injuring more than twice that number. This prompted inspections by American importers of factories in that area of the world that supplied clothing and other goods.

Edward Snowden disclosed the massive spying that the American government had been doing on unsuspecting citizens and others to journalists Glenn Greenwald, Laura Poitras, and Ewen MacAskill in Hong Kong. On June 21 the U.S. Department of Justice brought forth charges against Snowden on two counts of violating the Espionage Act of 1917 and theft of U.S. Government or foreign government property. He fled to Moscow, Russia, to seek asylum. Many thought him to be a hero for revealing an operation the extent of which had been hardly imagined, while others call him a whistleblower and a traitor.

In his sculpture *Anything to Say?* artist Davide Dormino (leftmost) celebrates whistleblowers Edward Snowden (left) and Chelsea Manning (right), along with WikiLeaks editor Julian Assange (middle).

Miley Cyrus, formerly "Hannah Montana" for Disney, twerked her way into controversy during her MTV Video Music Awards performance with Robin Thicke. 3D printing—using a computer and raw materials to form three-dimensional objects—made the news. The economy showed signs of recovery and by November, the Dow-Jones Industrial Average closed at 16,000 for the first time in history.

THE NUMISMATIC SCENE. On April 16 the ANA announced that Kim Kiick, a long-term staff member, would take the reins as the association's new executive director at its Colorado Springs headquarters.[35]

The annual World's Fair of Money was held at the Donald Stephens Convention Center in Rosemont, Illinois, close to Chicago O'Hare International Airport. It would also be held there in 2014 and 2015.

The U.S. Mint issued a special silver Presidential medal for Theodore Roosevelt, packaged in the 2013 Coin and Chronicles set. "This marked the first time the Mint struck a Presidential medal in .999 fine silver," says Dennis Tucker in *American Gold and Silver: U.S Mint Collector and Investor Coins and Medals, Bicentennial to Date.* Similar medals for other presidents would be issued in succeeding years.

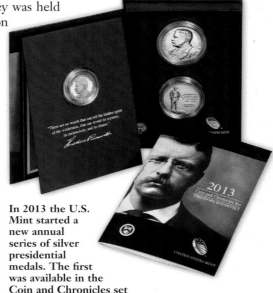

In 2013 the U.S. Mint started a new annual series of silver presidential medals. The first was available in the Coin and Chronicles set honoring President Theodore Roosevelt.

The Year 2014

CURRENT EVENTS. Racially motivated incidents and the unsupervised use of handguns was a national problem. In December President Barack Obama announced the resumption of normal relations with Cuba, which had been deemed a terrorist country since 1961.

In Africa the Ebola virus spread and many American medical professionals went to help. There was an ultimately unwarranted fear that an epidemic would sweep the United States. Russia annexed the independent country of Crimea, which also endangered the Ukraine, and caused many problems for those who had had cultural and commercial interchange with Russia earlier. A terrorist group founded in 1999 as Jama'at al-Tawhid wal-Jihad, which later took the name al-Qaeda in Iraq, rebranded itself as the Islamic State of Iraq and the Levant (often shortened to ISIL or ISIS), in an attempt to legitimize itself as a governing body. In reality this group, responsible for war crimes and genocide in Iraq and Syria, is a fringe group with no claim to statehood. Arab-language media call the group Daesh, which has pejorative undertones, and emphasizes worldwide Muslim refusal to legitimize the group as an Islamic state. This courageous refusal comes at great personal cost, as Daesh regularly publishes kill lists of prominent Western Muslims who refuse to support the group. Among American weapons were remote-controlled drone aircraft, while small "personal" drones equipped with cameras became popular with the public. The United Nations reported that more than 2,200 Palestinians, including 1,500 noncombatants (more than a third of whom were children), were killed as a result of escalating conflict in Gaza during July and August—more than had been killed in any year since 1967. The Israeli fatality toll from the hostilities also increased, to 71—66 soldiers, 4 civilian adults, and 1 child.

Huge cruise ships accommodated an ever-increasing number of passengers. New large-capacity cargo ships were launched as well. Singer-songwriter Taylor Swift's fifth studio album, *1989*, was the best-selling record of the year, and her third album in a row to go platinum—one million copies sold—within a week of its release. In Hollywood, *12 Years a Slave* earned the Academy Award for Best Picture.

In the automobile industry Mary Barra, the first woman president of General Motors, earned high marks from observers. Elon Musk, a billionaire from the field of technology, promoted his all-electric Tesla car and told of plans to build a huge factory to produce efficient storage batteries. Apple products including various iterations of the iPad and iPhone sold by the countless millions. By the second half of the year, oil prices fell by nearly 50 percent as a flood of crude oil extracted from shale by the fracking process made America self-sufficient and no longer reliant on foreign countries.

THE NUMISMATIC SCENE. With expanded programs such as the Code Talkers medal series, commemoratives, and more, the Mint solicited talent for its Artistic Infusion Program and received 123 submissions, from which up to 20 people were to be selected. Each finalist was to receive a fee plus $5,000 for any design used on a coin or medal. The cost of copper and nickel to make 5-cent pieces was more than face value. Testing was done on coins made of copper-plated zinc, but no change was made.

The Federal Reserve reported that it placed 240 million-dollar coins into circulation, but did not tell where they went other than 29 million to Latin America, El Salvador, and Ecuador. The last country had been using "golden dollars" for some time.

In January 2014 Charles Morgan was hired as editor of CoinWeek.com. Coin-Week, since its founding in 2011, had grown to be the hobby's most-read online news and information Web site. Later that year, CoinWeek published a video magnum opus, a three hour-long interview with Stack's Bowers founder Harvey Stack.

There was a zoo scene at the ANA World's Fair of Money in Chicago in August. The U.S. Mint stated that it would release the first 500 gold 1964–2014 Proof Kennedy half dollars to the public there for $1,240. Speculators paid people from off the street to wait in line. These people disrupted the scene, dirtied sanitation facilities, and created a large disturbance. The first coin sold on August 7 was certified by PCGS as such, changed hands, and was finally sold for $100,000 to a man who bought most of his coins on the Coin Vault television program. In the meantime, coins sold slightly later at other Mint outlets in Philadelphia, Denver, and the District of Columbia were purchased by speculators who flew to Chicago to have them (mis)labeled as early issues.[36]

Books by Q. David Bowers continued to reach wide audiences, including multiple titles in the "Bowers Series" by Whitman Publishing and titles by Stack's Bowers Galleries, including the 2015 award-winning *Treasures from the D. Brent Pogue Collection* and the related *Masterpieces of United States Coinage*. Leading periodicals with wide circulation included *Coin World, COINage, Coins Magazine, Numismatic News*, and *The Numismatist*. Online-exclusive media included CoinWeek and E-Sylum. The two leading national organizations continued to be the American Numismatic Association and the American Numismatic Society. Specialized societies included the Colonial Coin Collectors Club (C4), Early American Coppers, Fly-In Club, John Reich Collectors

In 2014 Karen M. Lee's *The Secret Sketchbook of George T. Morgan* won the A. George Mallis literary award.

Society, Liberty Seated Coin Club, Token and Medal Society, Civil War Token Society (which this year published the third edition of *U.S. Civil War Store Cards*), Society of Paper Money Collectors, and the Numismatic Bibliomania Society. The Professional Numismatists Guild (dealers) admitted members by application, and the Rittenhouse Society (published research scholars) admitted members by invitation.

During the spring and summer a crew from Odyssey Marine Exploration, Inc., revisited the side of the wreck of the SS *Central America* off the coast of North Carolina. Gold coins, ingots, and many silver dimes were recovered, but far less than had been found during the original salvages in the late 20th century.

The Year 2015

CURRENT EVENTS. Weather dominated headlines early in the year with record snowfall and cold east of the Mississippi with unprecedented drought persisting on the West Coast. Boston broke its own seasonal snowfall record with just over 108 inches of snow for the season. The snow storms, which fell in quick succession, paralyzed the region's public transportation system. A two-day blizzard in January affected 60 million people throughout New England and New York. New York City police reported no murders over a 12 day period, attributing the dip in homicides to the winter weather.

Uncertainty in distant lands including the Ukraine and the Middle East continued to trouble America and the world. Uncontrolled use of handguns kept the murder rate in America higher than in other Western countries. The shooting of unarmed African-Americans by police in recent years swelled into a major national concern. In June the killing of nine black worshipers in a Charleston, South Carolina, church by a young man who espoused Confederate values led to a reappraisal of the use of the Confederate States flag on public buildings in the South and on merchandise in general. ISIS, based in the Middle East, was involved in terrorism elsewhere, including in Paris in November 2015. This raised great alarm across the United States.

The economy enjoyed a rebound that had been in process for several years. The Dow-Jones Industrial Average crossed the 18,000 mark in the spring, but many if not most housing in America was valued less than it was in 2007. By early October, however, it had dipped below 16,000 in daily trading. In December the Federal Reserve raised the discount rate 0.25% to 0.50%, the first such raise since the business recession of the late 2000s. The introduction of the Apple electronic watch—a mini-computer and Internet portal—raised concerns for marketers of expensive

Swiss-made mechanical watches, some of which are priced in the tens of thousands of dollars. In November it was reported that Swiss watch sales were at a seven-year low.

In February, the New England Patriots beat the Seattle Seahawks 28 to 24 to win their fourth Super Bowl since the arrival of head coach Bill Belichik in 2000. They became the second team in NFL history, after the Dallas Cowboys, to win three Super Bowl championships within four years. Thoroughbred American Pharoah (whose name was an inadvertent misspelling) was the first horse in 37 years to take the coveted Triple Crown after winning the Kentucky Derby, the Preakness Stakes, and the Belmont Stakes.

Political candidates jumped into the 2016 presidential race early in the spring. At one time in late summer 16 Republicans and five Democrats were running for their party's respective nominations. New York real estate magnate Donald Trump became the darling of the media when he entered as a Republican candidate, sometimes making inflammatory and controversial remarks.

At the Oscars, *Birdman*, starring Michael Keaton, won the Academy Award for Best Picture. In Los Angeles the Eli and Edythe Broad Art Museum opened to the public. Pope Francis visited the United States in September and made stops at Washington, D.C., New York City (where he addressed the United Nations), and Philadelphia. The computer and Internet absorbed the vast majority of leisure time for most Americans to the detriment of hobbies, crafts, visits to museums and national parks, and other previously popular activities.

President Obama visited Cuba in March 2016 to cement the resumption of normal relations between Cuba and the U.S. Here, his daughter Malia translates a conversation with a Havana restauranteur.

The Numismatic Scene. Jeff Garrett, running without competition, became the president of the American Numismatic Association. The summer convention was held in Rosemont, Illinois, for the third year in a row (next year: Anaheim, California). In this era the five leading coin conventions were the World's Fair of Money (summer ANA show), Florida United Numismatists (FUN), and the three Whitman Coin and

The U.S. Mint debuted a remarkable innovation in 2015: the American Liberty High Relief .9999 fine gold coin, by designers Justin Kunz and Paul Balan. Shown at 125%.

Collectibles Expos held in Baltimore in March, June, and November. The Mint continued its research to find coinage metals to replace expensive copper and nickel. The Federal Reserve stated that its vaults held 857,000,000 "golden" dollars minted since 2000.

Whitman Publishing launched the Deluxe Edition of the *Guide Book of United States Coins*. Weighing-in at about 6 pounds and with 1,504 jam-packed pages the reference, with special features on half and large cents to be replaced by new special features on other denominations in subsequent editions, was well received from the outset. Stack's Bowers Galleries in partnership with Sotheby's held the first and second sales in the D. Brent Pogue Collection series, the most valuable collection ever to cross the auction block. Auction action was maintained by others as well, including Ira and Larry Goldberg and Heritage Auctions, including their recent and current Missouri, Eric P. Newman, and Eugene Gardner collections, among others. Increasingly, auctions with a combination of public attendance plus Internet and telephone bidding saw the majority of great collections sold. In some instances, public in-person attendance was modest while worldwide Internet participation was intense. On the Internet, eBay offered many coins for sale among other collectibles, although fakes remained a problem. The Eric P. Newman Numismatic Portal was launched with $2 million in funding from its namesake. A program of digitizing out-of-print numismatic publications and various documents was launched. The American Numismatic Association announced that digitized pages of *The Numismatist* from 1888 to date were available on the Internet.

EISENHOWER DOLLARS, 1971–1978

In 1969 Mint Director Mary Brooks advocated the resumption of the dollar coin, perhaps of silver-clad composition (outer layers of silver-and-copper alloy bonded to an inner core of lower-grade silver alloy) as used for the then-current Kennedy half dollars minted from 1965 up to that point. There had been a demand for dollars from Nevada casinos in particular. In addition it was desired that this denomination, a part of American history and tradition since 1794, would not be abandoned. An additional benefit and one that would help sell the idea to a budget-conscious Congress was that metal dollars were expected to last nearly 20 years in circulation, while the usefulness of a paper dollar was about 18 months. However, Wright Patman, chairman of the House Committee on Banking and Currency, opposed the idea. Seemingly, it would go nowhere.

President Dwight D. Eisenhower, in retirement for many years, died on March 28, 1969. New life was breathed into the dollar idea when Republican Representative Florence Dwyer of New Jersey suggested a coin with his image would be an appropriate

tribute. She discussed this with Democrat Representative Leonor Sullivan of Missouri. Both agreed that with John F. Kennedy already on the half dollar and Eisenhower potentially on the dollar there would be a balanced tribute to these past presidents, both of whom had been widely admired. On April 29, 1969, Representative Robert Casey of Texas introduced legislation providing for a new dollar coin to depict Eisenhower on the obverse and a motif relating to the Apollo 11 Moon mission on the reverse.

In the same timeframe other proposals to honor the late president were advanced, including naming the Interstate Highway System, a dam, and the proposed Moon landing-craft site for him. Other ideas, including those on 25 different bills before Congress, called

Official presidential portrait of Dwight D. Eisenhower.

for replacing George Washington's portrait on the quarter dollar and the $1 bill with Ike's visage and changing the name of Dulles Airport to Eisenhower Airport. The Eisenhower family stated it would be honored by such tributes, but did not have favorites.[1] Not long afterward a mountain in New Hampshire was named for him, which might be called, as humorously suggested, Ike's Peak.[2] Mount Eisenhower, earlier called Mount Pleasant, is southwest of Mount Washington in the Presidential Range of the White Mountains.

Mount Eisenhower in the White Mountains of New Hampshire.

On October 3, 1969, the House Banking Committee agreed to support legislation to create an Eisenhower dollar without silver content, to be of cupro-nickel–clad copper (outer layers of 75% copper and 25% nickel bonded to an inner core of pure copper; sometimes called "copper-nickel clad") as had been used for dimes and quarters since 1965.[3] Hopes were high that the House of Representatives and the Senate would both pass the bill on October 14, Eisenhower's birthday. The idea of a silverless dollar was not appealing to some. Colorado senator Peter Dominick suggested that the dollar be made with 40% silver content and supported his position with a letter from the late president's widow, Mamie Eisenhower, stating that her husband often tracked down silver dollars of his birth year, 1890, to give as gifts. The bill was amended to include silver coins in addition to cupro-nickel dollars and was passed by both houses of Congress on the desired date.

Chairman Wright Patman was still opposed to the use of silver. An amended bill was added as a rider to a bill favored by Patman relating to bank holding companies, to allow both silver-content and cupro-nickel coins, to eliminate silver in the current clad outer coating of half dollars, and to transfer several million long-stored 19th-century Morgan silver dollars, mostly from the Carson City Mint, then in a vault in the Treasury Building in Washington, to the General Services Administration to sell. President Richard M. Nixon signed the bill in the evening of December 31, New Year's Eve, just before the legislation was set to die.

The Apollo 11 Reverse Design

On October 29, 1969, Representative Robert R. Casey, who had introduced the original legislation for the dollar, proposed another bill to define the reverse as a tribute to the Apollo 11 Moon landing, one of America's proudest technological achievements, and was inspired by the mission's insignia. The Mint advised him that his suggested inscription, WE CAME IN PEACE FOR ALL MANKIND, was too long to include, in view of the other lettering required by law.

Chief Engraver Frank Gasparro, who had prepared sketches earlier, went to work to create two reverse motifs—one with an eagle landing on the Moon and another with a heraldic stance for the national bird.

The Apollo 11 insignia.

Congress mandated that the mission patch for Apollo 11 be used. The eagle depicted on the surface of the Moon was symbolic of the *Eagle* Lunar Module (LM), as it was called. The first iteration of the patch had the eagle holding an olive branch in its beak. In the final version the branch is on the surface of the Moon and the eagle is perched atop it.

On July 29, 1969, Captain Neil Armstrong had radioed to the National Aeronautics and Space Administration (NASA) headquarters at the Johnson Space Center in Houston, "The Eagle has landed." Accompanying him on the surface was LM pilot Edwin Eugene "Buzz" Aldrin Jr., while the third astronaut, Command Module pilot Michael Collins, remained aboard the command spacecraft.

The two motifs had a connection: Eisenhower as president had signed the 1958 legislation that created NASA. All was set!

Frank Gasparro Reminisces

Chief Engraver Frank Gasparro was assigned the Eisenhower dollar design project in a telephone call from Mint Director Mary T. Brooks. It was the usual but hardly the exclusive tradition for the holder of the highest office in the Engraving Department to create the motifs on new coinage. For the obverse he modeled the head of Eisenhower facing left, with LIBERTY above; at the lower left, in two lines, IN GOD WE / TRUST; and with the coin's date of mintage below. The reverse motif, from the Apollo 11 shoulder patch, showed an eagle perched on an olive branch on the Moon, with the Earth and the inscription E PLURIBUS UNUM above. UNITED STATES OF

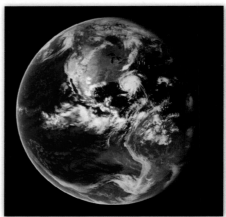

Earth as photographed from space by NASA.

AMERICA and ONE DOLLAR appear at the border. The size and proportion of the Earth was criticized by some, as the entire hemisphere view consists mostly of North America. Credit this to artistic license. The depiction of the Earth continued to create problems, and from the beginning until its final use (on the 1999 Susan B. Anthony dollar) many different versions were made in plaster, galvano, or finished coin form. None was geographically correct or even close.

Gasparro related this on November 21, 1991:

> The happiest and most rewarding experience in my Mint career was the day I was commissioned to design the Eisenhower dollar. It was like training daily for an athletic event. I was ready. Only I had to wait twenty-five years. This is my story.
>
> I remember that happy day in 1945 when I made every effort to take off from my Mint work to go to New York City from Philadelphia. I was to see the "D" Day–World War II victory parade down Broadway to honor our hero, General Eisenhower. I admired him greatly. I stood with the rest of the bystanders to celebrate Eisenhower's welcome home. Everyone shouted and waved.[4]
>
> Amidst all the rousing enthusiasm, I stepped back from the crowd and made a quick pencil profile sketch of our hero. I was pleased with my efforts. Then I took the train home to Philadelphia, and went back to work the next day.

In my off hours, I modeled in wax and then cast in plaster a life-size portrait of Eisenhower from memory and sketches, in the round. Meanwhile, I also started to chisel and engrave in soft steel, three inches in diameter a profile portrait of him. It took a long time; as you know steel is hard to move. Meanwhile, time moved on.

Late in 1970 (after twenty-five years), the director of the Mint, Mary T. Brooks, phoned me in Philadelphia from Washington (I was then chief engraver). She informed me that the Eisenhower dollar bill passed in Congress.

In my capacity, I was requested to design and produce working dies for the Eisenhower dollar, fast. I knew in my bones I could make it. Time was tight and there was no time for a national competition. So, I had to work hard and long hours. This was the Thanksgiving weekend, I started. The new dollar had to be struck January 2nd, 1971 (six weeks in planning).

I was ready; I had my Eisenhower early profile in hand. The dollar reverse had to portray the Apollo XI eagle insignia, as requested by the congressional bill. In this area I was fortunate, having pursued, for many years, research of the American eagle. Luckily my sketches were approved, with no changes. The rest is history.[5]

Frank Gasparro's self-portrait on a 1985 silver medal unrelated to the Eisenhower dollar, part of a signed private series created by him for Bowers and Merena Galleries. Shown at 125%.

Bust of Eisenhower sculpted by Frank Gasparro.

A photograph of President Dwight D. Eisenhower with Vice President Richard M. Nixon was one of the images used by Frank Gasparro to create the Eisenhower dollar.

Eisenhower: The Man, the Dollar, and the Stamps, by Thomas W. Becker, 1971, included comments from an interview with Frank Gasparro (edited excerpts):

Eisenhower was like a god in 1945. People spoke his name in awe and reverence. They regarded him as the world's savior. I don't think there was anyone in the country at the time who was willing to say anything against him. His own honesty and integrity had become a legend. You don't often find all these high qualities in the same man at one time.

I was a hero worshipper then, and Eisenhower measured up in every way to all my ideals of what a real hero ought to be. I remember that one time I drew a portrait of Charles Lindbergh and took it to the Philadelphia *Public Ledger* newspaper editor's desk to use. I guess I was about 17 at the time. The people at the *Public Ledger* were happy with the drawing, and it was put in the newspaper. I was always doing this sort of thing.

Sketch made by Frank Gasparro in 1945.

In the 1945 parade Ike stood up with his arms raised over his head giving the V-for-victory sign with both hands. I could tell that he knew he was the man of the hour; he had an excited look on his face. He had been in the sun a long time, and his face had a ruddy complexion. He had a very winning smile that made you like him right away. The people around me were jumping and shouting, and many of them had tears in their eyes—some of them were just crying outright with the tears streaming down their faces.

Early state of a model made in 1945 by Frank Gasparro.

That day, the moment he passed by, he seemed to be the embodiment of everything that would lead people to have confidence in him—and we felt this man would pull us through, because Roosevelt had just died and Ike was really the only man now who was close enough to the war to hold our trust.

Designing the New Dollars

Eager to get started, and with the legislation a virtual certainty, Gasparro contemplated his earlier sketch and profile and made several sketches over the Thanksgiving weekend in late November 1970. He had studied eagles for many years, as he recalled, but in 1970 he visited the Philadelphia Zoo to see if he could learn more. Soon drawings, models, plasters, and galvanos with the date of 1970 were prepared. A Treasury circular of December 1970 included this:

Much attention was given to the "character" of the emblematic eagle of Apollo 11 landing on the Moon. Mint Director Mary T. Brooks requested the artist to draw a "peaceful eagle." Mr. Gasparro describes his rendition as a "pleasant looking eagle."

President Nixon, Treasury Department and Mint officials, and the Fine Arts Commission approved the sketches Mr. Gasparro submitted for the obverse and reverse designs of the Eisenhower coin.

Subsequently the plastilene models (modeling wax) were approved. Eugene Rossides, the Treasury's assistant secretary for enforcement and operations, and Mint

Director Mary T. Brooks then met with Mrs. Dwight D. Eisenhower and secured her approval of the design of the coin. Mrs. Eisenhower was especially pleased with the portrait of her late husband.

Public Law 91-607, December 31, 1970, contained specifications for the Eisenhower coins:

Sec. 101 (d) The Secretary is authorized to mint and issue not more than one hundred and fifty million one-dollar pieces which shall have (1) a diameter of 1.500 inches; (2) a cladding of an alloy of eight hundred parts of silver and two hundred parts of copper; and (3) A core of an alloy of silver and copper such that the whole coin weighs 24.562 grams and contains 9.837 grams of silver and 14.755 grams of copper.

Sec. 203. The dollars . . . shall bear the likeness of the late president of the United States, Dwight David Eisenhower, and on the other side thereof a design which is emblematic of the symbolic eagle of Apollo 11 landing on the Moon.

Galvanos made in 1970 for the impending coinage of Eisenhower dollars, version 1. Note the eagle's breast feathers. The Earth is not round at the upper left. The reverse, with minutely detailed craters, was never used on regular circulation-strike or Proof coins but is likely the type or one of the types used for experimental strikes in January 1971. The Dwight D. Eisenhower Library in Abilene, Kansas, possesses similar galvanos, but of silver color.

Galvanos made in 1970, version 2. On the obverse the hair details are softer and the ear is slightly different. On the reverse the features have been softened. The island below Florida is unlike that later used in coinage.

On New Year's Day 1971 two of the galvanos used to make the pattern die hubs (the positive-image punches used to impress coin designs into dies for coinage) were presented to widow Mamie Eisenhower. By January 2, 1971, hubs and working dies were ready.

Trial Strikes

On January 25 the first two "official" trial or pattern strikings were made, although some had been made earlier in soft metal. The reverse of some of these had the minutely detailed eagle and Moon surface used in the earliest galvano. At the suggestion of Frank Gasparro the minute details in the craters were reduced and smoothed, lest they catch dirt on the finished coins. The features of the Earth were changed, but,still no attention seems to have been given to geographical reality. The two January 25 coins were examined and then destroyed.

A Mint circular noted:

> Several trial working dies of the obverse and reverse of the Eisenhower dollar coin have been prepared by the Mint's engraver. Because dies of identical design may vary in height of relief and shape of the basin (background), a succession of preliminary strikes is necessary to determine the best combination of dies to use to produce the best coin within the limitations of coining press equipment and die tools.
>
> For example, too high relief or improper shape of the basin would result in improper flow of the metal in the blanks and consequent damage to the dies or the coining press itself. (Too much pressure would be required to bring up all of the design elements.)

Mint Director Mary T. Brooks
watches a transfer lathe reducing
an obverse Eisenhower dollar galvano.

The transfer lathe.

A small-size hub
made by the transfer
lathe, an exact copy
of the galvano.

The 40% silver blanks used today for the trial strikes of the Eisenhower dollar were especially prepared by the coiner, and the strikes you are witnessing involve the final step in determining the best combination of dies, collars, and shape of the upset blank.

However, the prototype dies in use are not the final product. The engraver still has several weeks' work to do with the preparation of official master dies and hubs. Such work involves the painstaking removal of every tiny defect and the sharpening up of each design detail.

All trial strikes must take place in the presence of the Mint Director's Trial Strike Committee—today composed of the director's representative, superintendent of the Philadelphia Mint or his representative, the chief engraver, and the superintendent of the Coining Division.

In accordance with regulations, all of the prototype trial strikes must be and will be destroyed by the Director's Committee.[6]

Then and now there was no policy in place to save examples of pattern and experimental coins for archiving or display in the National Numismatic Collection in the Smithsonian Institution, although in the past some have been given on an irregular and inconsistent basis.

Obverse galvano for a
1971 Eisenhower dollar.

A pair of 1971 Eisenhower dollar
dies, Proof, without mintmark.

Eisenhower dollar hubs and dies.

Obverse Hub Changes, 1970–1978

In 1970 and 1971 many changes were made to the designs, mostly on the reverse, but obverse variants were also made. Various plasters, galvanos, and struck coins show differences, often minute.

Type I, Low Relief: For the first Eisenhower coinage of 1971 two sets of galvanos—electrolytic transfers from Frank Gasparro's models—were made.[7] The Type I or low relief was used to make hubs, master dies, and, eventually, working dies for circulation-strike dollars of that year.

On Type I the upright of the R in LIBERTY has flared serifs to the left and the right of its base with each ending in a point. *The lower right or tail of the R ends in a curve*, this being definitive. The base of the upright is much closer to the head than is the base of the tail of the R.

Herbert P. Hicks described Type I coins as such:

> Low Relief, Variety I: *Forehead:* Furrows either are not there or are too weak and are indistinguishable. One faint line is at a 45 degree angle. *Relief:* Low. *Extreme upper left hair line:* With a glass the design seems to consist of a pattern of valleys, two of which intersect. Unfortunately, later strikes are indistinct in this area. *Neck:* [no comment]. *B in LIBERTY:* Lower-left corner has tail (longer on some coins than on others). *R in LIBERTY:* Lack of serifs has no bearing on I and II issues. Both come both ways, although I would say Variety II is more apt to lose it. *FG (designer's initials):* Area above FG blends into the neck. No marks left or right of FG.

Type I was used exclusively on circulation strikes of all 1971 dollars from the three mints and on 1972 dollars from Philadelphia and Denver.

These obverse hub types or varieties have not gained wide popularity in the general marketplace as all issues except 1971-S Proofs are of one type or another, and the 1971-S Type II and III are from the same hub and differ mainly in the letter R in LIBERTY.

Type II, High Relief: On Type II the upright of the R is distinctive with the lower-left serif of the upright having a sharp tip on the upper side and extending to the left. The right tail of the R is long, straight, and pointed on this and the next two types. The letters in LIBERTY are thicker and the styling of the hair strands is different from types II to IV.

Plaster of a prototype 1970 dollar with heavier letters than are known to have been used on trial strikes.

1971-D Eisenhower dollar obverse, Type I.

Herbert P. Hicks described Type II coins as such:

High Relief, Variety II: *Forehead:* Three furrows are visible. *Relief:* High. *Extreme upper left hair line:* The design seems to consist of ridges. The pattern is definitely different from the Variety I strikes. The valleys do not cross each other. *Neck:* Furrows are stronger. *B in LIBERTY:* No tail. Upper-left corner bump is longer than the lower-left bump. *R in LIBERTY:* See preceding. *FG (designer's initials):* Sharp border above FG between truncation and neck. No marks to left of FG. Faint indentation at lower right of G and touching it.

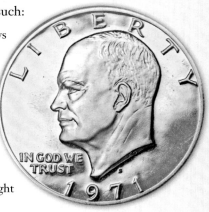

1971-S Eisenhower dollar obverse, Type II.

Type II was used on most Proof 1971-S dollars and not elsewhere. It is a variation of Type I.

The 1971-S Proofs can be found with Type II or Type III.

Type III, High Relief: On Type III the upright of the R loses a serif or projection at the lower left and is slightly indented at that point. This has been nicknamed the "Peg Leg."

Type III was used on a minority of 1971-S Proofs and on all 1972-S circulation strikes and Proofs.

Type IV, Modified High Relief: Type IV is a close copy of Type II. The left serif is slightly differently styled, and the bottom of the tail of the R is slightly lower than on Type II.

Herbert P. Hicks described Type IV coins as such:

1972-S Eisenhower dollar obverse, Type III.

Modified High Relief, Variety III: *Forehead:* Three furrows are visible. *Relief:* High. *Extreme upper left hair line:* Similar to Variety II. *Neck:* Furrows are stronger. *B in LIBERTY:* Similar to Variety II. *R in LIBERTY:* Base of left leg of R is stabilized. It is no longer parallel to the head but is tilted upward to the right. It is farther from the head and has squatter serifs. *FG (designer's initials):* Area above FG blends into design similar to Variety I. Proof forms are sharper, but still weaker than on II. A horizontal line is visible to the left of FG. A faint indentation is visible at the lower right of G and is separated from it.

Type IV was used on all circulation-strike and Proof coinage for 1973, 1974, 1977, and 1978.

1973-D Eisenhower dollar obverse, Type IV.

Prototype Reverses of 1970 and 1971

Several different prototype reverses were made in 1970 and 1971 that are not known to have been used for production coinage, although in some instances pattern coins were made. Points of observation include the distant Earth (the Mint struggled seemingly endlessly and never did get an accurate representation), the head and feathers of the eagle, and the craters on the surface of the Moon.

Mint policy was to destroy all such struck pieces, although it would have been a nod to numismatics and posterity if some had been given to the National Numismatic Collection at the Smithsonian Institution. In addition to the reverses of the 1970 and 1971 era, see those made for the 1776–1976 Bicentennial coinage later in this chapter.

Prototype 1: Reverse as used on the earlier of two 1970 known galvano types and probably on dies used for experimental strikes in January 1971 (also illustrated earlier). The Earth is not round at the upper left, the continents have light outlines, Canada is very irregular, the peninsula of Florida is fairly prominent, and at its lower right is one large island and faint traces of others. At the lower right of the Earth is the northwest coast of Africa.

The extremely detailed eagle feathers and craters have counterpart on later circulation strikes. At the suggestion of Chief Engraver Frank Gasparro these were reduced in sharpness and somewhat smoothed, for fear that coins with these details would catch dirt and grime in circulation. This variety has been generally unknown to Eisenhower dollar specialists.[8]

Prototype 2: The details on prototype 2, as shown earlier, feature considerable modification. The Earth is round, the continents are better defined, Africa is omitted, Canada is simpler, and the islands below Florida are different. The feathers of the eagle and the interiors of the craters have been smoothed.

Eisenhower dollar Prototype 1
(with 1970 obverse).

Eisenhower dollar Prototype 2
(with 1970 obverse).

Earth detail, Prototype 1 galvano.

Earth detail, Prototype 2 galvano.

1971 Prototype 3: Plaster prototype circa 1971, but probably made after Reverse A (see next page). Earth is flat at the upper left. The geography details are minimal, with the Florida peninsula being the easiest seen. At the lower right are hints of the northwest of Africa. The eagle's feathers are not sharply defined and the craters have minimal detail; some are barely defined, such as those to the right of FG.

1971 Prototype 4: Earth is round, Baja California is bold, and the northwest part of Africa is seen to the lower right. The letters are heavier than on any known production die. The eagle's feathers are not sharply defined and the crater interiors have little detail.

1971 Prototype 5: Baja California is distinct, as are Central America and the outline of South America. No trace of Africa is visible. Canada and the Arctic areas are very lumpy. An island is seen off the coast of Maine. Other islands are mostly in the Atlantic Ocean, east of Florida. The eagle's feathers are not sharply defined and the crater interiors have little detail.

Eisenhower dollar Prototype 3 galvano.

Earth detail, Prototype 3 galvano.

Eisenhower dollar Prototype 4 plaster.

Earth detail, Prototype 4 plaster.

Eisenhower dollar Prototype 5 galvano.

Earth detail, Prototype 5 galvano.

Regular Reverses of 1971 and 1972

In 1971 and 1972 the Mint produced several reverses for Ike dollars, all of the standard Moon, eagle, and Earth design, but with noticeable differences, again observable in the details of the Earth, the eagle, and the Moon craters. The outlines and geography of the Earth in particular permit easy attribution.

Reverse A: Low relief. *The State of Maine is huge and with a flat top.* Earth is flattened at the upper left. The north part of the Gulf of Mexico has a downward bulge. Mexico is a raised blob. The Florida peninsula can be raised overall or have a raised lump at the tip. The Eastern Seaboard is flat. Canada is almost non-existent. Below Florida is an island with another to its right and slightly lower. Beneath the first is a smaller island. South America has a prominent raised ridge at the lower right. The Ike Group identifies Reverse A as the Type 1 Reverse.

Reverse A was used on all cupro-nickel coins of 1971 of all three mints, on circulation-strike 1971-S silver coins, on a few Proof 1971-S dollars (not identified in this context until 2007), on many 1972 coins, and on all 1972-D coins. The details can vary depending on the strike and dies.

Reverse B: Earth is flattened at the upper left. *The northern part of the Gulf of Mexico is nearly round.* California, Oregon, and Washington are a raised lump as is Mexico. The eagle has no eyebrow, giving the nickname "Friendly Eagle," sometimes listed as FEV (Friendly Eagle Variety); CONECA: RDV-006; FS-C1-1971D-901.[9] In the Caribbean three islands slant down slightly to the right of the tip of Florida; these can appear to be joined or can be weak and almost invisible, depending on the impression. A smaller island below is in a line with the Florida peninsula.

Reverse B was used on the earlier strikings of 1971-D. Its coinage production was very small.

Eisenhower dollar regular Reverse A.

Eisenhower dollar Reverse B.

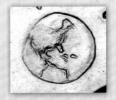

Earth detail, regular Reverse A.

Earth detail, Reverse B.

Reverse C: Aspects include a higher relief, round Earth, and continents redesigned to better match reality, but still in the same proportion. A very large low-relief amorphous island extends downward to the right, starting below the tip of Florida. The eagle's eye is different, and the breast feathers have been redone. The Moon craters have been strengthened by giving them higher rims.

Reverse C was used on most 1971-S Proofs.[10]

Reverse D: Round earth. The United States is represented as a flat country, with Maine and nearby states higher and slightly rounded. A large amorphous low-relief island(s) is seen to the lower right of Florida. South America is flat. Reverse D is identified by the Ike Group as 1972 Type 2.

Reverse D was used on some 1972 dollars.

Eisenhower dollar Reverse C.

Reverse E: Modified high relief. The Earth is round but the outline of North America has been changed to have a very heavy ridge on the left; a prominent south coast; Florida raised and prominent; and a raised ridge along the coast from Florida to Maine. Canada is mostly absent. One large lumpy island is below Florida, a smaller lump is below the left side of

Earth detail,
Reverse C.

the island, and a low-relief island more or less rectangular in shape is to the lower right of the first island. South America is outlined by a ridge, heaviest to the right. There is a hint of northwest Africa. The Ike Group identifies Reverse E as 1972 Type 3.

Eisenhower dollar Reverse D.

Eisenhower dollar Reverse E.

Earth detail, Reverse D.

Earth detail, Reverse E.

Reverse E was introduced late in 1972 for most 1972-P cupro-nickel coins, and carried over into the next several years of production.[11] It was used on some but not all 1972 coins, and was not used for the Bicentennial coins.

Circulation Strikes Coined

In early 1971 dies were sent to the Denver Mint and to the San Francisco Assay Office (henceforth called the San Francisco Mint in this text), the latter having been renamed in 1962 as no coins had been struck there since 1955.[12] On February 3, 1971, the first production of circulation-strike Eisenhower dollars took place at the Denver Mint, apparently without a public ceremony.

On March 31, a first-strike ceremony was held at the San Francisco Mint. I and certain others from the numismatic community were invited guests, including American Numismatic Association president Herbert M. Bergen. The highest-ranking Treasury Department official was Assistant Secretary Eugene T. Rossides. Tours of the mint were given. At 11:00 in the morning Mint Director Mary T. Brooks welcomed the guests and invited everyone into a room where four old-style knuckle-action presses with Eisenhower dies were set up. The first examples struck on 40% silver planchets were reserved to be given to members of the Eisenhower family, President Nixon, and select others. None were available for the visitors (this being normal policy at first-strike ceremonies). San Francisco Mint Superintendent John F. Breckle stated that an eight-hour shift on the presses could produce 240,000 coins.

In the meantime collectors eagerly awaited further news about methods of production, metallic content, and distribution policies for the coins. On June 18, according to an announcement, order forms for the new Eisenhower dollar coins would be made available. After that time approximately 53 million order blanks were sent to 84,000 distribution centers including 35,000 banks and branches and 44,000 post offices, and others to congressional offices, to the armed forces, and to customers on the Mint mailing list.[13]

The order period opened on July 1, 1971, and orders were limited to five Proof and five Uncirculated coins per person. The initial cost of the 40% silver coins in the Proof format was $10, and the Uncirculated coins were offered at $3 each. None were included in the Treasury's offering of Mint sets for $3.50 per set, which held coins from the cent to the half dollar.

On July 27, 1971, President Richard M. Nixon presented the first Proof Eisenhower dollar to Mrs. Eisenhower in a White House ceremony that included Mint Director Brooks and Secretary of the Treasury John Connally. In Abilene, Kansas, at

President Richard M. Nixon presenting the first 1971-S Proof dollar to Mrs. Dwight D. Eisenhower. Secretary of the Treasury John Connally and Mint Director Mary Brooks are to the left.

11:00 a.m. August 18, Director Brooks presented a pair of galvanos to Dr. John E. Wickman, director of the Dwight D. Eisenhower Library.[14]

At the Post Office within the Treasury Building in Washington on Eisenhower's birthday, October 14, 1971, Assistant Secretary of the Treasury Eugene T. Rossides and Mint Director Brooks mailed the first order containing a Proof Eisenhower dollar. In the meantime Uncirculated 1971-S 40% silver dollars were put up in bags of 1,000 coins and shipped from San Francisco to the New York Assay Office, where they were packaged and scheduled to be sent to buyers by registered mail.

Circulation-strike Eisenhower dollars were released by the Federal Reserve System and distributed through banks beginning on November 1, 1971. The coins had attracted a lot of interest, and many people bought them. Contemporary news articles, including those sent out by the Mint, said little about the mints that produced them and rarely mentioned that certain coins had D or S mintmarks.

Hardness of Die Steel

In 1971 thought was given at the Mint to using a new type of hardened steel to prolong die life, which was done in 1972. Meanwhile in calendar year 1971 the die life was:

> Obverse circulation-strike die: 100,000 coins
> Reverse circulation-strike die: 120,000 coins
> Obverse Proof die: 2,500 coins
> Reverse Proof die: 3,500 coins[15]

The use of harder steel was implemented in 1972 as described in the following article in *Coin World*, August 30, 1972. Mint Director Brooks was exceptionally interested in the numismatic community, attended many hobby events, and shared technical information more openly and quickly than did any of her predecessors in that office, many of whom felt that numismatists were a nuisance.

Mint Changes Dollar Dies

Mrs. Mary Brooks, director of the Mint, announced at the American Numismatic Association Convention in New Orleans that Mint officials had made a midyear change in the dies used to strike the cupronickel Eisenhower dollars for circulation, and that coins from the new dies were being released by Federal Reserve Banks throughout the country on Friday, August 18.

The most unusual development, Mrs. Brooks said, came about as the result of a decision "to take advantage of a technological advance on our die steel." The new variety of circulating "Ike" dollars will have "the identical design and relief of the Proof dollars," she said.

"The coins are struck only once and do not, of course, have the surface luster of the Proof dollar, but do have a considerably improved appearance compared with the circulating dollars manufactured heretofore," she explained.

"The use of . . . hardened tool steel," she said, "has eliminated the sinking tendencies which were encountered earlier when an attempt was made to strike the circulating cupronickel clad dollars with the high relief dies."

It is anticipated that approximately 20 million pieces of the new 1972 dollar variety will be struck at the Philadelphia Mint during the remaining months of 1972.

Dollar production for the year has been terminated at Denver and will not be resumed unless dictated by increased demands the director said.

A related article appeared in *Numismatic News*, September 26, 1972:

Eagle-Eyed Collectors Get New Coin to Ogle

The new version of the clad dollar metal Eisenhower dollar, with its high relief reverse, is easily discernible from the old low-relief model. The differences are clearly visible . . . in 1972 Philadelphia strikes before and after the change, and it's easy to identify the new varieties without the aid of a magnifying glass when examining actual specimens.

All features on the high relief version of the coin appear appreciably bolder than those on the low relief specimens. The differences are particularly noticeable on the stronger lettering, the relief of the craters on the lunar surface, the configuration of the sphere representing the Earth which appears above the eagle's right wing, and the feathers on the eagle.

The eagle on the high relief version seems to be almost soaring off the coin. Its feathers, particularly those on the left wing and on the tail, appear more realistic in form, almost as though the eagle were a full sculpture rather than a bas-relief rendering.

The high relief version of the Ike dollar, represented only in the Proof edition in 1971, was adopted for use on the Philadelphia production line in mid-July when the availability of a stronger die steel made such a move practical.

As detailed above in the reverse-die descriptions, the circulation-strike 1971 coins were in lower relief with Reverse A, and the 1971-S Proofs were in higher relief with Reverse C. Other changes were made. In 1972 Reverse E was introduced; it was continued through to the end of the Eisenhower series in 1978, except for the 1776–1976 Bicentennial dollars, which had a special reverse. Sometimes circulation-strike dies toward the end of their service life showed certain features weakly, and in some instances the reverse details seem to have been touched up slightly. There were minor changes made in the obverse dies, not as distinctive as for the reverse dies.

The new hard steel increased die life about 50%.

Eisenhower Dollars in Circulation

One welcome use of the Eisenhower dollars came from the Nevada casinos at Las Vegas, Reno, and Lake Tahoe, where hungry slot machines were to gobble millions of the coins during the next several years and had mechanisms to accommodate them. They were also familiar sights on roulette, blackjack, and other gaming tables. Most of these were Denver Mint coins. Silver dollars of like diameter had been last used in casinos in 1964, by which time most were Morgan dollars dated 1921 and Peace dollars from 1921 to 1935, nearly all in worn grades with none of numismatic value at the time.

After then the casinos used metal tokens (many made by the Franklin Mint) and colored chips made of various material. Widespread use of Ikes in the casinos proved to be short-lived, and did not continue past the early 1970s, although some stray pieces were seen on gaming tables as late as 1977. Colored chips made of composite material were the order of the day and took precedence. These also had an added advantage: many gamblers took chips home as souvenirs rather than cashing them in, yielding a profit to the issuers.

Although it was hoped that Eisenhower dollars would circulate in everyday commerce, that did not happen. The public was used to paper dollars that were lighter and easier to carry, without caring that their life expectancy in circulation was short. The new dollars might have found use in vending machines, but that is improbable, as by 1971 the largest coin of the realm in wide use was the quarter dollar. Half dollars were available in quantity in Treasury and other storage vaults, but they were hardly ever seen in pocket change. The last half dollars used in everyday transactions—and I remember them well—were Franklins, which started disappearing from circulation in 1964 and were mostly gone by late 1965. Silver-content Kennedy half dollars, launched in March 1964, were hoarded and never used in circulation.

The first Uncirculated silver-clad dollars were housed in Pliofilm packages in a navy blue envelope, earning the nickname "blue" Ikes. These were released beginning on March 31, 1971. The Proof versions of the silver-content coins were housed in large, somewhat awkward plastic holders, and came in a brown wood-grain box with a gold embossed eagle design on the front, giving rise to the nickname "brown" Ikes. The "blue" and "brown" nicknames were in use through the late 20th century, but are seldom heard today as so many of the original holders have been replaced by certified "slabs." In 1972 the Uncirculated and Proof silver-content dollars were each packaged in the same-style boxes.

As many cash drawers did not have a space for dollars, merchants disliked them and on the rare occasions they were received the cashiers would sometimes keep the Eisenhower coins in a separate box. The vast majority of vending machines, turnpike toll machines, and other devices would not accept them.

During 1971, 1972, and 1973 the dies were modified several times to make changes in the relief and other minor details. On July 31, 1972, Treasury vaults held 30.7 million Eisenhower dollars, and Federal Reserve Banks stored an additional 49.5 million. All official news releases proclaimed the Eisenhower dollar to be a great success, quite contrary to the real situation.

THE 1971
EISENHOWER
SILVER DOLLAR

From a Mint order form. Dollars with silver content were made in San Francisco and bore an S mintmark. Mintmarks were not mentioned often in Mint sales literature.

Mint Director Brooks presents the first 1973 Proof set to Secretary of the Treasury George P. Schultz. For the first time Proof sets included the Eisenhower dollar. In 1971 and 1972 these had to be ordered separately.

Numismatists and their societies and journals were very supportive of the Eisenhower dollars, but, save for limited use in casinos during the first several years, the public did not take a fancy to them. A later study showed that cupro-nickel Ike dollars paid out by banks, excepting those taken by casinos, were quickly returned and did not pass hand to hand. In contrast, cents, nickels, dimes, and quarters remained in circulation for years.

The Irrelevance of Eisenhower College

Public Law 93-441, October 11, 1974, diverted some Eisenhower dollar receipts:

> Sec. 2. (a) Except as provided by subsection (b) and after receiving the assurances described in subsection (c) the secretary of the Treasury is authorized to take one-tenth of all moneys derived from the sale of $1 Proof coins minted and issued under section 101(d) of the Coinage Act of 1965 (31 U.S.C. 391(d))[16] and section 203 of the Bank Holding Company Act Amendments of 1970 (31 U.S.C. 324b) which bear the likeness of the late president of the United States, Dwight David Eisenhower, and transfer such amount of moneys to Eisenhower College, Seneca Falls, New York.
>
> (b) For the purposes of carrying out this section, there is authorized not to be appropriated not to exceed $10,000,000.
>
> (c) Before the secretary of the Treasury may transfer any moneys to Eisenhower College under this Act, Eisenhower College must make satisfactory assurances to him that an amount equal to 10 per centum of the total amount of moneys received by Eisenhower College under this Act shall be transferred to the Samuel Rayburn Library in Bonham, Texas.[17]

Eisenhower College had no connection whatever with the coins, the Mint, or President Eisenhower and simply traded on his name. This small liberal-arts institution was established on September 21, 1965, with $14.5 million in private and federal funds. Collectors felt strongly that they did not want to pay for this involuntary and irrelevant "charitable donation" over which they had no control. Logic and common sense played no part, and about $9 million from sale of the Proof coins went to the college by the time the Eisenhower dollar was discontinued.

By 1979 Eisenhower College had an enrollment of only about 460 students and was deep in financial trouble. In March of that year it was taken over by the Rochester Institute of Technology. That didn't help, and on July 22, 1982, RIT announced the imminent closing of the institution.[18]

The 1976 Bicentennial Celebration

The Advisory Panel on Coins and Medals of the American Revolution Bicentennial Commission (ARBC) held its first meeting in January 1970 in Washington, D.C.[19] The field of numismatics was well represented by Margo Russell, editor of *Coin World*; Clifford Mishler, editor of *Numismatic News*; Herbert M. Bergen, president of the American Numismatic Association; and others.

The group proposed a sweeping program to change all of the coin designs from the cent to the dollar. In opposition, the Mint and Treasury Department officials were dead set against the idea of creating coins for collectors and other souvenir hunters. To back up their position, spokespeople recounted the irregular distribution, false marketing statements, and other ghosts from certain commemorative coin programs from 1935 to 1946. Abuses were many during that time as most coins were distributed by private individuals or groups without government or other oversight. For some exploitative issues few records were kept, false "sold out" information was given, profits disappeared, and there were other irregularities.[20] Mint Director Mary T. Brooks stated that issuing commemoratives was counter to the Mint's business of producing regular coinage. Indeed, none had been made since 1954, when the star-crossed Carver-Washington series of half dollars expired.

Bicentennial insignia.

The Treasury thought that a line of Mint-made medals would be ideal to observe the Bicentennial, an idea opposed by the Medallic Art Company and the Franklin Mint, large private producers of such. Their argument was that the Mint could not market medals in quantity.

The Treasury's opposition to a Bicentennial coinage changed when Wright Patman, chairman of the House Banking Committee, wrote to ARBC chairman David J. Mahoney on October 1, 1970, stating that the Committee would be willing to give careful consideration to such an idea. It is to be remembered that at this time the Eisenhower dollar was not a reality yet, and it does not seem to have been proposed in any Bicentennial discussions.

Meetings of the ARBC continued, and on March 5, 1973, Treasury Secretary George Schultz sent the Nixon administration's proposal for a Bicentennial coinage to Capitol Hill. It was to consist of cupro-nickel–clad coins for general circulation and silver-content coins for sale to collectors and other buyers at a premium. Two denominations were proposed: the half dollar and dollar. In time the quarter denomination was added. After many meetings and discussions Public Law 93-127 authorizing the Bicentennial coinage was passed by both houses of Congress. President Nixon signed it into law on October 18, 1973.

Public Invited to Submit Designs

Instead of using the many ideas proposed by the sculptor-engravers on the Mint staff the Treasury Department invited citizens with artistic talent to submit ideas. These had to be emblematic of the 1776–1976 Bicentennial and had to include UNITED STATES OF AMERICA and E PLURIBUS UNUM as inscriptions. The rules stated that entries had to be from citizens of the United States; had to be accompanied by a black-and-white sketch or drawing within a 10-inch circle or a photograph of like diameter of a model, either to be mounted on an 11-by-14–inch illustration board; and had to be received by December 14, 1973. Semi-finalists would be required to submit a model not to exceed 8-1/2 inches in diameter and with the relief not to exceed 5/32 of an inch. "For coinability, areas of high relief on the obverse side should be opposite areas of low relief on the reverse." Those interested were invited to write to the National Sculpture Society, c/o the U.S. Bullion Depository, West Point, New York 20096 for "formal printed instructions."[21]

Mint Director Brooks also sent out notices to art schools and colleges to stir up interest. During the competition she went on a three-week trip around the United States to give television, radio, and newspaper interviews. These designs were to be of the people, by the people, and for the people—created by citizens.

The contest drew 884 qualified entries. These were forwarded to the Philadelphia Mint. Beginning at 11.00 a.m., January 9, 1974, these were reviewed by a panel of judges chaired by Robert Weinman, president of the National Sculpture Society, which included Adlai S. Hardin, sculptor; Julius Lauth, vice president of the Medallic Art Company; Gilroy Roberts, former chief engraver at the Mint, now sculptor and executive with the Franklin Mint; and Elvira Clain-Stefanelli, curator of the National Numismatic Collection at the Smithsonian Institution. Interested media people were invited to watch the judging. The panel selected 12 semi-finalists, each of whom was invited to submit his design in the form of a plaster model, for which the Treasury Department would pay $750 each.[22] The semi-finalists were:

Professor Ogden Dalrymple, Augustana College, Sioux Falls, South Dakota
Dean McMullen, 913 Southwest Fir Grove Lane, Portland, Oregon
Margaret Grigor, P.O. Box 326, Stellacoom, Washington
Seth G. Huntington, 4153 Aldrich Avenue, Minneapolis, Minnesota
Jack L. Ahr, 1802 South Highland, Arlington Heights, Illinois
Albert B. D'Andrea, 2121 Bay Avenue, Brooklyn, New York
George Haessler, 4216 Bishop Road, Detroit, Michigan
Dennis R. Williams, 880 East Broad Street, Columbus, Ohio
Dean Millman, 94 North 400 West Street, Provo, Utah
Brydon Stuart, 1106 South 30th Avenue, Yakima, Washington
Pierce Rice, 2001 16th Street NW, Washington, D.C.
John Th. Bischof, 828 2nd Street, Rensselaer, New York

Finalists were to receive $5,000 each and to be announced after George Washington's birthday, February 22, 1974.[23]

It was not until March 6 that Secretary of the Treasury George Shultz and Mint Director Mary Brooks announced the winners: Jack L. Ahr for the quarter, Seth G. Huntington for the half dollar, and Dennis R. Williams for the dollar. Later, chairman Weinberg commented, "I really don't think what we got was a great bargain. Nothing we selected was a real winner that I'd fight to the death for. In terms of what we had to work with, though, I think we did the best we could."[24] Indeed, Huntington's depiction on the half dollar was virtually identical to John R. Sinnock's design for the 1926 Sesquicentennial quarter eagle. The Mint could have saved $5,000 by simply copying the original.

The news release included this about Williams:

Dennis R. Williams . . . designed the Liberty Bell extending over the Moon that was selected for the back of the one dollar coin . . . He is 21 years old and in his junior year at the Columbus College of Art and Design in Columbus, Ohio, majoring in sculpture. His sculpture instructor assigned him the National Bicentennial Coin Design Competition as a design problem.

Mr. Williams was born in Erie, Pennsylvania, October 26, 1952, but resides at 880 East Broad Street in Columbus while attending school. He says he would eventually like to teach sculpture at the college level and plans to use his $5,000 award to continue his education.

In the March 1974 issue of *The Numismatist*, American Numismatic Association president Virginia Culver included this as part of her monthly message:

The upcoming bicentennial of our country's independence is drawing closer at hand and its celebration should affect every person in the United States. Coin collectors all over the world are going to be able to add specimens to their collections that will mark this commemoration.

It was a rare privilege for me to be able to view the submitted entries for our coinage change at the Philadelphia Mint in January. History was being made as the five eminent judges reviewed the almost 1,000 entries. It was intriguing to see the varied submissions of the artists, knowing these were their interpretations of our country's birthday. In many, one could see the similarity of design that had been used before on either our coinage or on various tokens and medals. On some, one wondered just what connection the theme would have with our bicentennial.

In choosing the semi-finalists, the judges not only had to consider the design, but if it would be effective when struck on the reverse of one of our coins. Our Mint Director, Mrs. Mary T. Brooks, is certainly to be commended for the interest she stimulated across this country for the almost 1,000 entries.

Contemplating the future Mint Director Brooks "suggested that the dollar might be released on July 5, 1975, the half dollar on September 1, 1975, and if the quarter were changed, it might be released on January 2, 1976."[25] At that time there was some debate about eliminating the quarter, as this denomination was common in circulation, and a new design might interrupt the distribution. On the other hand, half dollars were rarely seen in commerce, and dollars had not been coined for circulation since 1935. Indeed, some Treasury documents mention only the two higher denominations. Distribution was to be through the 12 Federal Reserve Banks and their 25 branches.

For the dollar a sketch for a *quarter* by Dennis R. Williams was selected—the Liberty Bell partly superimposed on the Moon. At the Mint the lettering was changed from QUARTER DOLLAR to ONE DOLLAR. E / PLURIBUS / UNUM was changed to three lines instead of two.

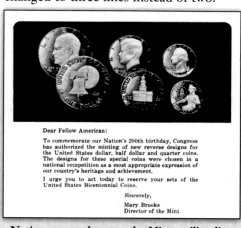

Notice sent to those on the Mint mailing list.

Dennis R. Williams's entry was for a *quarter dollar.* The original artwork is shown here. The border is with heavy block letters. This image was distributed to the media in early 1974.

Plaster model for Williams's quarter dollar design.

The Dennis R. Williams imaginative pockmarked Moon and a photograph of the real Moon.

Proposed and Accepted Designs

At the Philadelphia Mint, Chief Engraver Frank Gasparro and others proposed new designs for the Bicentennial, mostly for the dollar's reverse. Some galvanos and plasters from various motifs made but not used in earlier years were dusted off and reviewed. These featured eagles and/or Independence Hall.

In the proposed and final versions of Dennis Williams's reverse, artistic license was used for the surface of the Moon. Rather than having craters with flat centers, round semi-spherical depressions or pockmarks were shown on the left side of the Moon and only a few on the right side. Apparently, no one looked at a picture of Earth's satellite, or, if they did, it was ignored.

A Frank Gasparro doodle or semi-sketch on a picture of a woman printed in a magazine—part of his search for an ideal Miss Liberty.

Gasparro's further development of Miss Liberty.

Benjamin Franklin proposed as the obverse for the Bicentennial dollar. The artist signed as F. GASPARRO.

Signed Frank Gasparro design for a bold American eagle on a cliff.

Galvano of Frank Gasparro's
adopted 1776–1976 die.

Plaster with clay overlay idea
for the Bicentennial dollar reverse
(one of several eagle designs).

Eagle perched on a mountaintop
with stars and a glory of the
sun's rays in the background.

Eagle with Independence Hall.
BICENTENNIAL 1976 is lightly
lettered at the top border, FREEDOM
at the bottom border. Plaster and clay.

Finessed plaster version
of the preceding motif.

Eagle with Independence Hall, another pose. This plaster from the Mint's archives was among the motifs reviewed for the 1976 Bicentennial. In 1926 sculptor Albert Laessle (March 28, 1877–September 4, 1954) created the design for use on a 76-mm gold Medal of Award for the Sesquicentennial Exposition held in Philadelphia. Additional strikings were made in bronze. He also sculpted "America – Abundance," 1934, the 10th medal in the Society of Medalists series.

The 1926 Sesquicentennial of American Independence medal by Albert Laessle, struck by Bailey, Banks & Biddle, prominent Philadelphia jewelers. Bronze striking.

Reverse Varieties 1 and 2 of 1976

The following images show the regular reverse varieties of 1976 as well as some pattern variants.

Variety 1: *Quick identifier:* The E is directly over the I in PLURIBUS. This is Dennis R. Williams's original design. Its heavy block letters are without serifs. The O in OF is thick with a smaller center than on the following.

The block letters on the Bicentennial reverse were viewed as being too harsh and modernistic, and late in 1975 a second variety was made, first with heavy letters and, finally, a version was made by Mint sculptor-engraver Philip Fowler featuring delicate lettering with light serifs.

Variety 2: *Quick identifier:* The E is directly over the RI in PLURIBUS. The letters are lighter and thinner, with small serifs on most. The O in OF is thin, with a larger center. This is a modification by Mint sculptor-engraver Philip Fowler. Called *Light Letters* at the Mint.

Galvano of the first reverse
of the 1776–1976 dollar with
block letters without serifs.

A plaster of the Bicentennial dollar
reverse, Variety 1. The craters are not
as prominent as on the final version.

Coin showing the
adopted 1776–1976
Bicentennial dollar
reverse Variety 1.
These were struck in
calendar-year 1975.

Galvano for a (presumably)
unadopted variant of
1776–1976 dollar,
Variety 2. The E
is directly over the
I in PLURIBUS,
as on Variety 1.

Galvano for a presumably
(but it might pay to
look among existing
coins) unadopted
variant of Variety 2.
Some letters in the
motto have serifs.

Motto detail on the
variant of Variety 2.

The new 1776–1976 Variety 2 reverse was done by sculptor-engraver Philip Fowler. The letters are lighter and have traces of serifs. The position of the E over the I in PLURIBUS is farther to the left.

Galvano of the 1776–1976 Bicentennial dollar reverse, Variety 2. Called *Light Letters* at the Mint, as tagged here.

Coin with the adopted 1976 Bicentennial dollar reverse, Variety 2, as used for coinage.

Announcements and Preparation

In 1974 National Coin Week, sponsored by the American Numismatic Association, began on April 21. This event dated back to its first observation, February 9 to 16, 1924.[26] For the first time in history, in 1974 under Proclamation 4286 (dated April 19, 1974), the chief executive of the United States, Richard M. Nixon, made it a government-authorized occasion with focus on the Bicentennial. The text of his proclamation began:

A Proclamation

Since the beginning of history, coins have helped tell the story of civilization. They frequently reflect the economic development of their country of origin as well as the scientific advancement and artistic values of the people who produce and use them. Today more than ten million Americans collect coins both for pleasure and for profit.[27]

In honor of our Bicentennial year we are changing the designs on the backs of three United States coins. The new designs were selected through competition among the nation's sculptors [*sic*] and will appear on the backs of the dollar, half dollar, and quarter. The double date 1776–1976 will appear on the front of the three coins.

When in circulation these Bicentennial coins will reach every citizen and serve as reminders of our rich national heritage and continuing dedication to freedom and self-government . . .

On April 24 the three winning coin designers—Jack Ahr for the quarter, Seth Huntington for the half dollar, and Williams for the dollar—joined Director Brooks, ANA president Culver, and others for a reception at the White House hosted by Counselor to the President Anne Armstrong on behalf of Richard Nixon (who was immersed in the Watergate scandal at the time and was fighting for his political life, unsuccessfully as it turned out).

The winners then adjourned to the Treasury Building, where at 5:00 p.m. William E. Simon, designated to be the next secretary of the Treasury, presented each winner with a check for $5,000. On the 26th the group visited the Philadelphia Mint to watch the process of making dies. This was covered in a June 1974 article in *The Numismatist*, "Coin Design Winners Visit Washington, D.C. and the Philadelphia Mint," which further noted:

> It is expected that 1.4 billion quarters, 400 million half dollars, and 225 million dollars will be struck to meet commercial demand for the three new circulating bicentennial coins. In addition, at least 45 million silver-clad Proof and Uncirculated specimens of the new coins will be struck for sale to the public.
>
> As Mary T. Brooks so aptly stated, "Each (coin) will place a bit of our history into the hands of every man, woman and child in the country."

Director Brooks spent an unrelenting effort to promote the coins and made many appearances around the nation. As one example, at 8:00 in the evening of May 3 she was the featured speaker at the Educational Forum held at the Greater New York Coin Convention at the New York Sheraton Hotel. "We can all look forward to using Bicentennial coins after July 4, 1975," she said.

On August 9 President Nixon resigned in disgrace, and Vice President Gerald R. Ford became chief executive. From this time onward Ford was kept apprised of various Bicentennial coinage activities and events.

On April 24, 1974, a reception at the White House was held for the contest winners. Left to right: Dennis R. Williams, designer of the dollar; Seth G. Huntington, designer of the half dollar; John W. Warner, head of the American Revolution Bicentennial Administration; Mint Director Mary T. Brooks; Jack L. Ahr, designer of the quarter; and Counsellor Anne Armstrong.

Bicentennial Dollars Coined

At 11:00 a.m. August 12, 1974, the first-strike ceremony for the 1976 Bicentennial coins was held at the Philadelphia Mint with the three designers in attendance. Some of the coins and the galvanos were given to Mint Director Mary Brooks, who took them to the 83rd anniversary convention of the American Numismatic Association, which started in Bal Harbour, Florida (Miami Beach), on August 13, where they were displayed and admired. At 11:00 a.m. on Saturday the 17th she gave extended remarks about the program, including:

> The ANA has asked us for an old coin press. Right now we are holding on to every piece of equipment we have in our possession. If it runs we are using it. If it is out of order we are fixing it.
>
> In fact, until the Bicentennial crunch is over we are shipping old presses, ordinarily due for replacement, to West Point to be put to work again. One day this pressure has to subside. When it does the ANA will be the first in line for one of these presses that has done more than its share in helping the Mint break production records never before thought attainable with present equipment and facilities.[28]

In the White House on November 13, 1974, Mint Director Brooks presented President Gerald Ford with the first Bicentennial Proof set. An accompanying news release told of Bicentennial coins and order periods.

On November 15 the U.S. Mint began accepting orders for silver-content 1976-S coins. A three-coin Uncirculated set was priced at $9 and Proofs at $15 for the trio, with a limit of five sets per customer for each of the two options.

A dedication ceremony for the ANA Museum at its Colorado Springs headquarters was held on January 18, 1975. Director Brooks was on hand and presented a set of Bicentennial Proof coins. On January 19, 1975, the Mint announced a price reduction from $15 to $12 for 40% silver Bicentennial Proof sets and the removal of order limits. The same news release stated this:

> The new Automatic Proof Coin Handling System automates the feeding of blanks to a Proof coin press and places the finished coin into a color-coded coin tray providing faster inspection of the finished product. Minimal handling also results in fewer rejects due to accidental scratching.
>
> The prototype system is presently operational to handle dollar coins at the rate of 22 per minute and, by spring, will be further developed to handle 25 and 50 cent pieces.

Promoting the Bicentennial Coins

In 1975 a constant stream of articles based on interviews with Mint Director Mary Brooks and others appeared in newspapers nationwide. No campaign like this had ever been mounted. The mints geared up for nationwide excitement and unprecedented demand for the new coins.

In an Associated Press release of January 15, 1975, Director Brooks commented that the silver issues in particular would please coin collectors because they "are going to be very unique, and in the future probably very valuable. I don't like the idea that people collect coins just for the prospect of making money. I like the idea of their collecting them because of the history they teach people. . . ."

She commented further that with all of the "wrangling the last time over whose face to stamp on the silver dollars" she feared that if it were left to Congress "the House and Senate might insist on Sam Rayburn."[29] This lament was an old one:

despite the wishes, talents, and experience of the Mint artists, numismatists, and various fine-arts commissions and advisories, only Congress had the final say.

The Mint began accepting orders for three-piece sets of 1776–1976 Proof coins at $15, per earlier announcements. Director Brooks anticipated that the public demand for the Bicentennial quarters, half dollars, and dollars would be so great that she closed down the production of regular issues of these denominations! An article by Gary Palmer in the *Boston Herald*, February 2, 1975, told the story:

U.S. '75 Minting in Doubt

The government's failure to think far enough ahead in terms of the Bicentennial is liable to cost the nation's numismatists large denomination 1975 coins.

Mrs. Mary T. Brooks, director of the Mint, said no 1975-dated quarters, halves, or dollars will be struck during the first quarter of this year. In all likelihood that means they won't be struck—period. The government coining presses are going to be going full bore just to meet the public demand for the three coins which will bear the new Bicentennial designs.

In fact, such a demand is seen for these coins that the government has given Mrs. Brooks the go-ahead to produce the new design coins a full year ahead of the six months permitted under previous law.

In all, the Mint expects to coin 1.4 billion quarters, 400 million halves, and 85 million dollar with the Bicentennial reverse designs. Distribution to banks is scheduled to allow circulation beginning July 4. . . . The decision is probably a costly one which the government apparently gave little thought to when the Bicentennial coin decision was made.

If the nation had been given a full set of Bicentennial coins—penny to dollar—the problem would have been resolved quite easily. Perhaps someone will leave notes for the generation which celebrates the nation's 300th birthday. Maybe the same mistake can be avoided for the Tricentennial.[30] Here's hoping.

Storm clouds were rising on the sales horizon, although this was not publicly acknowledged. By this time the Mint had dropped the price for a three-coin Proof set to $12 and stated that an unlimited quantity could be ordered of Proof coins as well as Uncirculated silver-content pieces. Those who had already paid $15 were to be sent refunds beginning on March 15, 1975. Uncirculated sets cost $9, a price that was not changed. Furthermore:

Mrs. Mary T. Brooks, director of the Mint, said the old price of $15 per set was determined during the oil embargo, a time of uncertainty as to the availability, price, and future delivery of crucial packing materials.

"Our added production capacity together was the extended 18-month ordering period will greatly help toward reaching our goal of making these sets available to every American wanting them," Mrs. Brooks said.[31]

On April 23, 1975, production began at the San Francisco Mint of the Mint State or Uncirculated-surface strikes of the 40% silver Bicentennial coins. Mailing of such sets was to start on July 7.[32]

To stimulate demand the Treasury Department arranged to have order forms available at post offices, these including a detachable envelope and illustrations of the three coins. As portrayed by the Treasury Department and the Mint enthusiasm knew no bounds—clearly this distribution would create demand from citizens everywhere. Perhaps the congressional limits on coinage quantities were too low.

Bicentennial Coins Released

In June 1975 the Treasury announced that as of July 7 the circulating Bicentennial coins would be available for face value at banks.[33] This news was later revised to state that on the Monday, July 7, the 12 Federal Reserve Banks and their branches would begin shipping coins to their bank affiliates. Further changes were made in the schedule, and it was announced that Bicentennial half dollars would be distributed "on a limited basis" in July, and launching of the quarters would not be until August, in Chicago (held there as the designer of that coin, Jack L. Ahr, was from Arlington Heights, a suburb). The dollars were expected to be released in September.

To the public this was very confusing. Citizens who expected to go to banks in early July and buy as many quarters, half dollars, and dollars as desired now did not know what to do. In mid-July many banks had half dollars on hand, but in limited quantity. As an example, in Centre County, Pennsylvania, a newspaper reported that the Centre County Bank, Union National Bank, and Peoples National Bank "should receive shipments of the half dollars on Thursday [July 17] with the regular shipment from the Federal Reserve Bank in Philadelphia. The coins would be available Friday at those banks if they arrive with the shipment." However, Paul W. Beirly, president of People's National Bank, stated that he had already received $3,000 worth.[34]

In July some collectors across the country reported receiving Proof sets. Confusion continued everywhere. Unsure of where the circulation-strike half dollars could be purchased, and with uncertainty as when quarters and half dollars would become available, the public responded with a large collective yawn. There were no lines of waiting buyers at banks. There were no shortages except in a few isolated instances. Shortfalls did not last long as the Federal Reserve Banks were stuffed with half dollars with nowhere to send them.

Not helping matters was the fact that reviews of the half dollar were often negative. At the First National Bank on Broad Street in Charleston, South Carolina, Mrs. Becky Thompson, head teller, told a reporter from the *Charleston News and Courier* that demand was light as people did not know which banks had the coins. Furthermore:

> One of the reasons the coin is not going at a faster pace, Mrs. Thompson said, it that "People just don't like half dollars. The Bicentennial quarter and dollar coins should go over better."[35]

Results were mixed. As supplies were limited, some banks rationed them. The Preston Bank in Dallas, Texas, for example, received only 1,000 coins to begin with, then some more, and had to limit the number paid out. Within a few days more than 2,500 were paid out.[36]

Continuing News in 1975

In 1975 many newspapers had weekly columns on coin collecting, sometimes syndicated, other times custom-written for a given area. The authors of these seem to have received little or no official information about the Bicentennial coins from the Treasury Department and were as confused as was the general public. Information of great importance to collectors, such as where coins from the different mints were being paid out, was not given. In retrospect this seems strange, as Director Brooks was interested in and quite close to the numismatic community, with *Coin World* editor Margo Russell in particular being a fine friend. Brooks, however, had no say in Treasury planning, publicity, or distribution.

In early August the Treasury Department announced:

> A new quarter for a new century will be put into circulation August 18. The 25-cent piece will depict a Revolutionary era drummer boy on the back, instead of the American eagle, and will keep the likeliness of George Washington on the front. The coin will have the dates 1776–1976 below the head.[37]
>
> The quarter is the second of the three coins issued for the Bicentennial. The half dollar was issued a month ago, and a new version of the Eisenhower dollar will come out in October.[38]

On Friday, August 15, the Bicentennial quarter was launched in a special ceremony in Chicago. Designer Jack L. Ahr was honored. The Federal Reserve announced that the quarters were being released through more than 14,000 member banks as well as their branches. Director Brooks stated that the quarter was the "workhorse" of the Bicentennial coins, and that "at least 1.6 billion will be put in circulation."[39] This was done, indeed, but based on speculation, not on demand. Official optimism prevailed, and the mintage estimate on the dollars, yet to be released, was upped from 225 million to 300 million.[40]

Coins for Sale Everywhere

Sales of 40% silver circulation-strike Bicentennial coins were falling far behind the Treasury's predictions, while Treasury officials were scratching their heads in bewilderment. On September 11, 1975, Mint Director Brooks put into effect a new plan. Henceforth financial institutions such as banks and credit unions could take part in a bulk program to order silver sets in groups of 50. The announcement included this:

> Enclosed with this letter are the following: (1) Fact Sheet, (2) Blanks, (3) Suggested radio and newspaper copy for your individual promotion.
>
> Each order of 50 sets will be mailed directly to you from the San Francisco Mint [*sic*; it was called the San Francisco Assay Office in nearly all other announcements] and will also contain two teller counter-top posters as well as teller fact sheets designed to be responsive to customers.
>
> We earnestly solicit your cooperation and support in making the nation's 200th birthday an overwhelming success.

One of the suggested radio texts:

> The United States Mint and the (Name of Your Bank) are proud to present 40% silver Uncirculated Bicentennial coin sets for your memento of 200 years as a nation. Priced at $9.00 these beautiful coins were especially minted to mark this historic event. You will want to own some of these sets and find them to be beautiful gifts. Visit (Your Bank) today and purchase yours—40% silver Bicentennial Uncirculated coin sets.

AD #2

Join in our Bicentennial Celebration

Now available at our teller's windows

U. S. Mint Bicentennial Silver Coin Sets

Congress has directed that the dollar, half dollar and quarter be redesigned for the Bicentennial. The U. S. Mint has struck these three new coins in 40 percent silver sets, packaged handsomely, making beautiful mementos or gifts honoring our nation's 200 years of Independence.

Visit

(Your Logo)

Advertisement No. 2 on sheets of ready-made notices for banks and other outlets to publicize sets of Uncirculated 1976-S silver-content coins. The Treasury Department had an overwhelming quantity of unsold sets.

Eventually, more than 2.2 million sets were sold under this program.[41]

On October 11 Mamie (Mrs. Dwight) Eisenhower was on hand in Newport News, Virginia to christen the nuclear-powered aircraft carrier named for her husband, the USS *Dwight D. Eisenhower*. Mint Director Brooks was on hand to present Proof Bicentennial dollars to her and to Secretary of the Navy J. William Middendorf (for later installation on the ship's ceremonial quarter deck). Vice President Nelson Rockefeller was the main speaker.

The Bicentennial Dollar Ceremony

In comparison to the release of circulation strikes of the Bicentennial quarters and half dollars, the launching of the dollar was a quiet affair. Monroe Kimbrel, president of the Federal Reserve Bank of Atlanta, invited Mint Director Brooks and designer Williams to a "ceremonial function" at the Monetary Museum at the bank at 10:30 a.m. on Monday, October 13. The event garnered hardly any nationwide interest or attention.

On the same day circulation strikes of the Bicentennial dollars were shipped to commercial banks. Distribution began on Tuesday the 14th. The event was not well coordinated as a regional newspaper noted:

Bureaucratic Bungle

When the Federal Reserve Bank of Atlanta sent out a notice last week announcing the new Bicentennial dollar coins would be moved into circulation on Monday, it placed an embargo on the media forbidding them to say anything about it until after noon on Monday.

In the same envelope the Federal Reserve enclosed a similar notice about the new coins issued by the Department of the Mint in Washington. It was dated Oct. 1 and marked "For Immediate Release."

One wonders why a public announcement made in the nation's capital had to remain a closely guarded official secret in Atlanta for nearly two weeks.[42]

Clearly, as 1975 drew to a close the Bicentennial coins were no longer newsworthy on a national basis. Of the three denominations released, the dollar received only a tiny fraction of the coverage accorded to the half dollar and quarter. It was late at the gate.

During 1976, sales of Bicentennial coins were satisfactory in terms of exceeding past annual sales of Proof sets and related collector coins. The last 40% silver coins were struck in a special ceremony in San Francisco on June 22, with Director Brooks on hand. The event was closed to the public due to unspecified security concerns.[43]

On September 11 the Treasury stated that since the release of circulation strikes in 1975 "143 million Liberty Bell with Moon dollars" had been paid out, far exceeding comparable-period distribution of earlier regular-design Eisenhower dollars. This amounted to more than one coin for every family in America. In reality, few citizens ever saw one of the coins.

During the holiday season a push was made for sales by new packaging, "a scenic view of Independence Hall" on the Uncirculated silver sets, many of which were shipped from San Francisco to be offered at the shops in the Denver and San Francisco mints. Some banks and financial institutions continued offering Bicentennial coins in the two metal types. There was no particular rush to buy them, as they were old news by that time.

The glowing mintage production figures anticipated by Mint Director Brooks fell far short of her expectations. According to later government statistics a nationwide recession began in November 1973 and lasted until March 1975; during which time the Gross Domestic Product lost 3.2%. No doubt this dramatically affected the public demand for Bicentennial coins, causing production figures to fall far short of their predictions. This economic situation was not mentioned in any of the contemporary Treasury publicity I have seen about the coins.

After the Bicentennial celebration ended the Treasury Department came to the realization that Eisenhower dollars of either the old design or with the Bicentennial motif were never going to be popular in circulation. By that time the Nevada casinos had long since stopped ordering quantities. Gasparro's old reverse was put back in service in 1977.

Unrelated to numismatics and coinage there was wild speculation in the silver bullion market, and the use of this metal was discontinued for coinage of silver-content Ikes for the numismatic market. Production was slowed, and in 1978 the last Eisenhower dollars were coined. A core of collectors had kept the faith, however, and Proofs and circulation strikes remained popular until the end.

The Leftover Bicentennial Coins

In the late 1970s the Hunt brothers, business tycoons based in Dallas, Texas, were speculating in the silver market, causing its spot price to multiply several times. On Wednesday, September 19, 1979, the Mint suspended sales from its inventory of Uncirculated 40% silver coins as the meltdown value exceeded the list price of $9 per three-coin set. The bulk-purchase program was discontinued as well. Proof sets at $12 each were still available, and about 400,000 remained on hand.

The record high price of silver bullion was $50.35 per ounce, reached in trading on the Comex on January 18, 1980. By April 1980, the price of silver dropped to about $10.80 at one point.

In March 1980 the *investment market* for rare coins collapsed, and the prices of many "investment grade" coins (generally, MS-65 and Proof-65 or finer silver and gold coins sold through telemarketing and other aggressive sales techniques) fell sharply. Many other areas of numismatics, such as colonial and pre-federal copper coins, tokens, medals, and bank notes, were not affected.

In San Francisco in 1980 silver-content Bicentennial sets of Uncirculated and Proof coins remained on hand. On September 1, 1981, Mint Director Donna Pope, successor to Mary Brooks in that office, announced the resumption of Bicentennial silver-content set sales at $15 for Proofs and $12 for Uncirculated. Regular Bicentennial Proof sets were dropped from $20 to $15 with a limit of 100 sets per order. Uncirculated sets were dropped from $15 to $12 with no limit. In 1982, with the silver price still falling, the prices were changed to $12 and $9 respectively, with no limits. In fiscal-year 1983 sales of silver-content Bicentennial Proof sets totaled 40,004 and Uncirculated sets 19,633.

In March 1985 the last Bicentennial silver Proof sets were sold. In fiscal-year 1986 28,379 Uncirculated silver sets were sold. It was stated that sales would end on December 31, after which any remaining coins would be melted. I have learned no numismatic details concerning such destruction.

Eisenhower Dollars in Later Years

In January 1993 Joe Coyne, assistant to the board at the Office of Board Members, Federal Reserve Board Public Affairs Office, told Frank Van Valen, who was assisting me in research, that the Federal Reserve had no stockpiles of Eisenhower dollars at any of the 12 Federal Reserve Banks. All Ikes had been dispersed to smaller banks throughout the system.[44] In a visit to the vault in the San Francisco Federal Reserve Bank in April 2015 I was informed that there were many 20th-century dollars in storage there, but only a stray bag or two or three of Eisenhower or Anthony dollars, if any at all. No numismatically useful records were on hand.

Special Coins for the Smithsonian

In 1962 Eva Adams, then director of the Mint, the predecessor of Mary Brooks, directed the Denver Mint to make special strikings of current coins for the Smithsonian Institution. These pieces were especially carefully made with satiny "Special Mint Set"–type finishes, likely first strikes carefully made from new dies.[45] Later, during the Eisenhower dollar era, at least two each of the following varieties were made: 1971-D, 1973-D, 1776–1976-D, and 1977-D, as evidenced by examples held by the Smithsonian today. These were in the National Numismatic Collection but not tagged or recognized until Jeff Garrett came across them while doing other research under the aegis of NNC curator Dr. Richard Doty in 2013.[46] Nothing about them had ever been mentioned in Mint reports or publicity, nor had such special strikings been made available to collectors.

Specimen strike of a 1973-D Eisenhower dollar in the National Numismatic Collection in the Smithsonian Institution.

A Remarkable Hoard

In 2011 the Big Sky Hoard was announced by Littleton Coin Company:

> After thirty years in a Montana bank vault, a previously unknown hoard of over 220,000 Eisenhower dollars was discovered in 2011. Put away for years by a prominent Montana family, most of the coins in this remarkable hoard were still in original mint-sewn bags and were untouched by the wear and tear of general circulation. Shipped from the Denver Mint right to a Federal Reserve Bank branch in Montana, the coins missed the traditional movement between the mint and local banks, and escaped the widespread use of "Ike" dollars in western casinos.

The majority of these were 1974-D and 1977-D and of above-average Mint State quality. These were offered to Littleton customers, and brisk sales resulted.

A small part of the Big Sky Hoard.

Grading Eisenhower Dollars

1971-S. Graded MS-65.

MS-60 to 70 (Mint State). *Obverse:* At MS-60, some abrasion and contact marks are evident, most noticeably on the cheek, jaw, and temple. Luster is present, but may be dull or lifeless. At MS-63, contact marks are extensive but not distracting. Abrasion still is evident, but less than at lower levels. MS-64 coins are slightly finer. An MS-65 coin may have minor abrasion, but contact marks are so minute as to require magnification. Luster should be full and rich. *Reverse:* At MS-60, some abrasion and contact marks are evident, most noticeably on the eagle's breast, head, and talons. Otherwise, the same comments apply as for the obverse.

1972. Graded AU-50.

AU-50, 53, 55, 58 (About Uncirculated). *Obverse:* Light wear is seen on the higher-relief areas of the portrait. At AU-58, the luster is extensive, but incomplete. At AU–50 and 53, luster is less but still present. *Reverse:* Further wear is evident on the eagle, particularly the head, breast, talons, and tops of the wings. Otherwise, the same comments apply as for the obverse.

The Eisenhower dollar is seldom collected in grades lower than AU-50.

1776–1976-S, Bicentennial. Graded PF-68.

PF-60 to 70 (Proof). *Obverse and Reverse:* Proofs that are extensively cleaned and have many hairlines, or that are dull and grainy, are lower level, such as PF–60 to 62. There are not many of these in the marketplace. With medium hairlines and good reflectivity, assigned grades of PF–63 or 64 are appropriate. With relatively few hairlines a rating of PF-65 can be given. PF-66 may have hairlines so delicate that magnification is needed to see them. Above that, a Proof should be free of any hairlines or other problems.

Collecting Eisenhower Dollars

The popularity of Eisenhower dollars has varied over the years. As noted above, during the time of their production there was a steady numismatic demand, particularly from 1971 until the Bicentennial confusion, but nothing special. After a spike in sales for the 1971 coins, including Proofs, demand fell. In later years fewer Ike Proof dollars were made than of the other denominations, cents to half dollars, sold in sets.

In *The Numismatist* in April 1974 a brilliant landmark article by Herbert P. Hicks, "Eisenhower Dollar Varieties," explored in depth the differences he noted on dies. This set the standard for later research and descriptions by others. The lack of excitement for the 1976 Bicentennial designs (of the copycat-motif half dollar in particular, but also the dollar) dampened collector enthusiasm with the result that the issues of 1977 and 1978 did not garner much notice. By that time news concerning the development of a reduced-diameter "mini-dollar" attracted a lot of attention.

When the Susan B. Anthony mini-dollars were launched in 1979, the Eisenhower dollars became history. Many numismatists had completed basic sets of dates, mintmarks, and the two metal compositions. Excepting for dedicated specialists who followed the 1974 Hicks article, the obverse and reverse die varieties were generally ignored until the publication of *Walter Breen's Complete Encyclopedia of U.S. and Colonial Coins* in 1988. That book created a sensation. In the first year my company sold more than 10,000 copies.

In the early 1990s when I was writing *Silver Dollars and Trade Dollars of the United States: A Complete Encyclopedia,* I interviewed many collectors, dealers, and researchers. Interest in Ike dollars was lackluster, to coin a pun. Mint State and Proof coins from earlier times continued to trade, but there were relatively few new specialists.

A complete set of basic dates and mintmarks was inexpensive at the time, and many dealers offered them in albums. Write a check, and a few minutes later you owned a complete set. It was my feeling that in the future these coins would be widely collected. By way of analogy, I recall that when I first started my coin business on a part-time basis in 1953, hardly anyone liked Franklin half dollars—the main exceptions being investors who bought bank-wrapped rolls of all coins and never looked at them. Sure enough, by the early 1990s Franklin half dollars had not been made for a long time—since 1963—and they were very popular and enjoyed a strong market as they continue to do today.

This happened with Eisenhower dollars. By the late 1990s they were in great demand, and a subculture had arisen of enthusiasts who examined coins under magnification to find doubled dies, to take notice of the variations in the depiction of Earth, and to otherwise note what differences they could find. The best-selling book by Bill Fivaz and J.T. Stanton, the *Cherrypickers' Guide to Rare Die Varieties,* created a dramatic spurt in interest in the 1990s as did the popular CONECA group (Combined Organizations of Numismatic Error Collectors of America). More specific and with more varieties is a book by John Wexler, *The Authoritative Reference on Eisenhower Dollars,* published in 1998, succeeded in 2007 by a book of the same title, now with three authors, John Wexler, Bill Crawford, and Kevin Flynn. Appendix I of that book, "Important Letters and Documents," includes extensive correspondence to and from Herbert P. Hicks and is a valuable resource. In more recent times the Ike Group has maintained an information-filled Web site at www.ikegroup.info. To this Robert Ezerman, lead author of the 2011 book *Collectible Ike Varieties—Facts, Photos and Theories,* has been a prime contributor. The site includes the Designated Ike Variety Attribution section listing varieties thought to be of interest to specialists. Also included is an illustrated section on fantasy Eisenhower dollars dated 1970 and 1975 made by Daniel Carr, who operates the Moonlight Mint in Colorado.[47]

CONECA has a marvelous Web site, www.varietyvista.com, that lists and describes doubled dies and mintmark variations and gives much other information, much of which has been provided by Dr. James Wiles from his careful and pioneering studies.

Today the formation of a set of Eisenhower dollars of the basic dates and mintmarks, circulation strikes as well as Proofs, is an interesting and affordable pursuit. There are no "impossible" rarities. The more popular and publicized obverse and reverse die varieties range from common to slightly scarce, but all are affordable. Many can be found by cherrypicking at numismatic conventions and in coin shops.

Uncirculated Eisenhower dollars of the various years 1971 to 1978 vary in sharpness from issue to issue. Most Eisenhower dollars that have circulated, such as those used in the Nevada casinos, are rather dull in appearance and, to state it bluntly, are unattractive. There is no particular reason to collect them, in view of Mint State coins being inexpensive. For the most part, the best specimens are represented by Proofs or by hand-selected high-grade Mint State coins.

A degree of connoisseurship is required to build a high-quality set. Eisenhower dollars produced for collectors—including Proofs and those sold in Mint sets—tend to be available in better grades, virtually as issued, which for Proof means PF-65 or much finer. However, circulation-strike coins taken from bags are apt to be a different story and are often heavily marked and fairly unattractive, this being particularly true of coins from the first two years.

Putting together a nicely matched MS-65 and PF-65 set can be a challenge, at least with respect to MS-65 coins of certain dates. As the individual date descriptions in this book indicate, there are some truly scarce issues, particularly among those that were not specifically sold to collectors, such as 1971 (scarcest), 1971-D Variety 1 reverse (second scarcest), 1972 Variety 2 reverse (slightly scarce, once considered a rarity), and 1972-D. The circulation-strike 1776–1976 Bicentennial dollars tend to have a lot of bagmarks, but such coins are plentiful in the marketplace and inexpensive, so tracking down an MS-65 or better example will not be difficult.

Due to the demand for registry sets (in which a set with the highest cumulative total of grading numbers wins), some buyers have paid tremendous premiums for certain Ike dollars beyond MS-65. As I warned earlier, use caution in this regard. Grading is a matter of opinion, and there are many MS-66 coins in the marketplace that are not as attractive overall as hand-selected MS–64 or 65 coins. In December 2015 I purchased a certified MS-62 1971-D dollar that was nicer overall than a clearly photographed eBay offering of a certified MS-65 coin. Also see Charles Morgan's comments in chapter 2, and the following remarks written by Morgan in *CoinWeek* on March 21, 2012:

> I stand in defense of Eisenhower dollars because of their endless complexity. It stands today as the greatest achievement in clad coinage in U.S. history. It was the most technically challenging coin ever attempted. Sorry, Saint-Gaudens; your 1907 double eagle was spectacular, but try to churn out eighty million Eisenhower dollars on [old] presses leading to a number of modifications and revisions, some of which are only now being identified by experts—and it is a series like this that calls into question how much experts really know about modern coinage.
>
> Researching the Eisenhower dollar is vital for numismatic historians who want to understand what the post-silver era was like. The Eisenhower dollar was a noble failure. In this respect, it truly is a perfect collectible coin.

1971–1974, Eisenhower, Eagle Reverse

Designer: Frank Gasparro.

Composition, Cupro-Nickel Clad: Outer layers of .750 copper and .250 nickel bonded to an inner core of pure copper.[48]

Composition, Silver Clad: Outer layers of .800 silver and .200 copper bonded to an inner core of .209 silver and .791 copper. Pure silver content: .3161 ounce. 4% tolerance permitted by law. Sometimes called "40% silver" coins, as this is the net precious-metal composition of the alloy.

Weight: *Cupro-nickel clad:* 22.680 grams; *Silver clad:* 24.592 grams.

Diameter: 38.1 mm (1.5 inches).

Edge: Reeded.

1971, Cupro-Nickel Clad

Circulation-strike mintage: 47,799,000

Reverse A.
actual size: 38.1 mm

Availability in Mint State, Reverse A on all: Among the regular-issue dates and mintmarks in the Eisenhower series the 1971 is the second most elusive, after 1971-D Reverse B. At the MS-65 or higher level they are hard to find in relation to the demand for them. As of October 2015 PCGS had certified 833 as MS-65 and 57 as MS-66 with none higher. NGC had certified 677 and 37 respectively.

In terms of basic date and mintmark issues this is the key to a set of high-grade Eisenhower dollars. There are enough MS-65 coins in the marketplace that finding one will be no problem at all. MS-64 coins are very common and cost a fraction of the price of MS-65.

Availability in circulated grades: *VF-20 to AU-58:* This issue is very common in circulated grades. The Treasury made vigorous efforts to put these into circulation. As a general statement, circulated Ikes are rarely collected as Mint State coins are readily available.

Characteristics of striking: These are of average striking quality. They are frequently seen with some obverse design weakness.

Charles Morgan commentary: Philadelphia began minting the 1971 Ike dollar within days of the coin going into production in Denver. The large-format cupro-nickel–clad dollar coin was struck up on World War II–era presses; the results were less than complimentary to Frank Gasparro's design. Evidence of striking weakness can often be noted in the prevalence of annealing chatter (the star field of crisscross cuts on a planchet that are imparted on the coin during the planchet making process). Even on the most desirable Ike dollars, these marks will be visible to the naked eye on Eisenhower's jawline and cheek. Another feature of Ike dollars struck in 1971 and 1972 is die sink, which renders the far left portion of IN GOD WE TRUST flat and lifeless.

Notes: The circulation-strike 1971 Eisenhower dollars from all three mints were *not* sold in 1971 Mint sets offered for sale for $3.50 to collectors. Acquisition was by a catch-as-catch-can basis, although dealers in modern coins stocked many. Dollars were sold separately for $3 each (see introductory information). None had been handled with particular care at the mints, with the result that most showed handling and bagmarks and graded MS-63 or lower.

About 478 obverse dies and 239 reverses were made, and most were probably used.[49]

	EF-40	MS-63	MS-65	MS-66
1971, Cupro-Nickel Clad	$2	$5	$150	$1,200

1971-D, Cupro-Nickel Clad

Circulation-strike mintage: 68,587,424

Reverse A.
actual size: 38.1 mm

1971-D, Reverse A: This is the standard reverse also used on 1971 Philadelphia Mint dollars. An irregular shape can be seen in the northern Gulf of Mexico, and certain other details slightly differ. It is called *Variety 2* in some listings, although it was the first variety made.

Availability in Mint State, Reverse A: The 1971-D is slightly scarce in the context of Ike dollars. MS-65 and higher coins are the third scarcest of the early issues, after the 1971-D, Reverse B and Philadelphia issue. Enough exist, however, that they are readily available. MS-64 coins are slightly scarce, and lower Mint State levels are common. Many are heavily bagmarked. As of October 2015 PCGS had certified 3,317 as MS-65; 1,001 as MS-66; and 21 as MS-67. NGC had certified 1,369 as MS-65; 631 as MS-66; and 45 as MS-67. Note that the grading services have not differentiated the two reverse varieties.

Availability in circulated grades, Reverse A: *VF-20 to AU-58:* Very common. The Treasury made vigorous efforts to put these into circulation. Many were used in Nevada casinos.

Characteristics of striking: These are usually sharp, although weakly struck examples are numerous. Sharp strikes can be located with regularity. The overall quality of this issue is above average.

Charles Morgan commentary: Throughout the entire run of the Eisenhower dollar series, the Denver Mint bettered the Philadelphia Mint in the quality of coins it struck for circulation. This holds true for all series of coins, from the Lincoln cent through to the Ike dollar. Of all of the D-Mint coins in the Ike series, the 1971-D and the 1976-D [Reverse A] are by far the nicest coins struck for circulation. The die-sink issue that plagues the 1971 also affects the 1971-D, however, it is possible to find exceptional Ike dollars from this issue in high numerical grades and very few if any detracting marks with die sink. Several PCGS-graded MS-67 coins exhibit this feature.

Special finish: The National Numismatic Collection has two "Special Mint Set" finish coins.

Notes: Production of Eisenhower dollars at the Denver Mint began on February 3, 1971. The author can locate no record of a first-strike ceremony, if there was one. Presumably many of the early issues had the Variety 1 reverse. There was a great demand for dollar-sized coins from the Nevada casinos. It is believed that many if not most of the cupro-nickel–clad dollar coins used in the gaming houses in that state were from the Denver Mint.

Approximately 686 obverse dies and 343 reverses were prepared.

1971-D, Reverse B: This reverse is different from all others in the Eisenhower series. Nicknamed the "Friendly Eagle," because there is no brow line over the eye of the national bird, this variety is most easily distinguished by the more nearly round shape of the northern Gulf of Mexico. Also, the Earth is rounder and the islands below Florida are shaped differently. James Sego has estimated that about 1 in 32 1971-D Ikes is of this variety, which gives an estimated mintage of about 2,000,000 coins out of the total given. Other estimates range from about 500,000 coins upward. Fivaz-Stanton-C1-1971D-901; CONECA: 1971-D, RDV-006.

Rob Ezerman commentary: Evaluating this variety seems to be especially difficult for third-party graders. The dies seemed to deteriorate rapidly so many Friendly Eagle varieties (FEVs) have strange features. Also, the Friendly Eagle dollars seem to have had a tendency to bond with whatever planchet and die cleaning fluids were in use on the old presses that stamped out the FEVs (my theory, no proof) so a substantial minority of FEVs look frankly corroded, except it's not corrosion, it's a bonded chemical toning that looks like corrosion.[50]

Availability in Mint State, Reverse B: The Reverse B in Mint State is very scarce and is the most elusive of the *Guide Book*–listed Ike dollars. This variety was not recognized by PCGS or NGC until 2015, giving the possibility that cherrypicking among "regular" 1971-D dollars from these services might yield some with Reverse B. ANACS does list them, but not many ANACS coins have been publicized in cataloged auctions. Listings on eBay often include them. Most that have been identified have been through the efforts of the Ike Group and other specialists. The *Collectible Die Varieties: Facts, Photos, and Theories,* by Rob Ezerman and associates devotes chapter 1 to this issue. Probably the number of Mint State coins in existence is fewer than 100,000 and the number in MS-65 grade or higher fewer than 10,000 or 5,000. Many of these are, shall I say, *miserable* in aesthetic appeal (see Rob Ezerman commentary). In some instances a certified MS-63 coin will be of finer overall quality than an MS-66. Cherrypicking for quality is the order of the day.

These are listed in *A Guide Book of United States Coins* as 1971-D Variety 1, beginning with the 2016 edition. With this publicity the elusive issue will in time no doubt increase in popularity.

Availability in circulated grades, Reverse B: *VF-20 to AU-58:* Examples of this coin are scarce in the context of Ike dollars; probably fewer than 100,000 are in existence. These sell at a modest premium in coin shops and on eBay, but are not valuable enough to be listed in cataloged auctions.

Peg Leg variety: Some circulation strikes lack the serifs on the upright of the R in LIBERTY. "Peg Leg" varieties occur for a number of other Eisenhower dollar dates and mintmarks as well. It is one of six Peg Leg dollars listed and priced on the Ike Group Web site.

	EF-40	MS-63	MS-65	MS-66
1971-D, Cupro-Nickel Clad, Reverse A	$3	$5	$125	$300

	EF-40	MS-63	MS-65	MS-66
1971-D, Cupro-Nickel Clad, Reverse B	$2	$5	$60	$150

1971-S, Silver Clad

Circulation-strike mintage: 6,868,530[51]

Proof mintage: 4,265,234

Availability in Mint State, Reverse A: These are very common in lower

Reverse A.
actual size: 38.1 mm

Mint State levels, as they were sold at a premium to collectors and others, and most still exist today. Most surviving coins are in this category and have many bag marks. Very little care was taken at the Mint during the minting and packaging stage and many coins were left marked and unattractive. This did not sit well with the collectors who paid a premium for these pieces. MS-65 and higher coins are scarce in relation to the demand for them.

Characteristics of striking, Reverse A: The Reverse A is usually seen with problems. It is possibly the most poorly struck issue in the series.

Charles Morgan commentary: The 1971-S circulation-strike Ikes were shipped in bags from the San Francisco Mint to a processing facility for packaging. They typically come in grades MS-64 or below, spotted and ugly. I believe that the Mint included a card in the "Blue Packs" of this year to explain to the collectors who paid a premium for the coin that it was struck up just as a circulation strike would have been, warts and all. This and the 1969 Philadelphia-strike quarter dollar stand as two of the worst coin issues struck by the U.S. Mint in the clad era. An indeterminate amount of these Ike dollars have been melted for their silver. I doubt that as many as three million survive, but that is speculation. The 1971-S remains plentiful. This is the toughest silver Mint State Ike to find in high grade.

James Sego commentary: There is a wide variance of quality even for graded specimens in MS-65 and above. True Superb Gems (MS-67) are very scarce in the marketplace even though the populations are relatively high. The grading services seem to be one-half point more lenient on this issue.[52]

Notes: For the entirety of 1971-S Ike coinage, there were approximately 69 obverse circulation-strike dies prepared and 35 for the reverse.

1971-S, Reverse A, Doubled Die Obverse: Several varieties of 1971-S coins are known with IN GOD WE TRUST doubled.

1971-S, Peg Leg, Reverse C: Those with Type III or the "Peg Leg" polished-die obverse are in the minority, perhaps 30.[53] FS-S1-1971S-401; CONECA: 1971-S, ODV-002; DDO-09.

James Sego commentary: This variety typically comes slightly prooflike on the obverse with typical Mint State surfaces on the reverse. It is a very difficult coin to find in high grades of MS-66 and above.[54]

1971-S, Silver-Clad, Mint State, Repunched Mintmark: Prominent remnants of an earlier, lighter S mintmark are seen partially extending northwest from the final mintmark. FS-S1-1971S-501; CONECA RPM-001.

Possible prototype: What has been called a possible prototype 1971-S dollar is described on the Ike Group Web site and in the 2011 book, *Collectible Die Varieties: Facts, Photos, and Theories.* There are some slight variations from the usually seen 1971-S, especially on the obverse.

Proofs, Reverse A: Reverse A Proofs have the low relief and are very rare. This variety was discovered by Andy Oskam in a rare wood-grain box with a golden Presidential Seal and a facsimile of President Richard M. Nixon's signature on the cover.[55] It was publicized in 2007, by which time two other examples had been found. Since then several others have been located, but the variety remains rare.

Proofs, Reverse C: Reverse C Proof coins are common; most can be found at PF-65 and higher.

Charles Morgan commentary: In 2013, a 1971-S Proof Eisenhower dollar appeared on eBay in a brown box that was very different from the typical Brown Pack Ike box. This box had a large seal of the President of the United States and a facsimile signature of President Richard Nixon in gilt. The coin was apparently packaged for VIPs, although I have found no record to confirm this. The seller claimed the coin was presented at a ceremony honoring Mamie Eisenhower. The coin inside was unusual as it was a Proof 1971-S with a circulation-strike die used for the reverse. It sold for $140. This muling of a Proof obverse and a circulation-strike reverse is extremely rare.

Notes: Proofs had approximately 1,706 obverse dies prepared and 1,219 for the reverse.

1971-S, Silver-Clad Proof, Doubled Die Obverse, Reverse C: This variety has a lower relief than the following entry. Several doubled-die obverses are known with IN GOD WE TRUST doubled; the strength of the doubling varies. FS-S1-1971S–103 and 106; CONECA: DDO–003 and 006.

	EF-40	MS-63	MS-65	MS-66	PF-65	PF-67Cam	PF-68DC
1971-S, Silver Clad	$5	$12	$25	$40	$12	$15	$25

1972, Cupro-Nickel Clad

Circulation-strike mintage: 75,890,000

Availability in Mint State, Reverse A (often called Variety 1): This variety is very common, nearly but

Reverse E.
actual size: 38.1 mm

not quite as much so as Reverse E. By October 2015 PCGS had certified 1,295 as MS-65, 242 as MS-66, and 4 as MS-67.

Charles Morgan commentary: Most coins are lacking in luster and are mushily struck. MS-63 or MS-64 is the typical grade.

Availability in circulated grades, Reverse A: Reverse A coins are very common in circulated grades.

Characteristics of striking, Reverse A: Striking of this issue varies, but sharp coins can be found.

Notes: The second year of cupro-nickel–clad Eisenhower dollar coinage saw tens of millions more coins issued from the Philadelphia Mint. In fact, the "mother mint" produced nearly twice as many Ikes this year than in the first year of the series. 1972 Mint sets, sold by the Treasury for $3.50 per set, did not contain Eisenhower dollars.

In the East, Eisenhower dollars were available at banks, but were rarely seen in everyday circulation.

For the entirety of 1972 Philadelphia Ike coinage approximately 759 circulation-strike obverse dies were prepared and 380 for the reverse.

Availability in Mint State, Reverse D (often called Variety 2): This is the scarcest of the three varieties, about twice as scarce as the other two. Most are found in lower Mint State levels with bagmarks. Many certified MS-65 coins are "low end" in quality. Herbert P. Hicks, who discovered the variety, stated the following: "In researching the matter further, I received a letter from a prominent numismatist quoting a Mint official who should know, saying 'Proof dies were accidentally sent to the coining room in Philadelphia.' Also, this official speculated on how long it would take collectors to discover this since the strikes were 'considerably different.' Please note the use of the plural 'dies' and the use of the term 'considerably different.'"[56] Most were distributed in and around eastern Pennsylvania and Delaware. This was not an issue included in mint sets. By October 2015 PCGS had certified 435 as MS-65 and 21 as MS-66. As for most other high-grade scarce varieties this numbers probably include many resubmissions. Simply stated, this is a rare issue in conservatively graded MS-65 or higher with good eye appeal.

James Sego commentary: This is the rarest Ike in Superb Gem condition in the entire series.[57]

Availability in circulated grades, Reverse D: Reverse D coins are scarcer than their Reverse E counterparts. These and other circulated coins are not widely collected due to the inexpensive nature of lower-range Mint State pieces.

Characteristics of striking, Reverse D: Striking on this issue varies, but sharp coins can be found.

Rob Ezerman commentary on Reverse D dollars: In my quest for clashed Ikes and other varieties, recognized and not yet recognized, in years past I searched maybe twenty bags of circulated Ikes gathering dust in brick and mortar coin shops on local and east coast trips. These bags were the dumping grounds for all the useless Ikes coin dealers often have to purchase from eager customers. The bags were uniformly grungy, black with dirt and whatever else. In those bags I found about 20 1972 Reverse D Ikes, half of which looked like possible MS-64s per PCGS grading standards. Understand that the average Reverse D may appear dull in spite of having no markers of sufficient wear to drop it into circulated grades. I sent in the best twelve to PCGS over time and received six MS-63s and six MS-64s, nicely sealed and labeled in their pristine plastic holders in spite of their humble and definitely circulated origins. I sold them all for $100–$200 each and helped fund my coin research.[58]

Availability in Mint State, Reverse E (often called Variety 3): In *lower* Mint State grades this is the most common of the three varieties of this year and mint. This is the general style reverse used in later years except for the Bicentennial coins. Most have many bagmarks, as no effort was made to preserve them for collectors. Enough MS-65 coins exist, however, that finding one will be no problem. By October 2015 PCGS had certified 1,295 as MS-65, 242 as MS-66, and 4 as MS-67. NGC does not differentiate the three varieties for this year.

James Sego commentary: This is the second toughest variety to find in MS-65 or better grade.[59]

Availability in circulated grades, Reverse E: *VF-20 to AU-58:* These are very common in circulated grades. The Treasury made strong efforts to put them into circulation.

Characteristics of striking, Reverse E: Striking of this issue varies, but sharp coins can be found.

	EF-40	MS-63	MS-65	MS-66
1972, Cupro-Nickel Clad, Reverse A	$2	$5	$150	$7,000

	EF-40	MS-63	MS-65	MS-66
1972, Cupro-Nickel Clad, Reverse D	$5	$100	$1,500	$12,000

	EF-40	MS-63	MS-65	MS-66
1972, Cupro-Nickel Clad, Reverse E	$3	$5	$125	$1,000

1972-D, Cupro-Nickel Clad

Circulation-strike mintage: 92,548,511

Reverse A.
actual size: 38.1 mm

Availability in Mint State, Reverse A on all: This issue in Mint State is common overall. Most are in lower Mint State grades, although thousands exist in MS-65 and finer. Occasionally a 1,000-coin bag turns up, but such events are now few and far between. MS-67 and higher coins are rare, as is true for other early circulation-strike years. This is the last issue of the Eisenhower dollar not sold in Mint sets by the government, thus they are scarcer than they would have been if they had been sold directly to collectors.

Availability in circulated grades: *VF-20 to AU-58:* These are very common in circulated grades. The Treasury made vigorous efforts to put them into circulation. Many were used in Nevada casinos.

Characteristics of striking: The 1972-D is usually found well struck and is unusual in this respect, in comparison to the Philadelphia coins.

Rob Ezerman commentary: Mike Lantz, the Denver die setter who went on to lower-level management in the Ike era, is fond of saying that Denver always pushed harder to make quotas and with better looking Ikes than Philadelphia. However, at the same time

Denver had to stretch the dies shipped to them by the Philadelphia die shop by erasing clashed dies as best they could. Philadelphia seemed to pull and discard problematic dies sooner than Denver with their in-house die shop, assuming Philadelphia had as many clash episodes. Philadelphia was more attentive to spotting errors, possibly because Gasparro lived there and they had more politically important visitors than Denver.[60]

Notes: In a further attempt to circulate the Eisenhower dollar, nearly 100 million specimens were struck at Denver this year. Many did circulate for a time, particularly in the Western gambling halls, but most eventually disappeared into bank vaults or the hands of the public.

Approximately 926 obverse dies and 463 reverses were prepared.

1972-D, Doubled Die: This variety has doubling on the 1 in 1972, on the G in GOD, and all around the rim. CONECA: 1972-D, DDO-001/DDR-001.

1972-D, Struck in silver (error planchet): "The Denver Mint silver strikes happened when the San Francisco Assay Office shipped rejected cupro-nickel–clad Proof planchets to Denver to be coined as circulation strikes, and some silver planchets got in by mistake. The Assay Office had never used cupro-nickel–clad dollar planchets before 1973."[61]

	EF-40	MS-63	MS-65	MS-66
1972-D, Cupro-Nickel Clad	$2	$5	$50	$175

1972-S, Silver Clad

Circulation-strike mintage: 2,193,056

Proof mintage: 1,811,631

Reverse D.
actual size: 38.1 mm

Availability in Mint State, Reverse D on all: A sharply struck MS-65 or finer example of this date can be readily located by the interested collector without too much difficulty; one of the few dates in the early range of the series this can be said for.

Charles Morgan commentary: Most of the coins of this issue were struck with a beautiful satin finish—a tacit acknowledgement of the subpar effort from the year before.

Characteristics of striking: Usually very well stuck. Many have a beautiful satin finish.

Rob Ezerman commentary: After the debacle of shipping the 1971-S, silver-clad Specimen Ikes to San Francisco by rail in 1,000-coin bags, the Mint shipped the 1972-S, silver-clad Specimen Ikes in 20-coin plastic tubes. That plus better handling at the Mint resulted in the highest quality silver clad Ikes of the series. For anyone looking for a single high-quality Ike for a type collection, look through 1972 "Blue Ike envelopes" at shows (you may have to ask the dealer) and you have a decent shot at finding a handsome MS-67 Ike for $5–10. Of course, this 2015 comment may change if the market advances.[62]

James Sego commentary: This is the most common Ike dollar to find in high grades.[63]

Notes: All 1972-S dollars are Peg Leg by design. Six varieties are listed and priced on the Ike Group Web site. Approximately 22 obverse circulation-strike dies were prepared and 11 for the reverse.

Proofs, Reverse D: Proof coins with Reverse D are easily enough found.

1972-S, Proof, Doubled Die Obverse: Nearly all are gems. Priced at high levels on the Ike Group website. This is an obvious candidate for cherrypicking. FS-S1-1972S-101; CONECA: DDP-009.

Notes: The second year of 40% silver Eisenhower dollar production saw a smaller mintage of Uncirculated and Proof coins. The mintage figure of the Uncirculated version dropped nearly 4.7 million coins, while the Proof mintage figure dropped by almost 2.5 million coins. As before, Proofs were sold separately from the regular Proof sets. Clearly, Eisenhower dollars were no longer a novelty.

About 725 obverse proof dies were prepared and 518 for the reverse.

	EF-40	MS-63	MS-65	MS-66	PF-65	PF-67Cam	PF-68DC
1972-S, Silver Clad		$12	$15	$20	$12	$15	$25

1973, Cupro-Nickel Clad

Circulation-strike mintage: 2,000,056

actual size: 38.1 mm

Availability in Mint State: No effort at the Mint was made to handle these carefully, and nearly all have bagmarks, from light to extensive, including those sold in mint sets. As a result only a small percentage are MS-65 or higher. By October 2015 PCGS had certified 1,358 as MS-65 and 102 as MS-66. NGC had certified 462 as MS-65, 27 as MS-66, and 1 as MS-67. It is to be remembered for all Eisenhower dollars that only a tiny percentage of each mintage has ever been submitted to PCGS or NGC for certification.

Rob Ezerman commentary: Ikes have more than their share of dings, nicks, and scratches, but more than that some planchets seemed to have had an annealing problem: the best (or worst) examples are the 1973-P and 1976-P Type 1 Ikes whose annealing drum-planchet damage was not struck out in the coin press as is usually the case. These Ikes look like they received significant post-mint damage but that's not the case—the damage is mostly from transiting the annealing chamber.[64]

Availability in circulated grades: *EF-40 to AU-58:* These are quite rare in circulated grades, but there is only a limited market as most buyers seek Mint State coins.

Characteristics of striking: This issue is usually well struck and is seen with excellent luster.[65]

Notes: The total mintage is projected at 2,000,056, but 230,798 unsold pieces were reportedly melted, leaving a net total of 1,769,258. The 1973 cupro-nickel Eisenhower dollars from the Philadelphia Mint were not made for general circulation, and were intended to be included only in this year's Mint sets (which had all coins from the cent to the dollar and sold for $6). The Mint was overly optimistic concerning the number it would sell, and 230,798 unsold pieces were later recycled, per a Mint statement, but some were released into commercial channels.[66] In the early 2000s collector Brian Vaile found a mint bag of 1,000 coins put into circulation from which a dealer had removed a hundred or so.[67]

Approximately 20 obverse dies and 10 reverses were prepared.

	EF-40	MS-63	MS-65	MS-66
1973, Cupro-Nickel Clad		$12	$75	$1,000

1973-D, Cupro-Nickel Clad

actual size: 38.1 mm

Circulation-strike mintage: 2,000,000

Availability in Mint State: Many thousands exist, including enough in MS-65 or slightly finer grades to satisfy numismatic demand. As a class these are usually found in higher grades than are their Philadelphia Mint counterparts.

Availability in circulated grades: *EF-40 to AU-58:* These are scarce in circulated grades, but aren't numismatically important.

Characteristics of striking: The striking of this issue is usually good. They are nearly always more attractive than Philadelphia Mint dollars of this year and the mint luster is usually well above average.[68]

Special finish: The National Numismatic Collection has two "Special Mint Set" finish coins.

Notes: The total mintage was 2,000,000, of which 1,769,258 were sold as part of sets, and the balance was destroyed. By this time casinos had enough Eisenhower dollars because they were going out of use and were being replaced by colored chips.

About 20 obverse dies and 10 reverses were prepared.

	EF-40	MS-63	MS-65	MS-66
1973-D, Cupro-Nickel Clad		$12	$50	$400

1973-S, Cupro-Nickel Clad

Circulation-strike mintage: *See planchet error below.*

Proof mintage: 2,760,339

actual size: 38.1 mm

Proofs: Cupro-nickel–clad proofs can be found easily enough.

Charles Morgan commentary: Many of these coins have been certified as PF-69 Deep Cameo (DCAM). By late 2015 many earned the once-thought- impossible PF-70 grade, indicating that interpretations of the standards for 70s in the series have been relaxed in recent years. Further, the frosting on the reverse areas in relief—the Moon surface and the distant Earth—is usually unsatisfactory.

Notes: For the entirety of 1973-S Ike coinage, there were approximately 1,104 obverse dies prepared and 789 for the reverse.

James Sego commentary: In late 1973 there was a great speculative flurry in these coins, rising up to $150 or so each, after which the price went down.[69]

1973-S, Cupro-Nickel–Clad circulation strike (planchet error): At least three are known; one is certified as MS-67 (NGC).[70] As of July 2012 there were three reported, one of which had been graded MS-66 by PCGS.[71] One coin sold for $19,925 in June 2013.

James Sego commentary: The third coin is graded AU-58 (PCGS); a customer of mine owns the coin. These errors look like silver coins at first glance, and even the edges look like silver. I am not sure why this is. Weighing these coins is key to their authentication.[72]

	PF-65	PF-67Cam	PF-68DC
1973-S, Cupro-Nickel Clad	$12	$15	$30

1973-S, Silver Clad

Circulation-strike mintage: 1,883,140

Proof mintage: 1,013,646

Proofs: Proof coins are readily available in high grades. Although the mintage is low in the

actual size: 38.1 mm

Eisenhower dollar context, there are more than enough to satisfy numismatic demand.

Charles Morgan commentary on circulation strikes: This is a tricky date for high grades. Many have a finish that lacks the desirability of the 1972 and the 1974. These coins physically do not resemble those two dates when seen in hand. Spotting is common on these coins. MS-66 and MS-67 coins are plentiful, attractive MS-68 coins are not.

Notes: The 1973-S, 40% silver circulation strikes and Proof coins have the lowest-mintage figures of all the 40% silver Eisenhower dollars. Because of this, the 1973-S, Proof, 40% silver Eisenhower dollar is generally regarded as the key date in the series.

	EF-40	MS-63	MS-65	MS-66	PF-65	PF-67Cam	PF-68DC
1973-S, Silver Clad		$15	$20	$40	$35	$37	$50

1974, Cupro-Nickel Clad

actual size: 38.1 mm

Circulation-strike mintage: 27,366,000

Availability in Mint State: This issue us very common in Mint State, mostly in grades below MS-65. MS-65 coins, while in the minority, are readily available in comparison to the demand for them. Carefully-graded MS-66 and higher coins are somewhat scarce, Charles Morgan reports.

Availability in circulated grades: *EF-40 to AU-58:* These aren't seen often, but they not rare.

Characteristics of striking: The striking on this issue is usually good and with excellent mint luster.

Notes: Mint sets sold at $6.00 each contained one each of all circulation-strike issues, cent through the Eisenhower dollar; 1,975,981 sets were sold.

Approximately 274 obverse dies and 137 reverses were prepared.

	EF-40	MS-63	MS-65	MS-66
1974, Cupro-Nickel Clad	$2	$5	$75	$750

1974-D, Cupro-Nickel Clad

actual size: 38.1 mm

Circulation-strike mintage: 45,517,000

Availability in Mint State: This issue is very common in Mint State. Most are less than MS-65, although enough in the latter grade exist that they are readily available. Tens of thousands were in the Big Sky Hoard marketed by Littleton Coin Company beginning in 2011.[73]

Across the board, grade for grade, the Denver coins have better eye appeal than do the Philadelphia issues.

Availability in circulated grades: *EF-40 to AU-58:* These are common and of little numismatic interest.

Characteristics of striking: The striking on this issue is usually good and with nice mint luster.

Notes: Some of the 1974-D coins were minted in calendar year 1975, technically making them restrikes. However, in recent decades the Mint has paid little attention to the nicety of dating coins in the year in which they were made. Numerous issues, especially commemoratives and other collector issues, have been "pre-struck" or restruck.

Approximately 456 obverse dies and 228 reverses were prepared.

1974-D, Struck in silver (error planchet): The first example is said to have been discovered by a croupier at a Las Vegas blackjack table.

James Sego commentary: Today about 25 to 30 coins of this variety are known. These are almost always in lower grades with average sharpness at best. The finest known is MS-65.[74]

Peg Leg variety: Some circulation strikes lack the serifs on the upright of the R in LIBERTY. It is one of six Peg Leg dollars listed and priced on the Ike Group Web site

	EF-40	MS-63	MS-65	MS-66
1974-D, Cupro-Nickel Clad	$2	$5	$40	$150

1974-S, Cupro-Nickel Clad

Proof mintage: 2,612,568

Proofs: Cupro-nickel–clad proof coins are readily available. The frosting on the areas on the reverse is often unsatisfactory, including coins in high grades.

actual size: 38.1 mm

Notes: Approximately 1,045 obverse dies and 747 reverses were prepared.

	PF-65	PF-67Cam	PF-68DC
1974-S, Cupro-Nickel Clad, Proof	$10	$15	$30

1974-S, Silver Clad

Circulation-strike mintage: 1,900,156

Proof mintage: 1,306,539

actual size: 38.1 mm

Circulation strikes: The U.S. Mint office in San Francisco began accepting orders for Uncirculated dollars at $3 each, limit five per person, on August 1, 1974. On September 26 the Mint announced it would discontinue accepting orders. These are common as all were purchased by buyers who paid a premium and kept them. However, superb gems of good overall quality are elusive.[75]

Proofs: Order cards for Proof dollars were mailed by the U.S. Mint on April 22, 1974, and orders were accepted beginning on May 1, 1974. The price per coin was $10 with a limit of five per person. On June 20 the Mint announced it would not accept any further orders after June 28. Today these are common.

Charles Morgan commentary: This is the second nicest Blue Pack Ike in the series, behind the 1972-S, referring to color of the circular labels in the original containers, of which many were discarded. 1974-S Brown Packs tend to develop colorful toning due to a trace chemical found in the red velvet packaging. This chemical does not appear to be present on the 1971–1973 issues.

Notes: The 1974-S Eisenhower dollar is the last date in the series that features the original reverse design (commemorating the landing of Apollo 11) in the 40% silver format. There were no Ikes dated 1975, and the 1776–1976 double-dated commemorative issue features a rendition of the Liberty Bell superimposed on the Moon. By the time the original reverse design was resumed in 1977, the 40% silver format had been discontinued.

Approximately 19 obverse circulation-strike dies were prepared and 10 for the reverse. Proofs had about 523 obverse dies and 373 reverses prepared.

	EF-40	MS-63	MS-65	MS-66	PF-65	PF-67Cam	PF-68DC
1974-S, Silver Clad		$12	$20	$25	$15	$20	$30

1975–1976, Eisenhower, Bicentennial Reverse

Designer: Frank Gasparro (obverse); Dennis R. Williams (reverse). Reverse modified by Philip Fowler.

Composition, Cupro-Nickel Clad: Outer layers of .750 copper and .250 nickel bonded to an inner core of pure copper.[48]

Composition, Silver Clad: Outer layers of .800 silver and .200 copper bonded to an inner core of .209 silver and .791 copper. Pure silver content: .3161 ounce. 4% tolerance permitted by law. Sometimes called "40% silver" coins, as this is the net precious-metal composition of the alloy.

Weight: *Cupro-nickel clad:* 22.680 grams; *Silver clad:* 24.592 grams.

Diameter: 38.1 mm (1.5 inches).

Edge: Reeded.

1776–1976, Cupro-Nickel Clad

Circulation-strike mintage, Variety 1: 4,019,000

Circulation-strike mintage, Variety 2: 113,318,000

Variety 2.
actual size: 38.1 mm

Availability in Mint State, Variety 1: Variety 1 is by far the scarcer of the two varieties in a relative sense. All known mint sets sold to collectors had Variety 1. However, as more than four million were struck they are common today in just about any grade desired through MS-66, but see attached commentary. Most coins are in lower grades and are bagmarked, often heavily.

Charles Morgan commentary: The Variety 1 is scarce in conservatively graded MS-65 and rare in MS-66. Loosely graded MS-65 coins are easily available as are MS-66s, often overgraded by a point or two. Be super careful.

James Sego commentary: This issue, in my opinion, is the most difficult to find in superb gem condition—well struck, free of marks, and with rich luster. Many of the certified MS-66 coins, I estimate 20% of the total, are misattributed Variety 1 coins, thus artificially inflating the population reports.[76]

Rob Ezerman commentary (repeated from the 1973 listing): Ikes have more than their share of dings, nicks, and scratches, but more than that some planchets seemed to have had an annealing problem: the best (or worst) examples are the 1973-P and 1976-P Type 1 Ikes whose annealing drum-planchet damage was not struck out in the coin press as is usually the case. These Ikes look like they received significant post-mint damage but that's not the case—the damage is mostly from transiting the annealing chamber.[77]

Availability in circulated grades, Variety 1: Variety 1 coins are common in circulated grades.

Characteristics of striking: Striking on this issue varies, but is usually good. They are typically seen with good luster.

Notes: Approximately 41 obverse dies and 21 reverses were prepared.

Availability in Mint State, Variety 2: Variety 2 coins are very common, including in any grade desired through MS-66.

Charles Morgan commentary: The typical Variety 2 is an all-round nicer coin than a Variety 1. MS-66 coins, while not common, are often seen. Obverse designs of the Variety 1 and Variety 2 are slightly different. This is a fact that usually goes unnoticed in published descriptions of the coins.

Availability in circulated grades, Variety 2: These coins are common in circulated grades.

Characteristics of striking: Striking of this issue varies, but is usually good.

Silver-Clad Proof without Mintmark, Variety 2: One coin is known to exist in Proof format, silver clad, but is lacking the S mintmark typically seen on Proofs of this year. Presumably, it was struck at the Philadelphia Mint where all of the Bicentennial dies were made. The author saw in 1976 a mintmarkless Proof obverse and an accompanying reverse-up coin (presumably without mintmark) at a Mint ceremony, but where these are today is unknown. From www.uspatterns.com: "The piece is unique and, according to the *Coin World Comprehensive Catalog & Encyclopedia*, was discovered in a cash register at Woodward and Lothrop Department store in Washington, D.C. in mid-1977. It is said to weigh 383. 25 grains instead of 350 grains, thus it was struck on a 40% silver planchet. Only the single example is known and it was offered in Superior's February 1997 and Bowers and Merena's September 2002 sales."[78]

Notes: Variety 1 dollars are thought to have been struck in calendar year 1975. Approximately 1,134 obverse dies and 567 reverses were prepared for all Philadelphia coins of this year. These figures include the Variety 1 numbers given previously.

This date has the dubious distinction of having the largest mintage in the Eisenhower dollar series. Indeed, it is the only date in the series with a mintage figure above one hundred million pieces, but hardly any ever went into the channels of commerce.

	EF-40	MS-63	MS-65	MS-66
1776–1976, Cupro-Nickel Clad, Variety 1	$2	$6	$200	$1,250

	EF-40	MS-63	MS-65	MS-66
1776–1976, Cupro-Nickel Clad, Variety 2	$2	$5	$30	$150

1776–1976-D, Cupro-Nickel Clad

Circulation-strike mintage, Variety 1: 21,048,710

Circulation-strike mintage, Variety 2: 82,179,564

Variety 1.
actual size: 38.1 mm

Availability in Mint State, Variety 1: Variety 1 coins are very common due to the large number struck, but most are bagmarked. Well-struck MS-65 or finer coins are on the scarce side.

James Sego commentary: In gem Mint State grades this is the most common of the Bicentennial dollars. It is pursued not only by Ike collectors, but is a favorite with type-set enthusiasts as well.[79]

Availability in circulated grades, Variety 1: This issue is very common in circulated grades.

Characteristics of striking: These are usually seen with problems and are considered by some to be the poorest-looking coins in the Eisenhower series.

Notes: Variety 1 dollars are thought to have been struck in calendar year 1975. Approximately 211 obverse dies and 106 reverses were prepared.

1976-D, Struck in silver (error planchet), Variety 1 (tentative listing): Per James Sego: "At one time I thought I saw one in a three-piece Bicentennial set. I now question myself on this, as neither it nor any others have ever surfaced again. Knowing that a Variety 2 silver strike is confirmed, it could have been one of those."[80]

Availability in Mint State, Variety 2: These are even more plentiful than the very common Variety 1. MS-66 and finer coins are common in relation to the demand for them.[81]

Availability in circulated grades, Variety 2: Variety 2 coins are very common.

Characteristics of striking: Many of these coins have striking problems.

Special finish: The National Numismatic Collection has two "Special Mint Set" finish coins.

Notes: Approximately 822 obverse dies and 411 reverses were prepared. Some 1776–1976-D dollars were shipped in 1,000-coin cloth bags imprinted "1975-D."[82]

1976-D, Struck in silver (error planchet), Variety 2: This variety is exceedingly rare, possibly unique. An MS-64 (PCGS) is owned by James Sego.[83]

Peg Leg variety, Variety 2: Some circulation strikes lack the serifs on the upright of the R in LIBERTY. It is one of six Peg Leg dollars listed and priced on the Ike Group Web site.

	EF-40	MS-63	MS-65	MS-66
1776–1976-D, Cupro-Nickel Clad, Variety 1	$2	$5	$50	$200

	EF-40	MS-63	MS-65	MS-66
1776–1976-D, Cupro-Nickel Clad, Variety 2	$2	$5	$30	$60

1776–1976-S, Cupro-Nickel Clad

Proof mintage, Variety 1: 2,845,450

Proof mintage, Variety 2: 4,149,730

Proofs, Variety 1: These are common in high grades as all were bought at a premium and saved.

Variety 1.
actual size: 38.1 mm

Notes: Variety 1 dollars were included in 1975 Proof sets.

Proofs, Variety 2: Variety 2 coins are common in high grades as all were bought at a premium and saved.

Notes: Approximately 1,138 obverse dies and 813 reverses were prepared for both varieties. Variety 2 dollars were included in the Proof sets that were actually minted in 1976, along with cents, nickels, and dimes dated 1976, and quarters and half dollars that bore the dual date 1776–1976. A variety of proof-only coins with thin, tall, oval letter O's were issued in regular six-piece Proof sets of 1976. The release for this set ended July 22, 1976.

	PF-65	PF-67Cam	PF-68DC
1776–1976-S, Cupro-Nickel Clad, Variety 1, Proof	$12	$15	$30

	PF-65	PF-67Cam	PF-68DC
1776–1976-S, Cupro-Nickel Clad, Variety 2, Proof	$8	$12	$30

1776–1976-S, Silver Clad

Circulation-strike mintage, Variety 1: 11,000,000

Proof mintage, Variety 1: 4,000,000

Availability in Mint State, Variety 1: These were sold only as part of Mint Sets. The mintage was an incredible 11,000,000 of which 4,294,081 were distributed.

Variety 1.
actual size: 38.1 mm

James Sego commentary: This is a very tough coin to find in ultra-high Mint State levels.[84]

Notes: Approximately 43 circulation-strike obverse dies and 43 reverses were prepared. The open areas and shallow relief of the reverse made the Bicentennial dollars more susceptible to gaining nicks and contact marks.[85]

The 40% silver Eisenhower dollar made its final appearance this year as a regular-issue coinage, with Uncirculated and Proof specimens made available to collectors in the three-piece Bicentennial sets. The authorizing law required the Mint to finish striking the silver Bicentennials by July 4, 1976. Up through mid-June or so they were struck in small quantities and packaged immediately to avoid handling and/or spotting. With time running out and sales poor, the Mint decided to coin the last 7 million or so Uncirculated sets on high-speed presses and bag the coins against unlikely future sales. However, sales of unsold stored coins jumped up in 1979 when silver shot up and the .53792 troy oz. of silver in one set became worth more than the bulk-sale price, and packaging resumed. The 40% silver dollars of this year are all of the Variety 1 style. Beginning the next year, 1977, the silver would disappear once more from America's coinage, not to reappear until the commemorative issues of the early 1980s. Coinage was overly optimistic, and it is believed that many were melted, although exact figures are not known.

Silver-Clad dollars without Mintmark, Variety 1: Certain sets of silver-clad Bicentennial coins, perhaps three sets, were made without an S mintmark. No such sets are known today. In 1977 Thomas DeLorey, then on the staff of *Coin World*, viewed a mintmarkless silver-content dollar found earlier that year in a cash register in a Woodward & Lathrop Department Store in Washington, D.C.[86]

James Sego commentary: This coin is currently in a PF-64 (PCGS) holder. I was able to examine the coin in the early 1990s and study it carefully before it was placed in a holder. It has a Variety 1 reverse.[87]

Proofs, Variety 1: Variety 1 Proofs are common in high grades as all were bought at a premium and saved.

Notes: On January 19, 1975, the Mint announced a reduction from $15 to $12 for 40% silver Bicentennial Proof sets and the removal of order limits. The 40% silver Eisenhower dollar made its final appearance this year as a regular issue coinage, with Uncirculated and Proof specimens made available to collectors in the three-piece Bicentennial sets.

Approximately 1,305 obverse dies and 933 reverses were prepared.

	EF-40	MS-63	MS-65	MS-66	PF-65	PF-67Cam	PF-68DC
1776–1976-S, Silver Clad, Variety 1		$15	$20	$30	$15	$20	$35

1977–1978, Eisenhower, Eagle Reverse Resumed

Designer: Frank Gasparro.

Composition, Cupro-Nickel Clad: Outer layers of .750 copper and .250 nickel bonded to an inner core of pure copper.[48]

Composition, Silver Clad: Outer layers of .800 silver and .200 copper bonded to an inner core of .209 silver and .791 copper. Pure silver content: .3161 ounce. 4% tolerance permitted by law. Sometimes called "40% silver" coins, as this is the net precious-metal composition of the alloy.

Weight: *Cupro-nickel clad:* 22.680 grams; *Silver clad:* 24.592 grams.

Diameter: 38.1 mm (1.5 inches).

Edge: Reeded.

1977, Cupro-Nickel Clad

Circulation-strike mintage: 12,596,000

Availability in Mint State: Most 1977 Philadelphia Ikes are bagmarked. MS-65 and higher coins are only a small percentage of the mintage.

actual size: 38.1 mm

Availability in circulated grades: *EF-40 to AU-58:* These are common in circulated grades.

Characteristics of striking: This issue is usually well struck.

James Sego commentary: These are usually seen with good luster. The number of superb gems graded is misleading, as three or four *bags* were submitted for grading in the last few years. The quality of those pieces is lacking, even though the assigned grades are high. Be very careful when purchasing a high-grade specimen as the holders say nothing about overall desirability.[88]

Notes: With the passing of the Bicentennial celebration, the original reverse design was restored to the Eisenhower dollar and would remain in use through the end of the series in 1978. From this point forward, the few remaining varieties in the series would all be struck in cupro-nickel–clad metal.

Mint sets sold for $7.00 contained one each of all circulation-strike issues, cent through the Eisenhower dollar; 2,006,869 sets were sold.

Approximately 126 obverse dies and 63 reverses were prepared.

	EF-40	MS-63	MS-65	MS-66
1977, Cupro-Nickel Clad	$2	$5	$40	$150

1977-D, Cupro-Nickel Clad

Circulation-strike mintage: 32,983,006

actual size: 38.1 mm

Availability in Mint State: The 1977-D is readily available in Mint State. Most coins found from various sources are in grades below MS-65 and are bagmarked. The exceptions to this general rule are the tens of thousands of Ikes in the Big Sky Hoard marketed by Littleton Coin Company beginning in 2011. [89]

Availability in circulated grades: *EF-40 to AU-58:* These are common in circulated grades.

Characteristics of striking: This issue is usually well struck.

Special finish: The National Numismatic Collection has two "Special Mint Set" finish coins.

Notes: Approximately 330 obverse dies and 165 reverses were prepared.

1977-D, Struck in silver (error planchet): The February 22, 1978, issue of *Coin World* reported the finding of several 1977-D Ikes struck on 40% silver planchets. Subsequently, more were located. These were on rejected blanks intended for S-mint Bicentennials, mistakenly included among nickel-clad blanks shipped from San Francisco to the Denver Mint. About 20 examples are known, and it is no. 65 in *100 Greatest U.S. Modern Coins.*

	EF-40	MS-63	MS-65	MS-66
1977-D, Cupro-Nickel Clad	$2	$5	$40	$175

1977-S, Cupro-Nickel Clad

actual size: 38.1 mm

Proof mintage: 3,251,152

Proofs: These are common; nearly all are in grades from PF-65 upward.

Notes: Approximately 1,300 obverse dies and 929 reverses were prepared.

	PF-65	PF-67Cam	PF-68DC
1977-S, Cupro-Nickel Clad, Proof	$10	$15	$25

1978, Cupro-Nickel Clad

actual size: 38.1 mm

Circulation-strike mintage: 25,702,000

Availability in Mint State: These are very common due to the large number struck. Most examples are MS-64 or lower and have bagmarks. However, enough MS-65 and higher coins survive to supply the demand for them, though minimally bagmarked coins are scarce.

Availability in circulated grades: *EF-40 to AU-58:* This issue is common in circulated grades.

Characteristics of striking: Most coins of this issue are well struck.

Notes: Approximately 257 obverse dies and 129 reverses were prepared. Certain chrome-plated–reverse dies used to make Proofs were placed into service for making circulation strikes after being retired from Proofs.

	EF-40	MS-63	MS-65	MS-66
1978, Cupro-Nickel Clad	$2	$5	$40	$175

1978-D, Cupro-Nickel Clad

Circulation-strike mintage: 33,012,890

Availability in Mint State: This issue is common in Mint State. Most are MS-64 or below and are

actual size: 38.1 mm

bagmarked. Attractive MS-65 and finer coins are in the minority.

James Sego commentary: Of all of the 1977 and 1978 varieties this is the most difficult to find in superb gem grade. As I write these words only one coin exists in certified MS-67, a PCGS coin. I have seen it, and it is of superior quality.[90]

Availability in circulated grades: *EF-40 to AU-58:* These are common in circulated grades.

Characteristics of striking: This issue is usually well struck.

Notes: Approximately 331 obverse dies and 166 reverses were prepared.

Peg Leg variety: Some circulation strikes lack the serifs on the upright of the R in LIBERTY. This is one of six Peg Leg dollars listed and priced on the Ike Group Web site.

	EF-40	MS-63	MS-65	MS-66
1978-D, Cupro-Nickel Clad	$2	$5	$40	$150

1978-S, Cupro-Nickel Clad

Proof mintage: 3,127,781

Proofs: Nearly all coins are in grades from PF-67 upward. These are common enough and are readily available.

actual size: 38.1 mm

Charles Morgan commentary: The Mint changed its procedure of creating cameo finish this year, with the result that nearly all have deep frost on the relief areas. A side-by-side comparison of a 1978-S with any other date of clad Eisenhower dollar will easily demonstrate this.

Notes: Approximately 1,251 obverse dies and 894 reverses were prepared.

	PF-65	PF-67Cam	PF-68DC
1978-S, Cupro-Nickel Clad, Proof	$10	$15	$25

5

5 5 5 5 5 5 5 5 5 5 5

SUSAN B. ANTHONY DOLLARS, 1979–1981; 1999

On May 12, 1975, the Treasury Department commissioned the Research Triangle Institute, a highly accomplished North Carolina non-profit study facility, to examine the panorama of American coinage and make recommendations for the future. The findings, released in early 1976, took 18 months to complete and cost $116,000. Recommendations covered wide territory and included the eventual discontinuation of the cent (to be replaced by a two-cent piece), the abolishment of mintmarks on coins, and the introduction of "a coin larger than the current 25-cent piece but smaller than the 50-cent piece."[1]

In August 1976 the Treasury issued a report, "New Small Dollar Coin—Technical Considerations." This was widely circulated and spawned many articles. The Washington Star Service, a news syndicate, issued a story in the same month August, stating in part:

> The current $1 coin, the Eisenhower dollar, is "too big and bulky; it just doesn't circulate," says James Parker, a spokesman for the U.S. Mint.
>
> Leading the cheers for the new coin are the makers and operators of vending machines, since a 30-cent sandwich or 60-cent pack of cigarettes could be purchased with less fumbling.
>
> "I think a new coin would be good for the whole country as well as our industry," said G. Richard Schreiber of the National Automatic Merchandising Association. "So many things are at a point today where a dollar coin makes sense," he added.
>
> "We've done studies that have proven conclusively that a single-coin purchase will outsell a two coin purchase, that a two-coin purchase will outsell one requiring three coins, and so on. The new coin would certainly help sales."

On September 15, 1976, the Treasury Department, citing increased coinage costs, announced it might do away with the penny and the half dollar and replace the dollar coin with a lighter version.[2]

Liberty Cap Design Proposed

The subject of a mini-dollar caught the nation's fancy, and many articles appeared concerning the Mint's own ideas and the Research Triangle Institute study. Mint Director Mary T. Brooks urged caution, stating that if changes were made they should come slowly.

Realizing that a new small-diameter dollar might become a reality, Chief Engraver Frank Gasparro created a prototype design featuring the head of Miss Liberty with a pole and cap, loosely adapted from the copper half cent and cent of the 1790s. Inside the rim on a later version was an 11-sided border to help distinguish it from the quarter. The reverse showed a soaring eagle. The motifs were approved by the Commission of Fine Arts.

On December 31, 1976, Secretary of the Treasury William E. Simon submitted to Congress a report, "The State of the United States Coinage," based in part on the Research Triangle Institute study. It recommended a 26.5 mm small dollar coin.

On April 7, 1977, Secretary of the Treasury W. Michael Blumenthal, Simon's successor in that office, wrote to the chairman of the House Committee on Banking, Finance, and Urban Affairs, noting in part, "The Treasury recommends that the present dollar coin be replaced with a smaller, more conveniently-sized dollar and that the 50-cent piece be eliminated."

Kennedy half dollars, including newer issues without silver content, were not seen in circulation at the time. Except for use in Nevada casinos during the early 1970s, Eisenhower dollars did not circulate. Large quantities remained in Treasury vaults.

Frank Gasparro with an early version of his 1977 Liberty Head mini-dollar and a sketch of his reverse design.

1977 "Liberty Head experimental dollar coin," as illustrated in *The Annual Report of the Director of the Mint*, 1978.

Early galvano dated 1977 of Frank Gasparro's design for the proposed small-diameter dollar with a "recessed border," per a notation on the galvano.

Gilded plaster cast, large diameter, dated 1977, of Frank Gasparro's design for the proposed small-diameter dollar. An 11-sided interior border has been added.

On April 17, 1978, the Jimmy Carter administration submitted a recommendation to Congress to adopt the small dollar. On May 1, this proposal was introduced to the House of Representatives by delegate Walter E. Fauntroy and was referred to the House Committee on Banking, Finance, and Urban Affairs. A Liberty Head motif was proposed.

This was followed on May 3 by bill S. 3036, calling for suffragette Susan B. Anthony to be portrayed. It was introduced into the Senate by William Proxmire, who was well known at the time for his campaign to cut costs and his satirical but often realistic "Golden Fleece Award" for abuses of spending.[3]

H.R. 12728, introduced on May 15, 1978, by Mary Rose Oakar for herself and for Patricia Schroeder, similarly called for the portrait of Anthony to be used.

The Anthony proposal did not sit well with the numismatic community. On May 17, Margo Russell, editor of *Coin World*, addressed the House Banking, Finance, and Urban Affairs Subcommittee on Historic Preservation and Coinage, praising the earlier recommendation: "We commend the Mint for its selection of the Liberty-Eagle personification on the coin, and we hope this beautiful allegorical design will be selected for the coin, should it become reality." On the same day Mint Director Stella B. Hackel addressed the same committee, noting in part:

One proposal within the Mint was to adapt the Eisenhower portrait for use on the mini-dollar. Trial pieces were struck but later all were destroyed.

Galvano dated 1978 of Frank Gasparro's design for the proposed small-diameter dollar.

Galvano dated 1979 of Frank Gasparro's design for the proposed small-diameter dollar.

The new dollar would be distinguishable from the quarter by touch as well as by sight. The design proposed would have an eleven-side inner border on both sides of the coin within the outer circular configuration. This design element would provide for tactile recognition by the visually handicapped. . . .

Many materials—including several copper alloys, titanium, and other clad combinations—were tested to determine the most suitable composition for the new coin. The results of the studies indicates that the best overall material is a 75% copper / 25% nickel alloy clad on a 100% copper core. . . .

The recommended design for the obverse is a modern or stylized female Liberty Head. This historic design appeared on the first U.S. coins minted in 1793, and appeared in various forms on almost all denominations of coins through modern times. The female Liberty Head is symbolic of and honors all women rather than any particular individual. It is accompanied by the Phrygian cap which has been a symbol of freedom for over 2500 years and has repeatedly appeared on our coins. It is most appropriate that such a historic American design once again return to an American coin.

The recommended design for the reverse is a Soaring or Volant Eagle. The eagle has appeared on the reverse of every dollar coin since 1794, with the exception of the gold coins.[4] The recommended design, which is similar to the 1916 quarter-dollar eagle, is a more vivid rendition emphasizing the independence and spirit which characterizes this national symbol. . . .

Later in May, other proposals were introduced into Congress, one suggesting dual portraits of Harriet Tubman and Susan B. Anthony (H.R. 12872, May 25), but most calling for Anthony alone. In June there were more proposals, including for the images of Abigail Adams, Georgia Neese Clarke Gray, and Elizabeth Pole. Within the engraving department at the Mint some ideas were translated into plasters and galvanos, but most were not.

The Anthony Portrait

In June 1978 the Treasury Department, influenced by Congress's social progress, discarded the highly praised Liberty Head motif and directed Frank Gasparro to depict Anthony on the obverse, as it seemed a certainty that Anthony would be the dollar coin's subject. For the reverse Congress and the Treasury wanted a reduced version of the Apollo 11 motif used in the Eisenhower dollar. The engraver gathered many different Anthony portraits adapted from prints, engravings, and photographs, all reproduced to be about the same size, and at one time had them on display in his office.

The following commentary by Frank Gasparro was written at my request on November 4, 1991, and gives his view of the creation of the Anthony dollar:

> The important question for me, that stood out in designing the Susan B. Anthony dollar was how the public would accept my interpretation of the great suffragist.
>
> My first plaster, June 1st, 1978, showed Susan B. Anthony's portrait at the age of twenty-eight. Considering the few photographs available, I chose this one. This was followed by a rejection by Susan B. Anthony, 2nd, a grandniece, then living. She stated that I portrayed her as "too pretty." So, I had to go back to the "drawing board." Then, the only other photograph I could obtain was showing her in her very old age. I had to "'toughen" the features of my present plaster model.
>
> Eventually, after much effort, I ended up with a portrait showing Susan B. Anthony in her fifties, at the height of her career. I had to sharpen her features giving her strength of character. I kept in mind, to make the coin artistic and still prove acceptable to the public.

Susan B. Anthony portrait from a steel engraving published in 1881 by G.E. Perine & Co. as part of the six-volume *History of Woman Suffrage*.

What followed is history. There was trouble with the coin size.

The next hurdle was to experiment with giving the coin a gold or brass finish and still keep the same size.

This proved too late. There were already 450 million of the small dollars deposited in the Federal Reserve vaults and they could not move. Meanwhile, this experiment was picked up and pursued by European countries to give the higher denomination small coin a gold or brass finish. This proved very successful.

For America, the future will see a small size dollar with a gold or brass plate or finish that may prove acceptable, favorably, by the public.

On July 17, Mint Director Hackel appeared before the Senate Committee on Banking, Housing, and Urban Affairs and reiterated her stance on using a Liberty Head, noting that more than 100 different women from history had been proposed. She urged that S. 3036 requiring Anthony's portrait not be passed. The legislators listened politely and then ignored what she said.

Hope springs eternal, it has been said and the Liberty Head idea remained alive, at least for a while. A poll of *Coin World* readers published on August 3, 1978, showed that Gasparro's preferred design gained 1,056 votes, with the suffragette turning in a miserable showing in seventh place with only 78 votes.

On August 22 the Senate approved S. 3036. *The Annual Report of the Director of the Mint*, 1978, illustrated the Anthony coin, but also showed the Gasparro Liberty Head as an "experimental coin." The features on the Anthony dollar were identical to the engraving published in 1881 by G.E. Perine & Co.

On September 26, 1978, the Commission of Fine Arts approved the Gasparro designs featuring Anthony. Often in history the Commission recommendations were ignored, but not in this instance.

Plaster showing a head-and-neck portrait of Susan B. Anthony, with light letters.

Plaster showing a head-and-neck portrait of Susan B. Anthony, with slightly heavier letters.

Galvano made in 1978 for a proposed reverse. Signed FG at the lower right.

Galvano for an unadopted reverse for the 1979 dollar. FG initials are below the 1.

Galvano for another unadopted reverse for the 1979 dollar, a variation of the above. This has an 11-sided interior border.

Galvanos with an unadopted obverse showing slightly different features (note the position of the second star at the left) and a reverse with slight differences from that adopted.

Galvano of the adopted obverse.

The Dollar Becomes a Reality

Representative Mary Rose Oakar, who had been particularly active in the program, acted on behalf of the Carter administration and introduced the required legislation into Congress. It was passed on September 26, 1978. A descendant of the portrait subject, Susan B. Anthony III, was on hand with an enlarged model of the coin's obverse. The bill was signed as Public Law 95-447 by President Carter on October 10, 1978. The legislation also provided for, as of December 31, 1978, the discontinuation of the Eisenhower dollar.

On December 13, 1978, a test run of about one million coins was made at the Philadelphia Mint, using 1979-dated dies. The event was opened to government officials and invited guests from the media and public sector. At 11:25 a.m. four presses were started simultaneously with two dignitaries attending each. Mint Director Stella B. Hackel and Philadelphia Mint Superintendent Shallie M. Bey were at Press No. 4.

On January 9, 1979, Colorado state officials, members of Congress, Treasury officials, and other government people took part in a reception at the Denver Mint to learn about the new dollar and to see the new coins, already in production.

Launching the Anthony Dollar

Early in 1979 I received this invitation from Mint Director Stella B. Hackel:

> It is a pleasure to request the honor of your attendance at a ceremony to commemorate the production striking of both the circulating and Proof Susan B. Anthony dollar coin. The guests will gather at the Bureau of the Mint Assay Office in San Francisco, California, at 7:30 a.m., on Friday, February 2, 1979.
>
> The ceremony will start at 8:00 a.m. The Assay Office is located at 155 Hermann Street, San Francisco. Please call to let us know if your schedule will permit you to join us on this historic occasion. We look forward to seeing you there.

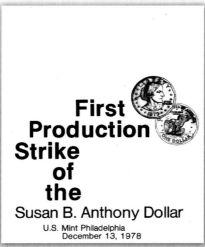

First Production Strike of the Susan B. Anthony Dollar
U.S. Mint Philadelphia
December 13, 1978

Denver Striking Susan B. Anthony Dollar
January 1979

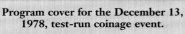

Program cover for the December 13, 1978, test-run coinage event.   **Mock-up of the Denver Mint program cover made before the date was finalized.**

I was delighted with the prospect and telephoned my acceptance. This was different from the other events in that Proof coins would be struck only at San Francisco. The ceremony was to be held at an early hour because the secretary of the Treasury, W. Michael Blumenthal, had to be in Los Angeles later in the day to give a speech.

Alighting from a taxi, I and my wife Christie proceeded up a sloping drive toward a huge, white granite building. Guards spaced at regular intervals around the outside apparently recognized us as guests and beckoned us to continue on the path that eventually led to the back side of the building. Against the building

Frank Gasparro holding one of "his" dollars before the ceremony.

wall on the front and on all sides were huge spools of tightly wound copper and nickel metal held together with bands, awaiting eventual transformation into coins. We later learned that the Assay Office had no facilities for tourists or casual visitors. Perhaps that is why the main entrance is on the far side of the building and is rather inconspicuous.

Walking up a few stairs and crossing a terrazzo-floor lobby (bearing a brass plaque patterned after the $50 gold Augustus Humbert slug of Gold Rush fame) we collected "Honored Guest" ribbons which had been prepared in advance. We were among the earliest arrivals and noted that ribbons had been prepared for several other numismatic personalities, including Margo Russell, editor of *Coin World*. Most of the audience consisted of numerous representatives of the general news media, Treasury and government officials, and people from the business community.

It was about 7:15 a.m. when we were among the first to enter a brightly lighted rectangular room in which two easels portrayed plaster casts, copper galvanos, and enlarged photographs relating to the Anthony dollar. On hand was Frank Gasparro, who had been a fine friend for many years. While other guests were drifting in I chatted with him about his latest thoughts on the new coinage. He had not been in favor of using an Anthony portrait, as I had known for a long time, and he had many who agreed with him, but once this was decided upon he went about to design the best image he could, and with enthusiasm.

At the beginning of our conversation a lady representative of the Daughters of the American Revolution came up to me, saw my camera, and asked me to take a picture of her together with Gasparro. Susan B. Anthony, it turned out, had been a D.A.R. member. Today this has a touch of irony, for Anthony is considered to be an archetype of liberal thinking, whereas the D.A.R. is known for its conservatism.

On display in the room, in addition to a long table filled with coffee and donuts, were die pairs used to create Susan B. Anthony dollars, both Proof and regular issues, as well as a made-up Proof set of the type that would be sold to collectors later in the year.

Although the scheduled production held during my visit was a "ceremonial striking" or "launch," test impressions had obviously been made earlier, as such a dollar was in the Proof set on display.

As 8:00 a.m. approached, the guests filed into an adjacent room filled with folding chairs arranged theater-style. At the front was a table and lectern, behind which was a green banner bearing the emblem of the United States Treasury Department. When Christie and I entered the room it was half full. I was eager to get an aisle seat, so as to be able to use my camera. Then at the last minute I noticed that several seats were vacant in the very first row as is so often the case at such events. So, there we went— a vantage point which was to give us a close view of all the proceedings.

At about 8:15 the luminaries assembled at the front table. Included were Mint Director Hackel; Treasury Under Secretary Bette Anderson; and Treasury Secretary W. Michael Blumenthal. In addition, other national and local officials were present.

Stella Hackel furnished an interesting introduction, giving a brief biography of Secretary Blumenthal. It turns out that he, a German immigrant, had his first job in San Francisco, where he counted cookies in a bakery. He then progressed, step by step, through an illustrious career, which culminated in the presidency of the Bendix Corporation and, in more recent times, to the position of the secretary of the Treasury, appointed by President Jimmy Carter.

Speaking from prepared notes, Blumenthal then told of the new Anthony dollar and the government's expectation for it. It would, he said, present great efficiencies, for the pieces would last longer in circulation than paper dollars and would be of a form easily handled by the public. It was expected this would effect an economy of $4.5 million a year, an important factor in an administration that was trying to cut costs, he emphasized. He then told a bit about Susan B. Anthony's life and how she came to be commemorated on the coin. "If Indians, buffalos, and eagles can be on coins, then a woman can be also," was a lighthearted comment that evoked laughter.[5]

> It's time the United States portrayed a woman on a coin, for we are one of the few countries which until now had no real female likeness represented on any of our coinage. Perhaps that is why the dollar was in some trouble. When Susan used to crusade from town to town to advocate women's rights she was backed by her father's money. Now we need Susan to back our money.
>
> When President Carter signed the new coin act he said, "This new coin will be a constant reminder of the continuing struggle for the equality of all Americans."
>
> It reminds me too of our constant struggle to stabilize the dollar. Susan Anthony, I sure hope you can help us now.

Following Blumenthal's remarks, the group went down one flight of stairs to the second floor to visit the production facility for Proof coinage. In a large room, presses were all set to stamp out Proof coins simultaneously. Blumenthal and several others gathered at a press and, with the aid of a press operator, produced the first "ceremonial" Proof dollar, holding it up proudly to display it before a large group of photographers and others. During the next 5 to 10 minutes several other pieces were coined, and many photographs were taken. Visitors were allowed to actuate the Proof press as well.

Each Proof coin was made by taking a blank or planchet from a group placed on a metal table in front of the operator, spread out like a fallen stack of poker chips. Each blank was carefully placed on the die and a lever was used to actuate the press to strike each coin twice. During the stamping process a protective glass plate came down between the operator and the die, thus making the coining process visible but at the same time protecting the operator from metal scraps. Then, as the die receded upward and after the glass plate lifted, the operator took a large forceps and extracted each coin, placing it on an easel, together with other pieces. During the whole process the dollars were not touched by human hands, nor were the faces of the coins allowed to come into contact with others. Each Proof die was good for about 4,000 strikes, creating 2,000 coins.

Following picture-taking and general discussions, all of which took perhaps 15 minutes, guests were invited to do one of two things: return upstairs to the reception area for additional refreshments, or go downstairs to visit the production facilities for ordinary circulating coinage.

A Tour of the Mint

Christie and I elected to do the latter, the only guests to do so, for we saw no others in evidence once we went down to the lower area. We were fortunate to have Don Butler, supervisor of the security staff, as our personal tour guide. The public is not admitted, and it wasn't very often that the San Francisco Assay Office had government or other authorized visitors, so giving us a tour was a special privilege, he told us.

Mint Director Stella B. Hackel at the podium and Secretary of the Treasury W. Michael Blumenthal at the Proof strike ceremony.

Dave Bowers, press attendant Cleveland Bias, and *Coin World* editor Margo Russell with a newly struck 1979-S Proof dollar.

Christie Bowers with a Proof dollar she struck, with press attendant Bias supervising.

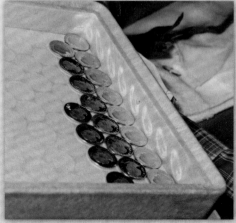

Proof dollars were placed carefully in a tray next to the press.

Going down to the lower level, we first saw several gigantic presses which took undulating wide strips of cupro-nickel–clad copper and stamped blank planchets from them, creating an ear-splitting din. One huge machine in particular churned out a whole handful of dollar planchets each time the punches came crashing down. Perhaps as a contrast to the white-painted Proof presses, the planchet punches and coining presses in the production level were all painted bright green.

Blanking press stamping Susan B. Anthony planchets from a strip of clad metal.

From that point we went into the production facility where many presses were busily churning out a coppery cascade of Lincoln cents and bins full of bright silvery Anthony dollars. The cents in particular were made in high-speed production and were being coined faster than the eye could follow. We spent nearly an hour watching thousands of coins being produced (cent and dollar denominations; other issues were not being made that day), the changing of dies, preparation of planchets, counting and handling, shaking of coins through a sieve (to remove oversize mint-error pieces), and other operations.

A bin being filled by a cascade of circulation-strike Susan B. Anthony dollars at the San Francisco Mint.

Advantages of the Anthony Dollar

At the ceremony the Treasury distributed an information packet. Included was a sheet, "Advantages / Comparisons," which began:

> The current [Eisenhower] cupro-nickel dollar does not circulate due primarily to its cumbersome size and weight. The recommended design for the $1 coin specifically addresses this problem of convenience. The $1 coin is only 9% greater in diameter than a quarter and only 43% heavier. Compared to the current $1 coin it is approximately 2/3 the diameter and 1/3 the weight.
>
> The current $1 coin costs about 8 cents each to produce as compared to the cost for the new coin which will be 3 cents each. This is a savings of greater than 60% per coin compared to the existing coin! Based on production figures for Fiscal Year 1978 the new coin would save about $4.5 million per year.
>
> Demand for one-dollar notes has been increasing steadily at the Bureau of Engraving and Printing. Current figures show that dollar notes represent 60% of currency production. A practical $1 note which circulates will displace $1 notes.
>
> One dollar notes wear out and must be replaced in approximately 18 months at a cost of 1.8 cents each. Since each coin will last at least 15 years, the coin has, at minimum, a tenfold service life advantage. Considering the cost of the coin compared to the note, each coin would save over 80% of the production costs for the notes displaced. With nearly 3 billion Federal Reserve Notes in circulation today, only modest displacement by $1 coins could result in savings of many millions of dollars in costs.

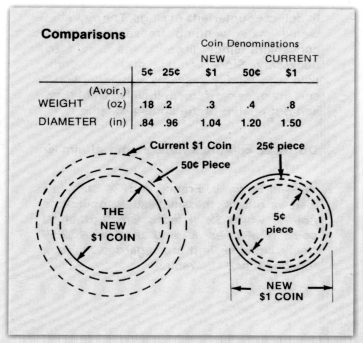

**"Comparisons" issued by the Treasury Department, showing
the size of the Susan B. Anthony dollar and other coins.**

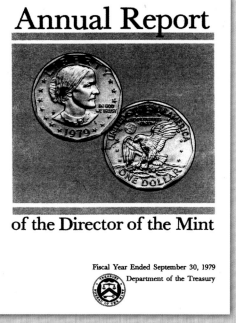

**Cover of the 1979 *Annual Report*
of the Director of the Mint.**

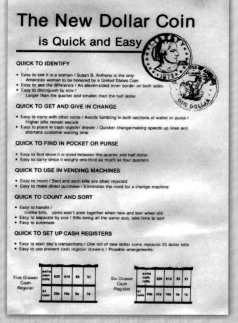

"Quick and Easy" information.

The Anthony Dollar in Circulation

The Treasury Department stated that before the first coins could be released to the general public, anticipated to happen in July 1979, it wanted to have 300 to 500 million on hand so that there would be enough to meet demand. On target, July 2 saw the official release. A ceremony was held in Rochester, New York, the city where Susan B. Anthony made her home. Among those in attendance was Mint Director Stella Hackel. Various philatelic/numismatic first-day covers were made privately, these typically enclosing an Anthony dollar obtained on July 2 and put in an envelope and postmarked.[6]

The initial production at the Philadelphia Mint amounted to a prodigious 360,222,000 coins, a figure that challenged the entire mintage of Morgan dollars from 1878 to 1904—and we thought *they* were made in large numbers!

Although certain representatives of the vending-machine industry expressed approval of the mini-dollar, it turned out that vendors took a wait-and-see attitude to assure that the public would be as eager to use them as the Treasury hoped. None of the Nevada gambling casinos showed any interest, as by that time they were all using their own chips. By year's end, more than 757,000,000 dollars had been struck, or more than two for every man, woman, and child in America.

Although the new dollars were available at banks, and some citizens obtained them as curiosities, they did not flow into circulation. If the Treasury would pay the several hundred million dollars needed to make new coin acceptors for vending machines, the Anthony might circulate, officials were advised, but the Treasury had no budget for such an expense. The matter was at a standstill, and only a few vending machines could use the coins.

Congressional Testimony

In diametric opposition to what the numismatic community and press had observed, Under Secretary of the Treasury Bette B. Anderson included this in September 25, 1979, testimony to the Subcommittee on Consumer Affairs of the House Committee on Banking, Finance and Urban Affairs:

> The initial reaction of the general public to the new coin has been essentially what the Department, and indeed the congressional committees, had anticipated. On the one hand there has been a favorable reception by many for this coin, which for the first time in our history, bears the image of an outstanding American woman.
>
> Beyond that, a number of nationwide retailers and local stores in various areas, which realized the advantages of using the new coin in commercial transactions, promptly began using and promoting the acceptance of the coin. Many communities and citizens' organizations have promoted use of the coin as well.

Anderson went on to say:

> At the same time we fully realized that there has been criticism of the new coin by many of our citizens. Perhaps the strongest objection we have heard is that, because of its size and color, the Anthony dollar coin can be mistaken for the quarter. During the past several months we have received suggestions for making the coin more distinct—there have been recommendations to increase the diameter, change the color or shape, or punch a hole in the middle of the coin.

She stated that all of these ideas had been considered earlier and had been rejected. It takes time for citizens to get used to a new coin. To help things along the Appropriations

Committee had approved $300,000 "for the Mint to conduct an educational circulation program." By the time of her speech nearly 400,000 kits had been distributed. It was only a matter of time, she suggested, before the Anthony dollar would save the Federal Reserve System $50 million yearly by replacing $1 bills in commerce.

Congressman Frank Annunzio, who shepherded many coinage proposals of the era, commented: "The new dollar coin may well go down in history as the only coin that more people wanted before it was released than after it was released."

Touché.

The preface to *The Annual Report of the Director of the Mint*, 1979, closed with this remark:

> Let me relate a piece of advice Susan Anthony received from an uncle. He said to her, "If you want to be a real success you have to make the world notice you." She replied, "I'll make them stare." Little did she know that the whole world would one day be staring at her likeness on a $1 coin.

There was an attempt, late in 1979, to use the smaller dollars to pay military personnel in Europe, but complaints forced an end to the practice. The coins could be used only on U.S. military bases because European banks discounted them heavily when making exchanges for local currency. In 1980 the Department of Defense did its best to work with the Treasury Department to circulate SBA dollars as well as generally unwanted $2 bills on military bases. While many coins and bills were used this way, they did not migrate into broader commerce outside of the military installations.

Treasury Efforts Continue

Even the United States Postal Service was enlisted in another vain attempt (February 1 to March 14, 1980) to distribute the coins. Signs were posted in 35,000 locations, and the coins were given out in change. This idea crashed after patrons made it clear to postal clerks that they did not want the "Susies" under any conditions. The New York Port Authority was persuaded to put up red-lettered signs at its tunnel and bridge toll booths on roads in and out of Manhattan advising that attendants would accept Anthony dollars, but few riders had such coins in their pockets. In time more than 9,000 stamp-vending machines in post offices accepted Anthony dollars, and in most instances the clerks supplied the coins. This did not seem to make much sense as most people in such offices bought stamps over the counter.

Ed Fulwider, a San Francisco Mint staffer with a deep interest in numismatics, wrote to me on January 18, 1980 (excerpt):

> July 2nd was the day that the Susan B. Anthony Dollar was released. What a fiasco that has turned out to be. The twenty cent piece all over again. I wonder if this coin will even last three years. I cannot believe the universal contempt for it. I have started giving talks again to coin clubs and other groups and even though I do not care for that coin I defend it. Numismatics has had enough bad press. The Mint really goofed on this one though.
>
> I gave a talk at the San Francisco Lighthouse for the Blind. The Assay Office gave me permission to take one of the new dollars over there, and not one of the forty five blind people could tell it from a quarter. I reported this to Mr. Brockenborough and he relayed my information to the people in Washington. Brock told me a couple of days later I really shook them up back there. I cannot figure out what kind of research they ran on that coin as far as the blind were concerned. . . .

History repeated itself, and echoing what happened with the twenty-cent pieces more than a century earlier in 1875, the public in 1979 confused the Susan B. Anthony dollars with the somewhat similarly sized quarters.

Frank Gasparro said that at the Philadelphia Mint cafeteria he tendered a new dollar for a small purchase, and the cashier gave him change thinking that a quarter had been paid. From the outset Gasparro had held the coin could confuse people, but no one paid attention to him.

Apropos of confusing the new dollars with quarters, numismatist David Sundman shared this experience:

> The only time in my life that I actually received a Susan B. Anthony dollar coin in change was from a cashier. The event was kind of humorous, at least to me.
>
> It was Memorial Day weekend 1980 and I was attending my 10th reunion at Gettysburg College, in Gettysburg, Pennsylvania. Directly across the street from my lodging was a nice 7-11 store, and in the morning I went over to it to get a cup of coffee and my favorite paper, the Sunday edition of the *New York Times*. When the cashier rang me up, and handed me my change, I looked at it and it contained a 1979 Susan B. Anthony dollar, and some other coins. The cashier had given me too much money. I pointed this out to him, and he counted it out for me—but he was figuring the SBA dollar as a quarter.
>
> I got a kick out of the whole thing, as that was a major problem with the coin. The cupro-nickel–clad coin was too similar in size and coloration to a quarter.[7]

In addition, there was a political aspect to the pieces. In times of double-digit inflation, President Jimmy Carter's novel new dollar was sometimes referred to as a "J.C. penny."

Circulation Campaign

In July 1980 the Mint mounted its "Anthony Dollar Circulation Campaign."

> The Bureau of the Mint has brochures, kits, posters, and informational materials on the Susan B. Anthony dollar. These materials are available to the public. If interested please write: Susan B. Anthony Circulation Program, Bureau of the Mint, Room 1020, 501 13th Street N.W., Washington, D.C. 20220.

A four-page letter was arranged by topics giving information and telling of past efforts. The following entries are the letter's headings and a synopsis of the information under each:

Why a re-sized dollar coin?

The Eisenhower dollar was cumbersome and inconvenient. The new dollar is more convenient. It will also save up to $50 million per year by replacing dollar bills. In addition a 20% displacement of one-dollar bills with one-dollar coins would indefinitely delay the need to build a new Bureau of Engraving & Printing at a cost of $100 million.

How was the size of the new dollar determined?

A Mint survey of world coins indicated that in order to provide a $1 coin that would circulate, the weight would have to be less than nine grams. In order to distinguish it from the 24.2 mm quarter the new coin would have to be from 26.0 to 28.0 mm. The size of the Anthony dollar is 26.5 mm in diameter. This size was selected so that the dollar coin could be distinguished from low-value foreign coins by automated counting, sorting, and vending machines.

Why wasn't the dollar made a different color?

Extensive testing was done on brass-colored materials bonded to a copper core. After months of handling the alloys deviated from their original brass color to various shades of yellow-green.[8] The silver-colored cupro-nickel metal was found to be ideal.

Why wasn't the dollar multi-sided?

Testing of multi-sided coins was conducted by Bell Laboratories and several other discriminator [coin-detecting device] manufacturers as well as the Bureau of the Mint. It was found that this would require many changes in coin devices and would be easier to slug [fraudulently pay with a fake coin] than a round coin.

Why not put a hole in the dollar?

Mechanisms would find it to be hard to discriminate from washers used as slugs. It would also affect the "electrical response" of vending machines.

How can the visually impaired distinguish the dollar from the quarter?

The high relief of the top of the eagle's head and wings on the reverse of the coin is tactilely distinguishable. No comparable area of high relief exists on either side of the quarter. This feature together with the difference in diameter and weight should enable the visually impaired to distinguish the new dollar from the quarter.

Why does the new dollar have an eleven-sided inner border?

This permits it to be easily distinguished from other coins. More than eleven sides would appear to be nearly circular and would defeat the idea.

Why not take the reeding off the coin?

The reeded edge acts as a deterrent to anyone who may attempt to pass slugs to the visually handicapped. Without reeds it is easier to manufacture slugs the size and weight of any coin.[9]

What about the additional weight of carrying dollar coins?

The Anthony dollar weights 0.3 ounce. This is approximately one-third as much as four quarters. Using the Anthony dollar would reduce the number of coins the average person carries, and therefore the weight of the change as well.

How many dollar coins were made and where can I get them?

The Mint produced 648.4 million Susan B. Anthony dollars in fiscal year 1979 [ended September 30, 1979]. Production of the dollars was divided between the Philadelphia Mint which produced 47%, the Denver Mint which produced 38%, and the San Francisco Assay Office which produced 15%. Production as of April 1980 totaled 845 million, and 462 million have been released into the Federal Reserve System. Dollars are available from commercial banks.

Is the Treasury planning to withdraw the $1 bill?

A study by the Treasury recommended a plan to replace dollar bills with dollar coins and to increase the use of the two dollar bill. These recommendations have not been adopted or endorsed by the Treasury Department. It is up to Congress to make changes.

How much was spent on promoting the $1 coin?

$300,000 was spent by the Mint and another $300,000 was allocated by the Federal Reserve Board. Part of the last was spent with a public relations firm.

In 1980 the production dropped to 89,660,708 coins, but it might as well have been zero, as hundreds of millions of 1979-dated dollars were still in storage. The Treasury threw in the towel in 1981 and made coins only for collectors. The game was over, or so it seemed.

The New Susan B. Anthony Sales Program

Galvano for the regular obverse of a 1981 Susan B. Anthony dollar. The 11-sided interior rim had not been added yet.

On January 30, 1985, Donna Pope, who had been Mint director since 1982, announced a new program to distribute Anthony dollars. "Since most banks do not inventory the coins because of their limited use in commerce, we have devised a system whereby collectors and the general public can buy them directly from the Mint."

Although nothing was said about dollars dated 1981, quantities of 1979 and 1980 dollars from all three mints were available. Offered were:

> **Option #1:** A complete set of six coins, one from each of the mints, for both production years. The coins are sealed in Mylar and sell for $10.00 per set.
>
> **Option #2:** A bag of 100 coins from a specific mint and year. Customers must specify what date and mintmark they desire. This bag is a smaller variety of the bag normally used to ship the coins to the Federal Reserve Banks. The mint and year of mintage is stamped on each bag. This bag will sell for $110.00.
>
> **Option #3:** An original bag of 2,000 coins direct from the Mint's vaults. Customers must specify what date and mintmark they desire. This bag sells for $2,050.00.
>
> Mint Director Pope emphasizes that this is not an attempt to promote the dollar coin, but that these procedures have been established as a service to the general public. There are no plans to produce any additional SBA dollars.

Prices included shipping. There was no limit to the number of coins that could be ordered. Subsequent issues of *The Annual Report of the Director of the Mint* for fiscal years ending on September 30 showed these sales figures:

> **1985:** Option 1: 20,442 • Option 2: 4,099 • Option 3: 173
>
> **1986:** Option 1: 101,050 • Option 2: 12,473 • Option 3: 149[10]
>
> **1987:** Option 1: 102,207 • Option 2: 13,899 • Option 3: 226.
>
> **1988:** Option 1: 83,101 • Option 2: 11,736 • Option 3: 510
>
> **1989:** Option 1: 87,862 • Option 2: 15,854 • Option 3: 164
>
> **1990:** Option 1: 26,172 • Option 2: 5,811 • Option 3: 54[11]
>
> **1991:** Option 1: 36,755 • Option 2: 6,249 • Option 3: 84
>
> **1992:** Option 1: 14,790 • 1979 sets of 3 coins, 1980 sets of 3 coins: 14,322 sold totally. Options 2 and 3 were not reported.

1993: Option 1: 36,176 • 3-coin 1979 sets: 7,784 • 3-coin 1980 sets: 5,932 • Sales of $100 bags: 1979-P 158; 1979-D 98; 1979-S 132; 1980-P 90; 1980-D 108; 1980-S 144 • Sales of $2000 bags: 1979-P 76; 1979-D 38; 1979-S 42; 1980-P 43; 1980-D 12; 1980-S 31 • Total revenue from sales of SBA dollars: $968,974. Last year of reports.

Where They Went

The following information is from Lauren Vaughan, United States Mint Office of Public Affairs, Washington, D.C., sent to me in January 1993, when I was trying to learn more about the distribution:[12]

Susan B. Anthony Dollars:

Calendar year 1979 production, all mints: 757.8 million.

Calendar year 1980 production, all mints: 89.7 million.

Calendar year 1981 production, all mints: 9.7 million.

Total production: 857.2 million paid out since 1979: 470.1 million.

Government inventory as of December 25, 1992:

Stored at the Philadelphia Mint: 111.2 million.

Stored at the Denver Mint: 14.2 million.

Stored at the San Francisco Mint: 55.2 million.

Total stored at all mints: 122.2 million.

Stored by Denver Federal Reserve Bank: 122.2 million.[13]

Stored by other Federal Reserve Banks: 84.3 million.

Total stored by government: 387.1 million.

A Later Idea for a Dollar Coin

The hope that a small-size dollar coin would eliminate the need for dollar bills did not go away. In the late 1990s some experimental coins were made to suggest that a coin with two metallic elements would not be confused with quarter dollars, and that Braille inscriptions would aid the blind. An example of such a privately made test piece appeared in the Americana Sale held by Stack's Bowers Galleries, February 2015, as lot 2736:

Experimental Model

26mm. 11.4 grams. Obv. Insert with a head facing left, wearing Phrygian cap of Liberty, the ring around inscribed EXPERIMENTAL/MODEL Rev. Insert with an eagle perched right, the ring around inscribed R&D/PROJECT on the reverse, with additional Braille characters at left and right indicating the reverse side. An interesting piece produced by Schuler, the German manufacturer of the Schuler coining presses that are widely used in mints throughout the world. Though undated, this piece was acquired by our consignor in 1999. Schuler produces complex presses that are used in striking bimetallic coins. According to the firm's website, theirs is a "press for hole-piercing, joining, coining, and separating . . . applicable as coin minting press for round, non-round and bi-metal coins, as a joining press, hole piercing press, and as a press to separate ring and core in the case of bi-metal coins taken out of circulation for recycling."

Schuler's 26 mm test-coin proposal for a new dollar with improved security and recognition features. Shown at 150%.

Research by Phillip Barnhart can be found on the Internet, and indicates that these bimetallic test pieces were struck in 1997 or 1998 by Schuler in their Michigan offices as demonstration pieces for the U.S. Mint and for exhibition at U.S. congressional hearings. The test pieces had two purposes. First, to demonstrate the addition of Braille elements to coinage in response to concerns of the Alliance for the Blind, and to promote their own technology to produce bimetallic coins as the U.S. Mint was investigating ideas for a new dollar coin. It is believed that approximately 20 pieces were struck.

Changes of the Late 1990s

Gradually, as new mechanisms were being made for vending machines, transit-system coin acceptors, and the like, provision was made to accommodate Anthony dollars. The idea of retrofitting existing mechanisms had not been successful.

This demand resulted in a steady outflow of SBA dollars from Treasury storage. The coins reached limited use, and relatively few were seen in everyday commerce.

On May 20, 1999, *Mint News*, an occasional newsletter, contained this:

U.S. Mint to Strike 1999 Susan B. Anthony Dollar Coins

Washington, D.C.—The U.S. Mint today announced plans to strike 1999-dated Susan B. Anthony dollar coins (SBAs) to ensure the availability of dollar coins until the introduction of the new [Sacagawea] dollar coin in early 2000. The Mint will announce the start date for 1999-dated production in the near future.

"Demand for dollar coins is growing as more mass transit authorities and vending operations convert to using the dollar coin," said Mint Director Philip N. Diehl. "As a result, we're likely to exhaust our current supply of SBA dollars before the new dollar coin is available in January. We're committed to providing an uninterrupted supply of dollar coins through this transaction. We also want to let collectors know that our annual Fall Catalog this year will feature a Proof version of the coin and a two-coin Uncirculated set including both P and D mintmark 1999-dated Susan B. Anthony dollar coins. We'll announce prices and estimated production levels for the sets when the catalog is released in the fall."

A total of 847.5 million Susan B. Anthony dollar coins were minted for circulation in 1979 and 1980 and 9.7 million for numismatic sets only in 1981. Because demand has increased for a dollar coin in commerce in recent years, the government's supply of SBA dollars is nearly exhausted. The increase in demand is attributable to a growing recognition in the vending industry of the efficiencies of using dollar coins, including the convenience that comes from more rapid transactions. . . .

For the 1999 Anthony dollars the dies were modified very slightly. On the obverse the 1999 coins have minor different spacing of the distances from the stars and the W in WE to the portrait, and slightly different spacing of IN GOD WE TRUST, among other slight changes visible only upon close inspection. On the reverse the lettering and features were adjusted after multiple efforts at modifying the craters and the Earth. This is noticeable, for example, in the relation of the stars and the A in STATES and AM in AMERICA. On the final reverse made for circulating coinage the Earth was changed noticeably from its appearance on the 1979, 1980, and 1981 coins. The 1999 reverse has no islands below Florida, and Mexico and Central America appear as a thin line.

Plasters for the 1999 Anthony dollar. Multiple ideas were tried for the reverse. On the illustrated plaster the Earth, which presented a continuing problem with regard to geographical accuracy, is outlined in ink (see detail). The craters also have strengthened vertical lines from their rims.

Another 1999 reverse plaster and Earth detail. The craters have minimal vertical lines. The islands below Florida are particularly extensive. Baja California is prominent.

A 1999 reverse plaster and Earth detail. The crater rims are mostly smooth. A small island is below Florida. A line seems to indicate the Mississippi River. Baja California is differently shaped than on the preceding.

Minting proceeded in due course. By the close of the fiscal year on September 30 the Philadelphia Mint had struck 13,750,000 of the new dollars, but none had been made yet in Denver. In October the first shipments were made to the Federal Reserve Banks. The use of SBA dollars had been increasing slowly, particularly within Midwest and Western transit systems, but the there was no danger of running short.

In the meantime there had been a lot of excitement about the upcoming mini-dollar of golden color with a new design (which would become a reality with the Sacagawea dollar of 2000, studied in the next chapter).

Plaster for the adopted obverse of the 1999-P Anthony dollar.

Much of the official Mint explanation (of the growing demand for dollar coins in 1999, and the desire to ensure enough supply to transition smoothly to the 2000 Sacagawea coins) was a cover, a highly placed Treasury official told me in an interview in 2015. This was the Treasury's idea, not the Mint's, and it seems that Mint officials were not advised at the time that there was no real coin shortage. The real reason the coins were minted was the Y2K scare—a dread of the chaos that might accompany the arrival of the year 2000. The fear was that many computer systems that dropped the first two digits of a 20th-century year (using, for example, *99* instead of *1999*) would be thrown into disarray once the year flipped over to 2000. The abbreviation of 00 would imply that data was from 1900, not 2000.

Earth as modified on a circulation-strike 1999-D Anthony dollar.

Fear that bank deposits would be lost, vital records would disappear, and government and business information would be destroyed gave the news media the opportunity to instill a lot concern, even panic, across the country. The Treasury Department realized that there might be a great rush by the public to get hard-metal coins. Making more Anthony dollars was done as a precaution. This was the *only* reason for making them, as otherwise Treasury supplies were already sufficient to take care of regular demand until the Sacagawea dollars were generally available.

What might have been, but wasn't. At the Philadelphia Mint plasters were prepared in case there was a further call for 2000-dated Susan B. Anthony dollars.

Forewarned, just about everyone with data missing the 19 part of the year date adjusted their computer systems. The stroke of midnight, December 31, 1999, came, and on New Year's Day, January 1, 2000, all remained just fine with computers, data storage, and the like. There was no problem at all. The media then turned to other things. The rush for coins that the Treasury had feared did not take place. Some citizens who had withdrawn bank savings as cash, nearly all in easy-to-handle high-denomination bills, returned it soon thereafter.

A Later Proposal

The Treasury held large stocks of 1999 SBA dollars after they were minted, hesitating to put quantities into circulation and thereby interfere with the promotion of the new Sacagawea "golden dollar." On September 20, 2011, Representative David Schweikert of Arizona introduced H.R. 2977, the Currency Optimization, Innovation, and National Savings Act—the COINS Act (how clever!)—in the House of Representatives.

> The bill calls for the sequestering of Susan B. Anthony dollars within six months of the bill's enactment. After one year the remaining quantities of Anthony dollars would be declared obsolete coins. The bill calls for the Federal Reserve to improve the circulation of dollar coins and conduct outreach and education programs to help businesses with the transition. It would require Federal Reserve Banks to stop issuing dollar notes four years after the enactment of the legislation or when circulation of dollar coins exceeds 600 million annually, whichever comes first.[14]

By this time Sacagawea and other dollars had been coined since 2000, but reserves of Anthony coins were still on hand. The bill did not become law. No specific accounting of later quantities of SBA dollars in government vaults has been located.

Grading Susan B. Anthony Dollars

1980-D. Graded MS-65.

MS-60 to 70 (Mint State). *Obverse:* At MS-60, some abrasion and contact marks are evident, most noticeably on the cheek and upper center of the hair. Luster is present, but may be dull or lifeless. At MS-63, contact marks are extensive but not distracting. Abrasion still is evident, but less than at lower levels. MS-64 coins are slightly finer. An MS-65 coin may have minor abrasion, but contact marks are so minute as to require magnification. Luster should be full and rich. *Reverse:* At MS-60, some abrasion and contact marks are evident, most noticeably on the eagle's breast, head, and talons. Otherwise, the same comments apply as for the obverse.

1979-D. Graded AU-50.

AU-50, 53, 55, 58 (About Uncirculated). *Obverse:* Light wear is seen on the higher-relief areas of the portrait. At AU-58, the luster is extensive but incomplete. At AU–50 and 53, luster is less but still present. *Reverse:* Further wear is evident on the eagle, particularly the head, breast, talons, and tops of the wings. Otherwise, the same comments apply as for the obverse.

The Susan B. Anthony dollar is seldom collected in grades lower than AU-50.

1979-S, Type 2. Graded PF-70 Deep Cameo.

PF-60 to 70 (Proof). *Obverse and Reverse:* Proofs that are extensively cleaned and have many hairlines, or that are dull and grainy, are lower level, such as PF–60 to 62. This comment is more theoretical than practical, as nearly all Proofs have been well kept. With medium hairlines and good reflectivity, assigned grades of PF–63 or 64 are appropriate. With relatively few hairlines a rating of PF-65 can be given. PF-66 may have hairlines so delicate that magnification is needed to see them. Above that, all the way to PF-70, a Proof should be free of any hairlines or other problems under strong magnification.

Collecting Susan B. Anthony Dollars

There is good news and bad news about building a collection of Susan B. Anthony dollars. The good news is that there are no rarities and that a full set in MS-65 and Proof-65 or finer grade is easy to assemble and is inexpensive. All are of cupro-nickel composition (no silver strikings). The bad news is that the series is short; that, except for the Wide Rim 1979-P, there are no significant varieties; and that it is difficult to make SBA dollars an in-depth specialty.

In general, circulation issues in MS–65 and 66 are easy to find and are inexpensive, the 1981-S being an exception as the average grade is lower. If they are in certified holders they are more costly, as the expense of such holders is often more than the value of the coins they contain. At the MS-67 or higher levels many are scarce in terms of certified coins, although this "scarcity" shouldn't be taken out of context; the vast majority have never been submitted for commercial grading. Auction records for certain early coins in ultra-high grades have run into four figures.

On the obverse the highest part of Susan B. Anthony's cheek often has contact marks or, in the case of coins not fully struck up, stray marks from the original planchet surface. The eagle's talons on the reverse of some coins are weakly defined. On the www.smalldollars.com Web site in January 2006 an article ("What are Full Talons?") by Robert Ezerman and David R Golan called attention to this area of sometime weakness. On the reverse of the 1999-P issues it is not unusual to find the entire branch on the reverse without details. As these aspects have not gained much publicity in the marketplace, anyone interested in obtaining sharply struck coins with minimal marks can do so by cherrypicking at regular prices.

Proof SBA dollars approach perfection, with such grades as 69 and 70 being common.

The registry-set specialty—trying to find coins with the highest grading numbers, for submission to audited competitions—was initiated a generation ago by David Hall of the Professional Coin Grading Service. As of 2016 there were about 4,000 participants assembling various sets from half cents to double eagles as well as other specialties. The Numismatic Guaranty Corporation has a registry-set program as well. Collectors building SBA sets have accounted for some of the lofty prices for early circulation-strike issues.

My own collection of Susan B. Anthony coins is mounted in a bookshelf-type album with clear sides to permit me to easily study and enjoy them. I selected the Mint State coins to include those MS-65 or finer, keeping an eye out for sharpness, and the Proofs were automatically of high quality, probably grading 69 or 70 if I were to submit them for certification. I have one of each date and mintmark, plus the added 1979-P Wide Rim variety. I have not collected the S mintmark "types," so called, of 1979-S and 1981-S as to me they are not very distinctive. They are widely listed, popular, and inexpensive, so if you want them they are easy to find.

Unless you are building a competitive registry set, collecting a hand-selected MS-65 and Proof–67 or 68 set is a nice way to go. The cost is very modest.

1979–1981, 1999, Susan B. Anthony Dollar

Designer: Frank Gasparro.

Composition: Outer layers of copper-nickel (.750 copper, .250 nickel) bonded to inner core of pure copper.

Weight: 8.1 grams.

Diameter: 26.5 mm.

Edge: Reeded.

1979-P, Narrow Rim

Circulation-strike mintage: 360,222,000

actual size: 26.5 mm

Availability in Mint State: This issue is common and probably 15% or so of survivors are MS-65 or better. Among certified coins, enough MS-66 coins exist to satisfy demands. MS-67 and higher coins are scarce. Only a tiny fraction of the mintage has ever been submitted for certification.

Detail of Narrow Rim.

Availability in circulated grades: Narrow Rim coins are common in circulated grades.

Characteristics of striking: The striking of this issue varies.

Notes: This design was launched with a narrow rim on the obverse. Most of the Philadelphia coins and all of the Denver and San Francisco coins have this feature. To help alleviate the numerous complaints that these coins could be confused with quarters, the obverse rim was widened. These new "Wide Rim" coins were first coined in July 1979. George W. Maschke, a New York collector, was the first numismatist to report the change. The numismatic community learned of this in an article by Herbert P. Hicks, "S.B.A. Dollar Varieties," in *Error-Variety News*, May 1980. Soon, theories were aplenty—such as this being the result of a worn hub and other opinions that the variety was either not real or significant. A detailed follow-up article appeared in the same publication in September 1981, "The 1979P Type 2 Dollars," by John A. Wexler, quoting Dr. Alan J. Goldman, deputy director of the Mint, who confirmed there had been a die change.[15]

George F. Hunter, assistant director for process and quality control at the Mint, stated that 643 working dies of the Wide Rim variety had been made, indicating an estimated mintage of 160,750,000 coins, a plentitude that does not square with the variety being very scarce. This comment has been widely questioned by numismatists.

In 1993 David M. Sundman, president of the Littleton Coin Company, wrote this to me:

> Apparently, the Near Date [Wide Rim] variety was only produced for a very short time in the Susan B. Anthony production. Since our company has sold over one million sets of 1979-P-D-S Susan B. Anthonys and only found 1,600 pieces of the 'Near Date' variety, we assume the production of this variety was very small. In the past year, I have sold more than half of what we found at $30 a coin. You still can find good coins today, if you are lucky. There is nothing remarkable about any of the other coins in the Susan Anthony dollar set from our point of view. I actually think that the "Near Date" variety is far more important and more noticeable than the Type II 1979-S Proof and the Type II 1981-S Proof mintmark varieties. The Near Date variety was really a design change.

Theories regarding the rarity of the Wide Rim coins have varied. The Mint may have prepared a large number of dies, but only used a few, and, as these coins were made after large quantities of Narrow Rim dollars had been struck, they were ready for release into circulation in early July. Coins struck in July or later were not needed for circulation and may have been bagged and stored.

2,526,000 Uncirculated each of the 1979-P and 1979-D Anthony dollars were included in Mint sets sold by the Treasury to collectors. These sets contained the 1979–P and D dollars only (not the S), plus other denominations cent through half dollar—total face value, $3.82; issue price of set: $8.00.

	MS-63	MS-64	MS-65	MS-66
1979-P, Narrow Rim	$5	$6	$10	$20

1979-P, Wide Rim

Circulation-strike mintage: Portion of the 1979-P, Narrow Rim mintage.

Availability in Mint State: Only a small percentage of coins are of this variety. They are rare in comparison to the Narrow Rim, but enough exist overall that finding one will be no problem. Several thousand have been certified MS-65 (mostly) or better by PCGS and NGC. Most are in

actual size: 26.5 mm

Detail of Wide Rim.

grades of MS-64 or less. FS-C1-1979P-301; CONECA: ODV-002.

James Sego commentary: In truly superb gem grade with excellent overall quality this is a very difficult variety to find.[16]

Availability in circulated grades: These are scarce in comparison to the Narrow Rim, but demand is low as nearly all buyers want Mint State coins. Still, they sell for a premium.

Characteristics of striking: The striking of the Wide Rim variety varies.

Notes: See Notes for 1979-P, Narrow Rim.

	MS-63	MS-64	MS-65	MS-66
1979-P, Wide Rim	$30	$40	$60	$150

1979-D

Circulation-strike mintage: 288,015,744

Availability in Mint State: This issue is very common, including in MS-65 and higher. For these and others, ultra-high grades exist and often sell for lofty prices to those who are building registry sets.

actual size: 26.5 mm

Availability in circulated grades: *EF-40 to AU-58:* These coins are very common in circulated grades.

Characteristics of striking: The striking of this issue varies.

Notes: All 1979-D coins are with Narrow Rim, the date farther from the inner edge of the border.

	MS-63	MS-64	MS-65	MS-66
1979-D	$5	$6	$10	$25

1979-S

Circulation-strike mintage: 109,576,000

Proof mintage: 3,677,175

Availability in Mint State: These are readily available through MS-65 and slightly higher grades.

actual size: 26.5 mm

Characteristics of striking: Striking of this issue varies, but they are usually sharp.

Proofs: Type 1: 1979-S, Filled S: The usually seen *variety* (the "type" designation is wrong, but seems to be here to stay), with interior spaces of the S mintmark appearing to be filled. This variety was created from the use of a worn mintmark punch. It is believed (by Alan Herbert, as quoted by Walter H. Breen in his 1988 *Encyclopedia*) that mintage of these took place from July to October. Probably about 80% to 85% of the mintage consisted of this style mintmark. One variety is from an over-polished die and has the third star too small.

Type 2: 1979-S, Clear S: This variety has the interior spaces of the S open. They are much scarcer than the preceding. It is believed that these were minted in November and December. Probably about 15% to 20% of the mintage consisted of this style mintmark.

Type 1 mintmark.

Type 2 mintmark.

Notes: All 1979-S coins are with Narrow Rim, the date farther from the inner edge of the border.

	MS-63	MS-64	MS-65	MS-66
1979-S	$5	$6	$10	$20

	PF-65	PF-68DC	PF-70
1979-S, Type 1 Proof	$7	$10	$110

	PF-65	PF-68DC	PF-70
1979-S, Type 2 Proof	$40	$75	$250

1980-P

Circulation-strike mintage: 27,610,000

actual size: 26.5 mm

Availability in Mint State: These are mostly seen in grades below MS-65, but enough have been certified MS-65 (mostly) to MS-67 to make them readily available.

Availability in circulated grades: *EF-40 to AU-58:* Coins in circulated grades are common, but are not widely desired.

Characteristics of striking: The striking of this issue varies. For any Susan B. Anthony dollar cherrypicking is advised. Oftentimes the lower center of the reverse has some weakness.

Notes: By 1980 the handwriting was on the wall, there was trouble in paradise, and it was evident that the Philadelphia Mint had struck enough coins for use from now to Kingdom Come. Accordingly, production was scaled back sharply, but to have stopped it completely would have been tantamount to admitting the whole idea was a poor one. Actually, the Jimmy Carter administration and his Mint director (Stella B. Hackel) never did face the facts. In time, the Anthony dollar simply faded away, at least for most of the decade.

2,815,066 Uncirculated 1980-P Anthony dollars were included in Mint sets sold by the Treasury to collectors; these sets contained the 1980–P, D and S dollars, plus other denominations cent through half dollar—total face value, $4.82; issue price of set: $9.00.

Walter H. Breen (*1988 Encyclopedia*, p. 472) suggested that some may exist with date distant from rim, but none has been reported.[17]

	MS-63	MS-64	MS-65	MS-66
1980-P	$5	$6	$10	$15

1980-D

Circulation-strike mintage: 41,628,708

actual size: 26.5 mm

Availability in Mint State: These are common in Mint State. Most coins are below MS-65 but, similar to 1980-P, many are available MS-65 and a couple grades higher.

Availability in circulated grades: *EF-40 to AU-58:* This issue is common in circulated grades, but they are not widely sought.

Characteristics of striking: The striking of this issue varies.

	MS-63	MS-64	MS-65	MS-66
1980-D	$5	$6	$10	$15

1980-S

Circulation-strike mintage: 20,422,000

Proof mintage: 3,554,806

Availability in Mint State: Similar comments as for 1980–P and D, but these are slightly scarcer. They are easy enough to find.

actual size: 26.5 mm

Characteristics of striking: The striking of this issue varies.

Proofs: All Proofs of this issue are of the same variety. They have the Open S mintmark, of the style made in November and December of 1979. Despite occasional rumors to the contrary, none of the old-style, Filled S mintmark variety have been reported.[18]

Notes: The 1980-S Anthony dollar has the lowest mintage of the three issues of the year. Relatively few circulated at the time. Proofs were sold in sets, cent through dollar, to collectors.

1980-S Proof, Repunched Mintmark: Enough of this variety is available to fill the numismatic demand. FS-C1-1980S-501.

	MS-63	MS-64	MS-65	MS-66	PF-65	PF-68DC	PF-70
1980-S	$10	$12	$15	$25	$6	$10	$85

1981-P

Circulation-strike mintage: 3,000,000

Availability in Mint State: This issue is common in Mint State. They are mostly found in grades MS–63 to 65, although MS-66 coins are readily available.

actual size: 26.5 mm

Availability in circulated grades: *EF-40 to AU-58:* These are very scarce as these did not circulate, but they are not numismatically important.

Characteristics of striking: The striking of this issue varies, but they are usually fairly sharp.

Notes: By 1981, the Anthony dollar was recognized as a failure as a circulating coin. To the incoming presidential administration of Ronald Reagan, the Anthony dollar was a relic of President Jimmy Carter's failed economic policies. With hundreds of millions of undistributed Anthony dollars piled up in government vaults, there was no reason to mint more for circulation. Three million were made for sale in Mint sets to collectors. Apparently, over 90,000 sets did not find buyers and remained undistributed by year's end.

	MS-63	MS-64	MS-65	MS-66
1981-P	$10	$14	$20	$50

1981-D

Circulation-strike mintage: 3,250,000

Availability in Mint State: This issue is common in Mint State. They are mostly found in grades MS–63 to 65, although MS-66 coins are readily available.

actual size: 26.5 mm

Availability in circulated grades: *EF-40 to AU-58:* These are very scarce as these did not circulate, but they are not numismatically important.

Characteristics of striking: The striking of this issue varies, but they are usually fairly sharp.

Notes: The 1981-D has the second lowest mintage (after 1981-P) of any Susan B. Anthony dollar. 2,908,145 Uncirculated 1981-D Anthony dollars were included in Mint sets sold by the Treasury to collectors; these sets contained the 1981–P, D and S dollars, plus other denominations, cent through half dollar—total face value, $4.82; issue price of set: $11.00 (an increase of $2 from the price of the previous year's set).

A burning question: What happened to the several hundred thousand 1981-D dollars not sold with the sets? In 1982 and 1983 I tried to find this out, also about the San Francisco coins, and was directed to the Federal Reserve System, after which I made several calls to individuals in Denver and elsewhere who were said to be familiar with the storage facilities. No one provided any useful information. I tried again in 1992 with no success at all.

	MS-63	MS-64	MS-65	MS-66
1981-D	$10	$12	$15	$25

1981-S

Circulation-strike mintage: 3,492,000

Proof mintage: 4,063,083

Availability in Mint State: This issue is common in Mint State. They are mostly seen in lower grades MS–62 to 64, as this is the scarcest of the circulation

actual size: 26.5 mm

strikes of the era to find MS-65 or higher. However, enough higher-grade coins exist to fill the demand for them, except at ultra levels.

James Sego commentary: This issue is by far the most difficult to find in superb gem grade with excellent overall quality. One would think with the high mintage this would not be the case.[19]

Availability in circulated grades: *EF-40 to AU-58:* These are very scarce as these did not circulate, but they are not numismatically important.

Characteristics of striking: Striking of this issue varies, but they are usually fairly sharp.

Proofs: Type 1, Filled S: There are two mintmark styles this year also, both very similar to those of 1979. This year's Type I appears to be a worn version of 1979's Type 2, while the 1981-S Type 2 is a new style, very open in the loops, and distinctly different from the Type 1 and Type 2 pieces of 1979, and the Type 2 issue of 1981.[20]

Type 1 mintmark.

Type 2, Clear S: These constitute the minority of the Proofs of this year, with a mintage of perhaps 10% or so of the Filled S.

Notes: The Filled S and Clear S mintmark varieties are quite similar in appearance and study under magnification is needed to differentiate them. The Filled S sometimes, but hardly always, appears as a blob under low magnification. Although these are popularly called "types," they are varieties, not a change in design.

Type 2 mintmark.

All 1981-S Anthony dollars, circulation strikes as well as Proofs, were minted especially for sale to collectors. What happened to the more than 500,000 1981-S Uncirculated dollars not sold with the Mint sets?

	MS-63	MS-64	MS-65	MS-66
1981-S	$20	$25	$40	$250

	PF-65	PF-68DC	PF-70
1981-S, Type 1 Proof	$6	$10	$85

	PF-65	PF-68DC	PF-70
1981-S, Type 2 Proof	$100	$175	$650

1999-P

Circulation-strike mintage: 29,592,000

Proof mintage: 750,000

Availability in Mint State: These are common in Mint State, but most are weakly struck (see Characteristics of striking).

actual size: 26.5 mm

Availability in circulated grades: *EF-40 to AU-58:* This issue is common, but is of no numismatic importance due to the availability of Mint State coins.

Characteristics of striking: These are usually seen with weakness at the centers, most noticeably on the branch on the reverse. This is the poorest-struck coin in the series.

Proofs: Proofs of this issue are easily available and all are in very high grades. The authorized mintage was 750,000. This was the second American Proof coin to bear a P mintmark, the earlier one being the 1942-P Jefferson nickel in silver-content "wartime" alloy.

1999-P, Struck on a Sacagawea planchet: In late 1999 both Anthony and Sacagawea dollars were being struck. Some "golden" planchets intended for Sacagawea dollars were inadvertently used for Susan B. Anthony dollars. Over a dozen examples are known. Conversely, some 2000-P Sacagawea dollars were struck on Anthony planchets.

	MS-63	MS-64	MS-65	MS-66	PF-65	PF-68DC	PF-70
1999-P	$3	$5	$10	$15	$20	$25	$85

1999-D

Circulation-strike mintage: 11,776,000

Availability in Mint State: This issue is common in Mint State.

Availability in circulated grades: *EF-40 to AU-58:*
These are common, but are of

actual size: 26.5 mm

no numismatic importance due to the availability of Mint State coins.

Characteristics of striking: This issue is often seen with weakness at the centers, most noticeably on the branch on the reverse.

Rob Ezerman commentary: These (and the almost as attractive 1999-Ps) are the only PCGS MS-68 SBAs one can acquire for reasonable money. They are usually gorgeous, even at MS–66 and 67, and today in 2015 some dealers at the larger coin shows regularly buy and sell the 1999 Special Mint Sets for under $20, each comes with a P and a D sealed in robust clear plastic so you can see the coins quite well.

About ten years ago I wanted to see what would happen if I purchased every PCGS 1999-D in MS-68 that popped up on eBay—at the time the PCGS population was in the 90s, way more than any other MS-68, but low enough to have a strong upside. Over the next 6 months I bought every one that was listed on eBay, well over twenty total, starting around $115 per and pushed the price well over $400 at the end of the six months. HOORAY! As much fun as this experiment was for me, I was going broke and had to sell them all over the next six months, bringing their price all the way back down to $115. Darn![21]

1999-D, Struck on a Sacagawea planchet: A few were struck on manganese-brass Sacagawea planchets. In 2011 an MS-65 sold for $7,762.

	MS-63	MS-64	MS-65	MS-66
1999-D	$3	$5	$10	$15

6 6 6 6 6 **6** 6 6 6 6 6

SACAGAWEA DOLLARS, 2000–2008

In 1997 several bills were introduced in Congress to mint more small-diameter dollars, but of a different appearance than the Susan B. Anthony coins, of which the Treasury Department still had large stocks on hand. Those coins were never popular with the public and few were seen in circulation. The Mint reported, however, that the SBA dollars had been finding increasing use in public transportation and in vending machines.

On March 20, Jim Kolbe, a representative from Arizona, forwarded the first bill for a further dollar coinage, but of a different appearance. He stated that Canada had been very successful with its brass dollar nicknamed the "loonie," featuring a loon, despite early opposition to the coin. The Canadian paper dollar was discontinued, and the coin became widely accepted in trade. Kolbe pointed out that the Anthony dollar had failed because it "looked and felt like the quarter" and also faced simultaneous circulation of paper dollar bills. The dollar bill should be phased out, he held. Representative Thomas M. Davis countered by saying that the public preferred dollar bills (which certainly had been the case during the SBA era) and, in any event, should not be told what type of money to use; furthermore, the American currency system was antiquated, and many universities, business, and people were switching to credit cards and other systems.

Theodore E. Allison, an assistant to the board of governors of the Federal Reserve System, recalled that before the SBA dollars were introduced, focus groups and retailers expressed reservation about a coin that could be confused with the quarter and would necessitate large costs to retrofit vending and amusement machines.[1] Debate continued pro and con.

On December 1, 1997, President Bill Clinton signed the 50 States Commemorative Coin Program Act, Public Law 105-124. Section 4, the United States $1 Coin Act of 1997, made the dollar a reality. The new coin was to be "golden in color, to have a distinctive edge, and have tactile and visual features that made the denomination of the coin readily discernible."

Seeking a New Design

Secretary of the Treasury Robert Rubin, by virtue of his office, had the final say in the design of the new coin. He appointed a Dollar Coin Design Advisory Committee with nine members charged to follow his instructions that it should show one or more women and not a living person. Members included Mint Director Philip N. Diehl,

Representative Michael Castle, Undersecretary of the Smithsonian Institution Constance Berry Newman, vice chair of the President's Committee on the Arts and Humanities Peggy Cooper Cafritz, president of the American Numismatic Society Arthur Houghton, architect Hilario Candela, sculptor Edward Vega, executive director of Business and Professional Women U.S.A. Gail Shaffer, and president of Trinity College Patricia McGuire.

With the exception of Diehl, Castle, and Houghton these names were unfamiliar to nearly all the numismatists who read the official Mint news release and *only* Houghton was a longtime numismatist.

Suggestions varied widely, from abstractions such as "Liberty" and "Peace" to individuals in history such as Eleanor Roosevelt, abolitionist Sojourner Truth, African-American aviatrix Bessie Coleman, and, of course, *Liberty Enlightening the World* (the Statue of Liberty).

On June 9, 1998, the committee, having reviewed the submissions, selected Sacagawea, the Shoshone interpreter for the Corps of Discovery, popularly known as the Lewis and Clark Expedition, which explored westward of the upper reaches of the Missouri River.

Michael Castle, who had a powerful influence in the House of Representatives and was also well known to the numismatic community, protested the choice and reiterated that the Statue of Liberty would be ideal as it was a popular and recognizable design and would facilitate the coin's use. At Castle's suggestion the General Accountability Office conducted a poll of citizens. The Statue of Liberty was preferred by 65%, Sacagawea by 27%, 5% said that either was acceptable, 3% liked neither, and 3% had no opinion. This effort came to naught, for Secretary Rubin chose Sacagawea. This was a poster example of an often-repeated scenario in American coinage history: polls, the Commission of Fine Arts, the Citizens Coinage Advisory Committee, numismatic groups, and others often favor or recommend designs, such sometimes being dismissed by the secretary of the Treasury. In this instance, however, after the coin became a reality nearly all in the numismatic community admired it greatly.

Invitations were sent to 23 artists to submit their interpretation of a design featuring Sacagawea on the obverse and on the reverse an eagle representing peace and freedom, their work to arrive at the Mint on or before October 28, 1998. No life portraits of Sacagawea are known to exist; the Mint's instructions were that she was to have the appearance of a Native American, not simply a generic woman. In November and December 1998 the Mint invited comments from government officials, numismatists, Native Americans, and others to review the designs submitted. This resulted in six obverse and seven reverse designs being named as semi-finalists. The creators of these were to receive $1,000 each, Mint employees excepted, and the designers for the final coin $5,000 each.

The Final Design

Using the Internet and other media the Mint also invited citizens to share their thoughts. The designs were then submitted to the Commission of Fine Arts. Chosen on December 17, 1998, was a representation of Sacagawea with her infant son Jean Baptiste Charbonneau, as submitted by talented sculptor Glenna Goodacre who had a studio in Santa Fe, New Mexico. The reverse chosen was the work of Mint sculptor-engraver Thomas D. Rogers Sr. depicting a soaring eagle. To the satisfaction of almost everyone, the secretary of the Treasury agreed.

As there are no contemporary portraits or other illustrations of Sacagawea, Good-acre went to the nearby American Indian Arts Museum in Santa Fe to see if she could find an appropriate model. She chose Randy'L He-dow Teton, daughter of a museum employee and a student at the University of New Mexico. Born in 1976, she is a Shoshone-Bannock-Cree woman from the Lincoln Creek District within the Fort Hall Reservation in Idaho. Selection as the coin's model brought her a degree of fame, and she was featured at several numismatic events, the first-ever living model for cir-culating coinage to appear at such gatherings.

An early plaster of Sacagawea as details were being added at the Mint.

A slightly later version with more details on Sacagawea's clothing.

The finessed final version with different details on Sacagawea's clothing, and no designer's initials.

The final version nearing readiness for the die-making process. Glenna Goodacre's GG initials are seen.

Notations on a plaster for determining the date style and position for 2005.

Sacagawea and the Expedition

The original Sacagawea, a Lemhi Shoshone woman, was born in May 1788. Her early life was mostly unfortunate. In 1800 she and some other girls were kidnapped by a group of Hidatsas and taken as captives. While there she was acquired as a wife by Toussaint Charbonneau, a Quebecois trapper who resided there, joining another of his wives. It is said that he won both women by gambling.

The author and Randy'L He-dow Teton at American Numismatic Association headquarters on July 14, 2001.

When the Lewis and Clark Expedition arrived at the Hidatsa settlement to stay the winter of 1804–1805 and build Fort Mandan, they hired Charbonneau as their interpreter. They learned that his captive wife spoke fluent Shoshone, providing an excellent possibility to join the group in their anticipated travels through Shoshone territory. Both husband and wife traveled with the adventurers. Their son Jean Baptiste was born on February 11, 1805.

Sacagawea's main activity with the travelers was as an interpreter, not as the guide mentioned in popular histories. The presence of a Native American in the group also assured other natives along the trip that their intent was peaceful, for a woman would not have been part of an invading force. The arrangement was very satisfactory. Along the way she negotiated the purchase of horses and at one time rescued the expedition's journal after a canoe accident. Several years later in 1809 Sacagawea and her husband accepted William Clark's invitation to relocate to St. Louis, where their child, nicknamed "Pomp" by the explorers, became enrolled into the St. Louis Academy boarding school. In the next year or shortly afterward, Sacagawea gave birth to a daughter, Lizette. She grew homesick and returned to the Northwest, leaving her two children behind for adoption. She died of "putrid fever" on December 20, 1812. It cannot be said that her life was a happy one, but we can hope she enjoyed at least part of it.

Controversy

News about the forthcoming Sacagawea dollar engendered much controversy, some of which was played out in the daily papers.[2] The Mount Vernon Ladies' Association strongly opposed the possible replacement of the familiar dollar bill, which featured George Washington's portrait. Other observers stated that the elimination of the paper dollar would cost 600 to 1,000 jobs at the Bureau of Engraving and Printing as about 40% of the Crane & Co. paper contract of $65 million per year was for dollar bills.

Standing to benefit from the coins was the vending-machine industry of about $40 billion revenue per year. It would not cost much to configure coin mechanisms to take dollar coins, replacing bill changers that cost $400 each. Beyond vending machines billions of dollars in coins, usually quarters, went through non-vending devices such as parking meters, washing machines, airport luggage carts, and even vibrating beds in motel rooms. The new coins replacing the paper dollar would result in increased employment at the various mints, offsetting to an unknown degree the job losses at the Bureau of Engraving and Printing (both entities are part of the Treasury Department). The seigniorage or profit made on each coin would be a benefit as well.

Sacagawea Coin News

On May 20, 1999, *Mint News*, an occasional newsletter, contained information about striking more Susan B. Anthony dollars, now with a 1999 date, and concluded with this information:

> Authorized by the United States $1 Coin Act of 1997, the new dollar coin's Sacagawea obverse design and Eagle reverse design were unveiled at a White House ceremony on May 4.
>
> Although the new dollar coin will be the same diameter as the Susan B. Anthony dollar coin it will have some new features to ensure it is easily discernible for both the sighted and the seeing-impaired. The new dollar will be golden in color, with a smooth edge—in contrast to the reeded edge of the Susan B. Anthony dollar coin—and have a wider border than current U.S. coinage. The Mint is currently completing research to develop an alloy to meet the requirements of the legislation, including mechanical and chemical simulated wear and tarnish testing.

Photographs of the White House event showed First Lady Hillary Rodham Clinton standing with Randy'L Teton, model of the coin, in front of a large cut-out of the new dollar. "Sacagawea played an unforgettable role in the history of our nation," Mrs. Clinton said. "Every day this coin will remind us we are a nation of many cultures."

The *Annual Report of the Director of the Mint* for the fiscal year ending September 30, 1999, included this:

> At year end we finalized the alloy for the Sacagawea dollar—or as we call it, the golden dollar—after almost two years of experimentation and coordination with business stakeholders.
>
> We'll produce more than 100 million golden dollars for release in February, when our consumer awareness and business education campaign ramps up. We're readying a national print and TV consumer campaign, and our business-to-business outreach team is finalizing materials, interactive displays, and schedules of appearances. We've met repeatedly with banking and retail organizations and tested public perception of the new coin.

Mint Director Jay Johnson

In August 1999 President Bill Clinton appointed Jay Johnson as director of the Mint, succeeding Philip Diehl. Johnson had served earlier in various government offices and at one time was a representative to Congress from Wisconsin. He had spent 36 years in media, including radio and television broadcasting. Confirmed by the Senate in May 2000, he served as Mint director until August 2001 when in the change of administration President George W. Bush appointed Henrietta Holsman Fore as director.

Mary Counts (later Mary Burleson), president of Whitman Publishing; Mint Director Henrietta H. Fore; and Fore's predecessor, Mint Director Jay Johnson, at the American Numismatic Association convention in August 2004.

Johnson embraced his post with passion and enthusiasm rarely seen. He helped create innovative advertising for the "golden dollars." One television spot featured George Washington holding one of the coins. Kermit the Mint Spokesfrog was on the screen as well, mainly promoting State quarters. Similar to what Mary T. Brooks had done during her tenure, Johnson was always available to the numismatic community, appeared at many events, and answered questions.[3]

A Great Success

As planned, in 1999 and 2000 the Mint promoted the Sacagawea dollars with advertisements on the radio and television as well as with print announcements. Kits were supplied to those interested and included a "Use the golden dollar here" decal that could be affixed to a glass entry door. The official view was that the launch was a spectacular success, per this in the *Annual Report of the Director of the Mint*, 2000:

> Formally introduced in January 2000 and propelled by full-scale outreach campaigns, the Mint's Sacagawea Golden Dollar has achieved overwhelming success in record time. In its first nine months, demand triggered the production and shipment of 979 million Golden Dollars—it took 14 years for the Susan B. Anthony dollars to reach demand at that level!
>
> By year's end, the billionth Golden Dollar rolled off our presses. Hundreds of millions of Americans are using the coins and collecting them. This enormous popularity resulted in a profit of over $800 million and was a major component of the Mint's record-breaking total revenues for the year.[4] The Golden Dollar's clearly successful introduction underscores the value of the Mint's vigorous market orientation. We were able to harness all of the marketing, partnering, and educational tools available to create, rather than merely respond to, demand—and in a single year have made the Golden Dollar a fixture in American coinage.
>
> A high-profile national multi-media campaign, featuring a contemporary George Washington as spokesperson, reached 92% of urban/suburban adults 15–18 times during the promotional period. Additional awareness came from media coverage, including appearances on the *Today Show*, on prime-time programs, and at the National Press Club.
>
> The business-to-business element of the U.S. Mint's marketing campaign involves targeting its resources and message. It identified eight sectors to focus its efforts to get more Golden dollars in customers' hands and circulating in commerce: financial institutions, retailers, the entertainment industry, grocery stores, fast food restaurants, government agencies, the vending industry, and transit authorities.
>
> Seventeen of the top 20 metro transit networks in the U.S. distribute and accept the Golden Dollar, including the country's two largest: New York and Chicago. Marketing materials sent to small financial institutions promoted the public's use of the Golden Dollar. A special direct-ship program assured their sufficient supply. Partnering with the Mint, Allfirst Financial, a 261-branch mid-Atlantic bank, launched a promotion that includes routinely paying Golden Dollars in change to customers.

The Rest of the Story

The above enthusiastic scenario was not visible at all to writers in the numismatic press or to collectors. In most areas of America the only Sacagawea dollars to be seen were on bank counters, available to those interested, this despite the huge mintage that equaled about three coins for every man, woman, and child in the United States! This was an era in which retail banking provided many services to over-the-counter customers, although ATMs and Internet banking were catching on and in time would replace much personal service. From this time through most of the rest of the decade, banks gladly supplied new dollar coins to their clients and often posted signs to this effect.

At the time I carefully studied the distribution. Then and at no later time did I ever receive even a single coin in change. The banks I surveyed often reported that the dollars they paid out were soon returned by merchant customers who hesitated to pass them on to general circulation. There was no action at all to reduce the production of $1 notes, which could have made the Sacagawea dollars successful, similar to the acceptance of Canada's dollar coin. Then came the recession of 2008: banks cut back, and within a few years hardly any banks made it known that they could order new coins for customers. Person-to-person interaction between tellers and customers was costly, and banks continued to try to minimize it.

At the same time the Sacagawea coins were warmly and enthusiastically embraced by the numismatic community. Nearly everyone loved them, a contrast to the rather mild reception given to SBA dollars.

The alloy used to make Sacagawea dollars was chemically active, causing many coins to become stained or spotted. The Mint tried several rinse compounds in an effort to prevent this. One, which was used on about 2,500 coins in 2001, imparted a distinctive pale patina. Faced with many complaints, mainly from collectors rather than the general public, the Mint issued this announcement:

> The different hues of the Golden Dollars now circulating are the result of the manganese-brass contained in the outer layer of the new coins. Like any brass, its color will eventually become darker, giving your coins an antique finish. As the coins are handled frequently, the darker "patina" may wear off the high points of the coin, leaving golden-colored highlights that accent the darker background around the border, lettering and other less exposed areas. The brighter, brass highlights, in contrast with the darker background, accentuate the profile and add a dimension of depth to the depiction of Sacagawea and her child.

In 2001 production dropped to 133,407,500 or about one-tenth of the 2000 figure. Beginning in 2002 the Mint limited the mintage to coins and sets sold to collectors. Uncirculated coins dated back to 2000 were available in rolls of 25 and in bags of 2,000. In 2005 the 2,000-coin bag was replaced by a 250-coin bag, bowing to the wishes of Mint customers, according to Mint spokesman Michael White.

Sacagawea Dollars Refused

In a retrospective editorial in *Coin World*, May 17, 2004, Beth Deisher laid out reasons why the high hopes for the Sacagawea dollars had been dashed:

> We hope that lawmakers and Treasury officials paid attention to what Tom McMahon, senior vice president and chief counsel of the National Automatic Merchandising Association, and Jeffrey Marquardt, association director for the Federal Reserve System's division of Reserve Bank Operations and Payment Systems, had to say [at an April 29 hearing in Congress]. Both deal in the practical world of coins being used—and not used-—in daily commerce.
>
> Both McMahon and Marquardt raised the same point: No new dollar coins will circulate in any meaningful way unless the Anthony dollar is extracted from the mix of coins in circulation. The reason is simple. The Anthony dollar coin is still

creating the same problem it did 25 years ago. It is too similar in color and size to the quarter dollar coin and is often mistaken for the lesser value coin. Therefore, retailers and banks refuse to use the Anthony dollar.

The Anthony dollar problem resurfaced anew shortly after the introduction of the Sacagawea "golden dollar" in 2000. Retailers across the country geared up to offer the new "golden dollars" to their customers. But after the initial round of receiving the new coins, they began receiving the Anthony and Sacagawea dollars co-mingled in rolls from the commercial banks.

Bank counting machines and vending machines don't distinguish between the Anthony dollar and the Sacagawea dollar because they have the same magnetic signature. As long as the co-mingled dollar coins were recirculated within a closed environment (such as a transit system) there was no problem. But as soon as the dollar coins began to be co-mingled in bank rolls, retailers began avoiding the dollar coins altogether. Not using any dollar coins became their only defense against receiving the unwanted Anthony dollar.

So how could you take the Anthony dollar out of circulation without demonetizing it? (The United States does not demonetize its coins. It still honors the face value of every coin made by the U.S. Mint.)

Marquardt suggested that the U.S. Mint buy back from the Federal Reserve all mixed rolls of dollar coins and sort them. Once sorted, the circulated Sacagaweas could be sold back to the Fed, which in turn would distribute them to all sectors of the economy through banks. He suggested that the Mint place the SBA dollars in long-term storage or destroy them. There's logic to Marquardt's suggestion. The Fed estimates it has 23 million Anthony dollars in inventory co-mingled with Sacagawea dollars. That's a far cry from the approximately 970 million SBAs originally minted or the 450 million once held in storage that Mint directors used to fret about having to incur reverse seigniorage on if they were destroyed.[5]

Editor Deisher suggested that the Mint buy from the Federal Reserve all stored small-size dollars, hire unemployed people to sort them (solving another problem), destroy the SBAs, and return the Sacagaweas to inventory for hoped-for further use.

The Ecuador Connection

Beginning early in the Susan B. Anthony dollar program many coins were sent to South American countries, but the Treasury Department declined to provide specific information. The story was told by Timothy Benford in "Sacagawea dollars, unwanted in U.S., 'most popular' form of exchange in Ecuador," in *Coin World*, May 31, 2004:

The Sacagawea dollar coin, unwanted, unused, and often verbally abused in the United States, may be the most recent of the US. Mint's metallic mistakes in a generation, but south of the border down Ecuador way, Sac dollars are a numero uno smash hit.

Several sources in Ecuador confirm that Ecuadorians love and use the coin more than any other form of legal tender. U.S. currency officially became legal tender throughout Ecuador in September 2000. The extraordinary action was an effort to stabilize the South American nation's shaky economy and to deal with rampant inflation of the up-til-then monetary unit, the sucre.

By New Year's Day 2003, the U.S. government had shipped more than 500 million of the dollar coins to Ecuador for use as circulating currency. With a lifespan considerably longer than paper currency the coins became an instant success in the often-humid climate. . . .

When Ecuadorians interviewed for this story were informed that there appears to be strong interest and support in the U.S. to replace the image of Sacagawea on the dollar coin with consecutive images of all the U.S. presidents their responses were emphatic.

"Oh, I hope not! I really hope they do not do that. Everybody likes the golden dollar coin very much here," said Monica Martinez, general manager of a Quito-based retail operation. She recalled that when many people received a Sacagawea dollar for the first time, they thought the obverse depicted an Ecuadorian Indian woman.

Martinez explained: "I thought that. I really did. The likeness is striking. The woman on the coin, she could be an Indian woman from the mountains selling hand woven rugs or artistic clay pots to tourists. Some people thought it was very nice for the U.S. to put an Ecuadorian Indian woman on these American coins they made especially for us! But now if they change it, then what? Who will know, or identify, with American presidents on our coins? It just won't be the same."

This was a godsend, as coins sent to South America tended to stay there!

By December 2009 the Federal Reserve System had 857 million Sacagawea dollars in storage. In early 2010 the Mint announced that 2000-P and D dollars that had been in storage for nine years were now part of its Direct Ship Program and could be ordered in any quantity desired. The Direct Ship Program was intended to promote circulation of the coins by offering rolls of the coins at face value with free shipping.

Grading Sacagawea Dollars

2006-D. Graded MS-65.

MS-60 to 70 (Mint State). *Obverse:* At MS-60, some abrasion and contact marks are evident, most noticeably on the cheekbone and the drapery near the baby's head. Luster is present, but may be dull or lifeless. At MS-63, contact marks are extensive but not distracting. Abrasion still is evident, but less than at lower levels. MS-64 coins are slightly finer. An MS-65 coin may have minor abrasion, but contact marks are so minute as to require magnification. Luster should be full and rich. *Reverse:* At MS-60, some abrasion and contact marks are evident, most noticeably on the eagle's breast. Otherwise, the same comments apply as for the obverse.

2000-P. Graded AU-55.

AU-50, 53, 55, 58 (About Uncirculated). *Obverse:* Light wear is seen on cheekbone, drapery, and elsewhere. At AU-58, the luster is extensive, but incomplete. At AU–50 and 53, luster is less but still present. *Reverse:* Further wear is evident on the eagle. Otherwise, the same comments apply as for the obverse.

The Sacagawea dollar is seldom collected in grades lower than AU-50.

2002-S. Graded PF-69.

PF-60 to 70 (Proof). *Obverse and Reverse:* Proofs that are extensively cleaned and have many hairlines, or that are dull and grainy, are lower level, such as PF–60 to 62. This comment is more theoretical than practical, as nearly all Proofs have been well kept. With medium hairlines and good reflectivity, assigned grades of PF–63 or 64 are appropriate. With relatively few hairlines a rating of PF–65 can be given. PF-66 may have hairlines so delicate that magnification is needed to see them. Above that, all the way to PF-70, a Proof should be free of any hairlines or other problems under strong magnification.

Collecting Sacagawea Dollars

A basic set of dates and mintmarks of Sacagawea dollars can be collected with ease. Most circulation strikes can be readily found in MS-65 grade, called "gem" Uncirculated. For countless generations coins of such a grade were pleasing to nearly all numismatists, including the most discriminating. That changed in the 1990s when certified coins became popular and went into the fast lane early in the present century when competing for PCGS and NGC registry-set listings became very popular. This has caused countless coins—not only dollars but also other denominations—that are very common in circulation-strike format and often inexpensive in MS-65—to be recognized as expensive rarities if in a grade such as MS–68, 69, or 70. Proofs with S mintmarks are typically found in 69 or 70 grades, although many uninformed buyers do not realize this and view these high grades as "rare."

Beyond the basics, there are three well-known varieties of special interest:

1. The 2000-P "Cheerios" dollar with a prototype reverse, of which fewer than 100 have been certified as of early 2016.

2. The Glenna Goodacre presentation coins, which are slightly scarce, typically sell into mid- to high three figures, and are readily found in the marketplace.

3. Satin Finish Sacagawea dollars made from 2005 to 2008 at the Philadelphia and Denver mints, which were included in Mint sets and have a special satiny surface. Many of these have surface marks from careless handling at the mints, but among them are some in very high grades. The difference between the Satin Finish coins and the regular Uncirculated coins is not sufficiently distinctive to inspire many collectors to desire one of each finish for a given date and mint. Certain varieties such as 2005-P, 2006-D, and 2008-D are rare in MS-65 grade but common in Satin Finish-65.

The 2000-D Millennial coins that seem to have been burnished after striking are interesting, but no great demand exists for them.

Paul Gilkes, in "Experimental washes, special strikings challenge to collect. Sacagawea dollar collections can include VIP strikings, toned pieces," *Coin World*, March 3, 2010, pointed out that due to experimental rinses, efforts to prevent tarnish, and other situations the mints turned out coins with varying surfaces:

> In 2006, Sacagawea dollars from the Denver and Philadelphia Mints appeared with discolored surfaces similar to the surfaces on the 2001-P strikes, although the discoloration did not necessarily cover the entire coin. The discoloration on the 2006 dollars was the result of a failure to properly rinse an anti-tarnishing agent used by the U.S. Mint, an agent that had originally been developed as a wood preservative. Although the 2006 issues were circulation strikes, the coins came from special Mint-wrapped circulation strikes offered to collectors as a numismatic product.

Because of uncertainties as well as toning and other home-made treatments added outside of the Mint, such coins have a limited popularity, and great caution should be used if you are considering such a purchase. Professional third-party certification is your best protection.

In a slightly different category are dollars struck from planchets improperly annealed during the heat-treating process. In the early 2010s certain certification services began calling these *sintered*. This term is metallurgically incorrect as sintering refers to compacting metal powder under great pressure to form a solid. *Mis-annealed* would be an accurate description, agreed to by error-coin expert Fred W. Weinberg.

2000–2008,
Sacagawea Dollar

Designer: Glenna Goodacre (obverse); Thomas D. Rogers Sr. (reverse).

Composition: Pure copper core with outer layers of manganese-brass (.770 copper, .070 manganese, .120 zinc, .040 nickel).

Weight: 8.1 grams.

Diameter: 26.5 mm.

Edge: Plain.

2000-P

Circulation-strike mintage: 767,140,000[6]

Collecting commentary:
So many of these were struck that today they are extremely common. Typical examples are in MS–63 and 64, but enough higher-grade MS coins exist that they are common in relation to

actual size: 26.5 mm

the demand for them. For these and all other Sacagawea dollars it is important to remember that only a tiny proportion of the mintage has ever been sent to the certification services for grading. A coin that may appear to be rare in population-report figures may actually be common. Several hundred million 2000–P and D dollars were shipped to Ecuador where they saw use in everyday commerce.

VIP strikes: On November 18, 1999, a first-strike ceremony was held at the Philadelphia Mint. Invited dignitaries and guests were on hand, and some were allowed to push a button to have a coin struck. A medal (not high-speed circulation) press was used. These coins had a special finish, lightly polished in appearance. It is thought that fewer than 600 were struck.[7] Some of these were later packaged and sent to those in attendance at the ceremony. The special characteristics of these have not been well defined in numismatic literature. Again, coins privately polished outside of the Mint have confused the matter.

Notes: Some 2000-P Sacagawea dollars were struck in error on clad planchets intended for 1999-P Susan B. Anthony dollars. Over a dozen are known.

More double-struck and other mint error coins are known of 2000-P than of any other date and mint issue.

	MS-64	MS-65	MS-66
2000-P	$3	$5	$12

2000-P, Goodacre Presentation Finish

Presentation Finish mintage: 5,000

actual size: 26.5 mm

Goodacre Presentation Finish: Glenna Goodacre received her $5,000 payment for designing the obverse in the form of as many Sacagawea dollars, but with a specially burnished and treated surface—unexpected by her and unannounced in advance. These proved to be a bonanza.

At the time the Mint was having some problems with discoloration, and this was the way to prevent that from happening with coins that no doubt would be given away or otherwise distributed by Goodacre, rather than being spent. Not all received this treatment, but most did. These coins were put up in cloth bags, resulting in some bagmarks, but not extensive.

These were delivered to her Santa Fe, New Mexico, studio by Mint Director Philip Diehl accompanied by two Mint police officers. A special ceremony was held there

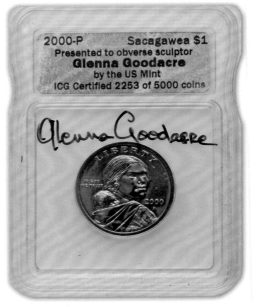

A Goodacre Presentation coin in the slab signed by Glenna Goodacre.

on April 5, 2000. Seeking to preserve them from handling, the artist had the Independent Coin Graders (ICG) encapsulate them without adding grades beginning on August 8. Many were broken out of their holders and sent to PCGS or NGC where they nearly all earned high grades. Goodacre kept 2,000 coins for herself. Nearly all of the others were sold for $200 each. The label on each read:

> 2000-P / Sacagawea $1
> Presented to obverse sculptor
> Glenna Goodacre
> By the U.S. Mint
> ICG Certified [number here] of 5000 coins

Many of these were broken out of their ICG holders and certified by PCGS and NGC, called "specimens," such as SP-65. At least 126 of the coins were found to have regular (not burnished) surfaces. These were referred to as Type 1 and the burnished coins as Type 2.[8]

From *Coin World*, April 11, 2011, reported by Paul Gilkes:

Nearly 2,000 of the remaining specially produced 2000-P Sacagawea dollars from among the 5,000 that sculptor Glenna Goodacre was presented as compensation for her adopted Sacagawea dollar obverse design were acquired in 2010 by Kentucky dealer Jeff Garrett, owner of Mid-American Rare Coin Gallery in Lexington. He had the coins removed from the Independent Coin Grading holders originally encapsulating them and had them resealed in Professional Coin Grading Service holders with grading inserts pedigreeing the coins to Goodacre. Garrett has since dispersed the PCGS-encapsulated coins into the market through dealers, except for a small number he retained for his personal collection.

Some regular 2000-P dollars have been privately burnished, creating deceptive pieces. Caution is advised when buying any coin not clearly certified and attributed to the Goodacre holding.

	MS-64	MS-65	MS-66
2000-P, Goodacre Presentation Finish	$500	$600	$800

2000-P, "Cheerios"

Prototype "Cheerios" mintage: 5,500

actual size: 26.5 mm

Early "Cheerios" "Prototype" Reverse: The most famous standard variety in the Sacagawea series is an early-release coin with the tail feathers showing prominent diagonal veins. This was the first type of die in use and had also been employed in making the 2000-W *gold* coins (see listing). The eagle was subsequently modified to show the tail feathers in parallel lines, this being the "regular" reverse.

The Mint was eager to promote public interest and acceptance of the new dollar. It arranged with General Mills, Inc., the Minneapolis manufacturer of cereals and other foods, to supply 5,500 coins struck in late summer or early autumn 1999 with a 2000-P obverse and the prototype reverse. The difference in the reverse details was not noticed at the time. General Mills advertised a "treasure hunt"—one in every 2,000 boxes of Cheerios would contain a new Sacagawea dollar, not yet in general release, and a 2000-dated Lincoln cent. "The only place to get either coin is in a box of Cheerios." Further, one box in every 4,400 had a certificate redeemable for 100 Susan B. Anthony dollars (finders who redeemed them received the dollars with the later-type reverse).

These coins were struck in advance of the regular quantity production run that started on November 19, 1999. The Cheerios dollars were indeed special for the recipients, as coins for general distribution were not released to the Federal Reserve Banks until January 26, 2000.

Detail of prototype or "Cheerios" reverse with diagonal veins in the tail feathers. Center line is raised.

Detail of later standard reverse without vein details in the tail feathers. The center line is recessed.

Walmart had an early supply of 100,000,000 coins, of the regular-reverse style, which it agreed not to release as change to its customers until January 30, so as not to eclipse the General Mills promotion. Remarkably, it was not until February 2005, or over five years later, that this special variety was recognized by numismatists when one was sent by California collector Pat Braddick to NGC.[9] By that time the Cheerios dollars had been widely dispersed, many had been spent, and those saved by chance could not be found other than by expensive and perhaps not fruitful advertising.

After the variety was discovered, coins appeared on eBay and other auctions, some selling for several thousand dollars with one bring a much higher price. Typical grades were MS-65 to MS-67.

Per Bill Gibbs in "Cheerios dollars soften," *Coin World,* June 29, 2009: "Prices falling from 2008 levels. When a new subtype or variety is discovered there is initial excitement, when over the next several years the market adjusts as the coin does (or doesn't) enter 'mainstream' collecting. A year ago an example of the 'Cheerios' dollar sold at auction for nearly $35,000! However, the initial excitement that accompanied its discovery has waned, and savvy collectors can now acquire an example for a fraction of its price at its market apex."

As of October 2015 PCGS had certified 1 as MS-64, 1 as MS-65, 8 as MS-66, 33 as MS-67, and 31 as MS-68 for a total of 74 occasions, some probably being resubmissions. NGC had certified 2, both MS-64. This would seem to indicate that fewer than 100 coins are in numismatic hands.[10] Prices on the market for grades of MS–66 and 67 vary widely, some being double or more than the price of others.

	MS-64	MS-65	MS-66
2000-P, Cheerios		$4,000	$6,000

2000-D

Circulation-strike mintage: 518,916,000

Burnished Millennium mintage: 75,000

Collecting commentary:
Typical coins of this issue are MS-63 to MS-65. Certified ultra- high Mint State coins are elusive in

actual size: 26.5 mm

proportion, but are much less often seen than are those of 2001-P. Large quantities were sent to Ecuador for use as legal tender in commerce (see introductory narrative).

2000-D from burnished millennium set: As a special promotion in its 2000 Holiday Catalog the U.S. Mint offered the United States Millennium Coin and Currency Set which contained a $1 Federal Reserve Note with the serial number starting with 2000, a 2000 American Eagle silver bullion coin, a 2000-D Sacagawea dollar. Also included was a booklet with information about each coin plus historical notes, including the tale about Benjamin Franklin preferring a wild turkey to a bald eagle as the national bird on the last page. These sets were offered at $39 each. Upon arrival of the sets, collectors noticed that the dollar was partially prooflike or burnished, reminiscent of the special coins given to Glenna Goodacre, and of a deeper golden color.

PCGS and ICG graders contended that the burnishing was post-strike. NGC graders had mixed opinions.

These became collectible in their own right, selling at a premium if submitted with original Mint packaging (so as to prevent home-burnished coins from being certified). PCGS and NGC certified such dollars with a "Millennial Set" notation and DPL suffix for "Deep Mirror Prooflike." The degree of the prooflike surface can vary, and some small percentage of sets contained dollars that were not prooflike. Again, the matter is confusing.

VIP strikes: On February 25, 2000, a first-strike ceremony was held at the Denver Mint. Invited dignitaries and guests were on hand, and some were allowed to push a button to have a coin struck. A medal (not high-speed circulation) press was used. These coins had a special finish, lightly polished in appearance. The mintage was just 120 pieces.

	MS-64	MS-65	MS-66
2000-D	$4	$8	$15

2000-S

Proof mintage: 4,047,904

Availability: Nearly all of these coins are gem Proofs approaching perfection.

Notes: 3,082,572 were sold as part of the 10-piece "clad" Proof sets;. 965,421 were sold as part of the 10-piece "silver"

actual size: 26.5 mm

Proof sets.[11] This was the high-water mark in terms of the number minted.

	PF-65	PF-69DC	PF-70
2000-S, Proof	$15	$25	$55

2000-W

Gold mintage: 39

Net mintage: 12

Notes: In June 1999 Mint Director Philip N. Diehl made the surprise announcement that 32 2000-W Sacagawea dollars had been struck in 22-karat gold. Although

actual size: 26.5 mm

they bore a W mintmark they were struck in Philadelphia, later research revealed.[12] He stated that more would be struck and these would be offered for sale. This caused quite a stir, the director was accused of exceeding his authority, and on August 12 he announced that all but 12 would be melted. Those surviving had been carried aboard the *Columbia* space shuttle launched on July 23, 1999, on a five-day mission under the command of Eileen Collins. On December 1, 1999, two more gold strikes were made.[13] In March 2000 Congress placed an indefinite moratorium on the striking of Sacagawea coinage in gold after lawmakers questioned whether the Mint had the legal authority to produce the coins in precious metal. The 12 Proof Sacagawea gold dollars sent into space were transferred to the Mint's gold-bullion depository at Fort Knox, Kentucky. The 12 coins were put on public display for the first time as a group during the American Numismatic Association's World's Fair of Money in Milwaukee in August. The remaining 27 Proof Sacagawea gold dollars struck were destroyed, according to U.S. Mint officials. Years later the West Point Mint actually struck Sacagawea dollars for the first time, the Native American 2015-W coins in manganese-brass limited to 90,000 coins.

2000-W, Sacagawea $5 patterns: In February and March 2000 the Philadelphia Mint struck 40 experimental circulation-strike and Proof $5 coins in gold. These had the higher denomination lettered on the reverse and bore W mintmarks. The tail feathers on the eagle were straight (the second style). Fifteen pairs of dies were prepared, the reverses denominated FIVE DOLLARS. It was thought that these might be a nice addition to the Mint's gold-bullion program. An original plaster is shown here. The idea was abandoned and all of the coins, hubs, and dies were destroyed. One reason was the fear that circulation-strike Sacagawea dollars could be gold plated and passed as $5 coins.[14]

2000, Sacagawea Dollar/ Washington Quarter Muling

Circulation-strike mintage: Unknown

actual size: 26.5 mm

Collecting commentary: It is thought that only 14 examples have been identified, all Mint State. These have captured the fancy of collectors, and several auction records into six figures have been recorded. Most are owned by a numismatist in the Southwest, as noted on the next page.

Sacagawea dollar/Washington quarter muling: At the Philadelphia Mint an undated Washington quarter obverse as used to strike State quarters was inadvertently combined with a Sacagawea dollar reverse with the soaring eagle, also undated. The first example was found in Ma y 2000 by Frank Wallis, a Mountain Home, Arkansas, collector, in a group of dollars obtained from the First National Bank & Trust Company in that town. It was brought to Bowers and Merena Galleries and auctioned in the 2000 ANA Convention Sale for $29,900, the buyer being Dwight Manley. This created no end of excitement. Here was a coin that was months old and worth tens of thousands of dollars—unprecedented in American numismatic history. Additional pieces came to light, each with publicity and each attracting attention, and along the way two press operators from the Philadelphia Mint were arrested. James Watkins and Raymond Jackson were charged with disposing of some of the coins, and were indicted on June 13, 2002. Jackson pleaded guilty, and Watkins became a fugitive. For a time the numismatic community feared that certain of the coins would be seized, but this did not happen.[15]

Careful examination revealed that three different die pairs were used to make them, indicating three different striking occasions and, perhaps, that they were "helped" out of the Mint. Some coins were recovered from a bin at the Mint and others at a wrapping facility and are thought to have been destroyed. The quantity made is not known, and the situation remains wrapped in mystery.

Tommy Bolack, a numismatist, rancher, and museum owner in Farmington, New Mexico, took a special fancy to these and has acquired at least eight pieces. The PCGS Web site devotes a page to these and lists past prices, all below $100,000, except for one that was sold in the 2012 ANA Sale by Stack's Bowers Galleries for $155,250. This coin is no. 5 in *100 Greatest U.S. Modern Coins.*

2001-P

Circulation-strike mintage: 62,468,000

Collecting commentary: Typical coins are MS-63 to MS-65. Ultra-high grade Mint State coins are elusive in proportion, but many exist due to the large quantities minted, although production was sharply

actual size: 26.5 mm

lower this year than in 2000. Many 2001 and 2002–P and D coins were sent to Ecuador for use as legal tender in commerce (see introductory narrative).

Experimental rinse: Spotting and staining was a problem with Sacagawea dollars in 2000, extending into 2001. Various rinses were tried in an effort to prevent this. One compound used on about 2,500 coins imparted a distinctive pale patina. Many of these were identified before being widely distributed and were sold into the numismatic market. Some were placed in holders by the Sovereign Entities Grading Service (SEGS) and labeled: "2001-P EXPERIMENTAL RINSE SAC $1 / EXPERIMENTAL RINSE BY U.S. MINT TO PREVENT SPOTS." (Also see 2006-D.)

	MS-64	MS-65	MS-66
2001-P	$2	$4	$6

2001-D

Circulation-strike mintage: 70,939,500

Collecting commentary: Typical coins are MS-63 to MS-64. In terms of certified coins, relatively few have been graded MS-68 or higher, with the result that they sell at sharp premiums, including to those in the PCGS registry-set program.

actual size: 26.5 mm

2001-D muling with South Carolina quarter reverse: At the Denver Mint in 2001 there were two cases of shenanigans when one or more coin-press operators intentionally created two mulings: (1) A 2001-D cent obverse with a Roosevelt dime reverse, struck on copper-plated–zinc planchets, and (2) A 2001-D Sacagawea dollar obverse mated with the reverse of a South Carolina State quarter. Investigators discovered these and are thought to have found and destroyed them all, but the matter was not certain. No examples have been reported on the coin market.[16]

	MS-64	MS-65	MS-66
2001-D	$2	$4	$6

2001-S

Proof mintage: 3,183,740

Availability: Nearly all of these coins are gem Proofs approaching perfection.

Notes: 2,294,909 were sold as part of the 10-piece "clad" Proof sets; 889,967 were sold as part of the 10-piece "silver" Proof sets.

actual size: 26.5 mm

Charles Morgan commentary: Once thought of as the "key-date" to the series, a lower mintage later occurred in 2008. Promoters pumped certified PF-70DC versions of this coin into the stratosphere with many selling for thousands of dollars. The open-market price for a PF-70DCAM was about $60 in 2015.[17]

	PF-65	PF-69DC	PF-70
2001-S, Proof	$50	$75	$85

2002-P

Circulation-strike mintage: 3,865,610

Collecting commentary: Typical grades are MS-64 to MS-66. From this year forward coins were only sold at a premium and were not available for general circulation. In terms of certified coins, MS-68 and finer examples are elusive and command strong premiums.

actual size: 26.5 mm

Notes: The U.S. Mint sold these and other regular circulation strikes at a premium in mint sets, rolls, and bags. Quantities for mint sets each year can be found in *A Guide Book of United States Coins*. Prices and quantities for rolls and bags can be found on www.smalldollars.com

	MS-64	MS-65	MS-66
2002-P	$2	$4	$10

2002-D

Circulation-strike mintage: 3,732,000

Collecting commentary: Typical grades are MS-62 to MS-64. Many if not most of these coins have bagmarks. In terms of certified coins, MS-68 and finer examples are elusive and command strong premiums.

actual size: 26.5 mm

Unusual die: A circulation-strike 2002-D dollar exists with die marks or evidence of adjustment at the D mintmark in the form of raised lines. The coin was found by R.A. Medina, a Texas collector. Bill Fivaz examined it and commented: "Obviously, there was something in the same area that was removed by the Mint prior to putting the Denver mintmark on the die. Because the coin is brilliant prooflike, I suspect it may have been an 'S' intended for Proof striking. Possibly some obverse 2002-S Proof dies were left over, and one or more were utilized for the Denver product after removing the 'S' and punching in a 'D.' You will note that the 'D' has surface doubling on the vertical portion, indicating that it was more than likely punched in more than once."[18]

	MS-64	MS-65	MS-66
2002-D	$2	$4	$8

2002-S

Proof mintage: 3,211,995

Availability: Nearly all are gem Proofs approaching perfection.

Notes: 2,319,766 were sold as part of the 10-piece "clad" Proof sets; 892,229 were sold as part of the 10-piece "silver" Proof sets.

actual size: 26.5 mm

	PF-65	PF-69DC	PF-70
2002-S, Proof	$18	$30	$55

2003-P

Circulation-strike mintage: 3,080,000

Collecting commentary: Typical grades are MS-64 to MS-66. Higher grades are available, and in MS-68 and higher grades this is one of the more easily found circulation strikes of the era.

actual size: 26.5 mm

	MS-64	MS-65	MS-66
2003-P	$2	$4	$8

2003-D

Circulation-strike mintage: 3,080,000

Collecting commentary: Typical grades are MS-63 to MS–64 or 65. In terms of certified coins, MS-68 and finer examples are elusive and command strong premiums.

actual size: 26.5 mm

	MS-64	MS-65	MS-66
2003-D	$2	$4	$8

2003-S

Proof mintage: 3,298,439

Availability: Nearly all are gem Proofs approaching perfection.

Notes: 2,172,684 were sold as part of the 10-piece "clad" Proof sets; 1,125,755 were sold as part of the 10-piece "silver" Proof sets.

actual size: 26.5 mm

	PF-65	PF-69DC	PF-70
2003-S, Proof	$18	$30	$85

2004-P

Circulation-strike mintage: 2,660,000

Collecting commentary: Typical grades are MS-63 to MS-65. In terms of certified coins, MS-68 and finer examples are elusive and command strong premiums, which is unusual for a Philadelphia issue.

actual size: 26.5 mm

	MS-64	MS-65	MS-66
2004-P	$2	$4	$8

2004-D

Circulation-strike mintage: 2,660,000

Collecting commentary: Typical grades are MS-64 to MS-66. Higher-grade coins are seen with frequency, but are scarcer in proportion.

actual size: 26.5 mm

	MS-64	MS-65	MS-66
2004-D	$2	$4	$8

2004-S

Proof mintage: 2,965,422

Availability: Nearly all are gem Proofs approaching perfection.

Notes: 1,804,396 were sold as part of the 11-piece "clad" Proof sets; 1,187,673 were sold as part of the 11-piece "silver" Proof sets.

actual size: 26.5 mm

In *Coin World*, June 5, 2006, a market analyst gave multiple examples of essentially the same coins selling for widely differing prices. An example: "I found two 2004-S Sacagawea dollars graded PF-70DC by PCGS that sold for $230 and $345, while three coins of that same issue and graded PF-70UC by NGC (the two firms use slightly different terms for the "same" grade), brought $138, $184, and $218.50. NGC's census lists a whopping 893 it has graded, while PCGS has graded just 184, according to its census. This compares to about 5,700 to 5,800 graded PF-69 deep or ultra cameo by each of these two services."

	PF-65	PF-69DC	PF-70
2004-S, Proof	$18	$30	$55

2005-P

Circulation-strike mintage: 2,520,000

Satin Finish mintage: 1,160,000

Collecting commentary, circulation strikes: This issue typically has many bagmarks, but enough MS-65 coins exist that

actual size: 26.5 mm

finding one will be no problem, although these are in the distinct minority. The demand for such is diluted by the ready availability of Satin Finish coins.

Collecting commentary, Satin Finish: These are typically graded 65 to 68, but selected coins are higher. Coins sold in mint sets have the Satin Finish, which is slightly different from the regular Uncirculated finish. This finish was continued through the end of the Sacagawea series in 2008. PCGS gives these a SP (Specimen) prefix and lists them separately in its population report. NGC designates these as SMS (Special Mint Set) and also lists them separately. According to David Lange: "The finish is similar to that on modern commemoratives that the U.S. Mint markets as Uncirculated."[19]

	MS-64	MS-65	MS-66
2005-P	$5	$10	$20
2005-P, Satin Finish	$3	$5	$12

2005-D

Circulation-strike mintage: 2,520,000

Satin Finish mintage: 1,160,000

actual size: 26.5 mm

Collecting commentary, circulation strikes: Enough MS-65 coins exist that finding one will be no problem, although these are in the distinct minority. The demand for such is diluted by the ready availability of Satin Finish coin.

Collecting commentary, Satin Finish: These are typically graded 65 to 68, but selected coins are higher. They are separately certified with an SP prefix by PCGS and with an SMS prefix by NGC.

	MS-64	MS-65	MS-66
2005-D	$5	$10	$20
2005-D, Satin Finish	$3	$5	$12

2005-S

Proof mintage: 3,344,679

Availability: Nearly all are gem Proofs approaching perfection.

Notes: 2,275,000 were sold as part of the 11-piece "clad" Proof sets; 998,000 were sold as part of the 11-piece "silver" Proof sets

actual size: 26.5 mm

	PF-65	PF-69DC	PF-70
2005-S, Proof	$15	$20	$55

2006-P

Circulation-strike mintage: 4,900,000

Satin Finish mintage: 847,361

Collecting commentary, circulation strikes: Finding an MS-64 coin is easily done, though MS-65 and higher coins

actual size: 26.5 mm

in PCGS and NGC holders are scarce. As is true of all of the later limited-issue circulation strikes, the vast majority have not been submitted to certification services.

Collecting commentary, Satin Finish: These are typically graded 65 to 68, but selected coins are higher. They are separately certified with an SP prefix by PCGS and with an SMS prefix by NGC.

	MS-64	MS-65	MS-66
2006-P	$2	$5	$8
2006-P, Satin Finish	$3	$5	$12

2006-D

Circulation-strike mintage: 2,800,000

Satin Finish mintage: 847,361

Collecting commentary, circulation strikes: MS–62 and 63 coins are easily available, but are slightly scarce. Coins certified MS-65 or higher are very rare. For regular Mint State coins (not Satin Finish) this is the key to the Sacagawea series dated after 2000. Demand for them is uncertain as MS-65 Satin Finish coins are easy to find.

actual size: 26.5 mm

Collecting commentary, Satin Finish: These are typically graded 65 to 68, but selected coins are higher. They are separately certified with an SP prefix by PCGS and with an SMS prefix by NGC.

Experimental rinse: An experimental rinse (see 2001-P) was also used on some 2006-D coins and gave them a distinctive hue. This discovery was made by Russ Flourney, whose coin was certified by PCGS with a special description.[20]

	MS-64	MS-65	MS-66
2006-D	$2	$5	$8
2006-D, Satin Finish	$3	$5	$12

2006-S

Proof mintage: 3,054,436

Availability: Nearly all are gem Proofs approaching perfection.

actual size: 26.5 mm

	PF-65	PF-69DC	PF-70
2006-S, Proof	$15	$20	$55

2007-P

Circulation-strike mintage: 3,640,000

Satin Finish mintage: 895,628

Collecting commentary, circulation strikes: MS–65 and 66 coins are readily available. MS-68 and higher coins constitute a tiny percentage of the series.

actual size: 26.5 mm

Collecting commentary, Satin Finish: These are typically graded 65 to 68, but selected coins are higher. They are separately certified with an SP prefix by PCGS and with an SMS prefix by NGC.

	MS-64	MS-65	MS-66
2007-P	$3	$5	$8
2007-P, Satin Finish	$3	$5	$12

2007-D

Circulation-strike mintage: 3,920,000

Satin Finish mintage: 895,628

Collecting commentary, circulation strikes: Certified MS-65 or higher coins are very scarce.

actual size: 26.5 mm

Collecting commentary, Satin Finish: These are typically graded 65 to 68, but selected coins are higher. They are separately certified with an SP prefix by PCGS and with an SMS prefix by NGC.

2007-D with lettered edge (error): The edge on these coins is lettered in error, as on a Presidential dollar. The first genuine specimen was found by Andrew Moores of Lakewood, New Jersey. Others were found later, but the variety remains scarce. Many fake lettered-edge dollars have lettering applied outside of the Mint.

	MS-64	MS-65	MS-66
2007-D	$3	$5	$8
2007-D, Satin Finish	$3	$5	$12

2007-S

Proof mintage: 2,577,166

Availability: Nearly all are gem Proofs approaching perfection.

actual size: 26.5 mm

	PF-65	PF-69DC	PF-70
2007-S, Proof	$15	$20	$55

2008-P

Circulation-strike mintage: 1,820,000

Satin Finish mintage: 745,464

Collecting commentary, circulation strikes: These are plentiful in MS–63 and 64 grades, but are scarce to rare at higher levels.

actual size: 26.5 mm

Collecting commentary, Satin Finish: These are typically graded 65 to 68, but selected coins are higher. They are separately certified with an SP prefix by PCGS and with an SMS prefix by NGC.

	MS-64	MS-65	MS-66
2008-P	$3	$5	$8
2008-P, Satin Finish	$3	$5	$12

2008-D

Circulation-strike mintage: 1,820,000

Satin Finish mintage: 745,464

Collecting commentary, circulation strikes: MS–62 and 63 coins are easily available, but are slightly scarce. Coins

actual size: 26.5 mm

certified MS-65 or higher are very rare. For regular Mint State coins (not Satin Finish) this is a key to the post-2000 Sacagawea series, second after the 2006-D. Demand for them is uncertain as MS-65 Satin Finish coins are easy to find.

Collecting commentary, Satin Finish: These are typically graded 65 to 68, but selected coins are higher. They are separately certified with an SP prefix by PCGS and with an SMS prefix by NGC.

	MS-64	MS-65	MS-66
2008-D	$3	$5	$8
2008-D, Satin Finish	$3	$5	$12

2008-S

Proof mintage: 2,169,561

Availability: Nearly all are gem Proofs approaching perfection. With its lower mintage this may be a potential "dark horse" issue.[21]

actual size: 26.5 mm

	PF-65	PF-69DC	PF-70
2008-S, Proof	$15	$20	$100

NATIVE AMERICAN DOLLARS, 2009 TO DATE

On September 20, 2007, the Native American $1 Coin Act, Public Law 110-82, was signed by President George W. Bush. The legislation specified that the coins shall have "images celebrating the important contributions made by Indian tribes and individual Native Americans to the development of the United States and the history of the United States." Such would appear on the reverse and would be different each year. The Sacagawea obverse was to be continued in use. The program had no expiration date.

In a curious twist that surprised numismatists and was possibly done in the name of "efficiency" so that new dies would not need to be made each year, the law dictated that the date be removed from the obverse and placed on the edge (where it would be impossible to see in an album or standard holder!). E PLURIBUS UNUM, on the reverse of the Sacagawea coins, was also relegated to the edge—actually making the reverse easier to design. The same edge treatment had been used for Presidential dollars starting in 2008 (see next chapter).

A Mint advertisement for the 2013 Native American dollar encouraging clients to collect rolls and bags of coins. (U.S. Mint catalog, 2013)

The following information is from the U.S. Mint:

The Program

In 2009, the United States Mint began minting and issuing $1 coins featuring designs celebrating the important contributions made by Indian tribes and individual Native Americans to the history and development of the United States. The Native American $1 Coin Program is authorized by the Native American $1 Coin Act (Public Law 110-82).

Design Requirements

The obverse (heads side) design retains the central figure of the "Sacagawea" design first produced in 2000 with the inscriptions *LIBERTY* and *IN GOD WE TRUST*. The reverse (tails) design changes each year to honor an important contribution of Indian tribes or individual Native Americans with the inscriptions *$1* and *UNITED STATES OF AMERICA*. Reverse designs for the Native American $1 Coin are selected by the Secretary of the Treasury after consulting with the U.S. Senate Committee on Indian Affairs, the Congressional Native American Caucus of the U.S. House of Representatives, the Commission of Fine Arts and the National Congress of American Indians, and after public review by the Citizens Coinage Advisory Committee. Like Presidential $1 Coins, Native American $1 Coins were mandated to have a distinctive edge, are golden in color, and feature edge-lettering of the year, mint mark and *E PLURIBUS UNUM*.

During the years of the program that correspond with the Presidential $1 Coin Program, Native American $1 Coins will be issued, to the maximum extent practicable, in the chronological order in which the Native Americans depicted lived or the events recognized occurred. Following the conclusion of the Presidential $1 Coin Program, the Native American $1 Coin Program coins will be issued in any order determined to be appropriate by the Secretary of the Treasury after consultation with the U.S. Senate Committee on Indian Affairs, the Congressional Native American Caucus of the U.S. House of Representatives, the Commission of Fine Arts, and the National Congress of American Indians, and after public review by the Citizens Coinage Advisory Committee.

The law also required that at least 20% of the dollars coined in any year be of the Native American type, thus tying production to the quantities made of Presidential dollars. The legislation stated that the designs may depict individuals and events such as the creation of the Cherokee written language, the Iroquois Confederacy, Wampanoag Chief Massasoit, the "Pueblo Revolt," Olympian Jim Thorpe, Ely S. Parker (a general on the staff of Ulysses S. Grant and later head of the Bureau of Indian Affairs), and Code Talkers who served the United States armed forces during World War I and World War II. Furthermore, "In the case of a design depicting the contribution of an individual Native American to the development of the United States and the history of the United States shall not depict the individual in a size such that the coin could be considered to be a '2-headed' coin."

By December 2009 the Federal Reserve System had 857 million Sacagawea dollars in storage. When the Native American dollars were first struck in 2009 the Federal Reserve stated that it did not need any, and said that none would be called for in 2010 either. The Mint by law was required to keep striking them. It was a win-win situation for the Treasury Department, as each coin cost about 8 cents to make and thus yielded 92 cents profit. This came to a halt in 2012 when mintages were limited to the quantities expected to be sold to collectors.

Plaster for the 2009, Three Sisters, dollar.   Master die for the 2009, Three Sisters, dollar.

Plaster for the 2010, Great Law of Peace, dollar.   Plaster for the 2012, Trade Routes, dollar.

$1 COINS

CHANGE IS EASY

The next time you're paying with cash, use $1 coins.
They last for decades. They save our Nation money.
And, they're 100% recyclable. To learn more, visit
www.usmint.gov/$1coin

2011 NATIVE AMERICAN $1 COIN

Sacagawea
Release Date: 1/3/2011

Wampanoag Treaty 1621
Reverse

Mint publicity for the 2011
Native American dollar.
Recipients were urged to
spend them in commerce.
This was the last year
Native American dollars
were made in large
quantities intended
for that purpose. Most
later issues were made
in smaller numbers and
sold at a premium.

A Schuler press used to coin Presidential (mainly) and Native American dollars at the San Francisco Mint. Two different presses were in operation to strike dollars.

Filling tubes with dollar planchets preparatory to striking 2015-S Native American dollars on a Gräbener press.

Inserting tubes of planchets into the right side of the press.

David Sundman striking 2015-S Proof Native American dollars on a Gräbener press.

Interior of the Gräbener press, and struck 2015-S dollars carefully arranged in slots as they emerge from the press.

Edge Orientation on Native American Dollars

Dollars with Uncirculated finish were made with the edge lettering oriented upright with regard to the obverse (Type B, or Type 2) or upside-down (Type A, or Type 1). There is no differentiation in numismatic market value. The following is derived from a PCGS news release of April 25, 2007, for Presidential dollars, later adopted for Native American dollars:

Effective immediately, PCGS will begin recognizing the up or down orientation of the edge lettering on Presidential Dollars, as follows:

POSITION A - Edge lettering reads upside-down when the President's portrait faces up.

POSITION B - Edge lettering reads normally when the President's portrait faces up.

This has caused some collectors to seek two examples of each Native American dollar to show each edge orientation. The edge lettering on Proofs was applied with a three-part segmented collar at the time of striking. In contrast, the lettering on circulation strikes was applied separately by a machine in one operation. All Proofs are Position B.

Surprises!

In 2014 at the Denver Mint 50,000 special coins with Enhanced Uncirculated finish were produced in addition to 2,080,000 regular Uncirculated coins. The special coins were sold at a premium. Collectors, dealers, and others had little advance notice, and existing albums had no

U.S. Mint gift catalog page describing the 2015-W special Native American $1 Coin & Currency Set. Curiously, the unique use of the West Point Mint was not mentioned. In the wide numismatic community this significance was not well known until news spread after the coins were sold out.

spaces for these or for the next unexpected issue (see below).

In 2015 the Mint introduced a new element to its ongoing Coin and Chronicles program. It packaged a *Reverse Proof* Philadelphia Mint Presidential dollar with a silver medal and other collectibles such as U.S. postage stamps. The new coinage style came as a surprise to collectors, dealers, and others. Holders and albums had no openings for these unanticipated coins.

In 2015 another unexpected twist was added to the series when for the first time the *West Point Mint* struck Native American dollars. In fact, this was the first time that institution made regular-issue (non-commemorative and non-bullion) dollars of any kind. These were limited in quantity to 90,000 and had a special finish. Hardly any promotional emphasis was put on the unique feature that these were the only such coins to be struck at the West Point Mint and have a W mintmark.

Whitman publisher Dennis Tucker (left), author Q. David Bowers, and Tom Jurkowsky of the U.S. Mint during a visit to the West Point Mint.

NEW FIRST FOR WEST POINT MINT

SET TO FEATURE ENHANCED UNCIRCULATED 2015-W DOLLAR

BY PAUL GILKES / COIN WORLD SENIOR EDITOR

The Enhanced Uncirculated 2015-W Native American dollar to be included in the 2015 American $1 Coin & Currency Set represents the first time a Native American dollar in any finish is being struck at the West Point Mint.

The set will go on sale from the U.S. Mint beginning at noon ET Aug. 24.

The product is limited to 90,000 sets, and the Mint will limit orders to five sets per household.

The set will be offered at $14.95.

The set will be held in a tri-fold presentation folder. It will include one Enhanced Uncirculated 2015-W Native American dollar and one Series 2013 $1 Federal Reserve note from the Federal Reserve Bank of New York.

Both the coin and the note are available only in this set.

The set will include historical information about the

The American $1 Coin & Currency set will feature an Enhanced Uncirculated 2015-W Native American dollar. Shown at top is a 2015-P coin from a 2015 Uncirculated Mint set and, at bottom, Enhanced Uncirculated 2014-D dollar.

Images courtesy of U.S. Mint.

Mohawk Ironworkers and their contributions to "high iron" construction work on New York City skyscrapers, including the World Trade Center.

The $1 note contains a serial number beginning with "911" in honor of the Mohawk Ironworkers' recovery efforts following the collapse of the World Trade Center twin towers in 2001.

A certificate of authenticity is printed on the packaging.

The idea of a limited edition Enhanced Uncirculated Native American dollar made its debut with the 2014 American $1 Coin & Currency set. That set contains a coin struck at the Denver Mint with the D Mint mark incuse on the edge.

The Enhanced Uncirculated dollars, according to U.S. Mint officials, are struck with dies that had details wire-brushed for brilliance or laser-frosted for contrast.

For more information on the 2015 set, visit the U.S. Mint's website at www.usmint.gov. ●

Coin World article by Paul Gilkes, August 12, 2015, describing the forthcoming 2015-W coins.

Grading Native American Dollars

2009-P, Three Sisters. Graded MS-68.

MS-60 to 70 (Mint State). *Obverse:* At MS-60, some abrasion and contact marks are evident, most noticeably on the cheekbone and the drapery near the baby's head. Luster is present, but may be dull or lifeless. At MS-63, contact marks are extensive but not distracting. Abrasion still is evident, but less than at lower levels. MS-64 coins are slightly finer. An MS-65 coin may have minor abrasion, but contact marks are so minute as to require magnification. Luster should be full and rich. *Reverse:* At MS-60, some abrasion and contact marks are evident, most noticeably on the eagle's breast. Otherwise, the same comments apply as for the obverse.

Native American dollars are seldom collected in grades lower than MS-60.

2009-S, Three Sisters. Graded PF-70 Deep Cameo.

PF-60 to 70 (Proof). *Obverse and Reverse:* Proofs that are extensively cleaned and have many hairlines, or that are dull and grainy, are lower level, such as PF-60 to 62. This comment is more theoretical than practical, as nearly all Proofs have been well kept. With medium hairlines and good reflectivity, assigned grades of PF–63 or 64 are appropriate. With relatively few hairlines a rating of PF-65 can be given. PF-66 may have hairlines so delicate that magnification is needed to see them. Above that, all the way to PF-70, a Proof should be free of any hairlines or other problems under strong magnification.

2009, Three Sisters

Designer: Glenna Goodacre (obverse); Norman E. Nemeth (reverse).

Composition: Pure copper core with outer layers of manganese-brass (.770 copper, .070 manganese, .120 zinc, .040 nickel).

Weight: 8.1 grams.

Diameter: 26.5 mm.

Edge: Lettered with date, mintmark, and E PLURIBUS UNUM.

2009-P, Three Sisters

Circulation-strike mintage: 39,200,000

Satin Finish mintage: 784,614

actual size: 26.5 mm

Collecting commentary, circulation strikes: MS-65 coins are common enough, but in terms of certified coins grading MS-68 and higher this issue is scarce.

Collecting commentary, Satin Finish: These are typically graded 65 to 68, but selected coins are higher. They are separately certified with an SP prefix by PCGS and with an SMS prefix by NGC.

Mint narrative: The reverse design features a Native American woman planting seeds in a field of corn, beans, and squash, and the inscriptions UNITED STATES OF AMERICA and $1.

Maize was domesticated in central Mexico and spread from the southwest through North America, along with symbiotic "Three Sisters" agriculture, in which corn, beans, and squash growing in the same mound enhanced the productivity of each plant. Native American skill in agriculture provided the margin of survival for the early European colonists, either through trade or direct sharing of expertise, and agricultural products native to the Americas quickly became staples throughout Europe.

Three Sisters symbiotic agriculture—planting corn, climbing beans, and squash together in the same plot—also originated in central Mexico and probably spread simultaneously with the corn. In this efficient planting method, corn stalks provided support for the bean vines, which added nitrogen to the soil. Squash provided ground cover, which discouraged weeds. Productivity was much higher (by some estimates as much as 30 percent!) for the three grown together than each grown separately.

Agriculture has always been an important subject in Native American culture—it emphasizes living with the land and understanding the surrounding natural resources. When Europeans first arrived in the "New World," one of the largest contributions and benefits of their relationships with Native Americans was the sharing of agricultural information. It is widely acknowledged that colonists would not have survived in the New World without the support and knowledge gained from Native American agricultural techniques.

Native Americans practiced crop rotation, round cropping, hybridizations, seed development, irrigation methods and many other agricultural techniques that are still used today.

Notes: These coins were released to the public on January 2, 2009, having been pre-struck in 2008. Purchases could be made of $25 bank-wrapped rolls in quantities of 250 or 500 coins, with shipping and handling paid by the Mint. This policy was changed on January 15, after which time they could be ordered in 25-coin rolls for $35.95, plus postage.

On January 17 in the Potomac Atrium of the Smithsonian Institution's National Museum of the American Indian a ceremonial "pour" of dollars from a hand-made Indian basket was made by Mint Director Edmund C. Moy and the Indian museum's director, Kevin Gover. Free coins were given to attendees 18 years old and younger, and nearby the Mint's "Real Change Exchange Truck" employees sold coins to the public for face value.

2009, Three Sisters, plain-edge error: Many coins were inadvertently issued without edge lettering and thus lack the date and mintmark. These are not identifiable to a particular mint. Probably close to 10,000 error coins have been identified by collectors and dealers.

	MS-64	MS-65	MS-66
2009-P, Three Sisters	$3	$5	$8
2009-P, Three Sisters, Satin Finish	$3	$5	$12

2009-D, Three Sisters

Circulation-strike mintage: 35,700,000

Satin Finish mintage: 784,614

Collecting commentary, circulation strikes: MS-65 coins are common enough, but in terms of certified coins grading MS-68 and higher this issue is scarce.

Collecting commentary, Satin Finish: These are typically graded 65 to 68, but selected coins are higher. They are separately certified with an SP prefix by PCGS and with an SMS prefix by NGC.

	MS-64	MS-65	MS-66
2009-D, Three Sisters	$3	$5	$8
2009-D, Three Sisters, Satin Finish	$3	$5	$12

2009-S, Three Sisters

Proof mintage: 2,179,867

Availability: Nearly all are gem Proofs approaching perfection.

	PF-65	PF-69DC	PF-70
2009-S, Three Sisters, Proof	$15	$17	$55

2010, Great Law of Peace

Designer: Glenna Goodacre (obverse); Thomas Cleveland (reverse).

Composition: Pure copper core with outer layers of manganese-brass (.770 copper, .070 manganese, .120 zinc, .040 nickel).

Weight: 8.1 grams.

Diameter: 26.5 mm.

Edge: Lettered with date, mintmark, and E PLURIBUS UNUM.

2010-P, Great Law of Peace

Circulation-strike mintage: 32,060,000

Satin Finish mintage: 583,897

actual size: 26.5 mm

Collecting commentary, circulation strikes: MS-65 coins are common enough, but in terms of certified coins grading MS-68 and higher this issue is scarce.

Collecting commentary, Satin Finish: These are typically graded 65 to 68, but selected coins are higher. They are separately certified with an SP prefix by PCGS and with an SMS prefix by NGC.

Mint narrative: The reverse design features an image of the Hiawatha Belt with five arrows bound together, along with the inscriptions UNITED STATES OF AMERICA, $1, HAUDENOSAUNEE, and GREAT LAW OF PEACE.

The Haudenosaunee Confederation, also known as the Iroquois Confederacy of upstate New York, was remarkable for being founded by two historic figures: the Peacemaker and his Onondaga spokesman, Hiawatha, who spent years preaching the need for a league. The Peacemaker sealed the treaty by symbolically burying weapons at the foot of a Great White Pine, or Great Tree of Peace, whose five-needle clusters stood for the original five nations: Mohawk, Oneida, Onondaga, Cayuga, and Seneca.

The Hiawatha Belt is a visual record of the creation of the Haudenosaunee dating back to the early 1400s, with five symbols representing the five original Nations. The Haudenosaunee symbol, the Great White Pine, is the central figure on the belt, also representing the Onondaga Nation. The four square symbols on the belt represent the Mohawk, Oneida, Cayuga, and Seneca nations. The bundle of five arrows symbolizes strength in unity for the Iroquois Confederacy.

Northern European settlers from France, England, and the Netherlands interacted with the Haudenosaunee as a separate diplomatic power. The success of the confederation showed the colonists that the Greek confederacies they had read about in the histories of Polybius were a viable political alternative to monarchy. The symbolism of the Great Tree of Peace and eagle sitting on its top were adopted as national icons during the American Revolutionary government

Some early narratives by explorers and missionaries introduced Europe to Native American societies which practiced equality and democratic self-government. These narratives quickly found their way into classics of European thought, including Sir Thomas More's *Utopia* and Montaigne's *Essays*. John Locke cited the Huron election of its chiefs in his refutation of the Divine Right of Kings (the idea that a monarch is subject to no earthly authority because they derive their right to rule directly from the will of God).

When the newly independent Americans devised a continental government they may have seen in these native societies living examples of the successful confederacies that they admired in the ancient Greek histories. Many tribal groups established confederations often based on linguistic affinity. One of the most famous and powerful of these Native leagues was the Iroquois Confederacy, known to its members as the Haudenosaunee ("People of the Longhouse"), or the Six Nations.

Notes: The reverse was designed by Thomas L. Cleveland of the Artistic Infusion Program and was engraved by Charles L. Vickers. The Artistic Infusion Program, begun in 2004, added talent to that already possessed by the Mint staff of highly accomplished artists and engravers.

The new dollars were made available to the public on January 4, 2010. The Mint's Direct Ship Program offered boxes of ten 25-coin bank-wrapped rolls for face value, delivered. A maximum of 20 boxes per household was set. On January 22 the Mint began offering 25-coin rolls in special wrappers for $35.95 per roll, plus shipping and handling, with no limit as to the quantity that could be ordered. Purchasers had their choice of Philadelphia or Denver coins.

On January 25, 2010, the official launch ceremony for the 2010 coins was conducted in the National Museum of the American Indian facility at the George Gustav Heye Center in the Alexander Hamilton U.S. Custom House in New York City. On hand were Mint Director Edmund C. Moy and John Haworth, director of the Heye Center.

2010, Great Law, plain-edge error: Several hundred coins were inadvertently issued without edge lettering and thus lack the date and mintmark. These are not identifiable to a particular mint.

	MS-64	MS-65	MS-66
2010-P, Great Law	$3	$5	$8
2010-P, Great Law, Satin Finish	$3	$5	$12

2010-D, Great Law of Peace

Circulation-strike mintage: 48,720,000

Satin Finish mintage: 583,897

Collecting commentary, circulation strikes: MS-65 coins are common enough, but in terms of certified coins grading MS-68 and higher this issue is scarce.

Collecting commentary, Satin Finish: These are typically graded 65 to 68, but selected coins are higher. They are separately certified with an SP prefix by PCGS and with an SMS prefix by NGC.

	MS-64	MS-65	MS-66
2010-D, Great Law	$3	$5	$8
2010-D, Great Law, Satin Finish	$3	$5	$12

2010-S, Great Law of Peace
Proof mintage: 1,689,216

Availability: Nearly all are gem Proofs approaching perfection.

	PF-65	PF-69DC	PF-70
2010-S, Great Law, Proof	$15	$17	$60

2011, Wampanoag Treaty

Designer: Glenna Goodacre (obverse); Richard Masters (reverse).

Composition: Pure copper core with outer layers of manganese-brass (.770 copper, .070 manganese, .120 zinc, .040 nickel).

Weight: 8.1 grams.

Diameter: 26.5 mm.

Edge: Lettered with date, mintmark, and E PLURIBUS UNUM.

2011-P, Wampanoag Treaty

Circulation-strike mintage: 29,400,000

Collecting commentary: Examples are readily available in almost any Mint State grade desired, although most are below MS-65.

actual size: 26.5 mm

Mint narrative: The theme for the 2011 Native American $1 coin is "Supreme Sachem Ousamequin, Massasoit of the Great Wampanoag Nation Creates Alliance with Settlers at Plymouth Bay (1621)." Its reverse design features hands of the Supreme Sachem Ousamequin Massasoit and Governor John Carver, symbolically offering the ceremonial peace pipe after the initiation of the first formal written peace alliance between the Wampanoag tribe and the European settlers. The design includes the required inscriptions, UNITED STATES OF AMERICA and $1, along with the additional inscription WAMPANOAG TREATY 1621.

Within Native American culture, the ability to make peace was historically as highly prized as leadership in war and was often conducted by a separate peace chief who stepped in when the time for the warriors had passed. For centuries, tribes created alliances with each other that spanned hundreds of miles. One of the first treaties for a mutual alliance with settlers in what became the United States of America occurred between the Puritan settlers at Plymouth and the Massasoit (a title meaning "head chief") of the Pokanoket Wampanoag in 1621. Historians credit the alliance with the Massasoit with ensuring survival of the Plymouth colony.

From the Declaration of Independence until 1868, the U.S. made some 370 treaties with American Indian tribes. Congress suspended formal treaty-making in 1868, but since then, government-to-government relations between the U.S. and sovereign tribes have taken a variety of other legal forms. Current U.S. policy states that federal relations with recognized tribes are conducted on a government-to-government basis.

In the spring of 1621, Ousamequin, the Massasoit of the Wampanoag Indians, made a formal treaty with the English who settled at Patuxet (in what is now Plymouth, Massachusetts). The document might well be the first written treaty between an indigenous people and European settlers in what is now the U.S. It consisted of six provisions, recorded in William Bradford's "History of Plimoth Plantation."

Massasoit promised to defend the Plymouth settlers against hostile tribes in return for their intervention if his people were attacked. His intermediaries—Tisquantum, Samoset, and Hobbamack—gave the settlers invaluable tips on survival.

The Plymouth settlers honored the treaty later that summer by coming to Massasoit's rescue when they thought he had been captured by enemies. In mid-October 1621, Massasoit and 90 of his tribesmen celebrated a harvest feast at Plymouth for three days (a traditional English folk celebration). The 1621 feast inspired the legend of the first Thanksgiving, as it was called 220 years later. The treaty at Patuxet lasted more than 50 years.

Notes: The reverse was designed by Richard Masters of the Artistic Infusion Program and engraved by Joseph Menna.

From *Numismatic News*, April 19, 2011:

> Almost 500 people witnessed the official introduction of the 2011 Native American $1 coin March 25 at a ceremony held at Plimoth Plantation in Plymouth, Mass. Eastern Suns Drum Circle, a Mashpee Wampanoag tribal group, performed. Associate Mint Director of Sales B.B. Craig formally introduced the new design. He was joined by Cheryl Andrews-Maltais, chairwoman of the Wampanoag Tribe of Gay Head; Cedric Cromwell, chairman of the Mashpee Wampanoag Tribe, and Jim Adams, senior historian of the Smithsonian Institution's National Museum of the American Indian. A coin pour was a highlight of the ceremony. Free examples of the new coin were given to the approximately 175 children [18 and younger] who attended. Adults were able to trade their folding money for $25 rolls at face value. A total of $5,000 was exchanged, or 200 rolls.

*2011, Wampanoag Treaty, **weak edge lettering:*** A number of coins were issued with the edge lettering weakly defined.

*2011, Wampanoag Treaty, **plain-edge error:*** A few coins were inadvertently issued without edge lettering and thus lack the date and mintmark, making them a great rarity. These are not identifiable to a particular mint.

	MS-64	MS-65	MS-66
2011-P, Wampanoag Treaty	$3	$5	$8

2011-D, Wampanoag Treaty

Circulation-strike mintage: 48,160,000

Collecting commentary: Examples are readily available in almost any Mint State grade desired, although most are below MS-65. Only a tiny percentage of the mintage has ever been certified.

	MS-64	MS-65	MS-66
2011-D, Wampanoag Treaty	$3	$5	$8

2011-S, Wampanoag Treaty

Proof mintage: 1,453,276

Availability: Nearly all are gem Proofs approaching perfection.

	PF-65	PF-69DC	PF-70
2011-S, Wampanoag Treaty, Proof	$15	$18	$55

2012, Trade Routes in the 17th Century

Designer: Glenna Goodacre (obverse); Thomas Cleveland (reverse).

Composition: Pure copper core with outer layers of manganese-brass (.770 copper, .070 manganese, .120 zinc, .040 nickel).

Weight: 8.1 grams.

Diameter: 26.5 mm.

Edge: Lettered with date, mintmark, and E PLURIBUS UNUM.

2012-P, Trade Routes

Circulation-strike mintage: 2,800,000

actual size: 26.5 mm

Collecting commentary: Typical grades for these coins are MS–64 to 66, although many higher-grade coins exist. This is the first year of restricted mintages. All dollars from this point onward exist in lower quantities than those of earlier times, however, there are more than enough to satisfy the numismatic demand for them.

Winning design by Thomas Cleveland.

Mint narrative: The theme for the 2012 Native American $1 Coin is "Trade Routes in the 17th century" in profile with horses running in the background, representing the historical spread of the horse. The design includes the required inscriptions, UNITED STATES OF AMERICA and $1.

American Indians maintained widespread transcontinental, inter-tribal trade for more than a millennium. The Native American trade infrastructure became the channel by which exploration, settlement, and economic development in the colonial period—and later of the young republic—ultimately thrived. When early European traders ventured from eastern city centers into the interior lands, they followed trading routes still in use, often in the company of Native American guides and traders who had used them for generations. By taking these routes they encountered an ecosystem and Native American culture already being transformed by European goods that had moved along the routes long before Europeans themselves arrived in the interior regions.

These routes showed the way to European explorers and traders and marked the corridors for future east-west travel. The Lewis and Clark Expedition in 1803 followed parts of this trail. This cross-continental trade infrastructure culminated in the construction of the modern-day interstate highway system. Trading routes centered on Zuni Pueblo in the Four Corners region of the southwest and the Mojave bead route to the California coast were incorporated into the Old Spanish Trail (now a National Park Service historic trail). The Old Snake Trade Route connected the pueblos of New Mexico north to the Mandan villages in the present-day Dakotas, branching to the west in present-day Wyoming and reaching the Columbia River at The Dalles in Oregon.

Of all the goods traded throughout the continent, the horse, spread by Indian tribes through Native American trade routes, is perhaps the most significant. Thanks to inter-tribal trade, horses had crossed the Rio Grande by 1600. This trade received a massive infusion in 1680, when the Pueblo Revolt released thousands of horses from the mission herds into Native American hands.

The horse became perhaps the most sought-after commodity in inter-tribal trade. The horse's spread in Native American hands was so prodigious that it became the primary means of transportation and the nucleus of the ranching economy already underway in the western territories. In the south, the Caddo trade center became a major entry point for the horse. Trade up the Old Snake Route brought horses as far north as the Mandan in North Dakota, who supplied them to the Lakota and Blackfeet. A parallel inter-mountain route brought horses to the northwest. By the time Lewis and Clark wintered with the Mandan in 1803, they encountered a well-established horse culture. These long-established Native American trade routes also provided the path for this primary means of transportation—a significant contribution to opening up the continental interior to the developing nation.

Notes: The reverse was designed by Thomas Cleveland of the Artistic Infusion Program and was engraved by Phebe Hemphill.

Beginning this year, the Mint discontinued launch events and special ceremonies for Native American dollars citing the expense involved.

	MS-64	MS-65	MS-66
2012-P, Trade Routes in the 17th Century	$3	$5	$8

2012-D, Trade Routes

Circulation-strike mintage: 3,080,000

Collecting commentary: The typical grades for these coins are MS–64 to 66, although many higher-grade coins exist.

	MS-64	MS-65	MS-66
2012-D, Trade Routes in the 17th Century	$3	$5	$8

2012-S, Trade Routes

Proof mintage: 1,189,445

Availability: Nearly all are gem Proofs approaching perfection.

	PF-65	PF-69DC	PF-70
2012-S, Trade Routes in the 17th Century, Proof	$15	$18	$125

2013, Treaty With the Delawares

Designer: Glenna Goodacre (obverse); Susan Gamble (reverse).

Composition: Pure copper core with outer layers of manganese-brass (.770 copper, .070 manganese, .120 zinc, .040 nickel).

Weight: 8.1 grams.

Diameter: 26.5 mm.

Edge: Lettered with date, mintmark, and E PLURIBUS UNUM.

2013-P, Treaty With the Delawares

actual size: 26.5 mm

Circulation-strike mintage: 1,820,000

Collecting commentary: Typical grades for this coin are MS–64 to 66, although many higher-grade coins exist.

Mint narrative: The 2013 Native American $1 coin commemorates the Delaware Treaty of 1778. Its reverse design features a turkey, howling wolf, and turtle (all symbols of the clans of the Delaware Tribe), and a ring of 13 stars to represent the Colonies. The design includes the required inscriptions UNITED STATES OF AMERICA and $1. The additional inscriptions include TREATY WITH THE DELAWARES and 1778.

Winning design by Susan Gamble.

When the American Revolution established a new sovereign government on the North American continent, its founders acknowledged the significance of Indian tribes as the new United States of America dealt with tribes government-to-government, making peace and winning allies through a series of treaties. The new Constitution in 1789 reserved the regulation of commerce with the tribes to the federal government—specifically in Article I, section 8, clause 3—putting them on the same footing as foreign governments. The First Congress affirmed this principle in major legislation on trade and land deals with Indians—laws that are still in effect. Treaty-making with the United States was the foundation for tribal relations with the new American government, but the legal theory underlying that relationship was sharply contested until Chief Justice John Marshall's pivotal 1832 decision in *Cherokee Nation v. Georgia*. In declaring tribes to be dependent nations, he started the process by which tribes were recognized under the American federal system, equal in status with state governments as the third leg of sovereign membership, but also diminished in stature under this system.

After declaring independence, the United States signed its first formal treaty with an Indian tribe, the Delaware, at Fort Pitt (now Pittsburgh, Pennsylvania) on September 17, 1778. The mutual defense treaty allowed American troops to pass through the Delaware Tribe's land to attack the British fort at Detroit, Michigan. Under the treaty, the United States recognized the Delaware Nation's sovereignty. The treaty also offered significant insight into the later process of incorporating tribes into the federal system. Article VI of the treaty gave the Delaware Nation the option of joining other tribes in the Ohio region to form a state with the Delaware Tribe at the head to become part of the U.S. confederation with representation in Congress. Although the statehood option was never taken up, it foreshadowed the later acknowledgment of tribes as partners in the federal system.

Notes: The reverse was designed by Susan Gamble of the Mint's Artistic Infusion Program and was engraved by Phebe Hemphill.

	MS-64	MS-65	MS-66
2013-P, Treaty with the Delawares	$3	$5	$8

2013-D, Treaty With the Delawares

Circulation-strike mintage: 1,820,000

Collecting commentary: Typical grades for this coin are MS–64 to 66, although many higher-grade coins exist.

	MS-64	MS-65	MS-66
2013-D, Treaty with the Delawares	$3	$5	$8

2013-S, Treaty With the Delawares

Proof mintage: 802,460

Collecting commentary: Nearly all are gem Proofs approaching perfection.

	PF-65	PF-69DC	PF-70
2013-S, Treaty with the Delawares, Proof	$15	$20	$150

2014, Native Hospitality

Designer: Glenna Goodacre (obverse); Chris Costello (reverse).

Composition: Pure copper core with outer layers of manganese-brass (.770 copper, .070 manganese, .120 zinc, .040 nickel).

Weight: 8.1 grams.

Diameter: 26.5 mm.

Edge: Lettered with date, mintmark, and E PLURIBUS UNUM.

2014-P, Native Hospitality

Circulation-strike mintage: 2,800,000

Collecting commentary: Typical grades for this coin are MS–64 to 66, although many higher-grade coins exist.[1]

actual size: 26.5 mm

Mint Narrative: The 2014 Native American $1 coin commemorates how Native American hospitality ensured the success of the Lewis and Clark Expedition. Its reverse design depicts a Native American man offering a pipe while his wife offers provisions of fish, corn, roots, and gourds. In the background is a stylized image of the face of William

Clark's compass highlighting "NW," the area in which the expedition occurred. It includes the required inscriptions UNITED STATES OF AMERICA and $1.

When the Lewis and Clark Expedition crossed the Continental Divide the nature of its mission fundamentally changed. Up to that point, the mission had been exploring territory that European powers would recognize as belonging to the United States through the Louisiana Purchase. Once past the headwaters of the Missouri River, the expedition was securing the American claim to a new accession of territory, the Pacific Northwest. More than ever before, success of the mission depended on help from the Indian tribes who might not have understood the long-term consequences of their hospitality. For every step of their way through the Rocky Mountains to the Pacific Coast, Lewis and Clark depended on the friendship, supplies, and logistical support of the tribes on their route. They camped in the midst of the Mandan and Hidatsa tribes in the winter of 1804–1805 and the Clatsop in 1806, and their cooperation was essential to the resounding success of this mission.

The Mandan and Hidatsa tribes of the Missouri River welcomed Lewis and Clark and their Corps of Discovery to their unique dome-shaped earthen-lodge villages, often sitting and talking by the campfire when meeting with Black Cat, the Mandan chief. The tribes were located in present-day North Dakota. Their village was the central marketplace for the northern plains. Lewis expressed the highest respect for Black Cat (Posecopsahe) and walked miles out of his way to smoke a pipe with him on the day of his departure. The expedition group traded for corn and gathered every scrap of intelligence they could about the route ahead. During the winter at Fort Mandan, the expedition blacksmith forged somewhat eccentric ax heads to trade for corn. Eighteen months later, the expedition found that some of the same ax heads had already been traded to the Nez Perce, which the expedition relied on to supply horses from their famous herd. Down the length of the Columbia River, the Americans traded with the Chinook and other tribes for provisions.

The Clatsop Indians were flourishing people who enjoyed plentiful amounts of fish and fur and occupied three villages on the southern side of the Columbia River. They were located in what is now known as Oregon. Some Clatsop tribesmen complained about the expedition's stinginess with gifts. Coboway, chief of one of the villages, visited the expedition group at its fort, which was still under construction. He exchanged some goods, including a sea otter pelt, for fishhooks and a small bag of Shoshone tobacco. Over the rest of the winter, Coboway would be a frequent and welcome visitor to this area they named Fort Clatsop. The Clatsop also aided the expedition both in preparing for, and dealing with, the northwest winter, and informed Lewis and Clark that there was a good amount of elk on the south side of the Columbia, information that influenced the location of Fort Clatsop. When the expedition's food supplies were running low, the Clatsop informed the corps that a whale had washed ashore some miles to the south.

At the expedition's departure from Fort Clatsop, Lewis wrote in his journal that Coboway "has been much more kind an[d] hospitable to us than any other Indian in this neighbourhood." Lewis committed the expedition's one act of pilferage, appropriating a Native canoe for the voyage up the river. (He later encountered a Lumhi Indian who claimed ownership of the vessel and paid him off with an elk skin.) This misdeed remained on the historical record, and late in 2011, the family of William Clark presented a replica of the original canoe to the Chinook tribe in recompense.

Notes: The reverse was designed by Chris Costello of the Artistic Infusion Program and was engraved by Joseph Menna. This depiction was approved on September 23, 2013, by Acting Deputy Treasury Secretary Mary J. Miller. The design had been recommended by both the Citizens Coinage Advisory Committee and the U.S. Mint.

	MS-64	MS-65	MS-66
2014-P, Native Hospitality	$3	$5	$8

2014-D, Native Hospitality

Circulation-strike mintage: 2,080,000

Enhanced Uncirculated mintage: 50,000

Collecting commentary, regular issue: Typical grades for these coins are MS–64 to 66, although many higher-grade coins exist.

Enhanced Uncirculated: The Enhanced Uncirculated coins were only sold with the 2014 Native American $1 Coin and Currency Set and are nearly all in higher grades. These went on sale as an American $1 Coin and Currency Set on November 13, 2014, with a Federal Reserve $1 bill accompanying each coin, priced at $13.95 for the set. In December the maximum authorized total of 50,000 sets had been reached, and distribution ceased.

From the Mint: "The 2014 American $1 Coin and Currency Set that went on sale November 20 for $13.95 has one Enhanced Uncirculated finish 2014 Native American $1 coin from Denver and one 2013 $1 note from the BEP. The enhanced finish coin is only available as part of the set and will not be sold individually. The base finish on the obverse and reverse was wire brushed, giving the coins a bright finish without appearing polished liked Proof coins. The obverse and reverse artwork was then frosted with different finishes."[2]

2014-D, plain-edge error (Enhanced Uncirculated): This variety is also called "missing edge lettering." In January 2015 ANACS reported that it had certified about 1,000 Enhanced Uncirculated coins, and that just one was missing the edge inscriptions. It was certified as MS-69.[3]

	MS-64	MS-65	MS-66
2014-D, Native Hospitality	$3	$5	$8

2014-S, Native Hospitality

Proof mintage: 665,100

Availability: Nearly all are gem Proofs approaching perfection.

	PF-65	PF-69DC	PF-70
2014-S, Native Hospitality, Proof	$15	$18	$130

2015, Mohawk Ironworkers

Designer: Glenna Goodacre (obverse); Ronald D. Sanders (reverse).

Composition: Pure copper core with outer layers of manganese-brass (.770 copper, .070 manganese, .120 zinc, .040 nickel).

Weight: 8.1 grams.

Diameter: 26.5 mm.

Edge: Lettered with date, mintmark, and E PLURIBUS UNUM.

2015-P, Mohawk Ironworkers

Circulation-strike mintage: 2,800,000

actual size: 26.5 mm

Collecting commentary: Most coins of this year and mintmark are in very high Mint State grades. Superb coins are the order of the day.

Mint narrative: The 2015 Native American $1 coin commemorates the contributions of the Kahnawake Mohawk and Mohawk Akwesasne communities to "high-iron"–construction work and the building of New York City skyscrapers. The reverse design depicts a Mohawk ironworker reaching for an I-beam that is swinging into position, rivets on the left and right side of the border, and a high elevation view of the city skyline in the background. The design includes the required inscriptions UNITED STATES OF AMERICA and $1, and the additional inscription MOHAWK IRONWORKERS.

Winning design by Ronald D. Sanders.

American Indians have become legendary figures in hazardous occupations. Tribes take great pride in the bravery of their people, whether displayed in high-iron–construction work on the tallest skyscrapers or fire jumping and brake-cutting in the face of the West's raging wildfires. These occupations receive the honor given to warriors in days past, and they carry on the ancient ethic of putting one's life on the line to protect the welfare and safety of the people. Just as the ancient warriors devoted themselves to preserving all the people of the tribe, the modern risk-takers see their occupations as a contribution to the public good.

Contribution: The tradition of Mohawk high-iron working dates to 1886, when the Dominion Bridge Company started a bridge from the Kahnawake Mohawk community across the St. Lawrence River. Mohawks were first employed as day laborers, but they insisted on working on the bridge itself, and supervisors were amazed at their ability to handle heights. The danger of the work became evident in 1907 at the Quebec Bridge project, designed to be the largest cantilevered bridge in the world. On August 29, the structure failed and the bridge collapsed into the river, killing 33 Mohawk workers. Four family names were wiped out. After the disaster the Kahnawake Clan Mothers ruled that large numbers of Mohawk men could not work on the same project at the same time.

Native ironworkers were in increasing demand in the 20th century as skyscrapers, tall bridges, and other high-elevation projects began to go up around North America. Crews from Kahnawake and the Mohawk Akwesasne communities in upstate New York and Canada made the trek to New York City to build its skyline, including the Empire State Building, the Chrysler Building, and work above the 80th floor on the World Trade Center twin towers. At one point, one in four men at Akwesasne worked in high-rise construction.

The tradition entered a new and poignant phase after the September 11, 2001, attacks on the World Trade Center, witnessed at close hand by a Mohawk construction crew on a nearby building. Dozens of Mohawk ironworkers volunteered for the dangerous job of removing debris. The venerated "9-11" flag displayed at the 2004 Winter Olympics was recovered from the lobby of Six World Trade Center by a Mohawk worker from Akwesasne on the day after the attack. The St. Regis Reservation Tribal Council—the government for the U.S. side of the Mohawk Akwesasne community that straddles the Canada/U.S. border—and the iron workers local union collected respirators to donate to the New York Fire Department for the recovery effort.

Notes: The reverse was designed by Ronald D. Sanders of the Artistic Infusion Program and was engraved by Phebe Hemphill.

	MS-64	MS-65	MS-66
2015-P, Mohawk Ironworkers	$3	$5	$8

2015-D, Mohawk Ironworkers

Circulation-strike mintage: 2,240,000

Collecting commentary: These are readily available in MS-65 and nearby grades.

	MS-64	MS-65	MS-66
2015-D, Mohawk Ironworkers	$3	$5	$8

2015-S, Mohawk Ironworkers

Proof mintage: 974,883

Availability: Nearly all are gem Proofs approaching perfection.

	PF-65	PF-69DC	PF-70
2015-S, Mohawk Ironworkers, Proof	$15	$18	$125

2015-W, Mohawk Ironworkers

Enhanced Uncirculated
mintage: 84,059

Collecting commentary: These are easily available in superb gem preservation as made. The combination of the unique W mintmark and the relatively low price for a limited-issue dollar has made these exceptionally popular.

Notes: The 2015-W was made available only in Enhanced Uncirculated form as part of the 2015 American $1 Coin and Currency Set that also included a Series 2013 Federal Reserve Bank of New York $1 note with the serial number starting with 911, in commemoration of the 9/11 World Trade Center disaster. The sets were priced at $14.95 each and went on sale on August 24, 2015. The production was limited to 90,000 sets with an initial household limit of five sets. The sets were packaged at the San Francisco Mint.

On August 25 the Mint announced that sales for the first day amounted to 44,344 sets. By the end of the second day the total was up to 48,272. Some collectors, probably in the distinct minority, experienced difficulties and delays in accessing the Mint's Web site and sent letters of complaint to *Coin World*.[4] Unsold sets remained on hand. At noon Eastern Standard Time on Monday, December 1, the limit of sets that could be sent to any given household was raised to 100, then not long afterward the household limit was lifted completely, but with a limit of 1,500 sets per day to any address. I ordered a quantity of sets myself as I felt that, as part of the series of American dollar coins, they would in time become appreciated and well known. As of the sales report on the morning of December 4 the Mint had sold 77,416 sets. On the evening of December 5 at about 10:25 the Mint Web site reported that only 18 sets were left. I relayed this to a correspondent, he ordered 18 sets, and at 10:30 the Mint posted a "no longer available" notice.

Little publicity was given to the fact, the seemingly superb selling point, that these were the only collectible 20th-century coins struck at the West Point Mint. The coins are very similar to a Reverse Proof (see 2015 Presidential dollars) but with the portrait and other features not quite as deeply polished. The three-panel fold-out holder for the coin and note includes a printed "Certificate of Authenticity" including: "2015 Enhanced Uncirculated Native American $1 Coin. The United States Mint certifies that this is a genuine coin, struck in accordance with the legislation signed by the President on November 20, 2007 (Public Law 110-82). This coin was minted by the Department of the Treasury, United States Mint. This coin is legal tender of the United States. Matthew Rhett Jeppson [below reproduction of inked signature]— Principal Deputy Director, United States Mint."

Edge style: In contrast with all earlier *Uncirculated-finish* issues of "golden dollars" in the various series—Sacagawea, Native American, and Presidential—which were struck with plain edges and later had the edge lettering with random orientation by another machine, the 2015-W coins had the lettering applied by a three-part segmented collar at the same time they were struck. As a result all 2015-W coins have the edge lettering oriented vertically in relation to the obverse as do Proofs from the San Francisco Mint.

	MS-64	MS-65	MS-66
2015-W, Mohawk Ironworkers	$15	$20	$25

2016, Code Talkers

Designer: Glenna Goodacre (obverse); Thomas D. Rogers Sr. (reverse).

Composition: Pure copper core with outer layers of manganese-brass (.770 copper, .070 manganese, .120 zinc, .040 nickel).

Weight: 8.1 grams.

Diameter: 26.5 mm.

Edge: Lettered with date, mintmark, and E PLURIBUS UNUM.

2016-P, Code Talkers

Circulation-strike mintage: Unknown at press time.

Collecting commentary: If this issue follows U.S. Mint tradition, the issued coins will be of gem Mint State quality.

Notes: These are readily available as all will be sold at a premium to collectors and others.

actual size: 26.5 mm

Mint narrative: The 2016 Native American $1 coin commemorates the code talkers from both World War I and World War II (1917–1945). The reverse design features two helmets with the inscriptions "WWI" and "WWII," and two feathers that form a "V," symbolizing victory, unity, and the important role that these code talkers played. It includes the required inscriptions UNITED STATES OF AMERICA and $1.

Notes: The reverse was designed by Thomas D. Rogers Sr., retired Mint sculptor-engraver. Two helmets are shown with a feather behind each.

On December 20, 2015, the U.S. Mint stated rolls, bags, and boxes of coins of the Philadelphia and Denver mints would be released on January 27, 2016.

	MS-64	MS-65	MS-66
2016-P, Code Talkers	$3	$5	$8

2016-D, Code Talkers

Circulation-strike mintage: Unknown at press time.

Collecting commentary: If this issue follows U.S. Mint tradition, the issued coins will be of gem Mint State quality.

Notes: These are readily available as all will be sold at a premium.

	MS-64	MS-65	MS-66
2016-D, Code Talkers	$3	$5	$8

2016-S, Code Talkers

Proof mintage: Unknown at press time.

Special finish mintage: Unknown at press time.

Availability: Nearly all of these coins are expected to be of gem Proof quality.

Notes: On December 20, 2015, the U.S. Mint stated that an American Coin and Currency Set of the San Francisco Mint would be released on March 14, 2016.

	PF-65	PF-69DC	PF-70
2016-S, Code Talkers, Proof	$15	$18	$125

PRESIDENTIAL DOLLARS, 2007–2016

Coin World editor Beth Deisher in the issue of May 17, 2004, wrote this (excerpted):

> Mistakes made in creating the small-sized circulating dollar coin a quarter century ago still haunt us today. And they will continue to impede the circulation of any dollar coin regardless of design or color unless and until someone in government figures out a way to remove all Susan B. Anthony dollar coins from circulation. . . .
>
> That's the dilemma two expert witnesses pointed out during a congressional hearing April 28. The hearing was a precursor to launching legislatively yet another plan to create yet another new small-sized dollar coin (Presidential series) that lawmakers are hoping beyond hope will be embraced and used by the public.

Coin programs then, earlier, and today are passed by Congress. Input from the Mint and Federal Reserve System is invited, and officials from such organizations attend hearings, but their experience and wisdom are often discarded. The result in the late 20th and early 21st centuries is that there have been many commemorative coins that have fallen below expectations, Kennedy half dollars piling up in Treasury storage, and, of course, hundreds of millions of unused small-diameter dollars.

On December 13, 2005, the House of Representatives passed one of the mostly widely sweeping pieces of coinage legislation in history. For the bicentennial of Abraham Lincoln's birth in 2009 the Mint was to create four special reverse designs for the cent, new $10 denomination .9999 fine gold bullion coins for the First Spouse series were authorized, a .9999 fine $50 one-ounce gold bullion coin with James Earle Fraser's buffalo (bison) design used on the 1913 nickel was authorized, and, among other things, the new Presidential series of manganese-brass dollars was legislated. These were to be issued at the rate of four per year and feature the chief executives in chronological order from George Washington onward until the last deceased president had been honored in 2016.

It was hoped the Presidential dollar would reverse the bad luck of its Susan B. Anthony and The primary advocate of the new Presidential dollar was Michael Castle, a congressman from Delaware, who for many years had taken a deep interest in coinage. It was his thought that if Sacagawea dollars were not popular with the public, ones featuring American presidents would be. He pointed to the fantastic success of the State quarter dollars launched in 1999 and minted at the rate of four per year since then. These had been widely accepted, and hundreds of millions of each issue reached circulation and stayed there. Banks stocked them in response to customer demand.

Sacagawea mini-dollar predecessors. Castle envisioned that bank customers would request them in quantity, and to promote goodwill various banks would gladly have them available.

In 2000 Mint Director Jay Johnson had stated that there were 140 million coin collectors in the United States. He was not referring to numismatists, but to the number of people he estimated were saving as souvenirs one or more of the State quarters. In Congressional discussions in 2005 this was brought up in a different context: there would be 140 million people who would desire one each of the Presidential dollars. Somehow, this would engender an enthusiasm for the long-neglected Sacagawea dollars.

Another proposal was that Sacagawea dollars should be minted in a quantity equal to 30% of the expected hundreds of millions of Presidential dollars each year. In 2004 just 2,600,000 Sacagawea dollars had been minted in circulation-strike format each at the two mints making these—Philadelphia and Denver. These went to numismatists. It was in 2002 that Sacagawea dollars were last coined in quantity for intended general circulation.

The Presidential Dollar Designs

Plans moved forward to create the Presidential dollars under the Presidential Coin Act of 2005, Public Law 109-145. Mint engravers were instructed to create a portrait of each president, using images from the bronze presidential medals that the Mint had been offering for sale for many years as inspiration, but to add their own interpretations. As a nod to Representative Michael Castle, the standard reverse was to feature the Statue of Liberty, a motif that in 1999 he strongly advocated for what became the Sacagawea dollar.

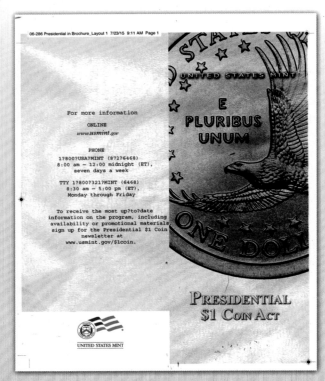

A mock-up draft proof sheet made in 2005 for a Mint brochure. At the time it was not realized that a new reverse would be made, and the eagle reverse from an earlier Sacagawea dollar was illustrated.

In January 2005 six variations in obverse inscriptions and ornamentation were made and were in time shown to the Commission of Fine Arts and, separately, the Citizens Coinage Advisory Committee for their review:

1st variant: Exhibits a braided rope border, the name of the president inscribed above the portrait, the number of the presidency below (i.e., 1ST PRESIDENT), and flanked by the dates of presidential service, not aligned with one another.

2nd variant: Similar to the preceding except that the border is beaded.

3rd variant: Exhibits larger lettering of the name of each president above the portrait, the flanking dates of service are aligned with one another, and the number of the presidency positioned within a scroll below the portrait. This version has no border design.

4th variant: With a change of the type face of the lettering of the president's name above the portrait, large sprigs of laurel emanate from the ends of a ribbon below, and the dates of service flanking the portrait are offset—the year of inauguration for Washington and Adams high on the left and end of service low on the right, and the order reversed for Jefferson and Madison.

5th variant: Features stylized laurel, reduced in size compared to the fourth variant, drops the scroll and fills the bottom border with the number of the presidency and the beginning and ending dates of service.

6th variant: Another typeface. The size and shape of the scroll is different, with the name of the president appearing in the scroll. The flanking beginning and ending dates of service for each presidency are positioned the same as on the fourth variant. The number of the presidency is at the top border above the presidential portrait. An oak branch with leaves appears to the left and a branch of laurel leaves with berries appears to the right. Oak is usually considered symbolic of strength and independence while laurel represents honor and glory for great achievements.[1]

Detail showing the initials of artist sculptor Don Everhart on a plaster of the reverse used on all Presidential dollars.

Plasters of the Presidential dollar dies for Garfield and Ford in the studio of Phebe Hemphill at the Philadelphia Mint.

Mint Publicity

Although the Mint had little to do with the Presidential dollar legislation, it and the Treasury Department of which it was a part were charged with the task of making the new dollars a success. A news release of January 20, 2005, included this:

> The United States Mint has produced presidential medals from the earliest days of the republic. Most of these medals were designed during the terms of the presidents with input from the administration and sometimes family of the president. The design process approvals originally came from the secretary of war.
>
> We'd like to think that this is how the presidents, themselves, would like to be portrayed. In most cases, these designs are classic when viewed today. But they are contemporary to the president's own lifetime and offer a historic window through which the public can view the time line of our nation. These are classic, beautiful designs, often from periods when sculpture and medallic design were regularly employed for the production of official United States Mint coins and medals.
>
> From the terms of Thomas Jefferson through Benjamin Harrison, a period of nearly 100 years, the presidential medals were used by the United States government in conjunction with official treaty negotiations.

The above was not pleasing to any numismatists with whom I discussed the matter at the time. Few people currently ordered bronze Mint medals. In *Coin World*, February 6, 2006, editor Beth Deisher spoke for many of her readers:

An ad from the U.S. Mint for the four Presidential dollars offered in 2007.

Retread Portraits Not Good Enough

Apparently there's not an ounce of creativity left at the U.S. Mint. Rather than let the artists participating in its Artistic Infusion Program and its full-time staff sculptor-engravers have an opportunity to create new and exciting likenesses of the presidents for the new Presidential dollar coin series, Mint officials are retreating to the Treasury bureaucracy mindset so pervasive 20 years ago.

At that time Treasury officials opposed any suggestion of changing designs on our circulating coins, stating that the presidential portraits in use had been "time honored." They even suggested that the American public could not or would not accept changes in the designs of its coins. We have the successful 50 State quarter dollars program and the Westward Journey Jefferson 5-cent coin series to prove just how wrong they were. Americans have demonstrated they like change in their change. In fact, the public has embraced coinage design changes. That's why it is so disappointing that the bureaucrats simply want to retread the portraits from the Mint's Presidential medal series for use on the new dollar coins.

Evidently, Mint officials paid no attention to chief sponsor Rep. Michael Castle, R-Del., and his vision of what the Presidential dollar series could and should be. In the "findings" section of the authorizing legislation, Castle states:

"In order to revitalize the design of United States coinage and return circulating coinage to its position as not only a necessary means of exchange in commerce, but also as an object of aesthetic beauty in its own right, it is appropriate to move many of the mottos and emblems, the inscription of the year, and the so-called 'mint marks' that currently appear on the 2 faces of each circulating coin to the edge of the coin, which would allow larger and more dramatic artwork on the coins reminiscent of the so-called 'Golden Age of Coinage' in the United States, at the beginning of the twentieth century, initiated by President Theodore Roosevelt, with the assistance of noted sculptors and medallic artists James Earle Fraser and Augustus Saint-Gaudens. . . ."

The repository of presidential likenesses is plentiful, and today's sculptor-engravers and artists are fully capable of rendering new and exciting designs for our coins, if U.S. Mint officials would only give them a chance. The Presidential dollar series is too important to simply rush through, just to be going through the motions. The justifications for using the Presidential medal portraits Mint officials espouse are merely excuses. Secretary of the Treasury John Snow should send the Mint back to the drawing boards and ask for great, memorable artistic treatment of our nation's leaders. Settling for anything less would reduce the eminence of our new dollar coins.

While Castle's dream of having beautiful art was rejected, the only unfortunate part of his proposal was accepted: moving the date and mintmark to the edge. As to the IN GOD WE TRUST and E PLURIBUS UNUM, few collectors cared. The latter had been lettered on edges before, such as on the Saint-Gaudens double eagles beginning in 1907. IN GOD WE TRUST had been on most coins, but not all (for example it was not on the Barber dime of 1892 to 1916). Putting the date and mintmark where it could not be seen if coins were in holders was heresy. It became a reality, and Presidential coins housed in Whitman, Littleton, Dansco, and other holders had this information hidden. When Native American dollars were introduced in 2008 they also had hidden dates and mintmarks. It can only be hoped that this will change for any issues beyond 2016, such as the ongoing Native American dollars.

Mint Director Edmund C. Moy

On September 5, 2006, Edmund C. Moy took the oath of office to become the 38th director of the U.S. Mint, succeeding Henrietta Holsman Fore. He inherited the responsibility of launching the Presidential dollars. In an October 3 interview with Paul Gilkes of *Coin World* he included these remarks:

"We're looking at strategies over the long term, but there are things we have to do really, really well right now, and one of them is implementation of the Presidential $1 Coin Act. I realize that regardless of what people think of the Mint, what its past history and accomplishments are, people are going to judge the Mint on the basis of how well this rollout is going to be. We've put a lot of attention into its being done right."

Moy says the enabling legislation for the Presidential dollar coin program requires the Mint to not only educate the public about the coins, but also to stage forums to receive input from the vending machine industry, the U.S. Postal Service, banks and other end-users to ensure the failure of the past are not repeated.

"It's a well-written bill that gives us a lot of tools that we didn't have before, so it gives me optimism that we are going to have a more successful rollout with this than we did in the past. We'll also have more long-term interest in this program. Our idea is that Americans will be interested in this program just as they are with the 50 State Quarters Program. Because it's a series instead of a 'one-off' like the Sacagawea dollar, hopefully that interest can be maintained over a longer period of time."[2]

Karen Springen wrote this in *Newsweek*, November 27, 2006:

The U.S Mint is hoping for the Midas touch with its February 15 launch of a series of "golden" $1 presidential coins. The touch was lacking with the $1 Sacagawea coins, 115 million of which the Mint still holds in "inventory." This time, government officials are applying a lesson from the successful 50-state quarters program—which has raked in $5 billion in profits since its 1999 debut. . . .

Mint director Edmund Moy notes that 140 million Americans collect the state quarters; he sees "a lot of parallels" between the two series. The $1 coins only cost about 20 cents to make (they're 88.5 percent copper, without a speck of real gold), and unlike paper bills, they'll last for decades. But will people spend them, or just hoard? "It's going to be like the Sacagawea dollar—nobody uses it in everyday commerce," says Shane Downing, publisher of the *Coin Dealer Newsletter*. Collector Mitch Sanders, chair of the Treasury's Citizens Coinage Advisory Committee, predicts many fans—among them, "the tooth fairy."

Mint Director Edmund C. Moy and images of the first four Presidential dollars.

Not All Presidents Notable

In "Other Side of the Coin," March 12, 2007, *Forbes* magazine printed this:

Perhaps the most striking thing about the new presidential coin is that Congress has asked the U.S. Mint to issue one for every President from George Washington to Gerald Ford. With four new coins coming out virtually every year, it will be hard to complain about the 2007 series, which offers a bumper crop of Founding Fathers.

The downside of this inclusive approach, though, is that not every year will be so glorious. The year 2010, for example, stands out as looking particularly dispiriting. The first coin will bear the likeness of Millard Fillmore, who may be best remembered today for signing the infamous Fugitive Slave Act into law. The next will belong to Franklin Pierce, a hard-drinking military man who was derided as the "victor of many a hard-fought bottle."

Collectors who hold out until 2014 will be rewarded with a dollar bearing the visage of Warren Harding. A shiny dollar may be a fit commemorative for a President whose administration is best remembered for the Teapot Dome scandal. And later that year there will be a coin for Herbert Hoover, who presided so unsatisfactorily over Depression-era America. From there is it a short two years until Americans get their hands on the first Richard Nixon dollar. The series will be a four-times-a-year reminder that not everyone who makes it to the White House belongs on Mount Rushmore.

Presidential Dollars Released

The first coin in the series depicted George Washington and was launched on February 16, 2007. For many years the Mint had honored February 22 as a special date, such as for the dedication of the Washington Cabinet in the Philadelphia Mint in 1860. Some students of history wondered why February 22 was not chosen in 2007. In actuality, quantities of Washington and other dollars were available to collectors before their general release to the public. The Mint put rolls and bags of the coins on sale on January 29.

On February 15 Mint Director Moy put the first coin "officially" into circulation. Dressed as George Washington, he dropped one in a parking meter (which was probably specially adapted). On this day more than 68,000 were distributed to the public. Joel Garreau reviewed the new coin in the *Washington Post*, March 21, 2007:

**Mint Director Moy and "George Washington"
during the launch of the first Presidential dollar.**

A Flip of the Coin: They're Bright, New and Shiny.
And You Can Bet Your Bottom Dollar, They're a Thing of the Past

The 1979 Susan B. Anthony dollar coin flopped. The 2000 Sacagawea dollar coin did little better. Nonetheless, the U.S. Mint in its infinite wisdom last month launched yet another new dollar coin.

Sit down in the handsome office of Edmund C. Moy, the director of the Mint. Ask him to comment on the quote attributed to Albert Einstein: "Insanity is doing the same thing over and over again, expecting different results."

Point out that the future of money is relentlessly shifting away from physical cash. Ask him if he has lost his blooming mind.

The Congress made me do it, he replies.

What *are* these things, these shiny new objects with a cartoonish George Washington on one side and the Statue of Liberty on the other that, like their two predecessor dollar coins, are not much bigger than quarters?

Release date for the John Adams dollar was May 18, for the Thomas Jefferson dollar August 17, and for the James Madison coin November 16.

The Mint announced that banks could order supplies from the Federal Reserve System two weeks prior to each launch and could continue requesting them for four months afterward. A huge demand was predicted, and to be sure that all citizens could have an adequate supply, more than 100,000,000 coins were made at each of the three mints. Proof set for collectors, containing the year's four coin designs and with 2007 and S on their edges, were made available at Mint stores and through the mail beginning on June 21, 2007.

Mint Director Moy at the launch of the John Adams dollar.

Mint Director Moy launching the Jefferson Presidential dollar, the third in the series.

Editor David C. Harper of *Numismatic News* did not envision much excitement, per this in the issue of February 13, 2007:

Are you waiting excitedly for the introduction of the new Presidential $1 coins February 15? Some collectors probably are, but if my mail and phone calls are any indication, the introduction of the Presidential dollar is a yawner compared to the Sacagawea dollar introduction seven years ago. Aside from a call and e-mail or two wondering only where "In God We Trust" is on the new coins (the edge), collectors seem to be from Missouri this time around. "Show me" seems to be the unspoken behavior guideline. . . .

The new gimmick for the Presidential dollars is the fact that there will be four designs a year instead of just one. The hope is that collectors and souvenir hunters will ask for them and collect the whole set. They will indeed ask for them, but that act will not make the coin a successful circulating coin . . . The first few of these will have higher mintages than the issues that come afterward, but the new coins will not circulate.

Applying the Edge Lettering

The Mint revealed that for circulation strikes the edge lettering was applied after the coins were struck. Paul Gilkes of *Coin World* describes the process:

For circulating and Uncirculated Mint set coins, after coins are struck on coinage presses, the struck coins are transported from the coin presses to the edge lettering equipment. The coins are fed in the lettering equipment horizontally at the rate of up to 1,000 coins per minute.

The coins pass through an edge-lettering segment or die bearing the raised lettering that is imparted incuse on the finished coin. A vertical wheel spinning counterclockwise grips the struck coin's plain edge on one side while the point of contact on the opposite side of the edge of the coin is directed through the edge segment bearing the raised inscriptions. The groove in the edge lettering segment resembles the bottom half of a compressed circle.

The orientation of the edge lettering to the obverse or reverse is random, as is the position on the edge where the lettering begins and ends.[3]

For Proofs the edge lettering was applied with a three-part segmented collar during the striking process. As a result all Proof coin lettering is upright in relation to the obverse.

For the Proof coins, the edge lettering is placed on the coins during the striking process. The edge die is a three-part, segmented collar that carries a portion of the edge lettering on each segment. The bottom anvil die, which can bear either the obverse or reverse design, is specially machined to include a donut-like projection around its center that triggers the opening and closing of the segmented collar.

At the moment of the striking, the segmented collar impacts the edge of the coin and forms the inscriptions. Then the edge collar segments separate as they pull away from the edge, permitting ejection of the coin without damage to the incused inscriptions from the raised numerals and lettering on the collar. The bottom die then helps position the finished coin for ejection from the coinage chamber.[4]

Some Presidential dollars, especially those of 2007, were accidentally made without edge lettering, giving them a plain edge. Plain-edge issues are highly collectible, but market values remain erratic. These were called "godless" dollars by some, and the Mint received complaints. On March 7, 2007, "A Statement from the United States Mint" included this:

The United States Mint has struck more than 300 million George Washington Presidential $1 coins. We have recently learned that an unspecified quantity of these coins inadvertently left the United States Mint at Philadelphia without edge lettering on them. . . .

The United States Mint understands the importance of the inscriptions "In God We Trust" and "E Pluribus Unum" as well as the mintmark and year on U.S. Coinage. We take this matter seriously. We also consider quality control a high priority. The agency is looking into the matter to determine a possible cause in the manufacturing process.

Production of the Presidential $1 coin, with its unique edge lettering,[5] is a new, complex, high volume manufacturing system, and the United States Mint is determined to make technical adjustments to perfect the process. . . .

Beginning in 2009 the motto IN GOD WE TRUST was moved near the lower rim on the obverse of each coin.

Overview of Edges
on Presidential Dollars

Dollars minted in 2007 have the edge lettered with the date, mintmark, and mottoes as:

> 2007 D E PLURIBUS UNUM • IN
> GOD WE TRUST •

Dollars of 2008 have a period after the mint-mark, as:

> 2008 D • E PLURIBUS UNUM • IN
> GOD WE TRUST •

Dollars were made with the lettering oriented upright with regard to the obverse (Type B or Type 2) or inverted (Type A or Type 1). There is no differentiation in numismatic market value. The following is derived from a PCGS news release of April 25, 2007:

> Effective immediately, PCGS will begin recognizing the up or down orientation of the edge lettering on Presidential Dollars, as follows:
>
> POSITION A—Edge lettering reads upside-down when the President's portrait faces up.
>
> POSITION B—Edge lettering reads normally when the President's portrait faces up.

This has caused some collectors to seek two examples of each Presidential dollar to show each edge orientation.

Continuing News

Although well over 800 million circulation strikes of Presidential dollars were made in 2007, few circulated. Most remained stored in Treasury vaults.

In October 2006 the Commission of Fine Arts reviewed dozens of proposed designs for the four 2008 coins, and the Citizens Coinage Advisory Committee did the same thing in November. Approved were facial portraits of James Monroe, John Quincy Adams, and Martin Van Buren adapted from paintings of full length figures in the National Portrait Gallery. The image of Andrew Jackson, who served between Adams and Van Buren, resembled that on the $20 bill.

On October 20, 2008, this appeared in *USA Today:*

Dollar Coins Get No Respect

The government is trying to convince consumers that dollar coins are greener than the dollar bill. The U.S. Mint is spending about $12 million on a pilot project to promote the presidential dollar coin by appealing to Americans' duty to protect the environment while saving the government money. The campaign, which may be expanded nationwide, stresses that coins last longer than dollar bills, are recyclable and could save tax money if more people used them.

"You'll want to get out and do your part, too," says one of the TV ads, which features an animated Statue of Liberty buying a hot dog on the streets of New York City with two dollar coins. In addition to TV, the four-month program includes radio, Web and newspaper advertising, and partnerships with banks and retailers that are giving out the coins as change.

Ads featuring the gold-colored coins are even plastered on city buses and trains. It is starting in four cities—Austin; Charlotte; Grand Rapids, Mich.; and Portland, Ore.—and may be expanded if successful. The Mint will be closely tracking bank orders for the coins in the four cities through November to gauge the program's success. . . .

The Mint has a constant reminder of its uphill battle: The agency holds in storage more than 92.7 million Uncirculated Sacagawea dollar coins created in 2000 and 2001. The Presidential dollar coin program, which began with George Washington in February 2007, is similar to the state quarters program. The Mint is introducing four $1 coins each year depicting the presidents in the order in which they served. The program is set to run at least through 2016 and will include only presidents who have died. Despite the popularity of the state quarters program, the presidential dollars have not taken off, and interest appears to be waning. . . .

In the meantime many "golden dollars" had become discolored, a problem dating back to the early days of testing the Sacagawea dollars before their release in 2000. In 2008 an independent scientific laboratory analyzed a tarnished 2008-P and found that manganese, one of four metals in the alloy, was the culprit as under certain conditions it could oxidize rapidly.[6]

Presidential dollars continued to pile up at the mints and in Treasury vaults. The numismatic press often ridiculed the quantities made and the perceived lack of artistry of the portraits, forgetting that the Mint had nothing to do with either. The decisions for coinage were made by others, and the secretary of the Treasury had the final say on the designs.

In June 2008 the $1 Coin Direct Ship Program was announced, whereby the Mint would ship up to $500 face value in rolls to financial and commercial entities as well as to individuals and would pay the postage. This was done in another effort to get the coins into circulation.

In 2009, mintages declined further, but still hundreds of millions of circulation-strike Presidential dollars were made—only to go into storage. In 2010 the Federal Reserve changed its ordering policies for Presidential dollars. Financial institutions could place their requests three weeks before the public launch date, instead of two as previously. The post-release ordering time was shortened from four weeks to two. The minimum quantity was $1,000 coins, with additional increments to be in the same quantity. These were put up in boxes of 40 25-coin rolls.

By 2009 a severe financial recession was underway, and many banks and financial institutions were experiencing losses, and some failed. Banks tried to reduce expenses. For many, no longer were supplies of new dollar coins offered and given out, with placards and notices nearby. Customers were told, in effect, "We do not handle new coins anymore."

2009 United States Mint Presidential $1 Coin Proof Set™

Presidential dollars of 2009.

Manganese-brass coins had surface tarnish problems from day one back in the Sacagawea dollar days. In 2009 the Mint revealed that for three years it had been using CarboShield BT, made by Lonza Inc., Allendale, New Jersey, a division of a Swiss firm. This product, originally developed as a wood preserver, was used to ameliorate the tarnish problem. "The CarboShield BT agent is applied during the burnishing process before the planchets are transferred to the coinage presses for striking into coins."[7]

"The Buck Stops Here"

On December 13, 2011, Secretary of the Treasury Timothy F. Geithner issued a directive suspending the production of all Presidential dollars intended for general circulation. Henceforth, mintage was to be limited to expected numismatic demand. He estimated that this would save $50 to $75 million annually in production costs. At the time the Federal Reserve Banks and storage facilities held 1.4 *billion* Presidential dollars. Even so, the subsequent figures exceeded sales to collectors.

Reflective of the preceding, the *Wall Street Journal* printed this article by Jeffrey Sparshott on December 14, 2011:

The Buck Stops Here: $1 Coins to Be Curtailed
Dead Presidents Go Way of Sacagawea

The U.S. government, its vaults stuffed with 1.4 billion one-dollar coins bearing the likenesses of dead presidents, has had enough of them. It is going to curtail production. "Nobody wants them," Vice President Joe Biden said Tuesday. That is for sure: The Mint says there are enough $1 coins sitting in Federal Reserve vaults to meet demand for a decade and the inventory was on track to hit two billion by 2016.

More than 40% of the coins that are minted are returned to the government unwanted, the Treasury said. The rest apparently sit in vending machines—one of the few places they are widely used—or in the drawers of coin collectors.

What the coins don't do is get around much. In fact, the Mint has never had much luck with dollar coins. The Susan B. Anthony dollar (1979–1981, revived for one year in 1999) never caught on; some people said it was too close in size to the quarter. Neither did the Sacagawea Golden Dollar (2000–2008) or its successor, the Native American $1 coin, which has the same front but a different back.

But that didn't discourage Congress. In 2005, it mandated that the Mint make $1 coins with the likenesses of the presidents, four each year from 2007 to 2016. So far, the Mint is up to James Garfield, the 20th president. Next up: Chester A. Arthur.

"And as it will shock you at all, the call for Chester A. Arthur coins is not there," Mr. Biden said at a Cabinet-level meeting of a White House campaign to cut government waste. Arthur fans needn't fret. The Mint will keep producing the presidential $1 coins on schedule but will only make enough to meet collector demand and no longer attempt to circulate them. By law, 20% of all dollar coins produced have to be Native American coins, so production of them will be reduced too.

The move, the Treasury said, will save taxpayers $50 million a year—or about 15 minutes' worth of the federal deficit. . . .

Per contra, there was a group who thought the hundreds of millions of dollars in profit made in seigniorage of unwanted dollars was a good idea. The Dollar Coin Alliance, a coalition of small businesses, budget watchdogs, transit agencies, and labor groups, stated that the suspension of production of Presidential dollar coins for circulation would cost taxpayers billions. While the government asserted that $50 to $70 million annually would be saved by stopping Presidential dollar production for circulation, the alliance cited the U.S. Mint's 2010 Annual report, which stated the dollar coin program made a net profit of $283 million.

The alliance also asserted that the best way to achieve real savings would be to replace the Federal Reserve Note paper dollar with dollar coins, which the Government Accountability Office reported in March 2011 would save the government an average of $184 million per year and approximately $5.5 billion over 30 years.[8]

Year after year different government offices and different surveys came up with widely differing "facts" on metal dollars versus paper dollars. In early 2012, for the fifth time in 22 years, the GAO offered an opinion on whether the dollar bill should replace the dollar coin. Contrary to previous recommendations, this time the GAO stated that the government would lose money in the first six years if it began to replace the dollar bill with dollar coins. While there still was anticipated savings over a 30-year time span, over 10 years the change would be unprofitable. One factor in the new scenario is that the GAO used an average life span for the bills of 56 months (per the Federal Reserve) as opposed to the Bureau of Engraving and Printing's previous estimate (quoted over the past 40 years) of about an 18-month life span.[9]

Launch Ceremonies

In early 2012 the Mint announced that as part of a program of cost savings it would no longer sponsor launch or related ceremonies for Presidential golden dollars.[10] This news was found to defy common sense, per *Coin World* editor Beth Deisher:

The U.S. Mint's decision to dispense with launch ceremonies for Presidential dollars is an example of a penny-wise, dollar-foolish reaction to the manic political atmosphere prevalent in Washington, D.C.

Mint officials justify the decision as one of cost-cutting, pointing to the fact that production of Presidential dollar coins for general circulation was suspended in December due to excessive inventories of the coins. The announcement was framed in a high-profile photo opportunity with Vice President Joe Biden in order to bring attention to the administration's determined attempt to trim government spending.

If the Mint were not producing any Presidential dollars in 2012, we could buy the logic. But, the fact is the Mint will produce four 2012 Presidential dollars in circulation and other qualities and sell the coins as numismatic products at premiums above face value.

Queried as to the cost of Presidential dollar launch events, a Mint official reported the average cost of prior Presidential dollar coin launch events has been about $10,000, depending on location. The direct costs have included travel expenses for two to three Mint staff members coordinating and speaking at the event, background materials for the media, and a free coin given to each child under the age of 18 attending the event.

Since 2007 when the series was introduced, Presidential dollar coin launch events have been held at ancestral homes or sites important to the president being depicted on the coin, with most being located in the Eastern portion of the country. Typically, the launch events have attracted many people in various age groups from the general population as well as collectors in the local communities. The launch events have brought renewed attention to the historical sites and generated stories and headlines featuring the coins that standard Mint advertising would never have produced.

Were the Mint a private enterprise, the $40,000 spent yearly on the launch events would be looked upon as marketing and advertising expenses, a rather modest sum for introducing and creating interest in four new products.[11]

In April 2012 the Chester A. Arthur dollar was launched, the first in the Presidential series to have a sharply reduced mintage aimed primarily at collectors. As expected there was no launch ceremony.

Another Surprise!

In 2015 the Mint introduced the Coin and Chronicles program pairing a *Reverse Proof* Philadelphia Mint Presidential dollar with a silver medal for $57.95. This came as a surprise to collectors, dealers, and others. Existing albums and folders had no provision for these varieties, a déjà vu scenario that took place with special strikings of the 2014-D Native American dollar (see previous chapter). The autumn 2015 Mint gift catalog included this description for the Johnson issue:

> The 2015 Coin and Chronicles Set—Lyndon B. Johnson features a Presidential $1 Reverse Proof coin (found only in this set!) and a Johnson Presidential silver medal. Also included is a U.S. postage stamp issued in 1973 to pay tribute to President Johnson. The set is perfect for the coin collector, history buff or as a special gift!
>
> The coin, medal and stamp are displayed in a grey folder covered in a soft–touch material with a handsome textured look that is very gift–worthy.
>
> The set includes:
> One Reverse Proof Finish 2015 Lyndon B. Johnson Presidential $1 coin
> One Lyndon B. Johnson Presidential Medal struck in .999 fine silver
> One Lyndon B. Johnson U.S. postage stamp issued in 1973
> One booklet including images from Johnson's life, military career and presidency
>
> *Presidential $1 Coin Design:*
> The obverse (heads) design of this Presidential $1 coin features a forward facing portrait of Lyndon B. Johnson. Inscriptions are "Lyndon B. Johnson," "IN GOD WE TRUST," "36th PRESIDENT" and "1963 – 1969."

The reverse (tails) design of the Presidential $1 Coin depicts a striking rendition of the Statue of Liberty.

This coin's designs feature large, dramatic artwork, as well as edge–incused inscriptions of the year of minting or issuance, "E PLURIBUS UNUM" and the mint mark. "IN GOD WE TRUST" appears on the face of the coin.

Presidential Silver Medal Design:
The obverse of the medal features a portrait of Lyndon B. Johnson with the inscription "LYNDON B. JOHNSON" centered along the border of the medal. The reverse of the medal features the inscriptions "PRESIDENT OF THE UNITED STATES," "NOVEMBER 22, 1963," "WE WILL SERVE ALL THE NATION: A UNITED PEOPLE WITH A UNITED PURPOSE: LYNDON B. JOHNSON."

No mention was made that all were Philadelphia Mint coins.

**U.S. Mint gift catalog page describing
the Johnson Coin and Chronicles package.**

Much to the dismay of many potential buyers, they were offered in sharply limited numbers, with the result that the first two—the Eisenhower and Truman issues— sold out quickly. Many if not most went to speculators rather than to longtime collectors loyal to the Mint. On eBay and elsewhere these were soon offered at figures that were multiples of the issue price. Complaints poured into the Mint as well as to *Coin World*, *Numismatic News*, and other numismatic media—collectors were not happy. Later issues were made in slightly larger numbers and were sold with less controversy.

Two dies for Harry S. Truman
Proof Presidential dollars.

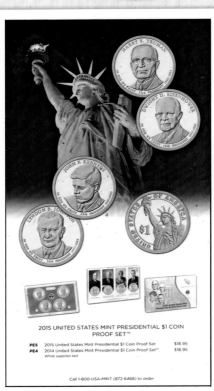

A die used to strike
Lyndon B. Johnson
Presidential Proof dollars.

Proof set of five
Presidential dollars
issued in 2015.

Dollar Coins at the San Francisco Mint

Under the aegis of Tom Jurkowsky of the U.S. Mint, the author and several others visited the San Francisco Mint on April 8, 2015, and documented the die-making and coining procedures for Presidential and Native American dollars, as well as other activities.[12]

Under careful supervision the author puts finishing touches on polishing a Proof Kennedy die at the San Francisco Mint.

A bin filled with blank planchets destined to be made into Native American and Presidential circulation-strike dollars.

Blank planchets in a Spaleck machine where they are mixed with tiny steel balls and a chemical solution and are intermixed at high speed.

Highly polished planchets being emptied from the Spaleck machine, destined to be made into Proof coins. From the machine the planchets are taken across a riddle-grid at which time the steel balls drop out to be re-used, and the polished planchets are put on a conveyor belt.

A tub with polished planchets at the end of the conveyor belt.

Polished manganese-brass Proof-coin planchets being dried on a Turkish towel.

Careful handling of the polished blanks before striking them with Proof dies.

Bulletin board showing images of dies and with lines indicating their alignment.

Grading Presidential Dollars

2007-P, Washington. Graded MS-68.

MS-60 to 70 (Mint State). *Obverse:* At MS-60, some abrasion and contact marks are evident, most noticeably on the highest-relief areas of the portrait, the exact location varying with the president depicted. Luster is present, but may be dull or lifeless. At MS-63, contact marks are extensive but not distracting. Abrasion still is evident, but less than at lower levels. MS-64 coins are slightly finer. An MS-65 coin may have minor abrasion, but contact marks are so minute as to require magnification. Luster should be full and rich. *Reverse:* At MS-60, some abrasion and contact marks are evident, most noticeably on the cheek and arm. Otherwise, the same comments apply as for the obverse.

2007-P, Madison. Graded AU-53.

AU-50, 53, 55, 58 (About Uncirculated). *Obverse:* Light wear is seen on the portrait, most prominently on the higher-relief areas. At AU-58, the luster is extensive, but incomplete. At AU–50 and 53, luster is less, but still is present. *Reverse:* Further wear is evident on statue. Otherwise, the same comments apply as for the obverse.

Presidential dollars are seldom collected in grades lower than AU-50.

2007-S, Madison. Graded PF-65.

PF-60 to 70 (Proof). *Obverse and Reverse:* Proofs that are extensively cleaned and have many hairlines, or that are dull and grainy, are lower level, such as PF–60 to 62. This comment is more theoretical than practical, as nearly all Proofs have been well kept. With medium hairlines and good reflectivity, assigned grades of PF–63 or 64 are appropriate. With relatively few hairlines a rating of PF-65 can be given. PF-66 may have hairlines so delicate that magnification is needed to see them. Above that, all the way to PF-70, a Proof should be free of any hairlines or other problems under strong magnification.

Specifications of the Presidential Dollar

Other than a change in the lettering on the edge, as discussed previously, the basic specifications for Presidential dollars did not change during its production run, and are listed below. See the individual entries for designer information.

Composition: Pure copper core with outer layers of manganese-brass (.770 copper, .070 manganese, .120 zinc, .040 nickel).

Weight: 8.1 grams.

Diameter: 26.5 mm.

Edge, 2007–2008: Lettered with date, mintmark, IN GOD WE TRUST, and E PLURIBUS UNUM.

Edge, 2009–2016: Lettered with date, mintmark, and E PLURIBUS UNUM. IN GOD WE TRUST was moved to the obverse.

2007, George Washington

Specifications: See pages 237 and 238 for details.

Designer: Joseph Menna (obverse); Don Everhart (reverse).

1st President (1789–1797)

Life dates: February 22, 1732–December 14, 1799.

Political party: None.

Vice president: John Adams, 1789 to 1797.

First lady: Married widow Martha Dandridge Custis in 1759. The couple raised two children by Martha's first marriage: John "Jack" Parke Custis and Martha "Patsy" Custis.

Especially remembered for: George Washington was known for his leadership during the Revolutionary War; for defining the duties of the office of president; and for his sterling character, which served as a shining example of integrity. He is known as "The Father of Our Country." He is the most popular president in terms of the number of different coins, tokens, medals, and currency notes with his portrait. He is one of four presidents honored on Mount Rushmore. His Mount Vernon home overlooking the Potomac River is a national landmark.

Coins and money: The Coinage Act of April 2, 1792, set in motion the establishment of the Philadelphia Mint and, eventually, the establishment of mints in other locations (beginning in 1838). Up to this time, coins of foreign countries were the only ones used in commerce, especially those of Europe, Mexico, Central America, and South America. Kentucky became the 15th state on June 15. Common in circulation were copper coins issued by Connecticut, Massachusetts, and New Jersey as well as the Republic of Vermont (which did not become a state until 1791). Paper currency was issued by a few state-chartered banks.

In July 1792 about 1,500 silver half dismes (later known as half dimes) were issued using Mint equipment in a nearby shop. The Mint buildings were not occupied until late summer. The Mint issued its first coins for circulation, copper cents, in March 1793. Half cents were first issued that summer. In 1794 the first silver half dollars and dollars were issued, and in 1795 the first half dimes of the Flowing Hair design (from dies dated 1794 but not used at that time) were issued. The first gold coins, $5 half eagles, and $10 eagles were also produced. In 1796 the first dimes, quarters, and $2.50 gold coins were made, thus completing all of the authorized denominations.

At the time a few museums in America displayed ancient and classical coins and medals, but there was little interest in the hobby of numismatics. In contrast there was great activity in Europe.

Notable sayings: In the first State of the Union address, on April 30, 1779, Washington said, "To be prepared for war is the most effective means of preserving peace."

"Few men have virtue to withstand the highest bidder."

"Associate with men of good quality if you esteem your own reputation, for it is better to be alone than in bad company."

"It is better to offer no excuse than a bad one."

"Beware entangling foreign alliances."

2007-P, George Washington

Circulation-strike mintage: 176,680,000

Satin Finish mintage: 895,628

actual size: 26.5 mm

Collecting commentary, circulation strikes: Typical Mint State grades hover around MS-65, although so many were minted that higher-grade coins can be found. Numismatists who purchase Presidential dollars in the aftermarket usually seek MS-65 or so. Coins saved by the general public in the early years when large quantities were made average MS–64 to 65. For all Presidential dollars issued with Satin Finish, many collectors buy these rather than regular circulation strikes.

Collecting commentary, Satin Finish: These are typically graded 65 to 68, but selected coins are higher. They are separately certified with an SP prefix by PCGS and with an SMS prefix by NGC.

Release of circulation strikes: A launch ceremony was held on February 15, 2007, at the venerable Grand Central Station in New York City. Mint Director Edmund C. Moy was there to meet and greet visitors and to "spend" some of the coins. Portrayers of Washington were on hand.

Notes: Presidential dollars of 2007 from the three mints do not have a dot after the date on the edge; a dot was added in 2008. Most of these and other early high-mintage dollars are in storage in Federal Reserve System vaults.

2007, Washington, plain-edge error: This variety is also called "missing edge lettering." Many of these coins were inadvertently issued without edge lettering and thus lack the date and mintmark. The 2007 Washington issues, not identifiable to a particular mint, are readily found in the marketplace today. Tens of thousands have been certified—more than all other plain-edge presidential dollars combined. It is thought that 200,000 or more were minted. These are no. 57 in *100 Greatest U.S. Modern Coins.*

	MS-64	MS-65	MS-66
2007-P, Washington	$2	$3	$6
2007-P, Washington, Satin Finish	$3	$5	$12

2007-D, George Washington

Circulation-strike mintage: 163,680,000

Satin Finish mintage: 895,628

Collecting commentary, circulation strikes: Typical Mint State grades hover around MS-65, although so many were minted that higher-grade coins can be found.

Collecting commentary, Satin Finish: These are typically graded 65 to 68, but selected coins are higher. They are separately certified with an SP prefix by PCGS and with an SMS prefix by NGC.

	MS-64	MS-65	MS-66
2007-D, Washington	$1.50	$3	$6
2007-D, Washington, Satin Finish	$3	$5	$12

2007-S, George Washington

Proof mintage: 3,965,989

Availability: Nearly all are gem Proofs approaching perfection.

Notes: 1,285,972 were sold by the U.S. Mint as part of four-coin Presidential dollar Proof sets.

2007-S, Out-of-sequence edge lettering (error): Normally the motto IN GOD WE TRUST is followed by the date and mintmark, but on some Proofs the lettering was out of normal sequence and the date and mintmark are found after E PLURIBUS UNUM.

	PF-65	PF-69DC	PF-70
2007-S, Washington, Proof	$10	$18	$190

2007, John Adams

Specifications: See pages 237 and 238 for details.

Designer: Joel Iskowitz (obverse); Don Everhart (reverse).

2nd President (1797–1801)

Life dates: October 30, 1735–July 4, 1826.

Political party: Federalist.

Vice president: Thomas Jefferson.

First lady: Married Abigail Smith on October 25, 1764. The couple had five children, including John Quincy Adams who also became president.

Especially remembered for: He was the first president to compete in a national election. He is also remembered for the XYZ Affair.

Coins and money: During the Adams administration federal coins struck at the Philadelphia Mint became familiar sights in American commerce, with copper cents being especially popular. Many silver and gold coins were exported, thus being of no practical use in domestic trade. State-chartered banks in certain of the larger Eastern cities issued their own paper money. There was no widely circulated federal paper money, nor would there be until years later in 1861.

Notable sayings: "Old minds are like old horses, you must exercise them if you want to keep them in working order."

"Facts are stubborn things."

Adams obverse plaster.

2007-P, John Adams

Circulation-strike mintage: 112,420,000

Satin Finish mintage: 895,628

Collecting commentary, circulation strikes: Typical Mint State grades hover around

actual size: 26.5 mm

MS-65, although so many were minted that higher-grade coins can be found.

Collecting commentary, Satin Finish: These are typically graded 65 to 68, but selected coins are higher. They are separately certified with an SP prefix by PCGS and with an SMS prefix by NGC.

Release of circulation strikes: The launch ceremony was held in Quincy, Massachusetts, on May 22, 2007, with Director Moy, Adams descendants, Mayor William J. Phelan, and others in attendance.

2007, John Adams, plain-edge error: Perhaps 10,000 or so were inadvertently issued without edge lettering and thus lack the date and mintmark. The 2007 Adams issues are not identifiable to a particular mint.

2007-P, doubled-edge lettering error: After they were struck these coins were run through the edge-lettering machine twice, giving IN GOD WE TRUST, E PLURIBUS UNUM, and 2007-P two impressions, off-register. It is thought that as many as 50,000 were made. These are no. 57 in *100 Greatest U.S. Modern Coins.* (Also see 2007-D.)

	MS-64	MS-65	MS-66
2007-P, J. Adams	$1.50	$3	$6
2007-P, J. Adams, Satin Finish	$3	$5	$12

2007-D, John Adams

Circulation-strike mintage: 112,140,000

Satin Finish mintage: 895,628

Collecting commentary, circulation strikes: Typical Mint State grades hover around MS-65, although so many were minted that higher-grade coins can be found.

Collecting commentary, Satin Finish: These are typically graded 65 to 68, but selected coins are higher. They are separately certified with an SP prefix by PCGS and with an SMS prefix by NGC.

2007-D, doubled-edge lettering error: After they were struck these coins were run through the edge-lettering machine twice, double impressions of the inscriptions, as was done for 2007-P (see previous). The mintage of these errors is estimated at fewer than 1,000 pieces. Some inscriptions are overlapped, while on others one inscription is inverted.

	MS-64	MS-65	MS-66
2007-D, J. Adams	$1.50	$3	$6
2007-D, J. Adams, Satin Finish	$3	$5	$12

2007-S, John Adams

Proof mintage: 3,965,989

Availability: Nearly all are gem Proofs approaching perfection.

Notes: 1,285,972 were sold by the U.S. Mint as part of four-coin Presidential dollar Proof sets.

	PF-65	PF-69DC	PF-70
2007-S, J. Adams, Proof	$10	$18	$70

2007, Thomas Jefferson

Specifications: See pages 237 and 238 for details.

Designer: Joseph Menna (obverse); Don Everhart (reverse).

3rd President (1801–1809)

Life dates: April 13, 1743–July 4, 1826.

Political party: Democrat-Republican.

Vice presidents: Aaron Burr, 1801 to 1805; George Clinton, 1805 to 1809.

First lady: Married 22-year-old widow Martha Wayles Skelton on January 1, 1772. The couple had six children. Jefferson formed an intimate relationship with one of his slaves, Sarah ("Sally") Hernings, who was a half-sister of his wife and sometimes traveled with him. She became the mother of six more of his children.

Especially remembered for: Jefferson was most famous for drafting the Declaration of Independence. He worked on finance during the Washington administration. The Louisiana Purchase of 1803, which more than doubled the size of the United States, was his doing, though his Embargo Act of 1807 was widely considered to be a failure. Jefferson designed his home (Monticello) and other buildings considered to be high examples of architecture. His nicknames included "Man of the People" and "Sage of Monticello." He is one of four presidents honored on Mount Rushmore. The Jefferson Memorial is a prime attraction today in Washington, D.C.

Coins and money: In 1804 the Corps of Discovery, best remembered as the Lewis and Clark Expedition, set out from St. Louis, Missouri, and went to the Pacific Northwest, finally reaching the Columbia River, then the Pacific Ocean, and then returning in 1806. The adventurers distributed silver Indian Peace medals to tribal chiefs along the way.

Notable sayings: "Banking establishments are more dangerous than standing armies."
   "That government is best which governs the least, because its people discipline themselves."
   "The price of freedom is eternal vigilance."
   "Delay is preferable to error."
   "If you want to know who you are don't ask. Act. Action will delineate and define you."
   "I cannot live without books."
   "The harder I work the more luck I seem to have."
   "Never spend your money before you've earned it."

2007-P, Thomas Jefferson

Circulation-strike mintage: 100,800,000

Satin Finish mintage: 895,628

actual size: 26.5 mm

Collecting commentary, circulation strikes: Typical Mint State grades hover around MS-65, although so many were minted that higher-grade coins can be found.

Collecting commentary, Satin Finish: These are typically graded 65 to 68, but selected coins are higher. They are separately certified with an SP prefix by PCGS and with an SMS prefix by NGC.

Release of circulation strikes: The official release date for these coins was August 16, 2007. However, on August 15 at the Jefferson Memorial in Washington a special ceremony was held in which citizens could exchange $1 bills for the new notes. Director Moy was present as was Daniel P. Jordan, president of the Thomas Jefferson Foundation.

2007, Jefferson, plain-edge error: Several thousand were inadvertently issued without edge lettering and thus lack the date and mintmark. The 2007 Jefferson issues are not identifiable to a particular mint.

	MS-64	MS-65	MS-66
2007-P, Jefferson	$1.50	$3	$6
2007-P, Jefferson, Satin Finish	$3	$5	$12

2007-D, Thomas Jefferson

Circulation-strike mintage: 102,810,000

Satin Finish mintage: 895,628

Collecting commentary, circulation strikes: Typical Mint State grades hover around MS-65, although so many were minted that higher-grade coins can be found.

Collecting commentary, Satin Finish: These are typically graded 65 to 68, but selected coins are higher. They are separately certified with an SP prefix by PCGS and with an SMS prefix by NGC.

	MS-64	MS-65	MS-66
2007-D, Jefferson	$1.50	$3	$6
2007-D, Jefferson, Satin Finish	$3	$5	$12

2007-S, Thomas Jefferson

Proof mintage: 3,965,989

Availability: Nearly all are gem Proofs approaching perfection.

Notes: 1,285,972 were sold by the U.S. Mint as part of four-coin Presidential dollar Proof sets.

2007-S, edge lettering out of sequence (error): Some 2007-S Proofs have the edge lettering out of sequence. Error coins have IN GOD WE TRUST followed immediately by E PLURIBUS UNUM. "As many as 100,000 may have been produced with this anomaly, according to Mint officials."[13]

	PF-65	PF-69DC	PF-70
2007-S, Jefferson, Proof	$10	$18	$55

2007, James Madison

Specifications: See pages 237 and 238 for details.

Designer: Joel Iskowitz (obverse); Don Everhart (reverse).

4th President (1809–1817)

Life dates: March 16, 1751–June 28, 1836.

Political party: Democrat-Republican.

Vice presidents: George Clinton, 1809 to 1812; none, 1812 and 1813; Elbridge Gerry, 1813 and 1814; none, 1814 to 1817.

First lady: Married Dolley Payne Todd on September 15, 1794. The couple had no children.

Especially remembered for: Madison is remembered for making a major contribution to the ratification of the Constitution by writing, with Alexander Hamilton and John Jay, the *Federalist* essays. He was a strong proponent of the Bill of Rights. Many historians view the War of 1812 as a tragic blunder by the president, as it had far-reaching negative effects on the economy of America. His nickname was "Father of the Constitution." His wife Dolley became one of the best-remembered first ladies.

Coins and money: Monetary conditions varied widely during the Madison administration. During the war coins were scarce in some areas and unavailable in others. The economy was uncertain. It was hoped that after the war normal conditions would resume, but this did not happen. In 1816 in particular a flood of small-denomination paper notes helped replace unavailable coins. In 1816 the Mint struck only one denomination: copper cents. This is unique in Mint history.

Notable saying: "The truth is that all men having power ought to be mistrusted."

Madison obverse plaster with clay overlay for finessing.

2007-P, James Madison

Circulation-strike mintage: 84,560,000

Satin Finish mintage: 895,628

Collecting commentary, circulation strikes: Typical Mint State grades hover around

actual size: 26.5 mm

MS-65, although so many were minted that higher-grade coins can be found.

Collecting commentary, Satin Finish: These are typically graded 65 to 68, but selected coins are higher. They are separately certified with an SP prefix by PCGS and with an SMS prefix by NGC.

Release of circulation strikes: The official release date was November 15, 2007, without ceremony.

2007, Madison, plain-edge error: Over one thousand were inadvertently issued without edge lettering and thus lack the date and mintmark. The 2007 Madison issues are not identifiable to a particular mint.

	MS-64	MS-65	MS-66
2007-P, Madison	$1.50	$3	$6
2007-P, Madison, Satin Finish	$3	$5	$12

2007-D, James Madison

Circulation-strike mintage: 87,780,000

Satin Finish mintage: 895,628

Collecting commentary, circulation strikes: Typical Mint State grades hover around MS-65, although so many were minted that higher-grade coins can be found.

Collecting commentary, Satin Finish: These are typically graded 65 to 68, but selected coins are higher. They are separately certified with an SP prefix by PCGS and with an SMS prefix by NGC.

	MS-64	MS-65	MS-66
2007-D, Madison	$1.50	$3	$6
2007-D, Madison, Satin Finish	$3	$5	$12

2007-S, James Madison

Proof mintage: 3,965,989

Availability: Nearly all are gem Proofs approaching perfection.

Notes: 1,285,972 were sold by the U.S. Mint as part of four-coin Presidential dollar Proof sets.

	PF-65	PF-69DC	PF-70
2007-S, Madison, Proof	$10	$18	$60

2008, James Monroe

Specifications: See pages 237 and 238 for details.

Designer: Joseph Menna (obverse); Don Everhart (reverse).

5th President (1817–1825)

Life dates: April 28, 1758–July 4, 1831.

Political party: Democrat-Republican.

Vice president: Daniel D. Tompkins, 1817 to 1825.

First lady: Married Elizabeth "Eliza" Kortright on February 16, 1786. The couple had three children.

Especially remembered for: Monroe is known for the Era of Good Feeling and for signing the Missouri Compromise bill. He had an extended tour visiting many states. The Monroe Doctrine (the name assigned years later to this policy) was celebrated in 1923 by a special commemorative half dollar.

Coins and money: On August 16, 1824, Lafayette, the French hero of the American Revolution, arrived in the United States to stay until September 7, 1825. Congress named him "the Nation's Guest." While here he visited all 16 states. Thousands of coins, mostly cents, were counterstamped with his portrait on one side and that of Washington on the other.

By 1821 the value of gold on the international market had risen to the point at which it cost more than face value to mint $2.50 and $5 coins (the only denominations being made at the time). Accordingly, from this time onward such coins, made to the order of bullion depositors, were mostly exported to foreign lands where they were received at their bullion value.

The 1923-S Monroe Doctrine Centennial half dollar bears his portrait on the obverse.

Notable saying: "A little flattery will support a man through great fatigue."

2008-P, James Monroe

Circulation-strike mintage: 64,260,000

Satin Finish mintage: 745,464

actual size: 26.5 mm

Collecting commentary, circulation strikes: Typical Mint State grades hover around MS-65, although so many were minted that higher-grade coins can be found.

Collecting commentary, Satin Finish: These are typically graded 65 to 68, but selected coins are higher. They are separately certified with an SP prefix by PCGS and with an SMS prefix by NGC.

Release of circulation strikes: On February 13 in heavy rain several hundred people attended an "official unveiling" of these coins at Ash Lawn-Highland, the Monroe homestead near Charlottesville, Virginia. Acting Deputy Director of the Mint Dan Shaver was on hand as were various other dignitaries. The official release date was a day later, February 14.

Notes: A large quantity of these were inadvertently struck on quarter planchets. Estimates suggested that many thousands of coins were involved, many of which were retrieved by Coin Wrap, Inc., a Harrisburg, Pennsylvania, contractor that put coins in 25-coin rolls and in 1,000-coin boxes to be shipped to banks that ordered them through the Federal Reserve System. The Mint was silent on how many coins were involved.[14]

2008, Monroe, plain-edge error: Hundreds of these coins were inadvertently issued without edge lettering and thus lack the date and mintmark. The 2008, Monroe error-edge issues, not identifiable as to mint, are rare today.

	MS-64	MS-65	MS-66
2008-P, Monroe	$1.50	$3	$6
2008-P, Monroe, Satin Finish	$3	$5	$12

2008-D, James Monroe

Circulation-strike mintage: 60,230,000

Satin Finish mintage: 745,464

Collecting commentary, circulation strikes: Typical Mint State grades hover around MS-65, although so many were minted that higher-grade coins can be found.

Collecting commentary, Satin Finish: These are typically graded 65 to 68, but selected coins are higher. They are separately certified with an SP prefix by PCGS and with an SMS prefix by NGC.

Notes: Despite the prodigious mintage figures for circulation strikes, few were actually distributed to the public. This comment applies to all in the series.

	MS-64	MS-65	MS-66
2008-D, Monroe	$1.50	$3	$6
2008-D, Monroe, Satin Finish	$3	$5	$12

2008-S, James Monroe

Proof mintage: 3,083,940

Availability: Nearly all are gem Proofs approaching perfection.

Notes: 836,730 were sold by the U.S. Mint as part of four-coin Presidential dollar Proof sets.

	PF-65	PF-69DC	PF-70
2008-S, Monroe, Proof	$10	$18	$140

2008, John Quincy Adams

Specifications: See pages 237 and 238 for details.

Designer: Don Everhart (obverse); Don Everhart (reverse).

6th President (1825–1829)

Life dates: July 11, 1767–February 23, 1848.

Political party: Democrat-Republican.

Vice president: John C. Calhoun, 1825 to 1829.

First lady: Married Louisa Catherine Johnson on July 26, 1797. The couple had four children.

Especially remembered for: John Quincy Adams is remembered for his foreign ministry, the development of the country's infrastructure, and his support of literature, art, and science.

Coins and money: During the mid-1820s there was a great expansion of private banks and insurance companies. However, the situation was short lived, and in 1825 many prices fell, causing an economic crisis in the United States. The controversial Bank of the United States was beset with many problems, had a shortage of gold and silver coins, and could not redeem its own notes. There was a business recession in 1826, but by 1827 conditions had improved.

Notable sayings: "May our country always be successful, but whether successful or otherwise, always right."

"If your action inspires others to dream more, learn more, do more and become more, you are a leader."

2008-P, John Quincy Adams

Circulation-strike mintage: 57,540,000

Satin Finish mintage: 745,464

actual size: 26.5 mm

Collecting commentary, circulation strikes: Typical Mint State grades hover around MS-65, although so many were minted that higher-grade coins can be found.

Collecting commentary, Satin Finish: These are typically graded 65 to 68, but selected coins are higher. They are separately certified with an SP prefix by PCGS and with an SMS prefix by NGC.

Release of circulation strikes: The official release date was May 15, 2008. On the same day, a ceremony not sponsored by the Mint but with coins available for face value was held at the visitor center of the Adams National Historical Park in Quincy, Massachusetts.

2008, Adams, plain-edge error: Over one thousand of these coins were inadvertently issued without edge lettering and thus lack the date and mintmark. The 2008 Adams issues, not identifiable as to mint, are scarce today.

	MS-64	MS-65	MS-66
2008-P, J.Q. Adams	$1.50	$3	$6
2008-P, J.Q. Adams, Satin Finish	$3	$5	$12

2008-D, John Quincy Adams

Circulation-strike mintage: 57,720,000

Satin Finish mintage: 745,464

Collecting commentary, circulation strikes: Typical Mint State grades hover around MS-65, although so many were minted that higher-grade coins can be found.

Collecting commentary, Satin Finish: These are typically graded 65 to 68, but selected coins are higher. They are separately certified with an SP prefix by PCGS and with an SMS prefix by NGC.

	MS-64	MS-65	MS-66
2008-D, J.Q. Adams	$1.50	$3	$6
2008-D, J.Q. Adams, Satin Finish	$3	$5	$12

2008-S, John Quincy Adams

Proof mintage: 3,083,940

Availability: Nearly all are gem Proofs approaching perfection.

Notes: 836,730 were sold by the U.S. Mint as part of four-coin Presidential dollar Proof sets.

	PF-65	PF-69DC	PF-70
2008-S, J.Q. Adams, Proof	$10	$18	$110

2008, Andrew Jackson

Specifications: See pages 237 and 238 for details.

Designer: Joel Iskowitz (obverse); Don Everhart (reverse).

7th President (1829–1837)

Life dates: March 15, 1767–June 8, 1845.

Political party: Democratic.

Vice presidents: John C. Calhoun, 1829 to 1832; none, 1832 to 1833; Martin Van Buren, 1833 to 1837.

First lady: Married Rachel Donelson Robards in August 1791, and again in a second ceremony on January 17, 1794, after it was learned that Rachel's earlier divorce had been invalid. They raised one child, Andrew Jackson Jr., who was adopted. Although Rachel did not live long enough to become first lady, during Jackson's tenure Rachel's niece, Emily Donelson, lived at the White House with her husband and served as hostess.

Especially remembered for: Jackson is remembered for having the greatest plurality of popular votes gained by any president to date. He is also known for his "The Union must and shall be preserved" statement during the political conflict with Senator John C. Calhoun. He vetoed the charter renewal for the 2nd Bank of the United States and had conflict with backers of the Bank. The tragic Indian Removal Act of 1830 was also under his watch. There was great prosperity during the early 1830s when he was President, including a Treasury surplus. The gossip about flirtatious Peggy Eaton and the "Petticoat Affair" resulted in the rearrangement of Jackson's Cabinet, followed by the "Kitchen Cabinet" of political cronies. The construction and occupation of the second Philadelphia Mint was under Jackson's presidency. His nickname was "Old Hickory."

Coins and money: In 1832 the second Philadelphia Mint went into operation, replacing the original facility in use since 1792. Steam power was introduced for coinage in 1839. Prosperity was the rule for most of the Jackson administration. The economy began to chill in 1836 and worsened in 1837 (see Van Buren listing for more).

Notable sayings: "The individual who refuses to defend his rights when called by his government deserves to be a slave, and must be punished as an enemy of the country and a friend to her foe."

"Internal improvement and the diffusion of knowledge, so far as they can be promoted by the constitutional acts of the federal government, are of high importance."

2008-P, Andrew Jackson

Circulation-strike mintage: 61,180,000

Satin Finish mintage: 745,464

actual size: 26.5 mm

Collecting commentary, circulation strikes: Typical Mint State grades hover around MS-65, although so many were minted that higher-grade coins can be found.

Collecting commentary, Satin Finish: These are typically graded 65 to 68, but selected coins are higher. They are separately certified with an SP prefix by PCGS and with an SMS prefix by NGC.

Release of circulation strikes: On August 24 the Mint arranged the official circulation launch of the new dollar (although quantities had been available to collectors earlier, as had Proofs). More than 400 students and others from the Nashville area attended the ceremony at The Hermitage, Jackson's home. Thousands of coins were poured onto a large table, and the public could exchange paper dollars for them. Youngsters under the age of 18 received free coins.

2008, Jackson, plain-edge error: Hundreds of these coins were inadvertently issued without edge lettering and thus lack the date and mintmark. The 2008 Jackson issues, not identifiable as to mint, are scarce today.

	MS-64	MS-65	MS-66
2008-P, Jackson	$1.50	$3	$6
2008-P, Jackson, Satin Finish	$3	$5	$12

2008-D, Andrew Jackson

Circulation-strike mintage: 61,070,000

Satin Finish mintage: 745,464

Collecting commentary, circulation strikes: Typical Mint State grades hover around MS-65, although so many were minted that higher-grade coins can be found.

Collecting commentary, Satin Finish: These are typically graded 65 to 68, but selected coins are higher. They are separately certified with an SP prefix by PCGS and with an SMS prefix by NGC.

	MS-64	MS-65	MS-66
2008-D, Jackson	$1.50	$3	$6
2008-D, Jackson, Satin Finish	$3	$5	$12

2008-S, Andrew Jackson

Proof mintage: 3,083,940

Availability: Nearly all are gem Proofs approaching perfection.

Notes: 836,730 were sold by the U.S. Mint as part of four-coin Presidential dollar Proof sets.

	PF-65	PF-69DC	PF-70
2008-S, Jackson, Proof	$10	$18	$135

2008, Martin Van Buren

Specifications: See pages 237 and 238 for details.

Designer: Joel Iskowitz (obverse); Don Everhart (reverse).

8th President (1837–1841)

Life dates: December 5, 1782–July 24, 1862.

Political party: Democratic.

Vice president: Richard M. Johnson, 1837 to 1841.

First lady: Married Hannah Hoes on February 21, 1807. They had four children: Abraham Van Buren (1807–1873); John Van Buren (1810–1866); Martin Van Buren (1812–1855); and Smith Thompson Van Buren (1817–1876).

Especially remembered for: Van Buren is remembered for his loyalty to President Jackson while serving as secretary of state and as vice president. The Panic of 1837 was an economic disaster that occurred under his watch. He had a lack of popularity throughout his presidency, and his 1840 bid for reelection was unsuccessful.

Coins and money: Van Buren's administration was dominated by the Hard Times era. Money became scarce and there was concern about the future of commerce and banking. On May 10, 1837, the leading banks in New York City and other Eastern metropolises suspended specie payments—no longer could their bank bills be exchanged for gold and silver coins. This precipitated the Panic of 1837 which quickly spread across the nation. Thousands of businesses and hundreds of banks failed. Today, numismatists enjoy many varieties of Hard Times tokens of the era and many currency notes that exist in large quantities as the banks that issued them failed.

Notable sayings: "It is easier to do a job right than to explain why you didn't."

"I tread in the footsteps of illustrious men . . . in receiving from the people the sacred trust confided to my illustrious predecessor." (The predecessor was Jackson; versions of this were used on Hard Times tokens.)

"As to the presidency, the two happiest days of my life were those of my entrance upon the office and my surrender of it."

2008-P, Martin Van Buren

Circulation-strike mintage: 51,520,000

Satin Finish mintage: 745,464

actual size: 26.5 mm

Collecting commentary, circulation strikes: Typical Mint State grades hover around MS-65, although so many were minted that higher-grade coins can be found.

Collecting commentary, Satin Finish: These are typically graded 65 to 68, but selected coins are higher. They are separately certified with an SP prefix by PCGS and with an SMS prefix by NGC.

Release of circulation strikes: On December 5, the president's birthday, a ceremony observing the coin was held at Van Buren's grave site in Kinderhook, New York, although such coins had already been released into general circulation. Deputy Director Andrew Brunhart was on hand from the Mint, joining local dignitaries.

2008, Van Buren, plain-edge error: Several thousands of these coins were inadvertently issued without edge lettering and thus lack the date and mintmark. The 2008 Van Buren issues are not identifiable to a particular mint.

	MS-64	MS-65	MS-66
2008-P, Van Buren	$1.50	$3	$6
2008-P, Van Buren, Satin Finish	$3	$5	$12

2008-D, Martin Van Buren

Circulation-strike mintage: 50,960,000

Satin Finish mintage: 745,464

Collecting commentary, circulation strikes: Typical Mint State grades hover around MS-65, although so many were minted that higher-grade coins can be found.

Collecting commentary, Satin Finish: These are typically graded 65 to 68, but selected coins are higher. They are separately certified with an SP prefix by PCGS and with an SMS prefix by NGC.

	MS-64	MS-65	MS-66
2008-D, Van Buren	$1.50	$3	$6
2008-D, Van Buren, Satin Finish	$3	$5	$12

2008-S, Martin Van Buren

Proof mintage: 3,083,940

Availability: Nearly all are gem Proofs approaching perfection.

Notes: 836,730 were sold by the U.S. Mint as part of four-coin Presidential dollar Proof sets.

	PF-65	PF-69DC	PF-70
2008-S, Van Buren, Proof	$10	$18	$140

2009, William Henry Harrison

Specifications: See pages 237 and 238 for details.

Designer: Joseph Menna (obverse); Don Everhart (reverse).

9th President (1841)

Life dates: February 9, 1773–April 4, 1841.

Political party: Whig.

Vice president: John Tyler, 1841.

First lady: Married Anna Tuthill Symmes on November 25, 1795. They had 10 children.

Especially remembered for: Harrison is remembered as the victor at the Battle of Tippecanoe against fractious Native Americans in 1811. He was the first president to die in office and had the shortest presidential term (one month). His nickname was "Old Tippecanoe," lending itself to the campaign slogan "Tippecanoe and Tyler too." Harrison caught pneumonia at his March 4 inauguration and died a month later.

Coins and money: Coins in circulation in 1841 included the copper half cent and cent, the silver half dime, dime, quarter dollar, half dollar, and dollar, and the gold $2.50, $5, and $10. Gold coins had returned to circulation after the Act of June 28, 1834, reduced their bullion content. In 1838 and later times branch mints at Dahlonega, Georgia; Charlotte, North Carolina; and New Orleans, Louisiana struck coins with D, C, and O mintmarks. Paper money was issued by many state-chartered banks primarily located in the East.

Notable sayings: "The prudent capitalist will never venture his capital . . . if there exists a state of uncertainty as to whether the government will repeal tomorrow what it has enacted today."

"A decent and manly examination of the acts of the government should be not only tolerated but encouraged."

2009-P, William Henry Harrison

Circulation-strike mintage: 43,260,000

Satin Finish mintage: 784,614

actual size: 26.5 mm

Collecting commentary, circulation strikes: Typical Mint State grades hover around MS-65, although so many were minted that higher-grade coins can be found.

Collecting commentary, Satin Finish: These are typically graded 65 to 68, but selected coins are higher. They are separately certified with an SP prefix by PCGS and with an SMS prefix by NGC.

Release of circulation strikes: On February 16 a special coin ceremony was held at Harrison's home, the Berkeley Plantation, near Charles City, Virginia. A group gathered, mostly of schoolchildren. By this time there was very little public interest in such events, some of which were held after the coins were in general release. With few exceptions, the numismatic media did not send representatives. The official public release of the Harrison coins was on February 19.

Notes: Nearly 100,000,000 circulation strikes were made—the lowest in the Presidential series to date—of which very few were circulated.

2009, Harrison, plain-edge error: Several thousands of these were inadvertently issued without edge lettering and thus lack the date and mintmark. These are not identifiable as to mint.

	MS-64	MS-65	MS-66
2009-P, W.H. Harrison	$1.50	$3	$6
2009-P, W.H. Harrison, Satin Finish	$3	$5	$12

2009-D, William Henry Harrison

Circulation-strike mintage: 55,160,000

Satin Finish mintage: 784,614

Collecting commentary, circulation strikes: Typical Mint State grades hover around MS-65, although so many were minted that higher-grade coins can be found.

Collecting commentary, Satin Finish: These are typically graded 65 to 68, but selected coins are higher. They are separately certified with an SP prefix by PCGS and with an SMS prefix by NGC.

	MS-64	MS-65	MS-66
2009-D, W.H. Harrison	$1.50	$3	$6
2009-D, W.H. Harrison, Satin Finish	$3	$5	$12

2009-S, William Henry Harrison

Proof mintage: 2,809,452

Availability: Nearly all are gem Proofs approaching perfection.

Notes: 629,585 were sold by the U.S. Mint as part of four-coin Presidential dollar Proof sets.

	PF-65	PF-69DC	PF-70
2009-S, W.H. Harrison, Proof	$8	$15	$60

2009, John Tyler

Specifications: See pages 237 and 238 for details.

Designer: Phebe Hemphill (obverse); Don Everhart (reverse).

10th President (1841–1845)

Life dates: March 29, 1790–January 18, 1862.

Political party: Whig.

Vice president: None.

First lady: Married Letitia Christian, on March 29, 1813; his second wife was Julia Gardiner, whom he married on June 26, 1844. They had 15 children.

Especially remembered for: Tyler is remembered for being the first vice president to be elevated to the office of president by the death of his predecessor—the "accidental president," as some opponents nicknamed him.

Coins and money: The Panic of 1837 wound down, and by the spring of 1845 the economy was on an upswing. Monetary and financial conditions were stable.

Notable sayings: "Popularity, I have always thought, may aptly be compared to a coquette—the more you woo her, the more apt she is to elude your embrace."

"Wealth can only be accumulated by the earnings of industry and the savings of frugality."

2009-P, John Tyler

Circulation-strike mintage: 43,540,000

Satin Finish mintage: 784,614

actual size: 26.5 mm

Collecting commentary, circulation strikes: Typical Mint State grades hover around MS-65, although so many were minted that higher-grade coins can be found.

Collecting commentary, Satin Finish: These are typically graded 65 to 68, but selected coins are higher. They are separately certified with an SP prefix by PCGS and with an SMS prefix by NGC.

Release of circulation strikes: On May 19 a dollar ceremony was held at Tyler's Sherwood Forest residence on the James River in Charles City County, Virginia. Deputy Director Andrew Brunhart represented the Mint. Youngsters

Tyler sketch by Phebe Hemphill.

under age 18 received coins for free, but no record has been found of a general exchange of other coins for face value to adults in attendance. The public release was two days later. Proofs of this and other issues had been made available earlier in the year.

2009, Tyler, plain-edge error: Over one thousand coins were inadvertently issued without edge lettering and thus lack the date and mintmark. These are not identifiable to a particular mint.

	MS-64	MS-65	MS-66
2009-P, Tyler	$1.50	$3	$6
2009-P, Tyler, Satin Finish	$3	$5	$12

2009-D, John Tyler

Circulation-strike mintage: 43,540,000

Satin Finish mintage: 784,614

Collecting commentary, circulation strikes: Typical Mint State grades hover around MS-65, although so many were minted that higher-grade coins can be found.

Collecting commentary, Satin Finish: These are typically graded 65 to 68, but selected coins are higher. They are separately certified with an SP prefix by PCGS and with an SMS prefix by NGC.

2009-D, Tyler, with 2010 edge date error: This error coin is exceedingly rare.

	MS-64	MS-65	MS-66
2009-D, Tyler	$1.50	$3	$6
2009-D, Tyler, Satin Finish	$3	$5	$12

2009-S, John Tyler

Proof mintage: 2,809,452

Availability: Nearly all are gem Proofs approaching perfection.

Notes: 629,585 were sold by the U.S. Mint as part of four-coin Presidential dollar Proof sets.

	PF-65	PF-69DC	PF-70
2009-S, Tyler, Proof	$8	$15	$36

2009, James K. Polk

Specifications: See pages 237 and 238 for details.

Designer: Susan Gamble (obverse); Don Everhart (reverse).

11th President (1845–1849)

Life dates: November 2, 1795–June 15, 1849.

Political party: Democratic.

Vice president: George M. Dallas, 1845 to 1849.

First lady: Married Sarah Childress on January 1, 1824. The union was a happy one, and Sarah worked closely with her husband, including as his secretary in the White House. The couple had no children.

Especially remembered for: Polk's dynamic administration included the expansion of the boundaries of the United States, reflecting imperialism and also adding acrimony to the long-standing differences between the North and the South concerning slavery in new states. During his tenure, the United States fought the War with Mexico, put in place new boundaries for the Oregon Territory, and saw the beginning of the California Gold Rush. Dancing and drinking were not allowed in the White House during Polk's administration in deference to Mrs. Polk's religious convictions.

On January 24, 1848, in California, in the tail race of a sawmill being built on the American River for ranch owner John Sutter, John Marshall glimpsed a golden flake. Thus was launched the Gold Rush, which soon defined the United States as extending from sea to shining sea. By a year later, in early 1849, the Gold Rush was in full force in California, and each tale of riches reaching the East seemed to be more fantastic than the one before it. The first Easterners to arrive in San Francisco docked in February aboard the SS *California*, pride of the Pacific Mail Steamship Company. In the meantime, tens of thousands of gold seekers were massing in Missouri, awaiting the chance to head westward as soon as spring conditions permitted travel.

Coins and money: In 1849 the influx of California gold on the world market caused the ratio to change in relation to silver, resulting in an increase in the price of the latter metal. Within a year it cost more than face value to mint silver coins.

Notable saying: "I am heartily rejoiced that my term is so near its close. I will soon cease to be a servant and will become a sovereign."

2009-P, James K. Polk

Circulation-strike mintage: 46,620,000

Satin Finish mintage: 784,614

actual size: 26.5 mm

Collecting commentary, circulation strikes: Typical Mint State grades hover around MS-65, although so many were minted that higher-grade coins can be found.

Collecting commentary, Satin Finish: These are typically graded 65 to 68, but selected coins are higher. They are separately certified with an SP prefix by PCGS and with an SMS prefix by NGC.

Release of circulation strikes: On August 20 a ceremonial release took place in Columbia, Tennessee, about 50 miles southwest of Nashville, at the location of the president's home. Deputy Director Andrew Brunhart represented the Mint. Youngsters were given coins for free, and adults could buy them for face value. By this time stockpiles of Presidential dollars were very large, and the Treasury was delighted when the public bought them.

2009, Polk, plain-edge error: Over one thousand coins were inadvertently issued without edge lettering and thus lack the date and mintmark. These are not identifiable to a particular mint.

	MS-64	MS-65	MS-66
2009-P, Polk	$1.50	$3	$6
2009-P, Polk, Satin Finish	$3	$5	$12

2009-D, James K. Polk

Circulation-strike mintage: 41,720,000

Satin Finish mintage: 784,614

Collecting commentary, circulation strikes: Typical Mint State grades hover around MS-65, although so many were minted that higher-grade coins can be found.

Collecting commentary, Satin Finish: These are typically graded 65 to 68, but selected coins are higher. They are separately certified with an SP prefix by PCGS and with an SMS prefix by NGC.

	MS-64	MS-65	MS-66
2009-D, Polk	$1.50	$3	$6
2009-D, Polk, Satin Finish	$3	$5	$12

2009-S, James K. Polk

Proof mintage: 2,809,452

Availability: Nearly all are gem Proofs approaching perfection.

Notes: 629,585 were sold by the U.S. Mint as part of four-coin Presidential dollar Proof sets.

	PF-65	PF-69DC	PF-70
2009-S, Polk, Proof	$8	$15	$65

2009, Zachary Taylor

Specifications: See pages 237 and 238 for details.

Designer: Don Everhart (obverse); Don Everhart (reverse).

12th President (1849–1850)

Life dates: November 24, 1784–July 9, 1850.

Political party: Whig.

Vice president: Millard Fillmore, 1849 and 1850.

First lady: Married Margaret Mackall Smith on June 21, 1810. In the White House Margaret was ill much of the time and did not attend most functions. The couple had six children.

Especially remembered for: As the hero of the War with Mexico he was admired by both the North and the South, while Southerners appreciated him as an owner of slaves. His brief presidency did not accomplish much in the way of national progress. His nickname was "Old Rough and Ready."

The California Gold Rush expanded, and as Taylor was spending his first months in the White House, tens of thousands of adventurers were heading to the land of seemingly unlimited opportunities. Most went overland by wagon, starting from Missouri or another jumping-off spot and continued west to lands now a part of Wyoming, Utah, and Nevada, then over the Sierra Nevada Mountains into California. Others came by sea, taking a steamship to Panama, crossing about 50 miles of rivers and jungle, and then taking passage on another steamer on the Pacific side, and from there north to San Francisco. This was the fastest way, but still took a few weeks. Still others sailed around the Cape Horn at the tip of South America, then north in the Pacific to California. San Francisco was the focal point of commerce, but towns and gold camps were scattered over a wide area. Other gold seekers arrived from Europe, Australia, Eastern Asia, and other places.

Coins and money: It cost more in silver bullion to mint coins from half dimes to dollars than their face value. Accordingly, such coins were delivered to depositors of silver who valued them for their metallic content. Vast quantities of silver coins were taken from circulation by hoarders and speculators. In 1849 gold dollars were introduced as a new denomination. These were minted continuously through 1889. In 1850 the first $20 gold double eagles were minted. The denomination proved to be very popular, and by the time they were last minted in 1933 over 75 percent of the gold converted into coins was made into double eagles.

Notable saying: "For more than half a century during which kingdoms and empires have fallen, the Union has stood unshaken. The patriots who formed it have long since descended to the grave; yet it still remains the proudest monument to their memory."

2009-P, Zachary Taylor

Circulation-strike mintage: 41,580,000

Satin Finish mintage: 784,614

Collecting commentary, circulation strikes: Typical Mint State grades hover around

actual size: 26.5 mm

MS-65, although so many were minted that higher-grade coins can be found.

Collecting commentary, Satin Finish: These are typically graded 65 to 68, but selected coins are higher. They are separately certified with an SP prefix by PCGS and with an SMS prefix by NGC.

Release of circulation strikes: Dollar coins went into general release on November 19, 2009. The official launch ceremony was held five days later on Taylor's birthday anniversary, November 24, 2009, in Taylor Park in the president's home town. Deputy Director Andrew Brunhart, a regular at these events, represented the Mint. The 392nd Army Band played music written in the 19th century to commemorate the president's military victories in the War with Mexico.

Notes: On January 22, 2009, the Commission of Fine Arts reviewed 22 obverse designs submitted for the four Presidential dollars of 2010. Secretary Thomas Luebke stated that "commission members would like, as a whole, to see better interpretations of the subjects by those preparing the designs rather than designs that are obviously lifted and scanned from known material."[15]

Defying logic (except for the tremendous seigniorage profit the Mint made on such coins), over 300 million Presidential dollars were struck in 2010. In yet another hope to force the coins into circulation, in August the Mint teamed with the Army and Air Force Exchange Service to use the coins on a test basis at stores at Fort Sam Houston, Texas; Fort Huachuca, Arizona; and Fort Carson, Peterson Air Force Base, and the Air Force Academy in Colorado, beginning on July 4. If the program proved to be successful it would be expanded to include all 1,703 such stores in the United States.

2009, Taylor, plain-edge error: Several thousand coins were inadvertently issued without edge lettering and thus lack the date and mintmark. These are not identifiable to a particular mint.

	MS-64	MS-65	MS-66
2009-P, Taylor	$1.50	$3	$6
2009-P, Taylor, Satin Finish	$3	$5	$12

2009-D, Zachary Taylor

Circulation-strike mintage: 36,680,000

Satin Finish mintage: 784,614

Collecting commentary, circulation strikes: Typical Mint State grades hover around MS-65, although so many were minted that higher-grade coins can be found.

Collecting commentary, Satin Finish: These are typically graded 65 to 68, but selected coins are higher. They are separately certified with an SP prefix by PCGS and with an SMS prefix by NGC.

2009-D, Taylor, with 2010 edge date error: In early 2010 a Zachary Taylor dollar was found by Gary D. Laird in a roll of 2010-D Native American dollars, with the 2010 date on the edge, and was certified by NGC. The Mint announced that 700,000 coins already shipped to the Federal Reserve would be recalled so the edges could be checked. A "hold" was placed on coins in the position of Coin Wrap, Inc., the Pennsylvania contractor who made shipments to various buyers.[16]

	MS-64	MS-65	MS-66
2009-D, Taylor	$1.50	$3	$6
2009-D, Taylor, Satin Finish	$3	$5	$12

2009-S, Zachary Taylor

Proof mintage: 2,809,452

Availability: Nearly all are gem Proofs approaching perfection.

Notes: 629,585 were sold by the U.S. Mint as part of four-coin Presidential dollar Proof sets.

	PF-65	PF-69DC	PF-70
2009-S, Taylor, Proof	$8	$15	$35

2010, Millard Fillmore

Specifications: See pages 237 and 238 for details.

Designer: Don Everhart (obverse); Don Everhart (reverse).

13th President (1850–1853)

Life dates: January 7, 1800–March 8, 1874.

Political party: Whig.

Vice president: None.

First lady: Married Abigail Powers on February 5, 1826. The union was blissful. The couple had two children. His second wife was Caroline Carmichael McIntosh, a wealthy widow whom he married on February 10, 1858.

Especially remembered for: Fillmore is remembered for the debates over the Compromise of 1850, which he favored, and for signing the unfortunate Fugitive Slave Act. The slavery question dominated Fillmore's administration, as it would his successors'. He was faithful to his duties and trust, but was undistinguished in the annals of the presidency. A good economy was fueled by the Gold Rush during his presidency.

In California, the Gold Rush continued, but by 1851 most of the easily accessible streamside deposits had been played out, and gold extraction was increasingly the province of large corporations.

Coins and money: In 1851 the silver three-cent piece or trime was introduced. Containing just 75% silver instead of the standard 90%, these coins cost less than face value to produce and helped alleviate the lack of federal silver in circulation. In1852, $45,506,177 worth of gold was sent by steamer from San Francisco. Of this amount, $39,007,367 was destined for New York City; $470,783 for New Orleans; $6,020,027 for London; $46,000 for Panama; and $15,000 for San Juan.

On February 21, 1853, the Coinage Act reduced the silver content of coins from the three-cent piece to the half dollar (but not the dollar). After this time they were once again seen with frequency in general circulation. In the meantime Spanish-American silver coins, legal tender at the time, served the needs of commerce. After this time the Liberty Seated silver dollar was a bullion issue that cost more than face value to coin and was valued at its metallic content. Nearly all were exported and melted.[17]

Notable saying: "An honorable defeat is better than a dishonorable victory."

"The man who can look upon a crisis without being willing to offer himself upon the altar of his country is not for public trust."

2010-P, Millard Fillmore

Circulation-strike mintage: 37,520,000

Satin Finish mintage: 583,897

actual size: 26.5 mm

Collecting commentary, circulation strikes: Typical Mint State grades hover around MS-65, although so many were minted that higher-grade coins can be found.

Collecting commentary, Satin Finish: These are typically graded 65 to 68, but selected coins are higher. They are separately certified with an SP prefix by PCGS and with an SMS prefix by NGC.

Release of circulation strikes: On February 18 two coin ceremonies were held—one at the Moravia Central School in Moravia, New York, the closest town to the president's birthplace, and the other in Buffalo, the city where he gained prominence as a politician. At the Moravia event Deputy Director Andrew Brunhart represented the Mint and made opening remarks. The Cayuga-Owasco Lakes Region Historical Society welcomed attendees. Youngsters received free coins.

2010, Fillmore, plain-edge error: Several thousand coins were inadvertently issued without edge lettering and thus lack the date and mintmark. These are not identifiable to a particular mint.

	MS-64	MS-65	MS-66
2010-P, Fillmore	$1.50	$3	$6
2010-P, Fillmore, Satin Finish	$3	$5	$12

2010-D, Millard Fillmore

Circulation-strike mintage: 36,960,000

Satin Finish mintage: 583,897

Collecting commentary, circulation strikes: Typical Mint State grades hover around MS-65, although so many were minted that higher-grade coins can be found.

Collecting commentary, Satin Finish: These are typically graded 65 to 68, but selected coins are higher. They are separately certified with an SP prefix by PCGS and with an SMS prefix by NGC.

	MS-64	MS-65	MS-66
2010-D, Fillmore	$1.50	$3	$6
2010-D, Fillmore, Satin Finish	$3	$5	$12

2010-S, Millard Fillmore

Proof mintage: 2,224,827

Availability: Nearly all are gem Proofs approaching perfection.

Notes: 535,397 were sold by the U.S. Mint as part of four-coin Presidential dollar Proof sets.

	PF-65	PF-69DC	PF-70
2010-S, Fillmore, Proof	$8	$15	$40

2010, Franklin Pierce

Specifications: See pages 237 and 238 for details.

Designer: Susan Gamble (obverse); Don Everhart (reverse).

14th President (1853–1857)

Life dates: November 23, 1804–October 8, 1869.

Political party: Democratic.

Vice president: William King, 1853; none, 1853 to 1857.

First lady: Married Jane Means Appleton on November 10, 1834. The couple had three children.

Especially remembered for: Pierce is remembered for being undistinguished as a leader and a minor presidential figure, as were his two predecessors. The prosperity of the Gold Rush continued throughout his term.

Coins and money: The economy was generally robust during the Pierce administration. "Free banking" laws made it easier for entrepreneurs to gain state charters for banks, and many were opened. In March 1854 the San Francisco Mint commenced operations in a remodeled and slightly expanded building earlier used by Moffat & Co., assayers and private minters of gold coins.

Notable sayings: "We have nothing in our history or position to invite aggression; have everything to beckon us to the cultivation of relations of peace and amity with all relations."

"The revenue of the country, levied almost insensibly to the tax payer, goes on from year to year, increasing beyond either the interest or prospective wants of the government."

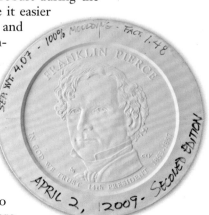

Pierce obverse plaster.

2010-P, Franklin Pierce

Circulation-strike mintage: 38,220,000

Satin Finish mintage: 583,897

actual size: 26.5 mm

Collecting commentary, circulation strikes: Typical Mint State grades hover around MS-65, although so many were minted that higher-grade coins can be found.

Collecting commentary, Satin Finish: These are typically graded 65 to 68, but selected coins are higher. They are separately certified with an SP prefix by PCGS and with an SMS prefix by NGC.

Release of circulation strikes: The launch ceremony was held at the Pierce mansion. Deputy Director Andrew Brunhart represented the Mint. Attendees 18 years old and younger received free coins. Peter Wallner, a Pierce historian and librarian of the New Hampshire Historical Society, was on hand as well. The public could buy coins at face value, including in $25 bank-wrapped rolls.

2010, Pierce, plain-edge error: Over one thousand coins were inadvertently issued without edge lettering and thus lack the date and mintmark. These are not identifiable to a particular mint.

	MS-64	MS-65	MS-66
2010-P, Pierce	$1.50	$3	$6
2010-P, Pierce, Satin Finish	$3	$5	$12

2010-D, Franklin Pierce

Circulation strike mintage: 38,360,000

Satin Finish mintage: 583,897

Collecting commentary, circulation strikes: Typical Mint State grades hover around MS-65, although so many were minted that higher-grade coins can be found.

Collecting commentary, Satin Finish: These are typically graded 65 to 68, but selected coins are higher. They are separately certified with an SP prefix by PCGS and with an SMS prefix by NGC.

	MS-64	MS-65	MS-66
2010-D, Pierce	$1.50	$3	$6
2010-D, Pierce, Satin Finish	$3	$5	$12

2010-S, Franklin Pierce

Proof mintage: 2,224,827

Availability: Nearly all are gem Proofs approaching perfection.

Notes: 535,397 were sold by the U.S. Mint as part of four-coin Presidential dollar Proof sets.

	PF-65	PF-69DC	PF-70
2010-S, Pierce, Proof	$8	$15	$35

2010, James Buchanan

Specifications: See pages 237 and 238 for details.

Designer: Phebe Hemphill (obverse); Don Everhart (reverse).

15th President (1857–1861)

Life dates: April 23, 1791–June 1, 1868.

Political party: Democratic.

Vice president: John C. Breckinridge, 1857 to 1861.

Marital status: The only president never to marry; he had been engaged earlier at age 28, but his fiancée committed suicide. A niece, Harriet Lane (1830–1904), orphaned at age 11 and his ward since that time, served as hostess at the White House.

Especially remembered for: Buchanan famously tried to appease both the North and the South and wound up pleasing neither. He was known as "Old Buck" because he pronounced his name similar to *buck-cannon*; indeed both items were shown on an 1856 campaign medal. He is considered by some historians to have been the worst American president, or tied with Warren Harding for that dubious distinction.

Coins and money: In 1857, the sidewheel steamer SS *Central America* was in service from New York City to the eastern side of the Isthmus of Panama. On September 9, while returning to New York on its 44th trip, the vessel ran into high seas whipped up by a hurricane. Shortly after eight in the evening on September 12, the *Central America* slipped below the waves and was no more. Over 300 men were drowned. Aboard was a vast store of gold being shipped to the East. The failure of the precious metal to arrive was a slight contributing factor to the economic difficulties that began in October and led to the Panic of 1857 when thousands of businesses failed.

In March 1858 teenaged Augustus B. Sage and his friends formed the American Numismatic Society, which would be active through 1859 and then expire. In the Kansas Territory the town of Denver was established, named after territorial governor James W. Denver. Placer gold was discovered at Cherry Creek, near Denver, setting off a gold rush which would see the flourishing of such mountain towns as Central City and Black Hawk. "Pikes Peak or Bust" became a popular slogan for Easterners who headed west in the hope of finding easy riches.

Notable saying: "There is nothing stable but heaven and the Constitution."

2010-P, James Buchanan

Circulation-strike mintage: 36,820,000

Satin Finish mintage: 583,897

actual size: 26.5 mm

Collecting commentary, circulation strikes: Typical Mint State grades hover around MS-65, although so many were minted that higher-grade coins can be found.

Collecting commentary, Satin Finish: These are typically graded 65 to 68, but selected coins are higher. They are separately certified with an SP prefix by PCGS and with an SMS prefix by NGC.

Release of circulation strikes: On August 19 a coin launch ceremony was held at Buchanan's Wheatland home in Lancaster, Pennsylvania. The event was announced then canceled when funding could not be found, as the Mint left it to local sources to finance these. An anonymous donor stepped up, and the Buchanan launch ceremony took place. Deputy Director Andrew Brunhart once again represented the Mint. Free coins were given to attendees 18 years old and younger. The public could buy them for face value.

Buchanan sketch by Phebe Hemphill completed on November 21, 2008.

2010, Buchanan, plain-edge error: Several thousand coins were inadvertently issued without edge lettering and thus lack the date and mintmark. These are not identifiable to a particular mint.

	MS-64	MS-65	MS-66
2010-P, Buchanan	$1.50	$3	$6
2010-P, Buchanan Satin Finish	$3	$5	$12

2010-D, James Buchanan

Circulation-strike mintage: 36,540,000

Satin Finish mintage: 583,897

Collecting commentary, circulation strikes: Typical Mint State grades hover around MS-65, although so many were minted that higher-grade coins can be found.

Collecting commentary, Satin Finish: These are typically graded 65 to 68, but selected coins are higher. They are separately certified with an SP prefix by PCGS and with an SMS prefix by NGC.

	MS-64	MS-65	MS-66
2010-D, Buchanan	$1.50	$3	$6
2010-D, Buchanan, Satin Finish	$3	$5	$12

2010-S, James Buchanan

Proof mintage: 2,224,827

Availability: Nearly all are gem Proofs approaching perfection.

Notes: 535,397 were sold by the U.S. Mint as part of four-coin Presidential dollar Proof sets.

	PF-65	PF-69DC	PF-70
2010-S, Buchanan, Proof	$8	$15	$35

2010, Abraham Lincoln

Specifications: See pages 237 and 238 for details.

Designer: Don Everhart (obverse); Don Everhart (reverse).

16th President (1861–1865)

Life dates: February 12, 1809–April 15, 1865.

Political party: Republican.

Vice presidents: Hannibal Hamlin, 1861 to 1865; Andrew Johnson, 1865.

First lady: Married Mary Todd on November 4, 1842. The couple had four sons (only one of whom lived to maturity).

Especially remembered for: Lincoln is remembered for his "log cabin" childhood and his leadership during the Civil War. During his tenure as president he passed the Emancipation Proclamation. Due to the Civil War, Lincoln was viewed as a hero by the North and as a scoundrel by the South. He was famously assassinated by John Wilkes Booth in Ford's Theater. His nicknames included "Honest Abe," "the Illinois railsplitter," and "the Great Emancipator." He is one of four presidents honored on Mount Rushmore.

Coins and money: The Civil War, which began in April 1861 and ended in April 1865, resulted in monetary chaos. After war was declared, President Lincoln called for three-month enlistments, for it was felt that the industrial Yankees in the North would soon subdue the rebellious Confederate States of America, which had been formed in January 1861. This was not what happened. The first major conflict, the Battle of Bull Run, did not begin until July 22, 1861. What was anticipated as an easy win for Union forces turned out to be an overwhelming victory for the Confederates.

By late December 1861 the outcome of the war remained uncertain and the Union Treasury was low on funds. Concerned citizens began hoarding gold coins, with the result that in January 1862 banks charged a premium for them. Matters went from bad to worse when Legal Tender Notes were issued in March. These were not redeemable at face value in gold or silver coins and could be exchanged at par only for other Legal Tender bills. During the spring, all silver coins disappeared from circulation in the East and Midwest, and in the second week of July all one-cent pieces were hoarded as well. There were no federal coins in circulation! An exception was in the West, where paper money did not circulate, and gold and silver remained in commerce. Anyone bringing Legal Tender Notes to that area could sell them only at a deep discount, conversely equal to the premium that silver and gold coins enjoyed in the East and Midwest.

On July 1862 ordinary postage stamps were made legal tender. Also helping to fill the void caused by the disappearance of coins were millions of copper (mostly) cent-sized tokens, an issue of Postage Currency (later succeeded by Fractional Currency), encased postage stamps, scrip notes, and more. Over 30 merchants advertised on the backs of brass encasements fronted by mica that revealed a postage stamp within. In 1863 National Banks were permitted to issue currency. These were exchangeable at par for other notes of National Banks and for Legal Tender Notes. Silver and gold coins were only available by paying a steep premium to banks and exchange brokers.

In 1864 the American Numismatic and Archaeological Society was formed in New York City, picking up the traces of the defunct American Numismatic Society.

Notable sayings: "You can fool some of the people all the time and all the people some of the time but you can't fool all the people all the time."

"If slavery is not wrong, nothing is wrong."

"Do I not destroy my enemies when I make them my friends?"

"Be sure to put your feet in the right place, then stand firm."

"No man has a good enough memory to be a successful liar."

"We can complain that rose bushes have thorns, or can rejoice that thorn bushes have roses."

"Better to remain silent and be thought a fool than to speak out and remove all doubt."

"Most folks are about as happy as they make up their minds to be."

"How many legs does a dog have if you call the tail a leg? Four. Calling a tail a leg doesn't make it a leg."

2010-P, Abraham Lincoln

Circulation-strike mintage: 49,000,000

Satin Finish mintage: 583,897

actual size: 26.5 mm

Collecting commentary, circulation strikes: Typical Mint State grades hover around MS-65, although so many were minted that higher-grade coins can be found.

Collecting commentary, Satin Finish: These are typically graded 65 to 68, but selected coins are higher. They are separately certified with an SP prefix by PCGS and with an SMS prefix by NGC.

Release of circulation strikes: The Lincoln dollars were released by the Federal Reserve on November 18, 2010. On the next day, November 19, the 147th anniversary of the Gettysburg Address, Mint Director Edmund C. Moy was the keynote speaker at a dollar ceremony held at Lincoln's Cottage on the grounds of the Armed Forces Retirement Home in Washington, D.C. Attendees 18 years old and younger received free coins, and the public could buy them at face value.

Notes: Larger quantities were made of Lincoln dollars at the Philadelphia and Denver Mints than were made of any other Presidential dollars that year. This was not necessary, as most coins were relegated to Treasury vaults.

	MS-64	MS-65	MS-66
2010-P, Lincoln	$1.50	$3	$6
2010-P, Lincoln, Satin Finish	$3	$5	$12

2010-D, Abraham Lincoln

Circulation-strike mintage: 48,020,000

Satin Finish mintage: 583,897

Collecting commentary, circulation strikes: Typical Mint State grades hover around MS-65, although so many were minted that higher-grade coins can be found.

Collecting commentary, Satin Finish: These are typically graded 65 to 68, but selected coins are higher. They are separately certified with an SP prefix by PCGS and with an SMS prefix by NGC.

	MS-64	MS-65	MS-66
2010-D, Lincoln	$1.50	$3	$6
2010-D, Lincoln, Satin Finish	$3	$5	$12

2010-S, Abraham Lincoln

Proof mintage: 2,224,827

Availability: Nearly all are gem Proofs approaching perfection.

Notes: 535,397 were sold by the U.S. Mint as part of four-coin Presidential dollar Proof sets.

	PF-65	PF-69DC	PF-70
2010-S, Lincoln, Proof	$8	$15	$185

2011, Andrew Johnson

Specifications: See pages 237 and 238 for details.

Designer: Don Everhart (obverse); Don Everhart (reverse).

17th President (1865–1869)

Life dates: December 29, 1808–July 31, 1875.

Political party: Democratic.

Vice president: None.

First lady: Married Eliza McCardle on May 5, 1827. The couple had five children.

Especially remembered for: Johnson is most famous for his impeachment and acquittal. He also put forth much effort to reconstruct the South after the Civil War. During his presidency the purchase of Alaska from Russia was finalized.

Coins and money: It was hoped that once the Civil War ended in April 1865 that silver and gold coins would again circulate in commerce. This did not happen, as citizens remained distrustful of the solidity of the Treasury Department.

Nickel three-cent pieces were introduced in 1865 and nickel five-cent pieces in 1866. Fractional Currency notes continued to be made and were widely circulated. Civil War tokens remained in circulation, but as the years passed fewer and fewer were seen. In 1866 the American Numismatic and Archaeological Society began issuing the *American Journal of Numismatics*, which remained the hobby's journal of record into the early 1900s.

Notable sayings: "If the rabble were lopped at one end and the aristocrats at the other, all would be well with the country."

"The goal to strive for is a poor government but a rich people."

2011-P, Andrew Johnson

Circulation strike-mintage: 35,560,000

Collecting commentary: Typical grades range from MS–64 to 66, but among the large number produced there are many higher-grade gems.

actual size: 26.5 mm

Release of circulation strikes: On February 17 there was an official unveiling of the coin at the Andrew Johnson National Historic Site in Greeneville, Tennessee. Attendees 18 years old and younger received free coins. Adults could buy them at face value, including, as usual, in $25 bank-wrapped rolls. The official release of the coins by the Federal Reserve was on the same day.

Johnson sketch by Don Everhart.

	MS-64	MS-65	MS-66
2011-P, A. Johnson	$1.50	$3	$6

2011-D, Andrew Johnson

Circulation-strike mintage: 37,100,000

Collecting commentary: Typical grades range from MS–64 to 66, but among the large number produced there are many higher-grade gems.

	MS-64	MS-65	MS-66
2011-D, A. Johnson	$1.50	$3	$6

2011-S, Andrew Johnson

Proof mintage: 1,972,863

Availability: Nearly all are gem Proofs approaching perfection.

Notes: 299,853 were sold by the U.S. Mint as part of four-coin Presidential dollar Proof sets. This marked a new low in sales.

	PF-65	PF-69DC	PF-70
2011-S, A. Johnson, Proof	$8	$15	$50

2011, Ulysses S. Grant

Specifications: See pages 237 and 238 for details.

Designer: Don Everhart (obverse); Don Everhart (reverse).

18th President (1869–1877)

Life dates: April 27, 1822–July 23, 1885.

Political party: Republican.

Vice presidents: Schuyler Colfax, 1869 to 1873; Henry Wilson, 1873 to 1875; none, 1875 to 1877.

First lady: Married Julia Boggs Dent on August 22, 1848. The couple had four children.

Especially remembered for: Grant is remembered for being a great general during his military service in the Civil War, but a below-average president. As president he allowed himself to be used by others. A depiction of his face is on several types of paper money (most famously the $50 bill) and on commemorative coins.

Coins and money: The Carson City Mint opened for business in 1870 and would continue to produce coins through 1873 with the addition of 1886 to 1888. The Coinage Act of February 12, 1873, discontinued the two-cent piece, the silver three-cent piece, and the standard (Liberty Seated) dollar. The trade dollar was introduced. In 1875 the

20-cent piece made its debut. It was easily confused with the quarter, and none were made for circulation after 1876. After April 20, 1876, Legal Tender Notes and National Bank bills circulated at par with silver coins. Long-hidden stores of hoarded silver were dumped on the market, resulting in a glut of such pieces.

Notable sayings: "I have never advocated war as a means of peace."
"My failures have been errs of judgment, not of intent."
"In every battle there comes a time when both sides consider themselves beaten. Then he who continues the attack wins."

2011-P, Ulysses S. Grant

Circulation-strike mintage: 38,080,000

actual size: 26.5 mm

Collecting commentary: Typical grades range from MS–64 to 66, but among the large number produced there are many higher-grade gems.

Release of circulation strikes: On May 19 a ceremony for the coin was held at the Ulysses S. Grant National Historic Site in St. Louis. The day marked the 148th anniversary of Grant's long and eventually successful campaign against Vicksburg overlooking and blockading the Mississippi River. Deputy Director Al Runnels represented the Mint. Distribution to youngsters and the public was as usual. The Federal Reserve released quantities of circulation strikes the same day.

Grant sketch by Don Everhart.

	MS-64	MS-65	MS-66
2011-P, Grant	$1.50	$3	$6

2011-D, Ulysses S. Grant

Circulation-strike mintage: 37,940,000

Collecting commentary: Typical grades range from MS–64 to 66, but among the large number produced there are many higher-grade gems.

	MS-64	MS-65	MS-66
2011-D, Grant	$1.50	$3	$6

2011-S, Ulysses S. Grant

Proof mintage: 1,972,863

Availability: Nearly all are gem Proofs approaching perfection.

Notes: 299,853 were sold by the U.S. Mint as part of four-coin Presidential dollar Proof sets.

	PF-65	PF-69DC	PF-70
2011-S, Grant, Proof	$8	$15	$55

2011, Rutherford B. Hayes

Specifications: See pages 237 and 238 for details.

Designer: Don Everhart (obverse); Don Everhart (reverse).

19th President (1877–1881)

Life dates: October 4, 1822–January 17, 1893.

Political party: Republican.

Vice president: William Wheeler, 1877 to 1881.

First lady: Married Lucy Ware Webb on December 30, 1852. The couple had eight children. In the White House the first lady was known as "Lemonade Lucy," as she forbid the serving of alcohol.

Especially remembered for: The results from Hayes's election were the most contested, controversial election results up to that time in history. He is remembered for his integrity and temperance, seemingly in contrast to the previous administration. His presidency was marked by a lack of cooperation between the Northern and Southern factions.

Coins and money: Gold coins, which had only been available by paying a sharp premium up to that point, reached parity with paper currency on December 17, 1878. The Treasury anticipated there would be a rush to convert paper to gold, but this did not happen, as citizens realized that bills were of solid value and could be exchanged for gold at any time.

In 1878 the trade dollar, highly successful as a bullion coin in the export trade with China, was discontinued by the Bland-Allison Act of February 28, which introduced the new Standard Silver dollar with a new design by George T. Morgan.

Notable sayings: "Amazing invention, who would ever want to use one of them?"

"Nothing brings out the lower traits of human nature like office seeking."

"It is now true that this is God's country if equal rights—a fair start and an equal chance at the race of life—are everywhere secured to all."

"Conscience is the authentic voice of God to you."

2011-P, Rutherford B. Hayes

Circulation-strike mintage: 37,660,000

actual size: 26.5 mm

Collecting commentary: Typical grades range from MS–64 to 66, but among the large number produced there are many higher-grade gems.

Release of circulation strikes: On August 18 a coin launch ceremony was held at the Rutherford B. Hayes Presidential Center in Spiegel Grove, the Fremont, Ohio, residence of the president. Opened to the public in May 1916, this was the first of many presidential centers in America. Free coins were given to younger attendees, and adults could buy them for face value. The Federal Reserve released quantities the same day.

Hayes sketch
by Don Everhart.

	MS-64	MS-65	MS-66
2011-P, Hayes	$1.50	$3	$6

2011-D, Rutherford B. Hayes

Circulation-strike mintage: 36,820,000

Collecting commentary: Typical grades range from MS-64 to 66, but among the large number produced there are many higher-grade gems.

	MS-64	MS-65	MS-66
2011-D, Hayes	$1.50	$3	$6

2011-S, Rutherford B. Hayes

Proof mintage: 1,972,863

Availability: Nearly all are gem Proofs approaching perfection.

Notes: 299,853 were sold by the U.S. Mint as part of four-coin Presidential dollar Proof sets.

	PF-65	PF-69DC	PF-70
2011-S, Hayes, Proof	$8	$15	$35

2011, James A. Garfield

Specifications: See pages 237 and 238 for details.

Designer: Phebe Hemphill (obverse); Don Everhart (reverse).

20th President (1881)

Life dates: November 19, 1831–September 19, 1881.

Political party: Republican.

Vice president: Chester Alan Arthur, 1881.

First lady: Married Lucretia Rudolph on November 11, 1858. She was well read in classics, designed the family's mansion, and was a devout adherent to the Disciples of Christ. The couple had seven children.

Especially remembered for: Garfields's brief presidency was terminated by his assassination. The assassin, Charles J. Guiteau, shot Garfield twice—one bullet grazing his arm and the other shattering a rib and lodging itself in his abdomen. It is widely believed that Garfield would have recovered from his wounds if modern medicine had existed by that point. He died two months later from a massive infection brought on from his doctors not having sterilized their hands before probing his abdomen for the stray bullet. He was widely mourned, and his portrait soon appeared on paper money.

Coins and money: Denominations in use included the Indian Head cent, bronze two-cent piece, nickel three-cent piece, Shield nickel five-cent piece, Liberty Seated dime, Liberty Seated quarter, Liberty Seated half dollar, Morgan silver dollar, and gold $1, $2.50, $3, $5, $10, and $20 coins. The Philadelphia, Carson City, New Orleans, and San Francisco mints were in operation.

Notable sayings: "I have many troubles in my life, but the worst of them never came."

"Whoever controls the volume of money in any country is absolute master of all industrial commerce."

"A brave man is a man who dares to look the devil in the face and tell him he is a devil."

2011-P, James A. Garfield

Circulation-strike mintage: 37,100,000

Collecting commentary: Typical grades range from MS–64 to 66, but among the large number produced there are many higher-grade gems.

actual size: 26.5 mm

Release of circulation strikes: The launch ceremony was held on November 17 at Garfield's home, Lawnfield, in Mentor, Ohio, at the James A. Garfield National Historic Site. Visitors 18 years old and younger received a free coin. The public could buy up to two $25 rolls for face value.

Buchanan sketch by Phebe Hemphill completed on October 29, 2009.

	MS-64	MS-65	MS-66
2011-P, Garfield	$1.50	$3	$6

2011-D, James A. Garfield

Circulation-strike mintage: 37,100,000

Collecting commentary: Typical grades range from MS–64 to 66, but among the large number produced there are many higher-grade gems.

	MS-64	MS-65	MS-66
2011-D, Garfield	$2	$3	$6

2011-S, James A. Garfield

Proof mintage: 1,972,863

Availability: Nearly all are gem Proofs approaching perfection.

Notes: 299,853 were sold by the U.S. Mint as part of four-coin Presidential dollar Proof sets.

	PF-65	PF-69DC	PF-70
2011-S, Garfield, Proof	$8	$15	$45

2012, Chester A. Arthur

Specifications: See pages 237 and 238 for details.

Designer: Don Everhart (obverse); Don Everhart (reverse).

21st President (1881–1885)

Life dates: October 5, 1829–November 18, 1886.

Political party: Republican.

Vice president: None.

First lady: Married Ellen Lewis Herndon (only child of Captain William Lewis Herndon, U.S. Navy, who had gone down with the SS *Central America* on September 12, 1857) on October 25, 1859. She died of pneumonia on January 12, 1880. The couple had three children. At the White House his sister Mary (Mrs. John E. McElroy) served as hostess and helped care for his daughter Ellen.

Especially remembered for: The first significant federal immigration law was enacted during Arthur's administration. His well-known dislike of the furnishings of the White House made him memorable as a president—he did not move in until it was redecorated in the Victorian style with everything new! (The old furniture was sold at auction.) Arthur is remembered for having changed his reputation from one of distrust when he became president to respect when he left office.

Coins and money: Coins in circulation consisted of the Indian Head cent, the nickel five-cent piece, the Liberty Seated dime, quarter, and half dollar, the Morgan dollar, and Liberty Head gold coins of the $1, $2.50, $3, $5, $10, and $20 denominations.

In January 1883 the Liberty Head nickel design was introduced, replacing the Shield motif. The denomination was expressed simply as V. Sharpers gold-plated the coins and passed them off as $5 gold pieces. The design was changed by adding the word CENTS. Rumors spread that the coins without CENTS would be recalled and would become very valuable—as such they were hoarded by the millions. This catalyzed a great nationwide interest in coins from rare to common, engendering a market boom that lasted until the waning years of the decade.

Notable sayings: "Good ballplayers will make good citizens."
"If it were not for the reporters I would tell you the truth."

2012-P, Chester A. Arthur

Circulation-strike mintage: 6,020,000

Collecting commentary: MS–64 to 66 coins are common, but at MS-68 and higher they are elusive.

actual size: 26.5 mm

Release of circulation strikes: In 2012 the Mint stopped conducting release ceremonies as a cost-cutting measure, although in relation to the quantities of Presidential dollars made the ceremonies had cost very little.

Notes: Circulation strikes went on sale to the general public on April 5. This began the era of lower-mintage circulation strikes.

2012, Arthur, plain-edge error: A few coins were inadvertently issued without edge lettering and thus lack the date and mintmark. These are not identifiable to a particular mint and are great rarities today.

Arthur sketch
by Don Everhart.

	MS-64	MS-65	MS-66
2012-P, Arthur	$2	$3	$6

2012-D, Chester A. Arthur

Circulation-strike mintage: 4,060,000

Collecting commentary: MS–64 to 66 coins are common, but at MS-68 and higher they are elusive.

	MS-64	MS-65	MS-66
2012-D, Arthur	$2	$3	$6

2012-S, Chester A. Arthur

Proof mintage: 1,438,743

Availability: Nearly all are gem Proofs approaching perfection.

Notes: 249,265 were sold by the U.S. Mint as part of four-coin Presidential dollar Proof sets. This was another record low for set sales.

	PF-65	PF-69DC	PF-70
2012-S, Arthur, Proof, Proof	$9	$16	$40

2012, Grover Cleveland, First Term

Specifications: See pages 237 and 238 for details.

Designer: Don Everhart (obverse); Don Everhart (reverse).

22nd President (1885–1889)

Life dates: March 18, 1837–June 24, 1908.

Political party: Democratic.

Vice president: Thomas Hendricks, 1885; none, 1885 to 1889.

First lady: Married Frances Folsom on June 2, 1886. She was the daughter of his late law partner, and he had been her legal guardian since she was 11. Although he had fathered a child earlier, he did not marry the mother. He was the only president to have his wedding ceremony in the White House. They had five children.

Especially remembered for: Cleveland is remembered for his objective evaluation of legislative proposals and his desire to be fair and benefit the citizenry. He took action against the scandals involving the railroad rates and passed the Interstate Commerce Act for regulation.

Coins and money (first term): These were boom times in America—commerce prospered, in the prairie states new cities arose like magic, and enthusiasm prevailed. Morgan silver dollars, made in large quantities under the mandate of the Bland-Allison Act, were mostly unwanted in commerce and piled up in 1,000-coin bags in Treasury and other storage vaults.

Notable sayings (both terms): "It is the responsibility of the citizens to support their government. It is not the responsibility of the government to support its citizens."

"Sensible and responsible women do not want to vote. The relative positions to be assumed by man and woman and the working out of our civilization were assigned long ago by a higher intelligence than ours."

"A man is known by the company he keeps, and also by the company from which he has kept out."

2012-P, Grover Cleveland, First Term

Circulation-strike mintage: 5,460,000

Collecting commentary: MS–64 to 66 coins are common, but at MS-68 and higher they are elusive.

actual size: 26.5 mm

2012, Cleveland, First Term, plain-edge error: Dozens of these coins were inadvertently issued without edge lettering and thus lack the date and mintmark. These are not identifiable to a particular mint and are rare today.

Cleveland, First Term, sketch by Don Everhart.

	MS-64	MS-65	MS-66
2012-P, Cleveland, First Term	$2	$3	$6

2012-D, Grover Cleveland, First Term

Circulation-strike mintage: 4,060,000

Collecting commentary: MS–64 to 66 coins are common, but at MS-68 and higher they are elusive.

	MS-64	MS-65	MS-66
2012-D, Cleveland, First Term	$2	$3	$6

2012-S, Grover Cleveland, First Term

Proof mintage: 1,438,743

Availability: Nearly all are gem Proofs approaching perfection.

Notes: 249,265 were sold by the U.S. Mint as part of four-coin Presidential dollar Proof sets.

	PF-65	PF-69DC	PF-70
2012-S, Cleveland, First Term, Proof	$9	$16	$60

2012, Benjamin Harrison

Specifications: See pages 237 and 238 for details.

Designer: Phebe Hemphill (obverse); Don Everhart (reverse).

23rd President (1889–1893)

Life dates: August 20, 1833–March 13, 1901.

Political party: Republican.

Vice president: Levi P. Morton, 1889 to 1893.

First lady: Married Caroline Lavinia Scott on October 20, 1853. After an extended illness she died in October 1892, near the end of his presidency. While serving as first lady she had the White House renovated and improved its appointments. His second wife was his wife's niece, the much younger widow Mary Scott Lord Dimmick (1858–1948), whom he married on April 6, 1896, much to the dismay of her three children who refused to attend the wedding. Benjamin Harrison had three children.

Especially remembered for: Harrison is remembered for his successful foreign policy, robust economy, and a Treasury surplus in the beginning of his administration. He was a staunch Presbyterian who often quoted the Bible and felt that God shepherded his presidency.

Coins and money: The American Numismatic Association was established at a gathering held in Chicago in November 1891. In time it grew to become the largest such group in the world and is still dynamic today. In 1892 the Liberty Head design of Charles E. Barber replaced the Liberty Seated design which had been in use on the dime, quarter, and half dollar since the late 1830s. The 1892 souvenir (as it was called) half dollar for the World's Columbian Exposition was the first U.S. commemorative coin that was sold widely.[18] Gold was discovered in Cripple Creek, a Colorado town on the western side of Pikes Peak; a great "rush" ensued.

Notable saying: "We Americans have no commission from God to police the world."

2012-P, Benjamin Harrison

Circulation-strike mintage: 5,640,001

actual size: 26.5 mm

Collecting commentary: MS–64 to 66 coins are common, but at MS-68 and higher they are elusive.

Notes: Coins went on general sale on August 16. Options and their prices were: 25-coin roll, $32.95; 100-coin bag, $111.95; 250-coin box, $275.95; 500-coin box $550.95, shipping and handling not included.

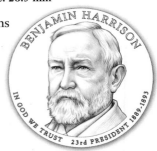

Benjamin Harrison sketch by Phebe Hemphill completed on May 26, 2010.

	MS-64	MS-65	MS-66
2012-P, B. Harrison	$2	$3	$6

2012-D, Benjamin Harrison

Circulation-strike mintage: 4,200,000

Collecting commentary: MS–64 to 66 coins are common, but at MS-68 and higher they are elusive.

	MS-64	MS-65	MS-66
2012-D, B. Harrison	$2	$3	$6

2012-S, Benjamin Harrison

Proof mintage: 1,438,743

Availability: Nearly all are gem Proofs approaching perfection.

Notes: 249,265 were sold by the U.S. Mint as part of four-coin Presidential dollar Proof sets.

	PF-65	PF-69DC	PF-70
2012-S, B. Harrison, Proof	$9	$16	$50

2012, Grover Cleveland, Second Term

Specifications: See pages 237 and 238 for details.

Designer: Don Everhart (obverse); Don Everhart (reverse).

24th President (1893 to 1897)

Life dates: March 18, 1837–June 24, 1908.

Political party: Democratic.

Vice president: Adlai E. Stevenson, 1893 to 1897.

First lady: Frances Folsom Cleveland (see details under First Term).

Especially remembered for: Grover Cleveland is the only president to have served two non-consecutive terms (a State Department ruling held that as his terms were not together, he should be considered as both the 22nd and 24th president). While president he maintained financial stability as gold reserves were being drained to overseas and worked to repeal the Sherman Silver Purchase Act.

Coins and money (second term): Poor conditions on the American financial markets, which had begun in 1890–1891 with defaults on Midwestern bonds, accelerating in 1892 when European investors withdrew funds, continued apace, creating the Panic of 1893. On May 5, 1893, the stock market dropped sharply, and a collapse occurred several weeks later on June 27. A depression was underway, and before the end of the year, over 500 banks failed, 15,000 businesses closed, and 74 railroads were bankrupted. The slump in the economy would last through at least 1897.

In June 1894 the Democratic Silver Convention was held in Omaha, Nebraska, with 1,000 attendees who listened to William Jennings Bryan extol the virtues of unlimited government purchases of silver and the adoption of a 16-to-1 ratio of silver to gold value. Throughout the United States, the "silver question" was the burning political issue of the day, although very few understood its intricacies. Bryan ran for the Senate in November, but lost. He kept busy, however, in his new post as editor of the Omaha *World-Herald* and as a popular speaker on the Chautauqua circuit.

In 1895, as the poor economic climate continued, funds in the U.S. Treasury reserves fell to $41 million, but bankers J.P. Morgan and August Belmont loaned the government $62 million in gold against bonds at an attractive rate in an effort to avert further financial problems. Gold became somewhat scarce because of exports and because the public began hoarding it, in view of the declining price of silver. Several conventions were staged by advocates of free and unlimited coinage of silver to support the diminishing market. In the meantime, gold discoveries in the Cripple Creek District of Colorado were bringing new supplies of the yellow metal onto the market.

On August 17, 1896, gold was discovered in the Klondike region of Alaska, setting off a new gold rush (beginning early in 1897) which would last for the next several years.

2012-P, Grover Cleveland, Second Term

Circulation-strike mintage: 10,680,000

actual size: 26.5 mm

Collecting commentary: MS–64 to 66 coins are common, but at MS-68 and higher they are elusive.

2012, Cleveland, Second Term, plain-edge error: A few coins were inadvertently issued without edge lettering and thus lack the date and mintmark. These are not identifiable to a particular mint and are great rarities today.

Cleveland, Second Term, sketch by Don Everhart.

	MS-64	MS-65	MS-66
2012-P, Cleveland, Second Term	$2	$3	$6

2012-D, Grover Cleveland, Second Term

Circulation-strike mintage: 3,920,000

Collecting commentary: MS–64 to 66 coins are common, but at MS-68 and higher they are elusive.

	MS-64	MS-65	MS-66
2012-D, Cleveland, Second Term	$2	$3	$6

2012-S, Grover Cleveland, Second Term

Proof mintage: 1,438,743

Availability: Nearly all are gem Proofs approaching perfection.

Notes: 249,265 were sold by the U.S. Mint as part of four-coin Presidential dollar Proof sets.

	PF-65	PF-69DC	PF-70
2012-S, Cleveland, Second Term, Proof	$9	$16	$60

2013, William McKinley

Specifications: See pages 237 and 238 for details.

Designer: Phebe Hemphill (obverse); Don Everhart (reverse).

25th President (1897–1901)

Life dates: January 29, 1843–September 14, 1901.

Political party: Republican.

Vice president: Garret Hobart, 1897 to 1901; Theodore Roosevelt, 1901.

First lady: Married Ida Saxton on January 25, 1871. The couple had two children, both of whom lived only a short time. After the death of her children, Ida led an emotionally distressed life, punctuated by seizures. Despite travails, the couple remained close.

Especially remembered for: McKinley is remembered for his tariff reform and changes, and his initiation of the Spanish-American War of 1898, which many felt was without real cause. He was also the first president in office to be photographed for motion pictures.

Coins and money: The 1896 Klondike gold discovery was publicized in the United States, and early in 1897 thousands of gold seekers headed north through Chilkoot Pass to Dawson and other outposts. By year's end an estimated $22 million worth of gold had been recovered. Optimism from the Klondike and Cripple Creek gold strikes and normal cyclical effects combined to continue to ease the economic depression which had been in effect since 1893.

On March 14, 1900, Congress passed an act setting a gold standard against which other monetary units including currency would be valued, thereby effectively ending the long-continuing controversy about the gold and silver ratio. Although gold coins had been minted since 1795, the country was not officially on the gold standard until now.

Notable sayings: "That's all a man can hope for during his lifetime—to set an example—and when he is dead, be an inspiration for history."

"In the times of darkest defeat victory may be nearest."

2013-P, William McKinley

Circulation-strike mintage: 4,760,000

actual size: 26.5 mm

Collecting commentary: MS–64 to 66 coins are common, but at MS–68 and higher they are elusive.

McKinley sketch by Phebe Hemphill.

	MS-64	MS-65	MS-66
2013-P, McKinley	$2	$3	$6

2013-D, William McKinley

Circulation-strike mintage: 3,365,100

Collecting commentary: MS–64 to 66 coins are common, but at MS–68 and higher they are elusive.

	MS-64	MS-65	MS-66
2013-D, McKinley	$2	$3	$6

2013-S, William McKinley

Proof mintage: 1,488,798

Availability: Nearly all are gem Proofs approaching perfection.

Notes: 266,677 were sold by the U.S. Mint as part of four-coin Presidential dollar Proof sets. Sales of sets saw a small uptick this year.

	PF-65	PF-69DC	PF-70
2013-S, McKinley, Proof	$9	$16	$40

2013, Theodore Roosevelt

Specifications: See pages 237 and 238 for details.

Designer: Joseph Menna (obverse); Don Everhart (reverse).

26th President (1901–1909)

Life dates: October 27, 1858–January 6, 1919.

Political party: Republican.

Vice president: None, 1901 to 1905; Charles Fairbanks, 1905 to 1909.

First lady: Married Alice Hathaway Lee on October 27, 1880. She died in childbirth. His second wife was Edith Kermit Carow (1861–1948), a friend since childhood, whom he married on December 2, 1886. Roosevelt had six children.

Especially remembered for: Theodore Roosevelt was one of the most interesting and admired presidents from the viewpoint of the public. He is remembered as the "trust-buster" for his extensive work to break up major companies. His "speak softly, but carry a big stick" idea of foreign policy, also known as "Big Stick Ideology," advocated for peaceful negotiations with the threat of violence if the negotiations did not work. The teddy bear was supposedly so called after his nickname, "Teddy." He had many accomplishments as an author, including the multi-volume *The Winning of the West* (essentially about disenfranchising Native Americans, but at that time few people cared). He was the originator of the terms "muckraker," "lunatic fringe," and "my hat is in the ring," among many others. Roosevelt was the only president who had ever worked closely on coin designs; curiously, he has been sadly neglected as a portrait figure on coins and currency. He is one of four presidents honored on Mount Rushmore.

Coins and money: In 1901 the third Philadelphia Mint opened, replacing the second Mint that had been in operation since 1832. Through a unique cooperation between President Roosevelt and Augustus Saint-Gaudens, America's most famous sculptor, an arrangement was made in 1905 for the artist to redesign all coinage from the cent to the double eagle. By the time of his death on August 3, 1907, preliminary designs for the Indian Head $10 and the MCMVII High Relief double eagle had been done. Both coins were released into circulation to high acclaim later that year. The Denver Mint opened in 1906. The American Numismatic Society, recently renamed from the American Numismatic and Archeological Society, moved into a beautiful new building in Audubon Terrace, 155th Street and Broadway, in New York City, the gift of railroad scion Archer Huntington.

Notable sayings: "It is hard to fail, but it is worse never to have tried to succeed. In this life we get nothing save by effort."

"Get action. Seize the moment. Man was never intended to become an oyster."

"To announce that there must be no criticism of the president, or that we are to stand by the president, right or wrong, is not only unpatriotic and servile, but is morally treasonable to the American public."

"Speak softly and carry a big stick."

"The only man who makes no mistake is the man who does nothing."

"It is common sense to take a method and try it. If it fails, admit it frankly and try another. But above all, try something."

"Believe you can and you are half way there."

"There's never yet been a man in our history that has led a life of ease whose name is worth remembering."

"Keep your eyes on the stars, and your feet on the ground."

"People ask the difference between a leader and a boss. The leader leads and the boss drives."

2013-P, Theodore Roosevelt

Circulation-strike mintage: 5,310,700

Collecting commentary: MS–64 to 66 coins are common, but at MS–68 and higher they are elusive.

actual size: 26.5 mm

	MS-64	MS-65	MS-66
2013-P, T. Roosevelt	$2	$3	$6

2013-D, Theodore Roosevelt

Circulation-strike mintage: 3,920,000

Collecting commentary: MS–64 to 66 coins are common, but at MS-68 and higher they are elusive.

	MS-64	MS-65	MS-66
2013-D, T. Roosevelt	$2	$3	$6

2013-S, Theodore Roosevelt

Proof mintage: 1,503,943

Availability: Nearly all are gem Proofs approaching perfection.

Notes: 266,677 were sold by the U.S. Mint as part of four-coin Presidential dollar Proof sets.

	PF-65	PF-69DC	PF-70
2013-S, T. Roosevelt, Proof	$9	$16	$35

2013, William Howard Taft

Specifications: See pages 237 and 238 for details.

Designer: Barbara Fox (obverse); Don Everhart (reverse).

27th President (1909–1913)

Life dates: September 15, 1857–March 8, 1930.

Political party: Republican.

Vice president: James S. Sherman, 1909 to 1912; none for the remainder of his term.

First lady: Married Helen Herron, on June 19, 1886. The couple had three children.

Especially remembered for: Due to his having been groomed by Theodore Roosevelt for presidency, Taft continued trust-busting and certain other of Roosevelt's policies. As his predecessor was a difficult act to follow in terms of public acclaim, and was often critical, Taft never achieved notable recognition in his own right.

Coins and money: In August 1909 the Lincoln cent replaced the Indian Head cent that had been standard since 1859. The initials of artist Victor D. Brenner (V.D.B.) on the reverse caused a problem when it was suggested that as Brenner was being paid, there was no need to "advertise" him. In an ill-considered move, in that artist's initials were prominent on other coins, the Mint removed the offending letters. In early 1913 James Earle Fraser's Indian/Buffalo (bison) design on the nickel five-cent piece replaced the Liberty Head motif that had been in use since 1883.

Notable sayings: "Politics, when I am in it, makes me sick."

"Next to the right of liberty, the right of property is the most important individual right guaranteed by the Constitution."

2013-P, William Howard Taft

Circulation-strike mintage: 4,760,000

Collecting commentary: MS–64 to 66 coins are common, but at MS-68 and higher they are elusive.

actual size: 26.5 mm

	MS-64	MS-65	MS-66
2013-P, Taft	$2	$3	$6

2013-D, William Howard Taft

Circulation-strike mintage: 3,360,000

Collecting commentary: MS–64 to 66 coins are common, but at MS-68 and higher they are elusive.

	MS-64	MS-65	MS-66
2013-D, Taft	$2	$3	$6

2013-S, William Howard Taft

Proof mintage: 1,488,798

Availability: Nearly all are gem Proofs approaching perfection.

Notes: 266,677 were sold by the U.S. Mint as part of four-coin Presidential dollar Proof sets.

	PF-65	PF-69DC	PF-70
2013-S, Taft, Proof	$9	$16	$40

2013, Woodrow Wilson

Specifications: See pages 237 and 238 for details.

Designer: Don Everhart (obverse); Don Everhart (reverse).

28th President (1913–1921)

Life dates: December 28, 1856–February 3, 1924.

Political party: Democratic.

Vice president: Thomas R. Marshall, 1913 to 1921.

First ladies: Married Ellen Louise Axson on June 24, 1885. As first lady she entertained effectively, but without pretense, and was admired by all. Interested in art, she installed a studio in the White House, complete with a skylight. Ellen died in the White House of Bright's disease on August 6, 1914. The couple had three children. His second wife was Edith Bolling Galt, a Washington widow, whom he married on December 18, 1915, amid criticism that such a brief mourning period might impair his chances for reelection. It didn't. She was a highly talented woman who added much to his presidency.

Especially remembered for: Wilson is remembered for his extreme racism, including prejudice against the black community and praise for the Ku Klux Klan. He also called Italian immigrants people of "the lowest class," and much more. He was also against women's right to vote. Despite his problematic personal viewpoints, he was widely praised for his academic knowledge. He passed the Federal Reserve Act and established the Federal Trade Commission. He is also remembered for his leadership during the Great War and his subsequent unsuccessful bid to have the United States join the League of Nations.

Coins and money: In 1916 beautiful new coin designs were introduced: the Mercury or Winged Liberty Head dime by Adolph A. Weinman, the Standing Liberty quarter by Hermon MacNeil, and the Walking Liberty half dollar also by Weinman.

The World War that began in Europe in August 1914 continued until the armistice in November 1918. Exports of war materiel to Allied forces stimulated the American economy and resulted in record production of some coinage denominations. Gold coins became scarce in commerce from 1917 through 1919 and some banks stopped paying them out.

Notable sayings: "Some people call me an idealist. Well, that is the way I know I am an American. America is the only idealistic nation in the world."

"We grow great by dreams. All big men are dreamers."

"If you want to make enemies, try to change something."

In his book, *History of the American People*, Wilson praised an organization many considered to be evil: "The white men were roused by a mere instinct of self-preservation . . . until at last there had sprung into existence a great Ku Klux Klan, a veritable empire of the South, to protect the Southern country."[19]

2013-P, Woodrow Wilson

Circulation-strike mintage: 4,620,000

Collecting commentary: MS–64 to 66 coins are common, but at MS-68 and higher they are elusive.

actual size: 26.5 mm

Wilson sketch
by Don Everhart.

	MS-64	MS-65	MS-66
2013-P, Wilson	$2	$3	$6

2013-D, Woodrow Wilson

Circulation-strike mintage: 3,360,000

Collecting commentary: MS–64 to 66 coins are common, but at MS-68 and higher they are elusive.

	MS-64	MS-65	MS-66
2013-D, Wilson	$2	$3	$6

2013-S, Woodrow Wilson

Proof mintage: 1,488,798

Availability: These are readily available in high gem Proof grades.

Notes: 266,677 were sold by the U.S. Mint as part of four-coin Presidential dollar Proof sets.

	PF-65	PF-69DC	PF-70
2013-S, Wilson, Proof	$9	$16	$45

2014, Warren G. Harding

Specifications: See pages 237 and 238 for details.

Designer: Michael Gaudioso (obverse); Don Everhart (reverse).

29th President (1921–1923)

Life dates: November 2, 1865–August 2, 1923.

Political party: Republican.

Vice president: Calvin Coolidge, 1921 to 1923.

First lady: Married Florence Kling De Wolfe on July 8, 1891. The couple was childless. Warren Harding fathered one child, Elizabeth Ann Christian (born in 1919), illegitimately by Nan Britton (according to Britton), one of several women with whom he had affairs.

Especially remembered for: Harding is remembered for the economic recession of 1921, cronyism in the White House, and the Teapot Dome and other scandals, most of which surfaced after his death. He is generally viewed as one of the poorest-performing presidents.

Coins and money: In 1921 the coinage of Morgan design silver dollars resumed, after a lapse since 1904. In December 1921 the silver Peace dollar was launched and would be coined intermittently through 1935. The economy was uncertain in 1921 and 1922, and production for most denominations was reduced from the heights registered during the World War.

Notable sayings: "My god, this is a hell of a job. I have no trouble with my enemies . . . but my damn friends, they are the ones that keep me walking the floor nights."

"The most dangerous tendency is to expect too much of government, and at the same time do for it too little."

2014-P, Warren G. Harding

Circulation-strike mintage: 6,160,000

Collecting commentary: MS–64 to 66 coins are common, but at MS-68 and higher they are elusive.

actual size: 26.5 mm

	MS-64	MS-65	MS-66
2014-P, Harding	$2	$3	$6

2014-D, Warren G. Harding

Circulation-strike mintage: 3,780,000

Collecting commentary: MS–64 to 66 coins are common, but at MS-68 and higher they are elusive.

	MS-64	MS-65	MS-66
2014-D, Harding	$2	$3	$6

2014-S, Warren G. Harding

Proof mintage: 1,373,569

Availability: These are readily available in high gem Proof grades.

Notes: 218,976 were sold by the U.S. Mint as part of four-coin Presidential dollar Proof sets. Sales of sets were at a new low this year.

	PF-65	PF-69DC	PF-70
2014-S, Harding, Proof	$9	$16	$40

2014, Calvin Coolidge

Specifications: See pages 237 and 238 for details.

Designer: Phebe Hemphill (obverse); Don Everhart (reverse).

30th President (1923–1929)

Life dates: July 4, 1872–January 5, 1933.

Political party: Republican.

Vice president: None, 1923 to 1925; Charles Dawes, 1925 to 1929.

First lady: Married Grace Anna Goodhue on October 4, 1905. During her stint as first lady the White House was no longer a social center for lavish parties and dinners. The couple had two children.

Especially remembered for: Coolidge's presidential term was an era of prosperity known as the "Roaring Twenties," but he was known as a "do-nothing" president. His nickname was "Silent Cal."

Coins and money: Coinage was generous for most denominations during this era. In 1926 Coolidge was featured on the obverse of the Sesquicentennial commemorative half dollar, the only living president in American history to be so honored.

Notable sayings: "Don't expect to build up the weak by pulling down the strong."

"Nothing in the world can take the place of persistence. Talent will not; nothing is more common than unsuccessful men with talent. Genius will not; unrewarded genius is almost a proverb. Education will not; the world is full of educated derelicts. Persistence and determination are omnipotent. The slogan, 'press on,' solved and always will solve the problems of the human race. No person is ever been honored for what he received. Honor has been the reward for what he gave."

When queried as to why he was not seeking reelection: "I do not choose to run."

2014-P, Calvin Coolidge

actual size: 26.5 mm

Circulation-strike mintage: 4,480,000

Collecting commentary: MS–64 to 66 coins are common, but at MS–68 and higher they are elusive.

2014, Coolidge, plain-edge error: A few coins were inadvertently issued without edge lettering and thus lack the date and mintmark. These are not identifiable to a particular mint and are great rarities today.

Sketch of Coolidge
by Phebe Hemphill.

	MS-64	MS-65	MS-66
2014-P, Coolidge	$2	$3	$6

2014-D, Calvin Coolidge

Circulation-strike mintage: 3,780,000

Collecting commentary: MS–64 to 66 coins are common, but at MS-68 and higher they are elusive.

	MS-64	MS-65	MS-66
2014-D, Coolidge	$2	$3	$6

2014-S, Calvin Coolidge

Proof mintage: 1,373,569

Availability: Nearly all are gem Proofs approaching perfection.

Notes: 218,976 were sold by the U.S. Mint as part of four-coin Presidential dollar Proof sets.

	PF-65	PF-69DC	PF-70
2014-S, Coolidge, Proof	$9	$16	$50

2014, Herbert Hoover

Specifications: See pages 237 and 238 for details.

Designer: Phebe Hemphill (obverse); Don Everhart (reverse).

31st President (1929–1933)

Life dates: August 10, 1874–October 20, 1964.

Political party: Republican.

Vice president: Charles Curtis, 1929 to 1933.

First lady: Married Lou Henry on February 10, 1899. The couple had two children.

Especially remembered for: Hoover is remembered for aiding in the recovery of Europe after the World War and for establishing the Reconstruction Finance Corporation in an unsuccessful attempt to end the economic Depression, for which many held him responsible. These were sad times for America.

Coins and money: Mintages of various denominations were sharply reduced in many instances due to the Depression. In 1932 the Washington quarter dollar was introduced.

Notable sayings: "Older men declare war. But it is youth who must fight and die."
"Blessed are the young, for they will inherit the national debt."
"Absolute freedom of the press to discuss public questions is a foundation stone of American liberty."
"Peace is not made at the counsel table or by treaties, but in the hearts of men."

2014-P, Herbert Hoover

Circulation-strike mintage: 4,480,000

Collecting commentary: MS–64 to 66 coins are common, but at MS-68 and higher they are elusive.

actual size: 26.5 mm

Sketch of Hoover by Phebe Hemphill.

	MS-64	MS-65	MS-66
2014-P, Hoover	$2	$3	$6

2014-D, Herbert Hoover

Circulation-strike mintage: 3,780,000

Collecting commentary: MS–64 to 66 coins are common, but at MS-68 and higher they are elusive.

	MS-64	MS-65	MS-66
2014-D, Hoover	$2	$3	$6

2014-S, Herbert Hoover

Proof mintage: 1,373,569

Availability: Nearly all are gem Proofs approaching perfection.

Notes: 218,976 were sold by the U.S. Mint as part of four-coin Presidential dollar Proof sets.

	PF-65	PF-69DC	PF-70
2014-S, Hoover, Proof	$9	$16	$45

2014, Franklin D. Roosevelt

Specifications: See pages 237 and 238 for details.

Designer: Joseph Menna (obverse); Don Everhart (reverse).

32nd President (1933–1945)

Life dates: January 30, 1882–April 12, 1945.

Political party: Democratic.

Vice presidents: John Nance Garner, 1933 to 1941; Henry A. Wallace, 1941 to 1945; Harry S. Truman, 1945.

First lady: Married a fifth cousin, Eleanor Roosevelt, on March 17, 1905, despite his mother's vehement objections. She became one of the most prominent and accomplished first ladies in American history, although the relationship with her husband was difficult at best, and in later years devoid of romance. He developed other liaisons. The couple had five children.

Especially remembered for: One of Franklin Roosevelt's most memorable moments was his inaugural address comment: "The only thing we have to fear is fear itself." During his presidency he established multiple federal agencies, such as TVA, CCC, and SEC (sometimes referred to as "alphabet soup"), and lifted the country from the Depression. He held "fireside chat" radio broadcasts to the public while quietly suffering with poliomyelitis. Roosevelt tried to pack the Supreme Court with his favorites while he was in office. He is remembered for his brilliant conduct of World War II with domestic and foreign policies, and for planning to establish the United Nations. He is a candidate for the most accomplished president, although not without many detractors, but he *is* the only president to have served for more than two terms. His nickname was "FDR." "Roosevelt is consistently rated by scholars as one of the top three presidents," notes *Wikipedia*, the other two being Washington and Lincoln.

Coins and money: America had been on the gold standard officially since 1900 and in practice since the first U.S. gold coins were minted in 1795. On April 5, 1933, Roosevelt declared a national emergency and issued Executive Order 6102, forbidding Americans to own bullion gold or coins except for certain numismatic purposes. The price of gold, earlier at $20.67 per ounce, was later raised to $35, in effect devaluing the dollar.

In 1935 a great boom in commemorative half dollars began with a flood of new issues. Prices multiplied, and excitement prevailed. The passion died in late 1936 and prices dropped. *The Numismatic Scrapbook Magazine* was launched and in time would become America's most popular coin-collecting publication, until being eclipsed by *Coin World* in 1960.

Notable sayings: "We have nothing to fear but fear itself."
   "A good leader can't get too far ahead of his followers."
   "Happiness lies in the joy of achievement and the thrill of creative effort."

2014-P, Franklin D. Roosevelt

Circulation-strike mintage: 4,760,000

Collecting commentary: MS–64 to 66 coins are common, but at MS-68 and higher they are elusive.

actual size: 26.5 mm

	MS-64	MS-65	MS-66
2014-P, F.D. Roosevelt	$2	$3	$6

2014-D, Franklin D. Roosevelt

Circulation-strike mintage: 3,920,000

Collecting commentary: MS–64 to 66 coins are common, but at MS-68 and higher they are elusive.

	MS-64	MS-65	MS-66
2014-D, F.D. Roosevelt	$2	$3	$6

2014-S, Franklin D. Roosevelt

Proof mintage: 1,392,619

Availability: Nearly all are gem Proofs approaching perfection.

Notes: 218,976 were sold by the U.S. Mint as part of four-coin Presidential dollar Proof sets.

	PF-65	PF-69DC	PF-70
2014-S, F.D. Roosevelt, Proof	$9	$16	$120

2015, Harry S. Truman

Specifications: See pages 237 and 238 for details.

Designer: Don Everhart (obverse); Don Everhart (reverse).

33rd President (1945–1953)

Life dates: May 8, 1884–December 26, 1972.

Political party: Democratic.

Vice president: None, 1945 to 1949; Alben Barkley, 1949 to 1953.

First lady: Married Elizabeth "Bess" Virginia Wallace on June 28, 1919. The couple had one child, Mary Margaret Truman (born in 1924).

Especially remembered for: President Truman famously ordered to drop atomic bombs on the Japanese cities of Hiroshima and Nagasaki, bringing a quick end to World War II, and possibly saving the millions of lives a land invasion might have cost. He also saw the "Cold War" with the Soviet Union and the start of the Korean War. His famous saying was, "The buck stops here," reflecting his courage to make decisions, and his nickname was "Give 'Em Hell Harry."

Coins and money: The Roosevelt dime was launched in 1946. The coin market was at a high in 1945 and 1946, but experienced hard times from 1949 to 1951, after which time it recovered with great strength.

Notable sayings: "A statesman is a politician who has been dead 10 or 15 years."

"America was not built on fear. America was built on courage, imagination, and unbeatable determination to do the job at hand."

"If you want a friend in Washington, get a dog."

"The buck stops here."

"You need not fear the expression of ideas—we do need to fear their suppression"

"You cannot stop the spread of an idea by passing a law against it."

"A pessimist is one who makes difficulties of his opportunities and an optimist is one who makes opportunities of its difficulties."

When Truman said upon being asked, "What did you think when the Republicans said you gave them hell?" he replied, "I never did give anybody hell. I just told the truth and they thought it was hell."

"It is amazing what you can accomplish if you do not care who gets the credit."

2015-P, Harry S. Truman

Circulation-strike mintage: 4,900,000

Reverse Proof mintage: 16,812

actual size: 26.5 mm

Collecting commentary: MS–64 to 66 coins are common, but at MS–68 and higher they are elusive.

Notes: At noon on February 5 the U.S. Mint began sales of circulation strikes to collectors for premium prices: 25-coin rolls for $32.95; 100-coin bags for $111.95; and 250-coin boxes for $275.95.

Availability of Reverse Proofs: Reverse Proofs are readily available as all were sold to speculators and collectors.

Notes: In the late spring of 2015 the Mint announced that Harry S. Truman Coin and Chronicles sets would contain

Truman sketch by Don Everhart.

a *Reverse Proof* dollar and would be available for $59.95 starting at noon on June 30. The news created a speculative rush, and the entire issue was sold out in three hours. Soon afterward quantities of sets were offered on eBay at prices from upwards of $150 each. Nearly all collectors desiring an example directly from the Mint were squeezed out. This caused no end of hard feelings with loyal Mint clients who were accustomed to routinely adding to their collections as new issues became available. Now, speculators took over and collectors were left in the lurch. Unfortunately, more was yet to come.

The Mint's description of the Truman set was as follows: "One of four presidential special sets to be available in 2015, includes a Presidential $1 Reverse Proof Coin minted in Philadelphia. Set also includes a silver presidential medal, presidential stamp and informative booklet about President Harry S. Truman. Look for additional Coin and Chronicles Sets this year for Eisenhower, Kennedy, and Johnson."

Reverse Proof.

The silver presidential medal, the stamp, and the booklet meant little or nothing to many buyers, who simply wanted the dollar coins for their collections.

	MS-64	MS-65	MS-66
2015-P, Truman	$2	$3	$5

2015-D, Harry S. Truman

Circulation-strike mintage: 3,500,000

Collecting commentary: MS–64 to 66 coins are common, but at MS-68 and higher they are elusive.

	MS-64	MS-65	MS-66
2015-D, Truman	$2	$3	$5

2015-S, Harry S. Truman

Regular Proof mintage: 1,191,876

Availability of regular Proofs: Nearly all are gem Proofs approaching perfection.

	PF-65	PF-69DC	PF-70
2015-S, Truman, Proof	$9	$16	$70
2015-S, Truman, Reverse Proof	$175	$225	

2015, Dwight D. Eisenhower

Specifications: See pages 237 and 238 for details.

Designer: Joseph Menna (obverse); Don Everhart (reverse).

34th President (1953–1961)

Life dates: October 14, 1890–March 28, 1969.

Political party: Republican.

Vice president: Richard M. Nixon, 1953 to 1961.

First lady: Married Mary "Mamie" Geneva Doud on July 1, 1916. The couple had two children.

Especially remembered for: Eisenhower's famous slogan during his presidential run was "I like Ike." He secured a truce in Korea and mandated desegregation of public schools and the armed forces. The Interstate Highway system was created under his leadership. He had an outgoing personality and enjoyed golf. Economic times were pleasant during his presidency.

Coins and money: Commemorative coins were discontinued after the last issue of Carver-Washington half dollars in 1954. In 1955 the San Francisco Mint struck cents and dimes, after which coinage was discontinued, seemingly forever. The name of the facility was then changed to the San Francisco Assay Office. Coinage was resumed there in the 1960s and the San Francisco Mint name was resumed in 1982.

Notable sayings: "We are going to have peace, even if we have to fight for it."
    "America is best described by one word: freedom."
    "There is nothing wrong with America that the faith, love of freedom, intelligence and energy of the citizens cannot cure."
    "I've never seen a pessimistic general win a battle."

2015-P, Dwight D. Eisenhower

Circulation-strike mintage: 4,900,000

Reverse Proof mintage: 16,744

Collecting commentary:
MS–64 to 66 coins are common, but at MS–68 and higher they are elusive.

actual size: 26.5 mm

Notes: On August 11, 2015, the U.S. Mint made available to
its customers the Dwight D. Eisenhower Coin and Chronicles Set. At first a limit of five sets per household was
placed, then was reduced to two by sale time. The set
contained a Reverse Proof 2015-P dollar with the lettering and devices polished to a mirror finish and the fields
with a laser-frosted matte surface. Reverse Proofs had
been sold in other denominations earlier, but this year was
the first time for Presidential dollars.

The offering was quickly sold out, with large quantities
going to speculators. Paul Gilkes told the story in *Coin
World*, August 31, 2015:

> Gone in 15 Minutes: The 2015 Dwight D. Eisenhower
> Coin and Chronicles set sold out within about 15 minutes
> of its noon Eastern Time Aug. 11 sales launch despite the
> U.S. Mint imposing a household ordering limit of two sets.
> The set had a product release limit of 17,000 sets, each
> priced at $57.95. The eBay auction site had confirmed sales
> as of Aug. 13 of Eisenhower sets in their original Mint packag-
> ing for between $250 and $400 per set. The sellout of the

Reverse Proof.

> Eisenhower sets follows the June 30 sellout, in 15 minutes, of the 17,000 Harry S.
> Truman Coin and Chronicles set, which had a household ordering limit of five sets.
> The two sets are in demand by dealers and collectors because of the Reverse Proof
> 2015-P Presidential dollar and 1-ounce .999 fine silver Presidential medal in each set
> are exclusive to the sets and not available for sale individually. The sets also include a
> U.S. postage stamp and information booklet on the featured president. The sets have
> been made available only through the Mint's website and telephone at 800-872-6468.
> None were made available at the sales outlet at U.S. Mint headquarters in Washing-
> ton, D.C., or contracted sales centers at the Denver and Philadelphia Mints. . . .

In the *Coin World* September 2015 issue, William T. Gibbs and Fern Loomis
wrote:

> Collectors Disgruntled with Buyers of Large Quantities for Resale: Some collec-
> tors upset with the 15-minute sellout of the Dwight D. Eisenhower Coin and
> Chronicles set are upset with firms they believe unfairly circumvented the mint's
> two-set-per-household limits or have some sort of special relationship with the
> Mint. A typical response came from collector Robert Savage, who said after
> recounting his inability to complete an order for the set: 'Meanwhile I checked
> eBay an hour after the sets went on sale and they were selling for $300–$600 each.
> Not what you know but who. Once again coin dealers get all the sets while the
> regular people get nothing.' Merle Norris wrote: 'The dealers and their agents log
> on to the website at the very instant the sales begin. By the time the average col-
> lector gets through, the sets are all sold out . . . The Mint HAS to know this. So
> who do they serve—the numismatist, or the for-profit dealer?' Norris wonders why
> the Mint doesn't make the sets to order. Buyers who were successful are profiting
> from their purchases when reselling them. Unopened U.S. Mint shipping boxes,
> each containing two sets, sold on eBay Aug. 20 for $385 and $400, a typical range
> for the sets. The original cost to the buyer: $57.95 a set. . . .

2015, Eisenhower, plain-edge error: A small number of coins were made without edge lettering. These are not identifiable to a particular mint.

	MS-64	MS-65	MS-66
2015-P, Eisenhower	$2	$3	$5

2015-D, Dwight D. Eisenhower
Circulation-strike mintage: 3,645,998

Collecting commentary: MS–64 to 66 coins are common, but at MS-68 and higher they are elusive.

	MS-64	MS-65	MS-66
2015-D, Eisenhower	$2	$3	$5

2015-S, Dwight D. Eisenhower
Proof mintage: 1,191,876

Availability: Nearly all are gem Proofs approaching perfection.

	PF-65	PF-69DC	PF-70
2015-S, Eisenhower, Proof	$9	$16	$30
2015-S, Eisenhower, Reverse Proof	$150	$200	

2015, John F. Kennedy

Specifications: See pages 237 and 238 for details.

Designer: Don Everhart (obverse); Don Everhart (reverse).

35th President (1961–1963)

Life dates: May 29, 1917–November 22, 1963.

Political party: Democratic.

Vice president: Lyndon B. Johnson, 1961 to 1963.

First lady: Married Jacqueline ("Jackie") Lee Bouvier on September 12, 1953. She was one of the most popular first ladies in American history, and until her death the media eagerly followed her activities. The couple had three children.

Especially remembered for: Kennedy was the first Roman Catholic president. On March 1, 1961, President Kennedy passed via Executive Order the Peace Corps Act. He is often remembered for his failed invasion of the Bay of Pigs and for the Cuban missile crisis. His family atmosphere in the White House was popular with news media and public alike—an aura called "Camelot," after the mythical kingdom, by some admirers. He was famous for his womanizing, although this did not seem to affect his presidential performance. Although his administration was unfortunately brief, he became remembered as one of the all-time favorite American presidents. His nicknames were "JFK" and "Jack."

Coins and money: Coins in circulation consisted of the Lincoln cent, Jefferson nickel, Roosevelt dime, Washington quarter, and Franklin half dollar. Silver dollars could be obtained from banks and were familiar sights on Nevada gaming tables, but were not used in general commerce.

In November 1962 a long-sealed vault was opened at the Philadelphia Mint, and hundreds of thousands of stored 1903-O silver dollars, at the time the rarest Mint State coin in the Morgan series, came to light. Other New Orleans dollars, rare and not-so-rare were also found. This set off a silver rush, and from that time until March 1964, hundreds of millions of silver dollars were obtained by collectors, dealers, and others from Treasury and bank vaults, until no more were available.

Notable sayings: "Ask not what your country can do for you—ask what you can do for your country."

"Forgive your enemies, but never forget their names."

"If we cannot end now our differences at least we can help make the world safe for diversity."

"The American, by nature, is optimistic. He is experimental, an inventor and a builder who builds best when called upon to build greatly."

2015-P, John F. Kennedy

Circulation-strike mintage: 6,160,000

Reverse Proof mintage: 49,051

actual size: 26.5 mm

Collecting commentary:
MS–64 to 66 coins are common, but at MS–68 and higher they are elusive.

Notes: In a discussion with the author Mint spokesman Tom Jurkowsky expressed regret at the limited numbers of Chronicles sets, but stated that as packaging had already been ordered, the program for this and the next Lyndon B. Johnson set could not be changed. Incoming Mint Principal Deputy Director Rhett Jeppson was aware of the problem, and it was hoped that in 2016 the distribution of special sets would be such that all who wanted them could order them easily.

Kennedy sketch
by Don Everhart.

	MS-64	MS-65	MS-66
2015-P, Kennedy	$2	$3	$5

2015-D, John F. Kennedy

Circulation strike mintage: 5,180,000

Collecting commentary: MS–64 to 66 coins are common, but at MS-68 and higher they are elusive.

	MS-64	MS-65	MS-66
2015-D, Kennedy	$2	$3	$5

2015-S, John F. Kennedy

Proof mintage: 1,191,876

Availability: Nearly all are gem Proofs approaching perfection.

	PF-65	PF-69DC	PF-70
2015-S, Kennedy, Proof	$9	$16	$85
2015-S, Kennedy, Reverse Proof	$80	$125	

2015, Lyndon B. Johnson

Specifications: See pages 237 and 238 for details.

Designer: Michael Gaudioso (obverse); Don Everhart (reverse).

36th President (1963–1969)

Life dates: August 27, 1908–January 22, 1973.

Political party: Democratic.

Vice president: Hubert H. Humphrey, 1965 to 1969.

First lady: Married Claudia ("Lady Bird") Alta Taylor on November 17, 1934. The couple had two children.

Especially remembered for: Johnson is remembered for his mixed legacy with pluses for the Great Society, Medicare, desegregation, and other programs, and minuses for the conduct of the Vietnam War and domestic racial unrest. He built a fortune through his political power. His nickname was "LBJ."

Coins and money: In March 1964 the Kennedy half dollar made its debut, replacing the Franklin design. The price of silver bullion had been rising on world markets. In 1964 it was realized that if the United States were to continue to produce silver coins beyond this time, they would cost more than face value to mint. Accordingly, beginning in 1965, clad alloy was used. Silver coinage became history, except for special pieces made to be sold at a premium to collectors. Proof sets, which had not been minted since 1964, were made again, now at the San Francisco Assay Office and with an S mintmark.

Notable sayings: "A president's hardest task is not to do what is right, but to know what is right."

"You ain't learnin nothin when you're talkin."

"If government is to serve any purpose it is to do for others what they are unable to do for themselves."

2015-P, Lyndon B. Johnson

Circulation-strike mintage: 7,840,000

Reverse Proof mintage: 23,905

actual size: 26.5 mm

Collecting commentary: MS–64 to 66 coins are common, but at MS-68 and higher they are elusive.

Reverse Proofs: From a U.S. Mint announcement by Michael White, October 27, 2015, 4:51 p.m. EDT:

> The United States Mint has sold the 25,000 units of the 2015 Coin and Chronicles Set - Lyndon B. Johnson. All accepted orders will be processed and fulfilled on a first-in, first-served basis according to existing United States Mint policies. The product inventory is at the fulfillment center for immediate shipment to customers. No additional inventory will be produced. Product shipments, returns and exchanges will be monitored daily over the next few weeks. To ensure fair and equitable access, a household order limit of two sets was established for the 2015 Coin and Chronicles Set–Lyndon B. Johnson. The product went on sale at noon Eastern Time October 27, 2015. By 3:57 p.m. (EST), available inventory had been depleted.

The next day, October 28, the Mint sent a notice, "Your U.S. Mint web order has shipped!" to a client for order USM03706646. Presumably this was also true for many other orders. The price was $57.95 per set.

The set included the Reverse Proof dollar, a one-ounce Johnson presidential medal (designs created in 1963, obverse by Chief Engraver Gilroy Roberts, reverse by Frank Gasparro), and a 1973 Johnson 8-cent postage stamp.

	MS-64	MS-65	MS-66
2015-P, L.B. Johnson	$2	$3	$5

2015-D, Lyndon B. Johnson

Circulation-strike mintage: 4,200,000

Collecting commentary: MS–64 to 66 coins are common, but at MS-68 and higher they are elusive.

	MS-64	MS-65	MS-66
2015-D, L.B. Johnson	$2	$3	$5

2015-S, Lyndon B. Johnson

Proof mintage: 1,191,876

Availability: Nearly all are gem Proofs approaching perfection.

	PF-65	PF-69DC	PF-70
2015-S, L.B. Johnson, Proof	$9	$16	$25
2015-S, L.B. Johnson, Reverse Proof			

2016, Richard Nixon

Specifications: See pages 237 and 238 for details.

Designer: Don Everhart (obverse); Don Everhart (reverse).

37th President (1969–1974)

Life dates: January 9, 1913–April 22, 1994.

Political party: Republican.

Vice presidents: Spiro Agnew, 1969 to 1973; none for part of 1973; Gerald Ford, 1973 to 1974.

First lady: Married Patricia Ryan on June 21, 1940. The couple had two children.

Especially remembered for: Nixon opened trade with China before his presidency went downhill. The resignation of dishonest and discredited Vice President Spiro Agnew was the beginning of Nixon's troubles. President Nixon is most often remembered for the Watergate cover-up and scandal, and the indictments of more than a dozen Cabinet and key officials. His unprecedented resignation in shame from the presidency in the aftermath was equally as memorable. He was perhaps the most troubled and dishonored of American presidents. His nickname given by detractors was "Tricky Dick."

Coins and money: In circulation all of the previous silver denominations were of clad metal. Half dollars, once a popular denomination, were nowhere to be seen in commerce, although collectors could buy them from the Mint. The largest circulating coin of the realm was the quarter dollar, which found wide use in vending and arcade machines.

Notable sayings: "I was not lying. I said things that later on seemed to be untrue."

"I am not a crook," a response to suggestions that he had a part in the Watergate affair.

"I like the job I have, but if I had to live my life over again I would like to have ended up a sports writer."

"Always give your best, never get discouraged, never be peppy; always remember, others may hate you. Those who hate you don't win unless you hate them. And then you destroy yourself."

2016-P, Richard Nixon

Circulation-strike mintage: Not known at press time.

Collecting commentary: Probably the usual will apply: MS–64 to 66 coins are common, but at MS-68 and higher they are elusive.

actual size: 26.5 mm

Notes: On December 20, 2015, the U.S. Mint stated rolls, bags, and boxes of coins of the Philadelphia and Denver mints would be released on February 3, 2016.

	MS-64	MS-65	MS-66
2016-P, Nixon	$2	$3	$5

2016-D, Richard Nixon

Circulation strike mintage: Not known at press time.

Collecting commentary: Probably the usual will apply: MS–64 to 66 coins are common, but at MS-68 and higher they are elusive.

	MS-64	MS-65	MS-66
2016-D, Nixon	$2	$3	$5

2016-S, Richard Nixon

Proof mintage: Not known at press time.

Availability: Probably most will be PF–69 and 70 gems.

	PF-65	PF-69DC	PF-70
2016-S, Nixon, Proof	$9	$16	$25

2016, Gerald Ford

Specifications: See pages 237 and 238 for details.

Designer: Phebe Hemphill (obverse); Don Everhart (reverse).

38th President (1974–1977)

Life dates: July 14, 1913–December 26, 2006.

Political party: Republican.

Vice president: None at the beginning; Nelson Rockefeller, 1974 to 1977.

First lady: Married Elizabeth ("Betty") Bloomer Warren on October 15, 1948. The couple had four children.

Especially remembered for: Ford was the first president to succeed a president who had resigned, and was the only president not elected to either the vice presidency or the presidency. He was widely criticized for his pardon of Richard Nixon (which probably cost him his election bid in 1976). He was, however, widely recognized as a fair, kind, and gentle man of good principles and intent. His nickname was "Jerry."

Coins and money: The 1976 Bicentennial of American independence was to have been a grand event, and years earlier it was hoped that a world's fair be held in Philadelphia, where in 1876 the Centennial Exhibition had taken place. However, it was thought that money should be spent on welfare and other programs instead of a grand celebration. When the Bicentennial arrived, many local historical societies published booklets, new coin designs were issued, and there were celebrations, but hardly any nationwide excitement. America was still preoccupied with inflation, unemployment, and other problems.

Notable sayings: "Things are more like they are now than they ever have been."

"Truth is the glue that holds governments together. Compromise is the oil that makes governments go."

"A government big enough to give you everything you want is a government big enough to take from you everything you have."

2016-P, Gerald Ford

Circulation-strike mintage: Not known at press time.

Collecting commentary: Probably the usual will apply: MS–64 to 66 coins are common, but at MS-68 and higher they are elusive.

actual size: 26.5 mm

Notes: On December 20, 2015, the U.S. Mint stated rolls, bags, and boxes of coins of the Philadelphia and Denver mints would be released on March 8, 2016.

Ford sketch
by Phebe Hemphill.

	MS-64	MS-65	MS-66
2016-P, Ford	$2	$3	$5

2016-D, Gerald Ford

Circulation-strike mintage: Not known at press time.

Collecting commentary: Probably the usual will apply: MS–64 to 66 coins are common, but at MS-68 and higher they are elusive.

	MS-64	MS-65	MS-66
2016-D, Ford	$2	$3	$5

2016-S, Gerald Ford

Proof mintage: Not known at press time.

Availability: Probably most will be PF–69 and 70 gems.

	PF-65	PF-69DC	PF-70
2016-S, Ford, Proof	$9	$16	$25

2016, Ronald Reagan

Specifications: See pages 237 and 238 for details.

Designer: Richard Masters (obverse); Don Everhart (reverse).

40th President (1981–1989)

Life dates: February 6, 1911–June 5, 2004.

Political party: Republican.

Vice-president: George Herbert Walker Bush, 1981 to 1989.

First lady: Married Jane Wyman (1914–2007) on June 25, 1940 (divorced in 1948). Jane was a well-known film actress. His second wife was Nancy Davis (1923–2016), whom he married on March 4, 1952.

Especially remembered for: Reagan is especially remembered for his career as a movie star, and his understanding of human nature, communication, and how to motivate his associates. An assassination attempt was made against him by deranged John Hinckley on March 30,1981, but he survived, making him the first U.S. president to survive an attempt at his life. He restored the national economy to normal interest and inflation rates, but the Iran Contra scandal engineered by his subordinates marred his presidential career. Reagan is credited with persuading Soviet leader Mikhail Gorbachev to tear down the concrete wall that enclosed Berlin. This event happened under the next administration, leading to the dissolution of the Communist bloc and freedom for many countries and is seen as one of the greatest diplomatic accomplishments in American history. He was a popular and highly respected president.

Coins and money: In 1982 the first commemorative coins since 1984 were launched, observing the 250th anniversary of George Washington's birth. The designer of the obverse was Reagan's appointee as chief engraver, artist-sculptor Elizabeth Jones, who served until her resignation in 1992 (after which there were no more presidential appointments to this office, although Mint Director Ed Moy later designated John Mercanti as *de facto* chief engraver). The commemoratives expanded into a large and dynamic program by the end of his presidency, something that has continued to the present day. Soon after the Washington half dollar became a reality Armand Hammer, CEO of the Occidental Petroleum Company, influenced California Senator Alan Cranston (who on a later matter was officially censured for misconduct) to initiate a proposal that Occidental should be given the exclusive marketing program for future commemoratives, as it could do better than the "sleepy" Mint. This precipitated the Treasury Department to call upon several hobby leaders (including Margo Russell, editor of *Coin World*; Q. David Bowers, president of the American Numismatic Association; and Edward Milas, president of the Professional Numismatists Guild) to testify before Congress on the Mint's behalf. They did this to good effect, and ever afterward the Mint remained in charge. Reagan had a personal interest in coinage as different issues were produced.

Notable sayings: (Among the presidents his comments are perhaps the most quotable and, often, humorous.)

"Mr. Gorbachev, please tear down that wall."

"Politics is supposed to be the second oldest profession. I have come to realize that it bears a very close resemblance to the first."

"In a world wracked by hatred, economic crisis, and political tension, America remains mankind's best hope."

"People don't start wars, governments do."

"The best minds are not in government. If any were, business would hire them away."

"The government's view of the economy could be summed up in a few short phrases: If it moves, tax it. If it keeps moving, regulate it. And if it stops moving, subsidize it."

"I have left orders to be awakened at any time in case of national emergency, even if I am in a Cabinet meeting."

"Abortion is advocated only by persons who have themselves been born."

"Entrepreneurs and their small enterprises are responsible for almost all the economic growth in the United States."

"Freedom is never more than one generation away from extinction. We didn't pass it to our children in the bloodstream. It must be fought for, protected, and handed on for them to do the same, or one day we will spend our sunset years telling our children and our children's children what it was once like in the United States where men were free."

"I don't believe in a government that protects us from ourselves."

2016-P, Ronald Reagan

Circulation-strike mintage:
Not known at press time.

Special finish mintage:
Not known at press time.

actual size: 26.5 mm

Collecting commentary: Probably the usual will apply: MS–64 to 66 coins are common, but at MS-68 and higher they are elusive.

Notes: On December 20, 2015, the U.S. Mint stated rolls, bags, and boxes of coins of the Philadelphia and Denver mints would be released in July 2016. It was also stated, date to be determined, that a Reagan Coin & Chronicles Sets would be issued with Philadelphia and Denver coins.

	MS-64	MS-65	MS-66
2016-P, Reagan	$2	$3	$5

2016-D, Ronald Reagan

Circulation-strike mintage: Not known at press time.

Collecting commentary: Probably the usual will apply: MS–64 to 66 coins are common, but at MS-68 and higher they are elusive.

	MS-64	MS-65	MS-66
2016-D, Reagan	$2	$3	$5

2016-S, Ronald Reagan

Proof mintage: Not known at press time.

Special finish mintage: Not known at press time.

Availability: Probably most will be PF–69 and 70 gems.

Notes: On December 20, 2015, the U.S. Mint stated a Reagan Coin & Chronicles Sets would be issued with Philadelphia and Denver coins.

	PF-65	PF-69DC	PF-70
2016-S, Reagan, Proof	$9	$16	$25
2015-S, Reagan, Reverse Proof	$75		

Epilogue

As the years slipped by on the calendar, additional presidents were honored—all by facial portraits on the obverse in combination with the Statue of Liberty motif on the reverse. It seems likely that the series would have generated more interest if varied image styles had been used on each obverse, and if each reverse had an American scene from the president's administration.

The placing of the date and mintmark on the edges of these and the Sacagawea dollars seems to have been a great mistake. Dates and mintmarks are essential for numismatists, and on the Sacagawea, Native American, and Presidential coins they can only be seen if they are *not* in an album or holder! If a holder has spacers or prongs to show the edge, a magnifying glass is still needed.

Collectors, dealers, and investors have been very loyal to the U.S. Mint for many years. To be sure, there are programs and pricing structures that have resulted in justified criticism, but it is to be remembered that Congress, not the Mint, specifies programs, designs, and quantities to be minted. Often, but not always, these decisions are made by well-intentioned senators and representatives that have little if any knowledge of the motif and spirit of collecting.

The Commission of Fine Arts and the Citizens Coinage Advisory Committee can make recommendations, but they are often ignored, such as frequent suggestions that classic motifs be used. It is the secretary of the Treasury who has the last word.

While officials of the U.S. Mint know full well what collectors like and do not like (collectors vote with their pocketbooks), members of Congress do not. Otherwise, why would the dates and mintmarks of certain coins be placed out of sight?

Ideal Designs

Much has been said in the numismatic press about the beauty and desirability of designs. The Winged Liberty Head ("Mercury") dime, Standing Liberty quarter, and Liberty Walking half dollar of 1916 have been held as ideals.

President Theodore Roosevelt, the only chief executive ever to immerse himself in studying and improving coin designs, commissioned America's most famous sculptor, Augustus Saint-Gaudens, to redesign all coins from the cent to the double eagle. The artist was in failing health, and by his passing in August 1907 he had done only the gold eagle and the MCMVII double eagle.

On October 24, 2008, the American Numismatic Society celebrated the opening of its new headquarters, rented premises on the 11th floor of what had been the *New York Herald Tribune* printing plant on Varick Street in lower Manhattan. At the event Mint Director Edmund Moy outlined five goals for designs:

1. To create a new American coinage that will be unmistakably American in style and imagery.

2. United States coinage should reflect the current times so that viewers 100 years hence will be able to link them to the periods in which they were created.

3. U.S. coins should tell the uniquely American story.

4. U.S. coins can and must be aesthetically beautiful, taking full advantage of 21st century technology and artistic ability.

5. Foster a new generation of American artists.

Number 5 is redundant, as through the Artistic Infusion Program, as well as the talents of the sculptor-engravers on the Mint staff, there are more American artists on tap than ever before. It is the other four points that need attention.

As former *Coin World* editor Beth Deisher pointed out in an editorial about the director's remarks:

> Interestingly, none of these ideas are really new. The numismatic community has long sought better coin designs and especially designs that would be reflective of current times on our circulating coins. Thousands of pages of testimony before congressional committees by various leaders in the numismatic community during the last 25 years have articulated the needs and benefits of improving the designs of U.S. coinage.[1]

It seems clear that the numismatic community knows what it wants and that Mint officials are fully aware of what appeals and does not appeal to collectors. To any ideal design, the reality of striking coins in quantities needs to be added.

The solution seems to be to educate Congress on what its constituency wants.

The Dollar Bill Problem
As of 2015:

> With roughly $1.36 billion in storage, the Fed is stuck with more metal dollars than it knows what to do with. The unwanted coins are bagged and stacked 30 inches high on pallets measuring 41 inches by 24 inches, which are distributed among the Federal Reserve's 28 bank offices around the country. If the waist-high pallets were laid end-to-end, they would cover about 1-1/2 football fields.[2]

Despite attempts from the 1971 Eisenhower dollar onward to substitute metal dollars for paper dollars, such efforts have never been successful. Paper dollars, now with new elements in their composition, were projected to last 5.9 years in circulation instead of the 18 months figure used earlier.

There was no prospect of reducing the federal stash of metal coins, as that would involve reverse seigniorage, or taking a loss on Mint and Treasury financial records. The situation may be saved by continuing to export these coins to Ecuador and a handful of other Latin American countries where they are regularly used in commerce as legal tender.

A

A A A A A **A** A A A A

THE EISENHOWER DOLLAR: TAKE A CLOSER LOOK

The Eisenhower dollar is certainly a curious coin.

Produced from 1971 to 1978, it is a coin that falls between two numismatic fault lines. In size, it resembles the glorious cartwheels of old (such as Morgan dollars and Peace dollars), but the coin's composition is firmly a part of the modern era of cupro-nickel–clad U.S. coinage. Yes, silver-clad (40% silver to be precise) versions of the Eisenhower dollar were produced, but these were special "numismatic" versions of the coin made for collectors and sold at a tremendous, almost unconscionable markup.

It's the cupro-nickel–clad aspect of the Ike dollar that has kept the coin on the numismatic fringes for so long—that and the fact that the hobby's fringe characters were the ones most eager to promote it as a collectible coin early on—but as the Eisenhower dollar gets older, collectors are becoming wiser to the series' complexity and appeal.

From a design perspective, the coin exhibits a Spartan, almost brutal simplicity. This is the medallic art of Frank Gasparro—a nice man and a true friend of numismatists, but a chief engraver from the Charles Barber school of design.

The coin honors Dwight D. Eisenhower and was issued two years after his passing. Eisenhower was the Supreme Commander of the Allied Forces in Europe during World War II and served as our nation's 34th president. At the time of its production, America's 32nd, 34th, and 35th presidents were honored on circulating coins, joining Washington (our 1st), Jefferson (our 3rd) and Lincoln (our 16th). The coin's reverse celebrates America's role as a pioneer in space exploration. As directed by Congress, Gasparro borrowed the design from the Apollo 11 mission insignia, designed by astronaut Michael Collins.

More than 40 years after the reverse's debut and subsequent repurposing for the Susan B. Anthony dollar in 1979, no other U.S. coin has been struck to celebrate NASA or space science and exploration. (Here's to the hope that Congress will see the error of its ways and change this precedent as we approach the 50th anniversary of the lunar landing!)

The Eisenhower dollar did circulate, mostly in the West and in and around Philadelphia (plus a handful of other eastern metropolitan areas). But for most Americans, the Eisenhower dollar was a curiosity and little more; a pocket coin or belt buckle centerpiece. Just as the case with the Peace and Morgan dollars before it, the Eisenhower dollar wasn't America's first choice for a spending dollar. Paper money—more convenient from a portability standpoint—held that position, but it's important not to dwell on the Eisenhower dollar's failure to penetrate the channels of commerce. Many of the most interesting coins issued in our country's history have failed to make a meaningful economic impact.

The situation in numismatics has been different. No new U.S. coin series issued within the last 50 years—with the possible exceptions of the American Silver Eagle and the State quarters—has been as enthusiastically well received by collectors as has the Ike dollar.

For me personally, the Ike dollar illustrates how much fun one can have and how much of an impact one can make in the hobby if you doggedly pursue goals and do the legwork necessary to become an "expert."

Through my work with the Ike Group I helped familiarize and popularize a number of interesting Ike dollar varieties. Much of the credit for our knowledge of the complexity of the series goes to the tireless efforts of Rob Ezerman, Andy Oskam, and Brian Vaile. Dave Bowers has graciously included a number of Ike Group DIVAS (Designated Ike Varieties) in this book, so now you, too, can go out and find them!

It was with the help of Andy Oskam and Troy Weaver (another top-tier collector) that the Eisenhower dollar found its way into the fold of CAC-submittable coins. For a series as difficult to find in nice condition and as difficult to grade consistently as this, CAC-certification is a necessary reinforcement of the major third-party grading services' grading opinion, as certified coins can be "low end" in quality, but are not indicated so on holders.

And finally, it was with the help of Ken Bressett and the editorial staff at the *Guide Book of United States Coins* that current collectors and potential new collectors were able to see a more realistic and accurate pricing portrayal of the series. Now, flipping to the Ike dollar section reveals just how scarce gems in this series truly are.

All of these efforts and the efforts of a growing number of enthusiastic collectors have breathed new life into the series and highlighted the fact that coins struck on this side of the great silver divide are worthy of study, admiration, and collecting. So whether you're new to Ike dollars, or considering them as a focus for your collection, know that this is a series that will keep you guessing and can be very rewarding if you keep your eyes open for condition rarities and coveted varieties.

The story of the modern dollar is the story of American coinage in transition, a story of trial and error, more errors than successes, and the existential question that faces all of our circulating coins: what is the practical value of base-metal monetary discs in an age of paper and plastic?

For numismatists, there is no other question that looms as large as we plant our feet firmly in the 21st century.

Charles Morgan
Editor of *CoinWeek*

APPENDIX

B

B B B B **B** B B B

ERROR DOLLARS, 1971 TO DATE

Mint Errors

When most factories make mistakes, criticism comes from all directions. When a mint makes mistakes, there is a fan club whose members cheer! As I wrote in the introduction to *100 Greatest U.S. Error Coins*, "to err is human, to forgive divine," as the saying goes.

There are two sides to the mint-error question. At the Philadelphia, Denver, San Francisco, and West Point mints—all of which I have visited on research trips—there are many signs posted as to how employees should prevent mistakes. In recent decades the coining and inspection processes have improved to the extent that mint errors are made less frequently than they were generations ago. A misstruck modern Presidential or Native American dollar is a great rarity, whereas misstruck coins of the late 20th century are readily available in proportion to the demand for them.

COMMON COIN DEFECTS

A Denver Mint bulletin board with illustrations of "common defects" to avoid.

On the other side is the Combined Organizations of Numismatic Error Collectors of America (CONECA) devoted to the study and appreciation of such coins.

In this appendix I illustrate and describe many mint errors from the Eisenhower series onward, mostly courtesy of the aforementioned *100 Greatest U.S. Error Coins* by Nicholas P. Brown, David J. Camire, and Fred Weinberg; of Fred Weinberg separately

Die-hubbing press at the Denver Mint and detail showing warning sign to prevent doubled dies.

A few of the high-speed Schuler presses at the Philadelphia Mint.

as he specializes in these as a business; and Littleton Coin Company, which has handled millions of modern dollars, mostly in original unsorted bags and sacks, and has found a number of errors along the way.

A selection of error coins can make a nice addition to a specialized collection. In general, the more unusual, or the more spectacular an error is, the more it is worth in the marketplace.

Part of the interior mechanism of a Schuler press.
These can strike a dozen or more coins *per second*.

Notice at the output end of a high-speed Schuler press. "Inspect coin quality—If unacceptable then shut off press, push scrap button, dump catch box into condemned coin tote." Great care is taken to prevent mint errors from going into circulation and relatively few escape.

Wrong Metal Dollar Planchet Errors

On several instances the Mint used the wrong metal-content planchets, such as 40% silver planchets for what should have been cupro-nickel Eisenhower dollars, manganese-brass planchets for 1999 Susan B. Anthony dollars that should have been on cupro-nickel planchets, and cupro-nickel planchets for 2000 Sacagawea dollars that should have been on manganese-brass planchets. Errors of this type are listed among the regular issues in earlier chapters and selected examples are given here.

Denver Mint Eisenhower dollars of 1972-D,
1974-D (illustrated), both types of 1776–1976-D,
and 1977-D are known on 40% silver planchets
instead of the intended cupro-nickel–clad planchets.

1999-P Susan B. Anthony dollar on a
manganese-brass Sacagawea planchet.
(No. 43 in *100 Greatest U.S. Error Coins*.)

2000-P Sacagawea dollar on a
cupro-nickel Susan B. Anthony planchet.
(No. 68 in *100 Greatest U.S. Error Coins*.)

Wrong Metal and Planchet Errors

Dollar dies struck on planchets intended for coins of other denominations include many variations.

Eisenhower dollar of
unknown date on
a bronze cent planchet.

1978 Eisenhower dollar
on a half dollar planchet.

1979-S Susan B.
Anthony dollar
on a cent planchet.

Eisenhower dollar of unknown
date on a clad dime planchet.

1979-S Susan B. Anthony
dollar on a dime planchet.

2007 Washington Presidential
dollar struck on a nickel planchet.

2008 Monroe
Presidential
dollar struck on
a dime planchet.

2000-P Sacagawea dollar struck on the
outer ring of a planchet intended for a
100-cedi coin of Ghana (the Mint struck
coins on contract for the African nation).
(No. 86 in *100 Greatest U.S. Error Coins*.)

Defective Planchet Errors

Defective planchets with parts of the top cladding layer missing, edges clipped by a
planchet cutter or otherwise irregular, discolored planchets from rinses or heat treat-
ing, called *mis-annealed* or improperly annealed manganese-brass planchets, and other
problems created errors.

1776–1976-D,
Type 1, dollar
with two clips
made by a
planchet cutter.

A so-called
"die cap"
1977-D
Eisenhower
dollar with a
plain reverse. It
was struck when
another 1977-D
dollar was still in the
press as multiple coins piled up in the machine.

1978 Eisenhower dollar
with the reverse cupro-
nickel–clad layer missing.

1979-S Susan B. Anthony
on a defective planchet
with the clad cupro-nickel
on the obverse partially
peeling away (see left).

1979-S Susan B. Anthony on a defective planchet, a die cap in this instance giving traces of the other coin that was still in the press on the reverse.

1979-S Susan B. Anthony on a planchet with a circular clip from a planchet cutter. The mintmark is not visible, but it was found in a bag of 1979-S dollars.

2001-P Sacagawea dollar on an improperly treated planchet. In the past some have been called "experimental rinse," "experimental planchet," "sintered," or similar, but it is thought that coins matching this one were improperly annealed during the heat-treating processes. Mis-annealed is the proper term.

2015 mis-annealed Truman dollar.

Off-Center and Double-Struck Errors

Off-center strikes are quite scarce in the Eisenhower, Susan B. Anthony, Sacagawea, Native American, and Presidential series. Double-struck coins are very rare.

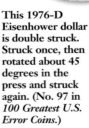

A double-struck 1973-S Proof Eisenhower dollar. Double-struck Proofs are very rare.

This 1976-D Eisenhower dollar is double struck. Struck once, then rotated about 45 degrees in the press and struck again. (No. 97 in *100 Greatest U.S. Error Coins*.)

1978 Eisenhower dollar struck 45% off center.

A double-struck 1999-P
Susan B. Anthony dollar.

1999-P Susan B. Anthony dollar
flip-over double strike, a particularly
desirable type of double strike.

A 1976-D Eisenhower
dollar die cap. No. 40 in
*100 Greatest U.S. Error
Coins:* "The dollar was
struck normally but
stuck to the obverse
die, gradually wrapping
itself around the die and
creating a deep die cap."

1999-P Susan B. Anthony dollar spectacularly
double struck so as to distend the planchet.

1999-P Susan B. Anthony
dollar struck 35% off center.

2000-P Sacagawea dollar struck off center.
(No. 77 in *100 Greatest U.S. Error Coins*.)

A triple-struck 2000-P Sacagawea dollar
with two of the strikes being prominent.
The third strike is best seen at the
border of the leftmost strike.

2000-P Sacagawea dollar slightly off center and on a clipped planchet.

2000-P Sacagawea dollar capped-obverse die.

2007 John Adams dollar double struck and without edge lettering.

2007 Washington dollar struck off center. (No. 70 in *100 Greatest U.S. Error Coins*.)

2009 Native American dollar double struck and without edge lettering.

Edge Lettering Errors

Many 20th-century dollars that were supposed to have edge lettering were not run through the lettering machine and henceforth have error-plan edges. These and other edge anomalies are discussed in earlier chapters under the various dates and mints.

Double Denomination Errors

Mint errors made by a dollar die impression on another denomination or vice versa are the rarest of the rare. Very few are known to exist.

1974-D Eisenhower dollar dies on a previously struck 1974-D dime.

Impression of part of a 1776–1976 Eisenhower dollar on a 1976 Lincoln cent. (No. 16 in *100 Greatest U.S. Error Coins*.)

Impression of part of a 1776–1976, Type 1, Eisenhower dollar on a 1976 quarter dollar.

1999-P Susan B. Anthony dollar struck over a 1999 Georgia State quarter dollar. Overstrikes on State quarters are rare as a class and are very rare in terms of specific states.

This 1979-S Susan B. Anthony dollar was struck in San Francisco and somehow crossed the country to be stamped with a cent die at the Philadelphia Mint in 1981. If only it could speak and tell its story!

Inadvertent (presumably) combination of a Washington quarter die with the reverse of a 2000 Sacagawea dollar (see listing under 2000-P Sacagawea). This is one of the most famous and valuable errors in the series. (No. 1 in *100 Greatest U.S. Error Coins*.)

2000-P Sacagawea dollar overstruck on a seven-sided 2000 Barbados dollar that had been struck by the Royal Canadian Mint in Winnipeg, Alberta. At the time the Mint was in high production gear and outsourced the milling (adding a raised rim) of planchets to Winnipeg on a contract basis. The Canadian Mint made coins on contract for Barbados. This is where the mix up occurred. (No. 66 in *100 Greatest U.S. Error Coins*.)

2000-P Sacagawea overstruck with dies for a 2000 Lincoln cent.

2000-P Sacagawea dollar struck over a 2000 Massachusetts State quarter dollar with abundant traces of the quarter still visible. (No. 59 in *100 Greatest U.S. Error Coins*.)

2000-P Sacagawea dollar struck over a 2000 Maryland State quarter dollar. Traces of the Maryland motifs are best seen at the bottom of the obverse and the top of the reverse.

2001-P Sacagawea dollar struck over a 2001 Kentucky State quarter dollar with tiny traces of the quarter still visible. Other State quarter undertypes exist.

2007 Washington Presidential dollar struck over a Jefferson nickel.

Odds and Ends

Certain miscellaneous and typically very rare errors are shown here.

This 1972 Eisenhower dollar was struck multiple times instead of
being ejected from the press. The result was metal splayed to the sides.

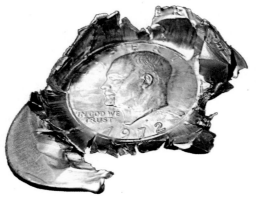

This 1972-D Eisenhower dollar was struck multiple times.

A bronze cent die was in the
press when this 1977-D
Eisenhower dollar was struck.

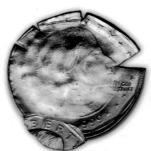

A blank planchet for a cent
was in the press when this
1974-D Eisenhower dollar
was struck. The cent left
an indented impression.

This 1999-P Susan B. Anthony dollar was
struck multiple times and was distorted.

An aluminum planchet-feeder finger on the coining press did not retract and was stamped multiple times by dies for a 2000-P Sacagawea dollar. Such errors are extreme rarities.

A stray washer (a machine part) was in the press when this 2004-P Sacagawea dollar was struck.

An unknown defect in the planchet of this 2000-D Sacagawea dollar caused it to split in two after striking. Consequently, a reverse image of the obverse strike is visible on the back side of this thin remainder.

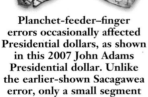

Planchet-feeder–finger errors occasionally affected Presidential dollars, as shown in this 2007 John Adams Presidential dollar. Unlike the earlier-shown Sacagawea error, only a small segment of the die is apparent.

Another feeding-finger strike, this on a 2007 James Madison Presidential dollar.

2007 Washington presidential dollar broadstruck without a retaining collar.

A set-up strike with the dies spaced too wide apart for a 2008 Andrew Jackson Presidential dollar.

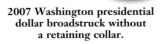

PROPOSED NATIVE AMERICAN DESIGNS

The Native American $1 Coin Act (Pub.L. 110-82) was signed into law on September 20, 2007, by President George W. Bush. In order to determine which design is depicted each year the National Congress of American Indians, the United States Senate Committee on Indian Affairs, and the Native American Caucus select a liaison to send to the U.S. Mint for discussion. From there, 12 to 15 themes are selected after consulting the National Museum of the American Indian and the Smithsonian Institute and receiving their comments regarding the themes. These suggestions are then sent to the Citizens Coinage Advisory Committee and the Commission of Fine Arts and a theme is recommended. After reviewing recommendations, the theme is finalized and the designing process begins. When finished, the various proposed designs are sent back to the consulting organizations before being sent to the CCAC for review. At this point all comments and recommendations are received, and the Mint will recommend a final design to the secretary of the Treasury for approval. The proposed designs for these coins (2009 to 2016) are shown here grouped together by year.

Proposed Designs, 2009

**Design by
Joseph Menna.**

**Design by
Phebe Hemphill.**

**Design by
Don Everhart.**

**Design by
Don Everhart.**

**Design by
Don Everhart.**

**Design by
Charles L. Vickers.**

**Design by
Don Everhart.**

**Design by
Don Everhart.**

Design by
Charles L. Vickers.

Design by
Don Everhart.

Design by
Don Everhart.

Design by
Norman E. Nemeth.

Design by
Don Everhart.

Design by
Don Everhart.

Design by
Joseph Menna.

Proposed Designs, 2010

Design by
Phebe Hemphill.

Design by
David Westwood.

Design by
Donna Weaver.

Design by
Barbara Fox.

Design by
Thomas Cleveland.

Proposed Designs, 2011

Design by
Susan Gamble.

Design by
Joel Iskowitz.

Design by
Joel Iskowitz.

Design by
Donna Weaver.

Design by
Jim Licaretz.

Design by
Richard Masters.

Proposed Designs, 2012

Design by
David Westwood.

Design by
David Westwood.

Design by
David Westwood.

Design by
Thomas Cleveland.

Design by
Donna Weaver.

Design by
Joseph Menna.

Design by
Donna Weaver.

Design by
Donna Weaver.

Design by
Donna Weaver.

Design by
Donna Weaver.

Design by
Phebe Hemphill.

Design by
Donna Weaver.

Proposed Designs, 2013

Design by
David Westwood.

Design by
David Westwood.

Design by
Thomas Cleveland.

Design by
Charles L. Vickers.

Design by
Charles L. Vickers.

Design by
Renata Gordon.

Design by
Charles L. Vickers.

Design by
Donna Weaver.

Design by
Richard Masters.

Design by
Susan Gamble.

Design by
Susan Gamble.

Design by
Joel Iskowitz.

Design by
Joel Iskowitz.

Proposed Designs, 2014

Design by
Paul Balan.

Design by
Paul Balan.

Design by
Chris Costello.

Design by
Chris Costello.

Design by
Chris Costello.

Design by
Ronald D. Sanders.

Design by
Don Everhart.

Proposed Designs, 2015

Design by
Paul Balan.

Design by
Chris Costello.

Design by
Chris Costello.

Design by
Donna Weaver.

Design by
Donna Weaver.

Design by
Donna Weaver.

Design by
Donna Weaver.

Design by
Donna Weaver.

Design by
Ronald D. Sanders.

Design by
Ronald D. Sanders.

Design by
Ronald D. Sanders.

Design by
Ronald D. Sanders.

Design by
Frank Morris.

Design by
Frank Morris.

Design by
Frank Morris.

Design by
Barbara Fox.

Design by
Barbara Fox.

Design by
Joseph Menna.

Design by
Phebe Hemphill.

Design by
Renata Gordon.

Proposed Designs, 2016

Design by
Joel Iskowitz.

Design by
Joel Iskowitz.

Design by
Joel Iskowitz.

Design by
Richard Masters.

Design by
Richard Masters.

Design by
Richard Masters.

Design by
Susan Gamble.

Design by
Susan Gamble.

Design by
Thomas D. Rogers Sr.

Design by
Donna Weaver.

Design by
Donna Weaver.

Design by
Donna Weaver.

Design by
Paul Balan.

Design by
Joseph Menna.

Design by
Don Everhart.

Design by
Don Everhart.

Design by
Ronald D. Sanders.

Design by
Ronald D. Sanders.

STYLE NOTES

Some historical and other quoted material has been lightly edited, but in no instance has meaning been changed.

The San Francisco Mint was known as the San Francisco Assay Office from 1962 to 1982, after which the earlier name was resumed. The facility is generally referred to as the San Francisco Mint throughout, as collectors and dealers did at the time, such as for Proof sets with S mintmarks.

Mintage figures for many coins represent authorized limits or numbers published by the Treasury Department. In many instances, especially for coins minted for the numismatic trade, some were held back for replacements and other purposes. In some instances, distribution continued years after the date on the coins. In 2015 the U.S. Mint Web site offered certain dollar coins dated back to 2009.

NOTES

Chapter 1

1. Per Mint Director Elias Boudinot's February 9, 1795, report to the congressional committee investigating the Mint.

2. 1795-dated half eagles with the Heraldic Eagle Reverse exist, but were struck in later years using 1795 dies still on hand at the Mint.

3. Italic type has been added to the above citation.

4. In actuality, some survived in archival storage, based upon the author's research and observations.

Chapter 2

1. Public Law 110-82. Some certified holders have air spaces around the edges of a coin so that by tilting it at an angle and looking carefully, the dates and mintmarks can be seen. However, this is counter to the idea that a holder should be relatively airtight. Ideally, a holder should be filled with an inert gas and then sealed, to prevent changes in the surfaces of coins.

2. Commentary, December 2, 2015.

3. Ibid.

4. In fact, some years ago I tapped Melissa Karstedt to build for me a set of certified Peace dollars in "high-end" MS-64. She spent two years doing this, with the result that most, if not all, coins in my set are nicer than some certified as MS-65.

5. Commentary, December 2, 2015.

6. Ibid.

Chapter 3

1. Until well into the 21st century there was no official or consistent way of tallying visitors. Those who filled out registration forms were usually far fewer than the stated attendance. Guesses were made as to how many friends and casual visitors were there.

2. In 1965 she harshly criticized numismatists for causing a nationwide coin shortage, and to punish them directed that no mintmarks be used on coins and production of Proof sets stopped. Later, she "got religion," but many were unhappy with her "conversion."

3. It was continued into the 21st century, and then closed.

4. "Are Congressmen Pinching Pennies," *Chicago Daily News*, April 21, 1975. David L. Ganz, "Aluminum Cents Look Legal to Own," *Numismatic News*, February 3, 2014, is definitive on the subject.

5. Both men wined and dined lavishly at ANA expense, often intimidated employees at Headquarters, and otherwise showcased their presumed importance.

6. Immediately prior to this, Richard Buffum, a columnist for the *Los Angeles Times*, interviewed coin dealers and others to ask their reaction to the coming gold boom. I was a solitary voice in the wilderness, and instead of urging *Times* readers to spend their money as soon as possible on anything that was round and yellow, I urged caution. I even had the audacity to say that the gold boom would be a fizzle. I was the only one who did so!

7. Details can be found in the May 1977 issue of *The Numismatist*.

8. Treasury document, March 9, 1979, with results of a survey conducted in September 1978.

9. For details see David Hall's commentary in the *Monthly Summary* of *The Coin Dealer Newsletter*, January 1981.

10. In actuality, but not related to grading, some coins were indeed extraterrestrial, including in this era 12 2000-P gold Sacagawea dollars, an Ohio state quarter, and even a 1793 copper cent.

11. May 31, 2004.

12. Interview with Paul Gilkes, *Coin World*, July 4, 2005.

13. Published August 22, 2005.

14. Issue of August 16, 2005. Both *Numismatic News* and *Coin World* covered the mess—which included leaking confidential matters, expelling an elected governor, and general turmoil. It would be the best part of a decade until the ANA governors and management straightened things out. Meanwhile, several executive directors were hired and fired.

15. "A Rebirth for Variety Collecting," January 2005.

16. *Business Week*, September 23, 2006, gave extensive details.

17. Paul Gilkes, "Cost of certain Mint products," *Coin World*, December 4, 2006.

18. Rita Laws, "Alphabet Explosion in 'Slab City'," *Coin World*, January 9, 2006, subtitled: "Slabs of lesser-known new grading services proliferate at general online auction sites."

19. Emily Mullins, "Inside Edition broadcasts program investigating TV shopping networks," *Coin World*, June 19, 2006.

20. *Business Week*, September 29, 2008.

21. *Coin World*, January 22, 2007.

22. Jeff Starck, "ANA names Larry Shepherd as new executive director," *Coin World*, March 31, 2008.

23. "Coin Values," *Coin World*, August 25, 2008.

24. May 12, 2009.

25. August 25, 2009.

26. May 5, 2009.

27. The *Wall Street Journal*, March 14, 2011.

28. *The Economist*, October 22, 2011.

29. David Harper, *Numismatic News*, March 1, 2011, giving a report by Executive Director Larry Shepherd.

30. *Latino Daily News*, May 12, 2014.

31. Beth Deisher, "Mint's new top leader brings wealth of experience to post," *Coin World*, April 4, 2011.

32. Reported by Paul Gilkes, *Coin World*, and April 4, 2011.

33. George Korte, "By George, $1 bill gets flipped into deficit-cutting debate," *USA Today*, October 25, 2011.

34. *Coin World*, June 6, 2012.

35. "ANA Board ousts another executive director," *Coin World*, May 20, 2013.

36. Mint launch of gold half dollar sales both exciting, troubling," *Coin World*, August 25, 2014; other sources.

Chapter 4

1. *Greensboro [North Carolina] Record*, May 9, 1969.

2. Register-Republic, Rockford, Illinois, July 2, 1969.

3. Cupro-nickel or cupronickel (one word) in Treasury reports. Copper nickel in many numismatic citations published elsewhere.

4. Held on Tuesday, June 19, 1945, with an estimated 4,000,000 people on hand. The day before he had been honored in a parade in Washington, after which he and his entourage went to New York City to stay in the Waldorf-Astoria Hotel in preparation for the next day. After the New York parade he went on a 50-mile parade north to the United States Military Academy at West Point.

5. This reminiscence by Frank Gasparro, former chief engraver of the United States Mint, was written expressly for the 1993 book: *Silver Dollars and Trade Dollars of the United States: A Complete Encyclopedia*.

6. January 25, 1971, handout sheet to those at the ceremony.

7. Information about obverse and reverse hub changes includes information adapted from Herbert P. Hicks, "Eisenhower Dollar Varieties," 1974 (primary source including some narrative describing differences), and John Wexler, Bill Crawford, and Kevin Crawford, and Kevin Flynn, *The Authoritative Reference on Eisenhower Dollars*, 2002.

8. Daniel Carr, proprietor of the Moonlight Mint in Colorado, produced a series of fantasy Eisenhower dollars including varieties with a 1970-dated obverse and Reverse A (see regular issue reverses). These were made from new dies struck on existing Eisenhower dollars, to avoid counterfeiting laws. The Ike Group Web site has a link illustrating and describing these and other Eisenhower fantasies.

9. First illustrated and described by Robert Ezerman in *Errorscope*, November–December 1999.

10. E-mail to Whitman Publishing, LLC, December 4, 2013.

11. Correspondence between Garn Smith and Q. David Bowers, October 6, 1992.

12. The San Francisco Mint name was officially restored in 1982.

13. *Annual Report*, 1971, p. 8.

14. For more information see http://www.coinweek.com/featured-news/nixon-presentation-ike-dollar-discovered.

15. Mint staff member Howard Johnson, letter to Russell Rulau of *Coin World*, July 24, 1974, cited in Wexler, et al., *The Authoritative Reference on Eisenhower Dollars*, 2007. The life for Proof coin dies was far longer, and over the years and for various denominations some dies, after striking a few thousand mirrored Proofs, were used to make large numbers of circulation strikes, some early impressions from which had prooflike surfaces.

16. This act authorized clad coinage and was not otherwise related to Bicentennial coins.

17. Known today as the Sam Rayburn Library, it was dedicated on October 9, 1957, to honor the long-time speaker of the House of Representatives.

18. In 1989 the campus was purchased and opened as the New York Chiropractic College.

19. For a detailed report of the numismatic aspects of the Bicentennial see David L. Ganz, "America's Bicentennial Dollar," 1992.

20. For extensive details see Q. David Bowers, *Commemorative Coins of the United States*, 1992. Perpetrators included L.W. Hoffecker, Thomas G. Melish, and C. Frank Dunn.

21. The National Sculpture Society, based in New York City, had no particular connection to the West Point facility. The U.S. Mint office there simply received mail to be forwarded.

22. Robert Alexander Weinman (March 19, 1919, to September 7, 2003) was a highly accomplished sculptor and medalist. His father, Adolph Alexander Weinman designed the 1916 Mercury dime and the 1916 Liberty Walking half dollar. His brother, Howard Kenneth Weinman, designed the 1936 Long Island Tercentenary commemorative half dollar.

23. Associated Press, January 22, 1974; several other sources.

24. Quoted by Ed Reiter, "Bicentennial hangover," *The New York Times*, July 8, 1979, p. D38.

25. *Annual Report*, 1973, p. 6.

26. National Coin Week was the brainchild of Julius Guttag, a member of the Guttag Brothers partnership—securities brokers (main business) and rare coin dealers in New York City. Later, the firm was an early casualty of the Depression. Julius remained active in numismatics and was involved with the 1938 New Rochelle commemorative half dollars.

27. Modern comment: No reliable estimates have ever been made of the number of coin collectors in America.

28. Later, the ANA received a Morgan & Orr coin press made in the 1870s to strike trade dollars. This refurbished unit is on display at the front of the Headquarters building in Colorado Springs.

29. *State-Journal Register*, Springfield, Illinois, January 15, 1974. Samuel Rayburn was a Democrat from Texas who served as speaker of the House of Representatives for three non-consecutive terms totaling 17 years, the longest tenure in history.

30. This will probably be known as the Tercentenary or Tercentennial.

31. *Richmond Times Dispatch*, Richmond, Virginia, February 2, 1975. At the time there were great difficulties with Middle East and other international oil producers, imports were restricted, long lines formed at gas pumps, and there were other related problems. Plastic used in coin packaging required chemicals including petroleum, and the idea that such material would cost $3 was absurd.

32. Treasury Department announcement April 10, 1975.

33. As a sidelight I mention that in the late 20th and early 21st centuries tens of thousands of bank offices and branches in America were willing partners in the distribution of new coins intended for circulation. It was common practice to display signs and to have stocks of coins on hand for customers who wanted them for face value. If desired, clients could order additional quantities. This nice arrangement came to an end, or nearly so, years later after the economic recession of 2008 set in. New issues were no longer available as desired by bank customers. The commemorative reverses used on Lincoln cents in 2009 were generally unavailable to those ordering them, and for the New Hampshire "America the Beautiful" White Mountain quarters of 2012, banks within New Hampshire could not order them! The Federal Reserve paid out coins to areas in which they were needed for general circulation, without regard to the wishes of the millions of collectors in the country. Most of the New Hampshire quarters were released in Maryland and Virginia!

34. *Centre Daily Times*, State College, Pennsylvania, July 15, 1975.

35. Issue of August 7, 1975.

36. *Dallas Morning News*, August 10, 1975.

37. Although the Treasury Department uses Revolutionary drummer boy, Dennis Tucker points out (communication, December 3, 2015) that some time ago the *Guide Book of United States Coins* changed the description to "military drummer," as the coin depicts a man of about 30 years of age and by the time of the Revolution he would not have been a boy any longer.

38. United Press International release, August 7, 1975.

39. *Register-Republic*, Rockford, Illinois, August 20, 1975.

40. Gary L. Palmer, Copley News Service, September 21, 1975.

41. 1978 *Annual Report*, p. 12.

42. *Marietta Journal*, Marietta, Georgia, October 15, 1975.

43. Treasury news release June 29, 1976.

44. Conversation, January 7, 1993.

45. Roger W. Burdette, communication, December 7, 2015. No documentation concerning the making of these survives at the National Archives.

46. The find was delineated by Jeff Garrett in "Hidden in Plain Sight," *Coin World*, August 2013. This describes other coins in the find, including two 1979-S Anthony dollars, the latest date for which special coins were made. Tom Mulvaney photographed the coins.

47. These include in order of production (which started in October 2011), new reference numbers added here: Carr-1 1975 overstruck on cupro-nickel 1976 Bicentennial $1 Var. 1, no mintmark, 94 made, issue $80; Carr-2, same but on 40% silver coin, 123 made, $85; Carr-3 1970 no mintmark, overstruck on 40% San Francisco silver coins of 1971-1974, matte finish, 5 made; Carr-4 1970 as above, struck on cupro-nickel dollars, matte finish, 13 made; Carr-5 1970 struck on San Francisco 50% silver coins, satin finish,149 made, $110; Carr-6 1970 struck on cupro-nickel dollars, 107 made $90; Carr-7 1975-S struck on 40% San Francisco dollars of 1971-1974, 103 made, $95; Carr-8 1975-D struck on cupro-nickel dollar, 87 made, $90; Carr-9 1975 struck on 40% silver dollar, 195 made; Carr-10, struck on cupro-nickel dollar, 155 made, $85. For more details see the Ike Group Web site.

48. Specifications from the *Annual Report*, 1971, p. 21.

49. Die production figures are based on 1971 Mint Bureau figures quoted in *Walter Breen's Complete Encyclopedia of U.S. and Colonial Coins*, p. 706. Proof dies: Obverses lasted on the average 2,500 impressions each, reverses 3500. Circulation-strike dies: Obverses, 100,000, reverses 200,000.

50. Commentary, December 3, 2015.

51. In the instance of certain Eisenhower dollars made primarily for collecting, the term "Uncirculated" may be more appropriate than "circulation strike," as the latter implies they were made for circulation. However, to maintain consistency, "circulation strike" is used.

52. Communication, December 21, 2015.

53. See Paul Gilkes, "1971-S Eisenhower may be prototype," *Coin World*, September 29, 2008. The discovery coin was found by Lee Lydston. Later, many more were found.

54. Communication, December 21, 2015.

55. Charles Morgan and Hubert Walker, "1971-S Type I Proof Reverse, Nixon Presentation Ike Dollar Discovered," 2013, Ike Group Web site.

56. "Eisenhower Dollar Varieties," *The Numismatist*, April 1974.

57. Communication, December 21, 2015.

58. Communication, December 4, 2015.

59. Communication, December 21, 2015.

60. Communication, December 11, 2015.

61. Thomas K. DeLorey, communication, June 11, 2015.

62. Communication, December 4, 2015.

63. Communication, December 21, 2015.

64. Communication, December 3, 2015.

65. James Sego, communication, December 21, 2015.

66. Thomas K. DeLorey, communication, June 11, 2015.

67. Charles Morgan, communication, October 15, 2015.

68. James Sego, communication, December 21, 2015.

69. Communication, December 21, 2015.

70. James Sego, communication, June 11, 2015.

71. William T. Gibbs, "Discovery coin out of hiding," *Coin World*, July 16, 2012.

72. Communication, December 21, 2015.

73. Most went to private customers and are not reflected in population reports.

74. Communication, December 21, 2015.

75. *Ibid.*

76. *Ibid.*

77. Communication, December 3, 2015.

78. Courtesy of Saul Teichman, December 14, 2015.

79. Communication, December 21, 2015.

80. Communication, June 11, 2015.

81. Charles Morgan, communication, October 15, 2015.

82. Some bags in the Littleton Coin Co. Sky Country Hoard were so imprinted. Some of these bags were not used at the time, and the 1975-D information was blanked out, and they were imprinted 1977 Denver Mint and used to ship 1977-D dollars.

83. *Ibid.*

84. Communication, June 11, 2015.

85. Charles Morgan, communication, October 15, 2015.

86. For details see DeLorey, "1976-S No S Proof Bicentennial Eisenhower Dollar" chapter in John Wexler, Bill Crawford, and Kevin Flynn, *The Authoritative Reference on Eisenhower Dollars*, 2002.

87. Communication, June 11, 2015.

88. Communication, June 11, 2015.

89. Most went to private customers and are not reflected in population reports.

90. Communication, June 11, 2015.

Chapter 5

1. Associated Press article with remarks by Frank H. MacDonald, deputy director of the Mint, February 1976 for nationwide release.

2. United Press International news release, September 16, 1976.

3. By the time he retired from the Senate in 1988 it had been awarded 168 times. The U.S. Department of Defense, the Bureau of Land Management, and the National Park Service were multiple winners.

4. In actuality the depiction of an eagle in flight only appeared on Gobrecht silver dollars of the 1836 to 1839 era. Other eagles were perched or displayed as in heraldry.

5. By 1979 women who had appeared on legal tender coins, commemoratives in silver, included Queen Isabella of Spain on the 1893 Isabella quarter and baby Virginia Dare and her mother on the 1937 Roanoke half dollar.

6. These never caught on with numismatic buyers, nor have any other related first-day covers, which date back to the release of Kennedy half dollars in 1964. Among the problems is that post offices often cancel letters at times other than on the calendar date imprint.

7. Communication, December 10, 2010.

8. As George Santayana said, "Those who do not learn the lessons of history are condemned to repeat its mistakes." Indeed, years later in 2000 the Mint tried new such "brass-colored materials" and found that the coins discolored (see the next chapter).

9. This was forgotten in 2000 when Sacagawea dollar became a reality; see next chapter.

10. Actually 149.

11. By this time the Mint had many other products to offer collectors—the usual yearly Proof sets, an increasing number of commemorative coins, and silver and gold eagles.

12. Fax communication received January 5, 1993.

13. May include some coins earlier designated for use in 1981 Mint sets; the Mint Office was not sure; if this is the case, some low-mintage 1981 coins could have still been in government hands.

14. Steve Roach, "Legislation seeks transition from $1 FRNs to dollar coins," *Coin World*, October 10, 2011.

15. Herbert P. Hicks, communication, December 18, 2015, provided extensive information on this issue, including from *Error-Variety News*.

16. Communication, June 11, 2015.

17. The Breen text has many speculative and incorrect entries and today is used only with a generous grain of the proverbial salt. For the first decade after its release it was heavily relied upon by almost everyone.

18. Per Alan Herbert and Walter H. Breen, communications to the author in 1993.

19. Communication, June 11, 2015.

20. This commentary per Frank Van Valen for *Silver Dollars and Trade Dollars of the United States: A Complete Encyclopedia*, 1993.

21. Communication, December 4, 2015.

Chapter 6

1. In actuality, in 1979 and earlier, few reservations about the coin being confused with the quarter were publicly expressed. The Treasury and the Department of the Mint pressed on with a publicity campaign for the new dollar, passing over such problems.

2. Certain of the following is from an article by Edward Dufner in *The Dallas Morning News*, reprinted as "Analysts disagree on whether coin version will be accepted," in *The Advocate and Greenwich Time*, Stamford, Connecticut, February 7, 1999.

3. Johnson died at his home in northern Virginia on October 17, 2009, from an apparent heart attack. He was widely mourned and favorably remembered.

4. Note: This aspect, little noticed by anyone at the time, explains in part why huge quantities of SBA and, now, Sacagawea dollars were minted, although there was relatively little public interest in them, this ebullient report notwithstanding.

5. Any destroyed coins would be charged against *current* operating profit of the Bureau of the Mint, resulting in congressmen and others viewing the Mint as operating in a reduced-profit or even loss mode, when the problem was that of earlier times.

6. Includes special finishes listed below.

7. www.smalldollars.com.

8. Paul Gilkes, "Goodacre received special Sacagawea dollars," *Coin World*, March 8, 2010.

9. Paul Gilkes, "Cereal promotion offers collectors welcome $1 surprise," *Coin World*, March 8, 2010.

10. More information can be found under No. 12 in Scott Schechter and Jeff Garrett. *100 Greatest U.S. Modern Coins*. Third edition.

11. In these and related sets not all coins in the "clad" Proof sets were clad and not all coins in the "silver" Proof sets were silver.

12. Paul Gilkes, "Mint confirms destruction of Sacagawea gold $5s," *Coin World*, October 22, 2007.

13. *Ibid.*

14. *Ibid.*

15. For more information see Paul Gilkes, "The Mule' Train Five Years since Errors Struck," *Coin World*, May 2, 2005.

16. Paul Gilkes, "Mint made, caught additional mules," *Coin World*, November 3, 2003.

17. See http://www.coinweek.com/modern-coins-the-collapse-of-the-2001-s-sacagawea-proof/

18. William T. Gibbs, "Dollar die scratches feed theory," *Coin World*, May 13, 2002.

19. Communication, October 20, 2015.

20. www.smalldollars.com.

21. Charles Morgan commentary December 2, 2015.

Chapter 7

1. The mintages given here for 2014-P and D dollars are those revised by the U.S. Mint in October 2015. Higher figures published earlier are incorrect. (Courtesy Lateefah Simms, U.S. Mint)

2. Debbie Bradley, "Coin in set has special finish," *Numismatic News*, December 23, 2014.

3. Paul Gilkes, "ANACS certifies enhanced Uncirculated dollar error," *Coin World*, February 9, 2015.

4. Paul Gilkes, "American $1 Set Sales Start," *Coin World*, September 14, 2015.

Chapter 8

1. Adapted from Paul Gilkes, "Mint uses Presidential Medal Portraits for New Dollar Coins," *Coin World*, February 6, 2006.

2. Published in the issue of October 23, 2006.

3. From Paul Gilkes, "Mint's Presidential Proof set for sale beginning June 21," *Coin World*, June 25, 2007.

4. *Ibid.*

5. In actuality, edge lettering was used on federal coins beginning in the early 1790s.

6. Paul Gilkes, "Manganese oxide discolors Monroe dollar," *Coin World*, November 3, 2008.

7. Paul Gilkes, "Anti-tarnishing agent for dollars originally wood preserver," *Coin World*, June 29, 2009.

8. Adapted from Michele Orzano, "Dollar Coin Alliance says decision will cost billions," *Coin World*, January 23, 2012.

9. Adapted from David L. Ganz, "Paper Dollar Gets a Boost," *Numismatic News*, March 13, 2012.

10. Mint spokesman Michael White as quoted in *Coin World*, March 26, 2012.

11. "Cutting Presidential launch events penny-wise, dollar-foolish?" *Coin World*, March 26, 2012.

12. Others on the trip included Dennis Tucker, David Sundman, Brian Kendrella, and Lee Bowers.

13. Paul Gilkes, "Mint aware of edge error on Proof 2007 Jefferson dollar," *Coin World*, April 24, 2008. Lancets.

14. Paul Gilkes, "Collectors wait to see if $1 coins circulate," *Coin World*, February 25, 2008.

15. Paul Gilkes, "CFA announces recommendations for 2010 dollar designs," *Coin World*, February 16, 2009.

16. Information and image from the NGC Web site.

17. In 1873 the new trade dollar denomination would replace the Liberty Seated dollar for the export trade.

18. In 1848, 1,389 quarter eagles were counterstamped with CAL. to indicate their production from California gold. While these were commemoratives in a way, at the time they were not billed as such, but were routinely placed into circulation.

19. D.W. Griffith's blatantly racist 1915 movie, *The Birth of a Nation*, included this quotation flashed on the screen.

Epilogue

1. *Coin World*, October 24, 2008.

2. Jo Craven McGinty, "Dollar Coin Loses Currency on Savings," *Wall Street Journal*, April 3, 2015.

SELECTED BIBLIOGRAPHY

Becker, Thomas W. *The Man, the Dollar and the Stamps*. Media, PA: American Mint and Postal Society, 1971.

Bowers, Q. David, "The Striking of the Susan B. Anthony Dollar," *The Numismatist*, July 1979.

— *American Numismatic Association Centennial History, 1891–1991*. Wolfeboro, NH: Bowers and Merena Galleries, Inc., 1991.

Bressett, Kenneth E. (senior editor). *A Guide Book of United States Coins*. Atlanta, GA: Whitman Publishing, various modern editions; earlier editions edited by Richard S. Yeoman.

Bressett, Kenneth E. (senior editor). *A Guide Book of United States Coins, Deluxe Edition*. Atlanta, GA: Whitman Publishing, 2015.

Bressett, Kenneth E. and Abe Kosoff. *The Official American Numismatic Association Grading Standards for United States Coins.* 4th edition. Colorado Springs, CO: American Numismatic Association, 1991.

Brown, Nicholas P., David J. Camire, and Fred Weinberg. *100 Greatest U.S. Error Coins.* Atlanta, GA: Whitman Publishing, 2010.

COINage. Behn-Miller Publishers and others, 1970 to date.

CoinWeek. (www.coinweek.com) Various issues, 2011 to date.

Coin Dealer Newsletter. Various locations, 1971 to date.

Coin World Almanac. Sidney, OH: Coin World, 2000.

Coin World. Sidney, OH: Amos Press, 1969 to date.

Combined Organizations of Numismatic Error Collectors of America (CONECA). (www.conecaonline.org) Publisher of Errorscope online.

Department of the Treasury News, Bureau of the Mint. News releases and announcements from 1969 to date.

The Dwight D. Eisenhower Presidential Library, Museum, and Boyhood Home. Abilene, KS. *Error-Variety News.* Various issues, especially the early 1980s issues discussing the Susan B. Anthony dollars.

Errorscope. Online publication of CONECA.

Ezerman, Robert. *Collectible Ike Varieties—Facts, Photos and Theories.* Lulu: 2011.

Fivaz, Bill, and J.T. Stanton. *Cherrypickers' Guide to Rare Die Varieties.* Fifth edition. Atlanta, GA: Whitman Publishing, 2012.

Ganz, David L. *The Story of America's Bicentennial Coinage.* Washington, D.C.: Three Continents Press, 1976.

— "America's Bicentennial Dollar." *The Comprehensive U.S. Silver Dollar Encyclopedia.* Chapter 71. 1992.

Hicks, Herbert P. "Eisenhower Dollar Varieties," *The Numismatist,* April 1974. This is *the* article that catalyzed interest in the title subject.

Highfill, John W. "The Eisenhower Dollar and the Coinage Act of 1965." *The Comprehensive U.S. Silver Dollar Encyclopedia.* Chapter 70. 1992.

www.ikegroup.info. The Ike Group. Web site.

Julian, R.W. "Anthony Dollars 1979–1981: Historical Background," *Silver Dollars and Trade Dollars of the United States: A Complete Encyclopedia.* Chapter 17. 1993.

Judd, J. Hewitt. *United States Pattern Coins.* Tenth edition. Atlanta, GA: Whitman Publishing, 2009.

Mint News. Occasional newsletter issued by the U.S. Mint.

Numismatic Guaranty Corporation of America Census Report. Sarasota, FL: Numismatic Guaranty Corporation of America, various issues.

Numismatic News. Iola, WI: Krause Publications, 1969 to date.

Numismatist, The. Colorado Springs, CO: The American Numismatic Association, various issues 1969 to date.

www.pcgscoinfacts.com. PCGS "CoinFacts" Web site.

Schechter, Scott, and Jeff Garrett. *100 Greatest U.S. Modern Coins.* Third edition. Atlanta, GA: Whitman Publishing, 2014.

www.silverinstitute.org. The Silver Institute Web site.

www.smalldollars.com. "United States Small Size Dollar Coins and Related Items." Web site.

www.wikipedia.org. General information on American history.

Tucker, Dennis. *American Gold and Silver: U.S. Mint Collector and Investor Coins and Medals, Bicentennial to Date.* Atlanta, GA: Whitman Publishing, 2016.

United States Treasury Department, United States Mint, *et al. Annual Report of the Director of the Mint.* 1969 to date.

www.uspatterns.com. U.S. patterns Web site conducted by Saul Teichman with updates of the latest news and discoveries.

Wexler, John. *The Authoritative Reference on Eisenhower Dollars.* Rancocas, NJ: Archive Press, Inc., 1998.

Wexler, John, Bill Crawford, and Kevin Flynn. *The Authoritative Reference on Eisenhower Dollars.* Roswell, GA: Kyle Vick, 2007.

Wiles, James. *The SBA Dollar Variety Book.* Free Internet book in the Variety Vista section of the CONECA Web site.

ACKNOWLEDGMENTS

These acknowledgments includes those who helped with Eisenhower and Anthony dollars for *Silver Dollars and Trade Dollars of the United States: A Complete Encyclopedia,* 1993. **Representative Frank Annunzio** answered research questions when he was involved in coinage affairs for the House of Representatives. The author's sons **Wynn, Lee, and Andrew Bowers,** helped on research visits to certain mints. **Kenneth Bressett,** editor of *A Guide Book of United States Coins,* made suggestions. Former Mint Director **Mary T. Brooks** arranged Mint visits and provided documents. **Patrick Brown** of the Denver Mint furnished selected images. **Roger W. Burdette** reviewed the manuscript and made suggestions. **William Creech** of the National Archives assisted with research. **John Dannreuther** assisted during mint visits and helped in other ways. **Tom DeLorey** shared recollections about Eisenhower and Sacagawea dollars. **Tom DiNardi,** deputy manager of the West Point Mint, assisted during a visit. **Rachel Dobkin** of the Heritage Assets Project helped in several ways. **Richard Doty,** curator of the National Numismatic Collection, provided access to archival material. **Larry Eckerman,** plant manager of the San Francisco Mint, facilitated research, photography, and other aspects of a 2005 visit. **Troy Elkins** of the Dwight D. Eisenhower Presidential Library and Museum corresponded and also furnished images. **Don Everhart,** sculptor-engraver at the U.S. Mint, helped in many ways. **Rob Ezerman,** who founded the Ike Group and whose published and Internet information on Eisenhower dollars is perhaps the most comprehensive ever, reviewed the manuscript and made contributions.

Tom Fesing of the Denver Mint provided historical information. **Bill Fivaz** helped with die varieties. **Kevin Flynn** shared information on Eisenhower dollars. **Francis B. (Barry) Frere** of the U.S. Mint assisted with research involving Eisenhower and Susan B. Anthony dollars in the 1980s and facilitated access to Mint correspondence and documents. **Ed Fulwider,** a numismatically informed member of the San Francisco Mint staff, answered many inquiries about Eisenhower and Susan B. Anthony dollars in correspondence over the years. **Jeff Garrett** assisted with research inquiries, including information about special strikings of Eisenhower dollars. **Frank Gasparro,** former chief engraver of the U.S. Mint, submitted first-hand recollections about how he designed the Eisenhower and Susan B. Anthony dollars. In addition, during his tenure he warmly greeted the author during various visits to the Philadelphia Mint. **Robert Goler,** Mint historian, cataloged many galvanos and plasters that were later available for study, and has been a very important factor with the extensive Mint archives. **Tim Grant** of the Philadelphia Mint helped with several visits to that institution. **Ron Guth** and PCGS CoinFacts provided information. **Stella B. Hackel,** director of the Mint from 1977 to 1981, made arrangements for the author to visit the Philadelphia, Denver, and San Francisco mints and to take photographs and do research there. **Michelle Hansen** provided an image. **Phebe Hemphill,** medallic sculptor at the U.S. Mint, helped in many ways. **Gerald Higgs** shared information on dollars with plain edges (missing edge lettering). **John W. Highfill** granted permission to use information in his book, *The Comprehensive U.S. Silver Dollar Encyclopedia*. **D. Wayne Johnson** provided information about a medal. Former Mint Director **Jay Johnson** provided much information about "golden dollars" and facilitated research. **Elizabeth Jones**, chief engraver of the U.S. Mint from 1981 to 1991, assisted the author with various research in Mint records and made available various historical galvanos and other items from the engraving department. **R.W. Julian's** "Anthony Dollars 1979–1981: Historical Background," chapter 17, in *Silver Dollars and Trade Dollars of the United States: A Complete Encyclopedia*, 1993, was helpful with the present book. **Thomas Jurkowsky** of the U.S. Mint provided extensive help including arranging visits to the four mints, directing inquiries, and providing archival information; he was key to the creation of this book.

David Lange provided information. **Michael Levin**, historian at the San Francisco Mint, helped in several ways. **Christine Matthews** provided the image of the Millennium Dome. **David McHenry** gave information about Eisenhower dollars. **Joseph Menna**, medallic sculptor at the U.S. Mint, provided images and information. **John Mercanti**, former lead engraver at the U.S. Mint, discussed various aspects of coinage. **Evelyn R. Mishkin** helped early on in the project. **Charles Morgan** of *CoinWeek* reviewed the manuscript and made many suggestions, especially relating to Eisenhower dollars, and contributed Appendix A, which shares his thoughts on Ike dollars. Charles and Rob Ezerman have been two of the foremost modern students of Eisenhower dollars. Former Mint Director **Edmund C. Moy** wrote the foreword, provided information, and also contributed U.S. Mint pictures, including of launch ceremonies. **Douglas Mudd**, curator of the ANA Museum, provided images. Certain pictures are courtesy of **Tom Mulvaney**, via Jeff Garrett or Whitman Publishing. **The National Archives and Records Administration (NARA)** provided much Mint data over a long period of years. **Andy Oskam** furnished images from his winning registry set of Eisenhower dollars; the pictures were taken by PCGS (as were images of the Troy Weaver coins in the same set).

Deputy Mint Director **Richard Peterson** helped in several ways, including arranging mint visits and facilitating research. **Donna Pope**, director of the Mint from 1981 to 1991, arranged for several visits to do research at various U.S. mints; in addition, through her office in Washington she and her staff helped in many ways. **Jim Reardon** furnished information concerning the availability of various issues of Eisenhower dollars. The **RIA Novosti** archive provided the image of the 1980 Olympiad (image #487026, Vladimir Vyatkin). **Jane Samuels** of the Heritage Assets Project helped in several ways. **Tracy Scelzo** of the U.S. Mint provided brochures and artwork. **Scott Schechter** provided grading information. **James Sego** helped with information on Eisenhower dollars and other matters and reviewed parts of the manuscript. **Roger Siboni** furnished an illustration. **Lateefah Simms** of the U.S. Mint helped with information, including updated mintage figures (different from some earlier-published numbers). **Garn Smith** corresponded about Eisenhower and Susan B. Anthony dollars. **The Smithsonian Institution** provided access to coins from the National Numismatic Collection and to items from the Frank Gasparro estate. **Adam Stump** of the U.S. Mint provided information. **David M. Sundman** of Littleton Coin Company helped in several ways. **Saul Teichman** provided images and helped with information on patterns. **Dennis Tucker** furnished images, including those on modern mint visits and made many suggestions. Over a long period of years, officers and employees of the **U.S. Mint and the U.S. Treasury Department** have facilitated visits to mints and access to archives and have helped in many ways. **Frank Van Valen** made important suggestions and contributed much to the Eisenhower and Susan B. Anthony sections. **Ken and Stephanie Westover** of Littleton Coin Company provided many images and much information. **Michael J. White** of the U.S. Mint gathered many documents, assisted with Mint visits and photography, and helped in other ways, being the most generous contributor of printed material to this book. **James Wiles** added information and helped with editing, with emphasis on Eisenhower dollars.

ABOUT THE AUTHOR

Q. David Bowers has been in the rare-coin business since he was a teenager, starting in 1953. He is a founder of Stack's Bowers Galleries and is numismatic director of Whitman Publishing. He is a recipient of the Pennsylvania State University College of Business Administration's Alumni Achievement Award (1976); he has served as president of the American Numismatic Association (1983–1985) and president of the Professional Numismatists Guild (1977–1979); he is a recipient of the highest honor bestowed by the ANA (the Farran Zerbe Award); he was the first ANA member to be named Numismatist of the Year (1995); and he has been inducted into the ANA Numismatic Hall of Fame maintained at ANA headquarters. He has also won the highest honors given by the Professional Numismatists Guild. In July 1999, in a poll published in *COINage*, "Numismatists of the Century," Dave was recognized as one of six living people in this list of just 18 names. He is the author of more than 50 books, hundreds of auction and other catalogs, and several thousand articles, including columns in *Coin World* (now the longest-running by any author in numismatic history), *The Numismatist*, and other publications. His books have earned more "Book of the Year Award" honors bestowed by the Numismatic Literary Guild than have those of any other author. He and his firms have presented the majority of the most valuable coin collections ever sold at auction. Dave is a trustee of the New Hampshire Historical Society and a fellow of the American Antiquarian Society, the American Numismatic Society, and the Massachusetts Historical Society. He has been a consultant for the Smithsonian Institution, the Treasury Department, and the U.S. Mint, and is research editor of *A Guide Book of United States Coins*. For many years he was a guest lecturer at Harvard University. This is a short list of his honors and accomplishments. In Wolfeboro, New Hampshire, he is on the Board of Selectmen and is the town historian.

INDEX